5 THE PILLARS OF LIFE

RECLAIMING OWNERSHIP
OF YOUR MIND, BODY, AND FUTURE

THE
5 PILLARS
OF
LIFE

HOW ANCIENT TRADITIONS
CAN GIVE YOU BACK
TRANQUILITY, CONTROL,
HEALTH, LOVE AND SECURITY

DR. SYMEON RODGER

Ottawa, Ontario

The 5 Pillars of Life:
Reclaiming Ownership of Your Mind, Body, and Future
Published by Core Systems Press
2251 Courtice Ave., Ottawa, ON K1H-7G5 CAN
www.rocksolidlife.com

Notice: This publication contains the opinions and ideas of the author. It is intended to provide helpful and informative material on the subject matters covered. The content of this book is not meant to replace the advice of mental or medical healthcare professionals or qualified counselors. The authors and publisher specifically disclaim any responsibility for any liability, loss, or risk, personal or otherwise, which is incurred as a consequence, directly or indirectly, of the use and/or application of any of the contents of this book.

Cover and interior design by Pneuma Books, LLC
Visit www.pneumabooks.com

Library and Archives Canada Cataloguing in Publication

Rodger, Symeon, 1959-
   The 5 pillars of life : reclaiming ownership of your mind, body
and future : how ancient traditions can give you back tranquility, control, health, love and security / Symeon Rodger.

(Rock solid life series)
Includes bibliographical references and index.
ISBN-13: 978-0-9738734-0-5 (bound).--ISBN-13: 978-0-9738734-1-2 (pbk.)
ISBN-10: 0-9738734-0-X (bound).--ISBN-10: 0-9738734-1-8 (pbk.)

   1.   Self-actualization (Psychology) I. Title. II. Title: Five pillars of life.
III. Series.

BF637.S4R64 2005   158.1
C2005-904913-8

09 08 07 06 05   5 4 3 2 1

PRINTED IN CANADA

First and foremost, to my lovely wife Larissa,
for her hard work as my first editor and for her constant inspiration.

To our son, Anthony, whose literary expertise and knowledge of the
sources undoubtedly improved this manuscript.

And to our daughters, Katherine and Juliana,
who with grace, good humor, and patience
put up with me while I was writing this!

To my dear parents, Foster and Lorna,
who did not remain on earth long enough to see this book finished, but
who are in so many ways responsible for it.

To Archpriest Georges Pokrowsky (1907-1999),
who demonstrated in his own person that the adversities of life are
powerless against the human spirit.

TABLE OF CONTENTS

PILLAR 1: TAKE BACK CONTROL OF YOUR CIRCUMSTANCES

PILLAR 2: MASTER YOUR INNER WORLD

PILLAR 3: BECOME UNSTOPPABLE

PILLAR 4: EMBRACE THE MOST EFFECTIVE LIFE PARADIGM

PILLAR 5: TURN LIFE INTO LOVE

APPENDICES

PREFACE

As far back as I can remember, I was blessed with a burning obsession: What does it mean to be human and how do you perfect human life?

From my early teenage years, as this single idea gathered strength, I began to judge everything I encountered in relation to it. Whatever led toward this goal was deemed useful, and whatever didn't was clearly irrelevant.

This was not idle, metaphysical curiosity on my part, but an urgent, driving force within. As a child, I grew up in a safe and loving home environment, but from an early age I was deeply tormented by the fear of losing it. Later, as a teenager and young adult, I suffered terribly from other equally ridiculous fears and the mental and physical pain they produced.

But there was more. In addition to my inner suffering (which no one ever noticed from the outside) I was also plagued by the fact that my typical modern life, however "safe" and "secure," was a *colossal bore*. My life and the lives of everyone around me were utterly bland. And it was certainly not for lack of entertainment. This boredom was a chasm that no amount of entertainment could ever fill. It was life without mystery, without heroism, without honor and finally without meaning. And in the midst of this kind of existence ("life" is too qualitative a word to use here!), my spirit felt like a caged tiger.

Strangely enough, I interpreted the obvious mental, emotional, spiritual, physical, and social dysfunction all around me as yet more proof that there must be such a thing as true life. This certainly wasn't it, but in my eyes this betrayal of life was proof that life had to exist.

I desperately wanted answers to real life problems, to the convulsive and disordered energies within me and within everyone else. My various church experiences from childhood to university were a singular disappointment in providing any answers. These churches were all more intent on selling me their ideologies than in answering my real needs. It quickly became obvious that they didn't have any viable or proven therapy for the real human condition.

From the time I was about ten years old I began to study oriental martial arts. I fell in love quite quickly with their spiritual content, but then I realized over the next decade that the martial arts schools here, no matter what the style, were largely ignorant of that content. I remember Judo and Karate instructors starting off their classes with "meditation" — they gave their students no instructions whatsoever on how to do it and exactly sixty seconds to do it in! The externals of the various martial arts had been retained but the soul that gave them life and breath was largely absent. So once again I found myself empty-handed at the doors of those who should have had answers.

In my mid-teens I began to read everything I could get my hands on that might have had the answers I was looking for. I read Hindu, Sufi, Buddhist, Taoist and Native American sources. I read self-help material, of which there was very little at the time compared to now. In particular I immersed myself in Tibetan Buddhism, where I discovered the criteria that would enable me to distinguish true paths from false ones. It was here, in my "Far Eastern" sojourn, that I first encountered people who had lived or were living amazing lives, and it was here that I found the first real proof that life can be totally transformed and that the potential inherent in human life is nearly limitless.

As you'll see later, I didn't stay in the Far East, though I certainly respect those who chose to do so. My research led me ultimately to the original Christian tradition, long dead in the Western world and replaced by a shadow of its former self. Here I went on to meet other incredible people who also knew exactly how to transform human life.

Over the course of thirty years of study and ten years of counseling others, I continually refined what I had seen and experienced. Eventually, I became convinced that there was no coherent explanation of the riches of the worldwide tradition of how to find true life. There was no single source that a Westerner could use to find his way. The ancient texts and many recent ones are available, to be sure, but they are often unhelpful to people like you and me living in a society and a mental universe that is very different from the ones that the texts were written for.

And moreover, people today are less willing than ever to "buy the car without test driving it." They don't want to become Buddhists or Taoists or Orthodox Christians or whatever else unless these traditions can first *prove* that they have something to offer. That is all the more reason to make the fundamentals of self-transformation available to a wider audience in a form that anyone can use, regardless of his or her metaphysical opinions.

In other words, this is the book I was desperately hoping to find for so many years. My greatest wish is that you would profit enormously from "test driving" its contents!

INTRODUCTION

Your life contains incredible potential and undreamt of possibilities. Every human life does, because this potential is innate in human nature and is just waiting for you to unlock it.

Science tells us that we use only about ten percent of our brain function. As it happens, there are some living traditions on our planet that have been well aware of this for centuries, and these traditions maintain that we have other capacities, not centered in our physical brains, that are even more amazing and even more essential to becoming an authentic human being.

But if you're like most people, it's not so much unrealized potential that's on your mind every day, as how you can free yourself from the killing psychological stress that's giving you that ulcer or those chest pains, or how you can build more fulfilling relationships, be entirely free from negative emotions, protect your physical health or just find a way to take back control of your time and your life.

All these things are possible and anyone can accomplish them, as long as they have the right methods and are willing to practice them consistently. To change your life, you clearly need to stop thinking and doing certain things, and to start thinking and doing other things. Whatever mess you're in right now, you can be sure that your own thoughts and actions have led to it. The good news is that if you start today to train new physical, mental, emotional and spiritual habits, time will compound your investment and completely transform your life in return. But this will only happen if your methods are correct.

The keys to this miracle of self-transformation have been known almost worldwide for millennia. They're not new. But they are only found within certain traditions and not in others. After thirty years of studying and living in these traditions, I can tell you that this book is the first systematic explanation of their best training methods and, more importantly, it's the first time anyone has pulled together the seldom discussed inner principles that make their training systems work. These principles make the difference between guaranteed success and inevitable failure.

We live in the information age, so we're overwhelmed by information in all areas of our lives. What we often lack, though, is reliable information. There are lots of books out there on how to change your life; how to become happier or more efficient or more spiritual or whatever else you could want. Unfortunately, much of the information they contain is partial, unreliable, impractical or just plain wrong. But it's only from the standpoint of traditions that really work that anyone can judge what information is useful and what is not.

This book is a training manual. It gives you all the theory you need in order to understand how to transform your life on every level, together with inspiring proof that these traditions actually live up to their promises. Most importantly, though, you will find in these pages the concrete "how to" instructions that will allow you to make a difference in the quality of your life and the lives of those around you every day.

Every one of us has a choice. We can choose to live a tormented and fruitless life or an excellent and powerful one. We can live a "safe" bourgeois life that condemns us to terminal boredom or we can live the ultimate adventure. We all make this choice, though most do it unconsciously.

I suggest that you first of all read through the entire book once, just so that you'll start with an outline of the whole picture in mind. Then begin to work your way through it, slowly and deliberately, doing the exercises in the order in which they are presented. The order of the presentation is very deliberate – it mirrors the training syllabus that has made ancient traditions so successful.

Remember, it's better to master the basics than to rush ahead and end up with nothing. We have a tendency to "gobble up" the latest information at breakneck speed and then wonder why it doesn't change our lives. Alas, this is not "fast food." It's a feast that has to be digested one course at a time. You need to take your time, savoring and enjoying the nuances of each flavor.

If you ever want more detail on the "how to" of any chapter, you can visit us at www.rocksolidlife.com. There you'll find courses based on the content of each chapter, courses that go into even more detail than I've been able to pack into this already sizable tome!

Whatever you do, don't skip the first chapter – it contains the background information and terminology you'll need to make sense out of everything that follows.

Next, we get down to work. Pillar One teaches you how to take charge of the externals of your life — your time, your energy, your health, your home environment, your interpersonal relationships and your economic situation. While it's true that lots of books, many of them excellent, have been written on each of these subjects, the purpose of the two chapters of Pillar One is to allow you to stabilize all these areas as quickly as possible.

Pillar Two introduces you to the one and only method that can lead you to complete mastery over your inner world, over your thoughts and emotions. Pillar Three leads you to experience and recapture the unstoppable willpower you already have but may not know how to harness. Pillar Four initiates you into the Warrior's World, into the most effective and satisfying life paradigm ever discovered. Pillar Five teaches you how to cultivate the transformative energy of love. Then there is an important chapter on how to overcome all of life's obstacles, on how to win all the time. And finally, there is a final challenge – your graduation.

Working your way through these exercises will take a long time — many months in fact. Do you find that daunting? You shouldn't. Ask yourself how long it took you to develop the professional qualifications, the marketable skills that allow you to work where you do. How much time, effort and money did you spend to acquire them? At a conservative estimate, you probably took four years, spent upwards of thirty to fifty thousand dollars or more, and put yourself through some tough situations. Wouldn't you be willing to spend just one year and the trivial cost of this book to live a life of indescribable inner solidity and joy, free from fears and neuroses, from chronic ill-health, from psychological stress and its physical consequences, from poor relationships, isolation and loneliness and from the countless other plagues that torment the masses of our fellow human beings? What price could you put on this knowledge?

Think of one person you really love deeply and whose welfare means a great deal to you. It could be your spouse, your child, your friend. In the final analysis, the greatest gift you can give to this person is the quality of your own life. That will do more to provide the person you love with inspiration, happiness and inner stability than any other gift you can give.

Shall we begin?

Chapter One

INTRODUCTION to THE ONLY PROVEN PATH to REAL HAPPINESS

M y dear brother or sister in the human race, I sincerely hope that you're well and enjoying a happy, healthy, and fulfilling life, but chances are that this is not the case. In fact, most people you know and perhaps you yourself are living what the great American philosopher Henry David Thoreau once called "lives of quiet desperation."

Here are a few key questions you can ask yourself that will help you evaluate the effectiveness of your current lifestyle and how happy (or unhappy) that lifestyle is making you:

Would you say that you live under uncomfortable psychological stress, and if so, do you suffer from any of its many physical and emotional consequences? Do you suffer from chronic anxiety, panic attacks, or a deep sense of insecurity about your health, appearance, relationships, or financial well-being? Has this begun to affect your health with ulcers, palpitations, sleep disorders, gastrointestinal problems, or other symptoms?

If you can answer yes to any of these questions, then you're just one of millions of victims of the greatest plague of modern times – the manmade evil of psychological stress, an evil you know you have to defeat but probably don't know how.

Are you at ease with the idea of being alone and in silence for a period of time, or would you immediately run to turn on the radio, television, or any other source of ambient noise? Do you find yourself constantly running away from a gnawing inner emptiness and deep lack of fulfillment, trying unsuccessfully to avoid it by immersing yourself in distractions and "entertainment"? Is there an endless and trivial dialogue in your head tormenting you with reminders of a thousand and one irrelevant things? Are you always worrying that you "should" be using your spare time to do this or that because "it needs doing"? Do you feel that you have lots you must do but no time to do it in? Are you surprised when emotional energies you either didn't recognize or couldn't control suddenly cause some debilitating physical symptom?

If you're nodding in agreement to any of this, you're one of millions suffering from a serious inner dysfunction that Western medicine and psychology only dimly understand and cannot cure. But not curing this affliction will cause your life to go to waste and probably cut it short as well.

Are the years gaining on you while you still feel unfulfilled on many levels? Have you given up on your economic dreams and settled for a dead-end job? Do you feel you have so much more to contribute to society and others but are hemmed in by circumstances? Does it seem that the demands of others control your time and energy? Do you feel like a caged animal, captured and domesticated by a tedious and meaningless life? Does your whole being cry out for a challenging and rewarding life?

If so, you are far from alone. You know instinctively that there has to be a better way, a way to take back control of your life.

Stressed out, crippled by emotional dysfunction, and a slave to a tedious treadmill existence in the rat race of modern life—this is the sad, not to say pathetic, condition of millions of people in the world's most "advanced" and "developed" nations. Amidst this sea of misery,

THE 5 PILLARS OF LIFE

all our talk about freedom, democracy, and the pursuit of happiness and the American dream seems rather pointless. The prisons, hospitals, and mental institutions are full, and together with the generalized hopelessness and despair of life, they convict us that our way of life doesn't work.

If any of this describes your life, then you know from bitter experience that you desperately need an entirely new way of life. And judging from all these symptoms, this new way of life must meet certain criteria if it is to be of any value to you at all:

1. It must be a *complete* way of life, one that addresses all aspects of your existence.
2. It must be an *authentic* way of life, capable of taking you to your ultimate potential as a human being.
3. It must be a *proven* way of life that has been clinically tested and proven successful over extremely long periods across various cultures.
4. It must be a *reliable* way of life, one that gets results reliably 100 percent of the time as long as you apply it properly.
5. It must be clearly explained as a *step-by-step* method so that you know how to implement it in your own daily life.

You have probably already tried to transform your life in some way, however small. Perhaps you've tried to quit smoking or lose weight. Perhaps you've tried to increase your income, improve a relationship, find some inner peace, or rescue your self-esteem. Whatever the case, the first step in transforming your life is to know where you are right now. The following questionnaire is designed to help you think through your state in various areas of your life. Unless you take the time to analyze your own situation, you are acting only on a vague impression and not on the facts. The second purpose of the questionnaire is to get you thinking about where you want to go. If possible, arrange for an hour or two, without interruption, so that you can think your answers through clearly. Please put your answers in writing; this is essential to achieving clarity of vision.

THE STATE YOUR LIFE IS IN TODAY

Take a few minutes to answer the following questions as honestly as possible.

1. Do you feel that you are in control of your life?

2. Do you feel stressed by too much to do and too little time in which to do it?

3. Does inadequate organization of your personal, family, and business affairs create problems?

4. Describe your difficulties in the area of time management as they relate to your relationships with people, to your work or business, to your health and fitness, and to your inner peace of mind.

5. Are you troubled by random emotional states and waves of thoughts that you cannot turn off?

6. Does this obsessive thinking prevent you from sleeping?

7. Do you have difficulty controlling your temper? Does anger surge up within you because of other peoples' faults? Do you yell at the kids, curse lousy drivers, stick pins in a voodoo doll of your boss?

8. Are you satisfied with your interpersonal relationships with your spouse/significant other, children, parents, siblings, other relatives, friends, colleagues, and neighbors?

9. Describe any difficulties you have or have had during your life in forming and maintaining fulfilling interpersonal relationships.

10. Do you make an effort to keep in good shape physically?

11. Have you taken steps to improve your diet?

12. Do you have a weight problem?

13. Describe any medical conditions you may have.

14. Describe any undiagnosed symptoms that you may have (e.g., sleep disorders, high blood pressure, constipation, diarrhea, bloating or gas, frequent indigestion, body odor, bad breath, skin problems, weight problems, fungal or yeast infections, allergies, water retention, memory problems, difficulty concentrating, frequent headaches, joint pain, muscle cramping, menstrual problems, premenstrual syndrome, menopausal problems, cellulite, heart palpitations, low energy level, frequent colds or flus, low sex drive).

15. Are you under frequent psychological stress?

16. Describe any noticeable physiological symptoms this produces.

17. Are you satisfied with your career and your financial situation? If not, describe what you would change.

18. When you are alone, are you content to dwell in silence, or do you automatically put on radio, television, or some other system just to produce noise or avoid boredom?

19. Do you belong to a particular "spiritual" tradition?

20. How do you see this tradition—its strong points and its limitations?

21. Do you have a sense of being trapped in your current life circumstances and unable to change them?

22. Have you failed so often at changing them that you no longer believe you can?

23. Do you think or has anyone ever told you that you have low self-esteem?

24. Do you pray or meditate on a regular basis?

25. Do you often judge or criticize others in your mind or in front of other people?

26. Are you or have you ever been tormented by fear of illness or death?

27. Is there anyone in your life whom you have been unable to forgive?

28. Are you a chronic overachiever who is still dissatisfied with life?

29. If your life were an airplane, would you be the pilot, or just a hostage tied up and blindfolded in the cargo hold?

30. Write down your major goals over the next year and the next five years in each of the following areas: inner life/self transformation, health and fitness, interpersonal relationships, career, and financial situation.

31. In each of these areas, describe what your life would look like if you could change anything you wanted.

Once you have answered all the questions as honestly and thoroughly as possible I'd like you to do something very particular with it. Put it

THE 5 PILLARS OF LIFE

in an envelope, label it, and then put it away in a place you will remember, because you're not going to look at it again until you've worked your way through the entire contents of this book!

If you've come this far, there's little doubt that you're seriously interested in changing your life. Chances are that you've already read some other books about changing some element in your life. Let me ask you this: Do you honestly believe that your generation is the first one on planet Earth to engage in a desperate search for happiness, fulfillment, and the meaning of life?

Obviously not! After three decades of research in this area, I can tell you this unequivocally: Any truly impartial historical study could not fail to conclude that the answers you are seeking have long since been found, tested, and clinically proven, and that furthermore these answers are available in one place only. That's right; any unbiased investigation would tell you that everything you seek — and more — is both possible and readily available. You just have to know where to look.

So where is this one place where the answers can be found? Everything you so desperately wish for is to be found exclusively within what I call *authentic ancient traditions of self-transformation*. These traditions are the sole repository of the three things you must have:

1. A correct understanding of the human psychosomatic structure and its relationship to the world in general. (This is where most of modern psychology gets off to a wrong start and why most of its methods are abject failures in practice.)
2. Correct training methods. (This is where the New Age material always goes off the rails: It presents secondary methods as if they were important.)
3. A repository of direct experience stretching back for centuries.

Millennia ago, authentic ancient traditions analyzed your own personal situation on a level so deep it defies comprehension. So perhaps the stupidest and the most dangerous thing you could possibly do is to ignore this huge body of knowledge and wisdom. If you have no experience in auto repair but have a problem with your car, you go to your auto mechanic. You don't try to do it yourself because you don't have the tools or the knowledge. And you certainly don't take your car to someone who specializes in interior decorating! And yet this is exactly the kind of thing that people today are doing when they seek answers to their questions in some of today's self-help literature.

Down through the ages, practitioners of many different authentic ancient traditions adopted a similar approach to life in order to help them attain self-transformation most effectively. Because so many features of this way of life resembled what was demanded of the best professional soldier or warrior, this came to be called the Warrior's way of life, or Warriorship — even though most of its practitioners have never even held a weapon, let alone taken a life. This alternate paradigm or way of life is in many ways the inverse of the ineffective lifestyle lived by the vast majority of people.

The purpose of *The Five Pillars of Life: Reclaiming Ownership of your Mind, Body, and Future* is to introduce you to this alternate paradigm and teach you how to repattern your life according to it. And the results will be these:

- A rock-solid inner peace and tranquility
- Harmony and order in your physical surroundings
- Fulfillment in your relationships with others
- Vastly improved health through specific diet and exercise programs
- Control of your time and energy
- Unbending willpower
- Mastery of thoughts, emotions, complexes, and hang-ups that had previously enslaved you
- Leaving the crippling stress of modern life behind
- Vanquishing anxiety, fear, and their source—the fear of death
- Defining and achieving your goals and objectives
- Distinguishing worthwhile goals from seductive traps
- Recognizing authentic traditions of self-transformation from their modern imitations

- Stepping onto the path leading to union with the Absolute
- Transforming your life into a work of art

The Five Pillars of Life will give you:

- The distilled wisdom from authentic traditions of self-transformation
- A systematic training method and timetable
- Access to the real and seldom explained training secrets of authentic ancient traditions

This book is the fruit of thirty years of research, both experiential and academic, into self-transformation. It will challenge most of your assumptions about your own possibilities; about religion, faith, and morality; and about the very origins of Western civilization itself. It will not fit on any continuum you are familiar with; it is neither liberal nor conservative, neither puritanical nor laissez-faire. It is unlikely you will be able to pigeonhole its conclusions in the neat categories of your intellectual universe. This book will alternately please and aggravate, enlighten and confuse, console and take to task, reassure and terrify. It is not easy or light reading, for it comes not from the everyday world we know, but from deep within the mysterious worlds of Eastern Orthodox Christianity ("Orthodoxy" for short), Taoism, Buddhism, and other authentic ancient traditions of self-transformation.

If you want remake your life, there are a few basic tenets you must keep in mind at all times. You will have to remind yourself of these principles every so often and make sure that you're following them:

- Your target must be the real thing. (Aiming at wrong goals is a waste of time and energy.)
- Your training methods must be correct. (Wrong practice leads to wrong results.)
- Your approach must be comprehensive. (Any area of life left out of the training syllabus will eventually sabotage you.)

- Your practice must be "24/7"—in other words, unending.
- Your energies must be concentrated.
- You must free yourself from cares and worries.

All this may sound a bit daunting, but this book will teach you how to accomplish all of this in a simple and systematic way.

IS THIS BOOK FOR YOU?

You want to be happy. Everybody does. If you think for a moment about the ingredients that go into that elusive feeling of "being happy," you'll see that your happiness is built on five pillars:

1. Inner (mental and emotional) peace
2. Feeling in control of your time and energy
3. A high level of mental and physical energy and health
4. Satisfying relationships (love and friendship)
5. Material success and security

These can be shortened as follows:

1. Tranquility
2. Control
3. Health
4. Love
5. Security

These are usually considered essential human needs for a happy and fulfilling life. If any one of the five pillars topples over, you feel off balance, anxious, and *un*happy. Brian Tracy, a superb coach of personal effectiveness, says that happiness is given to us as a kind of internal barometer, so that when we are unhappy, we need to ask ourselves some serious questions about our lifestyle and our choices. Despite what you might think, authentic ancient traditions would agree with this assessment:

Most of our unhappiness comes from our wrong approaches and choices, so that unhappiness can be considered a wake-up call.

They would add, though, that all five pillars of happiness are inherently vulnerable, so that to base your happiness on them is setting yourself up for a fall. Someone treats you badly and you lose your inner peace. Your girlfriend or boyfriend breaks up with you and you go into a funk. You get laid off. Face it, the five pillars are pretty precarious.... Moreover, the happiness you can get from the five pillars is not nearly as fulfilling as people think — that's why you so often hear about people who seem to "have it all" express disappointment and say, "Is that all there is?"

Fortunately the answer is no. There's more. There is a happiness that gives you everything the five pillars do, but in a permanent and indestructible form. There is a way of cultivating happiness that takes all of the pillars to a higher level and makes them into your permanent property.

The Five Pillars of Life will show you how to attain all five pillars of happiness and how to transform them into the indestructible basis of your life and your future by *not* aiming for them. That's right, the more you try to grasp the five pillars of happiness, the more they will elude you. You must aim at the five pillars of transformation instead.

According to the ancient systems of self-transformation, these five pillars of transformation are as follows:

1. *Overhauling the externals of your life* to bring them in line with self-transformation. This means mastering your use of your time, home environment, health, relationships, and financial situation.

2. *Applying the one and only method that can give you complete mastery of your inner world.* Unless you apply this one method you will never achieve any real progress; it is the basis of all the wonders of the ancient traditions.

3. *Rediscovering your unstoppable willpower.* This may seem

daunting, but anyone can learn the rules of willpower quickly and easily. We only fail because we don't play by the rules.

4. *Embracing the warrior's way of life*, the secret that will allow you to win the paradoxical war for inner peace.

5. *Learning to love*, that is, cultivating the virtues (patterns of thought and action) that act as guardians of the real transformative power in human life.

When you cultivate the five pillars of transformation, the five pillars of happiness gradually fall into your hands without any special effort on your part.

In general, three kinds of people read books like this, and each is looking for something in particular: The peace-seekers are looking for inner peace and relief from stress. The spiritual-seekers are looking for a greater feeling of being spiritually connected. The performance-seekers are looking for an effective lifestyle that will give them the tools they need to pursue their goals. *The Five Pillars of Life* answers all these needs by providing proven methods to defeat stress, to put you in control of your life, and to make you vastly more effective in everything you do.

But to each group, this book gives a particular message: Peace-seekers need to think more holistically, because they won't find what they're looking for unless they fix their whole life. Spiritual seekers need to realize that the spiritual "feelings" they often seek are not what real spiritual life is based on. And performance-seekers need to learn to relax and smell the roses, and to drill it into their heads that doing more of one thing means doing less of another.

Within all three groups there is a mixed bag of "spiritual" or "religious" backgrounds. If you can identify with any of the following points, *The Five Pillars of Life* will be exceptionally helpful to you.

- You are an ("Eastern") Orthodox Christian but are confused about how to put Orthodoxy into practice.

- You are a Western Christian (Roman Catholic, Eastern-Rite Catholic, or Protestant of any kind) but are dissatisfied with your spiritual life.
- You are a Buddhist, Taoist, or member of some other ancient tradition but are confused about how to make your tradition "work" here, in the urban civilization of the Western world.
- You are an atheist or agnostic searching for an approach to life that makes sense.

TERMINOLOGY

Like any other endeavor, self-transformation has its own jargon, and that jargon varies from one system of self-transformation to another. So to understand the rest of this book, you'll need to understand certain terms, elaborated in the next sections.

Authentic Ancient Traditions

Authentic ancient traditions are those whose sole purpose is to bring about the complete transformation of the practitioner's life on the ontological level. In other words, this transformation is so deep that it goes far beyond "being nice" or "feeling better" or "inner peace." It is not just a change of attitude, but an organic metamorphosis of the very "stuff" that your physical and psychological elements are made of. This process actualizes the incredible potential latent in every human being.

The authentic ancient traditions used here include Eastern Orthodox Christianity, Mahayana Buddhism (usually of the Tibetan variety and mostly from the Kagyü and Gelug schools), Taoism (usually the Northern or Southern Complete Reality schools), and some aboriginal traditions from the Americas. Although you probably think of these as "religions," they are in fact the opposite, as discussed subsequently.

Authentic ancient traditions are the most important treasures on the face of this earth. They are irreplaceable treasures because only they can explain what self-transformation is, teach the methods for achieving it, and show proven clinical results over a period of several centuries or even millennia.

Let's be clear that I am not proposing any kind of muddy relativism among traditions and still less any form of syncretism — in which you take the elements you like from different traditions and throw them together. The approach presented here is to insist on the integrity of each authentic tradition and to recommend that each person adopt one of these traditions without trying to mix and match elements from others. Each of these traditions has shed its blood to delve into the truth of human existence, and their findings and teachings are so deep that it is completely impossible to determine their relative worth by academic investigation alone.

I am an Orthodox Christian by conviction, but I include material here from a number of other traditions for two reasons. First, many of their conclusions about self-transformation are astonishingly similar — and sometimes identical — to those of Orthodoxy. And second, nothing has ever shaken my profound respect for these other traditions, a respect based in some cases on my personal participation in them.

There are also profound differences among these traditions, and I have no intention of glossing over them. However, most of them reside on the level of cosmology, of overall worldview, whereas on the basic level of how the human psychosomatic entity functions and how to heal it, there is considerable consensus.

God or the Absolute Reality

You may believe in God in some way, or perhaps you are an agnostic or an atheist. Whatever the case, I begin with a proposition that every intelligent person can subscribe to intellectually: There is an ultimate reality behind the universe we see and experience. This reality, whether personal or impersonal, is in some way the pattern for all that exists. For the purposes of this book, I refer to this reality as "the Absolute."

This is not a New Age attempt to dilute the concept of God, nor am I saying that your concept of God is unimportant — it is critical. But, it is not critical right now. Whether you believe that the

THE 5 PILLARS OF LIFE

Absolute reality is personal or impersonal, triune or one, will have little impact on your success in the preliminary work of self-transformation as found in this book. Here the Christian, the Buddhist, and the average agnostic are on a level playing field, as long as each is willing to keep an open mind.

If there is an ultimate reality of any kind behind our visible universe, then it follows that there is an ultimate truth to human existence. Consequently, there is also a right way to live in order to actualize your potential and become the person you're meant to be.

Likewise, there are also many wrong ways to live your life, ways that will not lead you to the goal of self-transformation. Therefore, your most important task in life is to find this truth behind human existence and assimilate it into your daily life.

Therapy, not "Religion"

Rev. Dr. John Romanides writes in "Religion as a Neurobiological Illness":

> All fantasies, especially that of religion, are caused by a short-circuit at the centre of the human personality. This short-circuit, which exists between the heart which pumps blood (the circulatory system) and the spinal cord which circulates spinal fluid (the nervous system) is only repaired by ceaseless prayer in the heart. It is only when the short-circuit is repaired that you begin to be liberated from the realm of fantasy.[1]

Startling, isn't it? A world-renowned Orthodox priest and theologian calling religion a "neurobiological illness"! But he's right—Orthodox

Christianity is *not* a religion in the conventional Western sense of that word. And for that matter, neither are other authentic ancient traditions. What Westerners conventionally call "religion" is a term that applies almost exclusively to their own approach to life as it has developed historically over the last thousand years or so.

"Religion" in the Western sense the word has a number of particular traits. And generally speaking these traits apply to the vast majority of Western people who "practice their religion":

1. Religious teachings are ideological statements divorced from real life that people subscribe to based on emotional considerations. Teachings of authentic traditions are based on an experience of true life, and practitioners adhere to them based on observable verification.

2. Religion provides psychological comfort and self-justification in the face of its failure to cure psychospiritual (noetic) illness, telling you your sickness is health. Authentic traditions take you from sickness to health.

3. Religion shifts the blame for good and evil, and for the final outcome of life, onto a deity or process (saying, e.g., that illness is a punishment from God or that God decides whether to forgive you and send you to heaven or to damn you to hell). Authentic traditions say that the Absolute Reality never does harm and that the only real danger to us in this world or hereafter comes from ourselves.

4. Religions and authentic traditions both have a ceremonial aspect or some collective manifestation, but the religious version exists to provide psychological comfort or aesthetic pleasure, whereas the authentic version is there to lead you to self-transformation.

5. Religion is always reduced to a compartment of life, whereas

training in any authentic tradition involves every moment of life.

6. Religion's "transformation" of human life is limited to the superficial aspects of the personality, is often based on a tedious list of prohibitions, and is geared toward social acceptability. Religion produces nice people; authentic traditions produce extraordinary ones.

7. Real self-transformation is not a goal of religion; the knowledge and methods required for self-transformation are absent, and there is no access to a lineage of transformed people. Life degenerates into salvation by association ("I'm saved because I'm part of the group") and salvation by conviction ("I'm saved because I hold a particular opinion").

8. Religion is ignorant of the technical terminology of self-transformation and interprets it in a general and nebulous way. The religious version of a tradition will seldom have any real idea what the authentic version is talking about, even if they use the same language.

9. Religion is comfort-loving and presents no real challenge to its adherents, whereas authentic traditions take you beyond your comfort zone and into realms that religion knows nothing of.

10. Religion abhors mystery and tries to explain everything with concepts. These concepts can be controlled and manipulated by a cadre of "experts" for the good of the institution, whereas transformed people—saints, immortals, or bodhisattvas — are notoriously hard to control.

Given these traits of religion, it is not too surprising that Fr. Romanides classifies religion as a "neurobiological illness." This means that religion has its origin in the fallen state — where the neurobiological malfunction characteristic of life in the fallen world has not been healed – and that it perpetuates this unhealed state as if it were normal. So it is not surprising that religion prevents countless millions of people from finding true fulfillment and happiness. And like all illness, it leads to untold suffering and misery.

The Nous and the Fallen State of Being

According to every authentic tradition, humankind's current state of existence is profoundly abnormal no matter how subjectively "happy" people may be. I use the Orthodox terminology of *fall* to describe humankind's current existence in a world ruled by time and death, where suffering and eventual disintegration are unavoidable. Buddhism refers to this existence as *Samsara*. This disintegration is primarily psycho-spiritual and manifests itself in the neuroses, emotional disequilibrium, fear, and egocentrism that follow us all like a shadow. Physical death is just the final stage of this inner corruption. Ancient traditions discovered that if you reverse this inner corruption – and there is a way – you free yourself from the power of death and achieve perfect peace, whether or not the body itself eventually dies.

The path to real healing looks like this: Your *nous* (rhymes with goose, not with house)—the innermost aspect of the human mind and consciousness—has been damaged in the fall. The rational mind–the reasoning faculty behind our conscious thought—then takes over and subjects you to the rule of random emotions through temporal conditioning. This gives rise to a false personality or "ego" and subsequently to the rule of fear. Healing is about rediscovering and curing the *nous* and all of the internal psychosomatic powers. Without this, people remain trapped in the delusion of individuality, living as isolated biological/psychological entities obsessed with survival. Religion only reinforces this approach — decorating the fall, in effect.

Once healed, you experience life as indescribable love for the other and realize you have transcended death and fear. Self-transformation returns the noetic energy (the energy of the *nous*) to the heart, restoring you to optimum functioning on all levels. It is the only complete

THE 5 PILLARS OF LIFE

fulfillment that exists. All other "fulfillments" are nothing but substitutes for the real thing, and so they are distracting, deceptive, and ultimately dangerous.

When noetic energy is restored to its proper place in the heart and a person is cleansed from all external influences, the main drives and powers are reeducated and returned to normal focus. Curing the *nous* requires considerable effort on our part, and that's why Taoism describes it as reversing the natural process. The process Taoism calls "natural" is the way most people think human life ought to be, according to their fallen perceptions, but in reality it leads to inner disintegration and death. So it is by going along with the natural process that we have gotten ourselves into our present mess. Only by reversing the course of our lives can we begin to make a difference. Going along produces mortals, say the Taoist texts, while reversal produces immortals.

To continue with a bit of extremely useful Taoist imagery, our predicament can be thought of this way: In our fallen state we are extremely vulnerable or yin to all the harmful energies in the world around us, but impervious or yang to the healing energies of the Absolute. Our goal is to reverse this situation completely, so that we are yang to the corrupt energy surrounding us, while increasingly yin or permeable to the influence of the Absolute Reality that is the ontological basis of ourselves and the universe.

Orthodoxy versus Western Christianity

Insofar as it even exists in the popular mind, Orthodoxy is just one of the three main types of Christianity, one of the "three branches on the tree." Alternatively, some would tell you it is one of the two "lungs" of Christianity—the Eastern and Western. The fact is, though, that Orthodoxy is not even on the same continuum as the Western Christianity of the past millennium.

It is vital for Western Christians to realize that what we now call Western Christianity is merely a pale reflection of its former self, which is Orthodoxy. It is also important for them to understand the difference between religion and therapy, and that it is possible for them, even individually, to begin to repair the damage to themselves, their churches, and their culture. And the only way to do this is to set out on the path to self-transformation.

Table 1.1 on page 27 gives some idea of the differences between Orthodoxy and Western Christianity, and the real significance of some of these differences will become apparent to you later in the book as you begin to see how they relate to self-transformation.

I don't have the time here to go into detail about the historical reasons for these deformations of Christian teaching in the West, but the thumbnail sketch looks something like this. From the ninth century onward most of Western Europe was conquered by the Frankish empire. The Franks then imposed their mistaken version of Christianity on the preexisting Orthodoxy of the West. Frankish Christianity was built almost exclusively on the interpretations of St. Augustine of Hippo, a fifth century North African bishop. Unfortunately, many of Augustine's teachings on the relationship between man and God, the nature of God, the nature of man, and self-transformation and how to accomplish it are grossly mistaken. This new Frankish Christianity became what is now called "Roman Catholicism" and forms the basis of all of the various Protestant sects. This is why Roman Catholic clergy are still referred to in Greek as "frangopapas" — Frankish priests.

This new "religious" version of Christianity taught that the highest faculty of the human person is the rational mind. I will go into considerable detail later as to why this teaching is exceptionally dangerous, and I will even show you how to verify for yourself that this is the case. No authentic ancient tradition has ever taught this.

The Frankish Christianity also reduces the relationship between man and God to juridical categories, so that salvation itself becomes a legal question. This is not only preposterous and unbelievable, but it also ends up portraying God as a kind of monstrous cosmic tyrant. In this view, God himself is responsible for all evil — he decided to banish Adam from Paradise, he decided to create death as a punishment, and he decides whom to send to Hell for eternal punishment. The original Christian tradition taught none of these things.

Unfortunately, the methods of self-transformation within any

Table 1.1: Western Christianity and Orthodoxy

Western Christianity	Orthodoxy
When Adam and Eve sinned, God invented death as a way of punishing them and their descendants.	Adam and Eve fell automatically into progressive decay when they chose to separate themselves from God's life-giving energies. God did not invent death.
As an infinite being, God was infinitely offended by their sin.	God is infinite love beyond comprehension, and cannot be offended by anything.
God would not relent in punishing the human race until He could punish someone as great as Himself — Jesus Christ.	God had no interest in punishing anyone. Christ assumed a human body and soul in order to destroy death in his own flesh, to destroy humanity's slavery to corruption.
Christ was punished in our place, so that we can receive forgiveness and go to Heaven.	God the Father was neither punishing His Son, nor looking for repayment of a mythical debt. God was willing to suffer to help humanity out of an impossible dilemma of its own making.
The merits Christ accumulated by doing this are distributed to those who believe in Him.	By overcoming death inside our human nature/organism, Christ has refashioned humanity on the ontological level.
God decides whether or not to forgive each person.	God forgives everyone everything at all times. The question is whether we are willing to receive this forgiveness.
Heaven and Hell are opposites — Hell is exile from God.	Heaven and Hell are the same. Hell, too, is intimacy with God, but is experienced as intolerable by those who have resisted His love all their lives.
Humanity's main problem is obtaining forgiveness from God.	Humanity's main problem is corruption/death.
Each person has inherited the guilt of Adam at the moment of conception ("Original Sin").	We inherit only mortality. No one is guilty of anything he or she did not do personally. Sexuality is not inherently tainted.

Table 1.1: Western Christianity and Orthodoxy (continued from p. 27)

Western Christianity	Orthodoxy
You cannot really know God in this life.	You really can know God in this life, becoming by participation everything that God is by nature — this is called "deification."
The Scriptures are God's revelation to us.	The Scriptures are about God's revelation to us: they describe how to participate in revelation. They are the map, not the territory.
The Scriptures are the only book written by God.	The Scriptures were written by people under divine inspiration. Many other books written by holy people are also inspired and error-free.
The Pope is infallible (Catholicism).	No human being is infallible, and one cannot become infallible by holding a particular job.
The mystical experience of the saints has no doctrinal authority.	The mystical experience of the saints has authoritative value.

authentic ancient tradition depend on and are expressed in certain doctrinal teachings. And when these teachings are perverted, the methods of self-transformation are undercut. So not surprisingly, the tradition of self-transformation was slowly extinguished by the new Frankish Christianity.

The authenticity of any ancient tradition can be verified easily by whether or not it produces the results that it claims. This is why Christ himself said, " You will know them by their fruits" (Matt.7:16; RSV). When any segment of any tradition fails to produce transformed human beings over a significant period of time, this is an infallible indication that it has gone seriously wrong.

People today idolize the rich and successful, the charismatic speaker, the icons of "personal effectiveness," "together" people and people who "make a difference" or "live their dreams." The transformed person may be any or none of the above. But the treasure he or

THE 5 PILLARS OF LIFE

she has is an inner joy that defies any description and that no change in circumstance can diminish in any way. Some of them can do many wondrous things as well, but those are just extras.

THE NEW AGE MOVEMENT

What is now called the "New Age Movement" (NAM) is really a twentieth-century North American cultural phenomenon. The NAM is notoriously difficult to identify in a concrete sense because it is not an institution and does not have membership cards. But one of its opponents has summed it up rather well as "a conglomeration of theologies, hopes and expectations held together with an eclectic teaching on salvation, of 'correct thinking' and 'correct knowledge.' It is the theology of 'feel-goodism,' 'universal tolerance' and 'moral relativism.'[2]

Of the large number of people who are dissatisfied with the institutional religion they know, a great many are being seduced by the NAM without even knowing it. It is often difficult for the novice to distinguish an authentic ancient tradition from the NAM version of that same tradition. And this is particularly a problem for Far Eastern traditions like Buddhism and Taoism, which have been in some measure hijacked by the NAM within North America.[3] Indigenous North American native traditions are also a NAM favorite.

The NAM perversion of any authentic tradition always has certain common traits:

- *It is comfortable* — Following this version of the tradition does not present any serious challenge and certainly won't subject you to any discomfort.

- *It is very North American in ethos* — The attitudes of the people will be typical of the surrounding society: lighthearted, fun-loving, and superficial. However, cult-like practices using painful methods and demanding blind obedience have occasionally been seen.

- NAM *teachings are very often based on an exaggeration of secondary methods* — This often comes across as a technique-centered method of transformation and is actually based on age-old deviations caused by Oriental misunderstandings of Oriental texts.

So it is extremely important for anyone thinking of getting involved in an ancient tradition to learn how to distinguish between the real thing and its NAM counterpart. The first reason for caution is this: The real thing shows how to train you and change your life. The best you can expect from the NAM version is to waste lots of time making little progress, and the worst is that you may fall into serious delusion and suffer physical or psychological damage.

There are a number of telltale signs that can help you to make this distinction. First of all, the NAM often makes references to a "higher self," to the "universe," to "your higher power," your "super conscious mind," to "cosmic energies," and to other similar amorphous concepts. The NAM is also wildly syncretistic by nature and will readily drag in material from all kinds of disparate sources.

Although some of the NAM is built on a Far Eastern traditional base, a great deal of it is not. Much of it is based on or purports to be based on older West European antecedents such as druidism, Gnosticism, magic/witchcraft or various forms of occultism. Conversely, it may claim to base itself on some indigenous shamanism from North America or elsewhere. In a great many cases, though, there is actually no real living connection with the tradition in question at all. It is simply all made up and entirely fraudulent. These things are often invented simply to seduce the gullible and curious and to make money for the inventors.

One particular segment of the NAM champions the "Gnostics" and the "Gnostic Gospels." This line of thinking asserts that the original tradition of Christianity was actually that of the Gnostics and that the institutional church — those would be the bad guys — hijacked the entire enterprise at a very early date. On the one hand, you can sympathize with these people for recognizing that the Christianity they know does not have much to offer. On the other hand, though, their hypothesis is historically plain wrong. Far from being mystical savants similar to the Buddhists, the Gnostics of early days were simply a conglomeration of extremely unimpressive cults. Their teachings were worthless, inconsistent gibberish, and there is no evidence that they ever produced a single transformed human being.

However, many of the accusations and criticisms leveled at the NAM from Western Christian sources are not entirely well-founded. They criticize the NAM for tolerating everything except Christianity (but it is by nature a rebellion against their version of Christianity, and NAM adherents do not know any other Christianity), for replacing sin as the central problem of human life with a "lack of knowledge" (but that is because the Western understanding of sin is both unbelievable and intolerable), for teaching that man is evolving to Godhood (but when you have lost the original Christian teaching on deification, you cannot blame these people for recognizing that something is missing—it is in human nature itself to seek deification), for seeing man as basically good (but the one-sided Augustinian pessimism about man found in the West is exaggerated. People react against what oppresses them). In other words, Western Christian critics of the NAM simply don't recognize that they themselves have created the NAM in the first place. If you oppress people and create a rebellion, then the existence of rebels shouldn't terribly surprise you!

THIRTY YEARS OF RESEARCH AND PRACTICE IN SELF-TRANSFORMATION

I have now spent more than thirty years of my life researching authentic ancient traditions and almost as long practicing what they teach in some form or other. In my youth I was blessed with a particular obsession — the search for the truth of human existence. It was then that I began reading material from ancient traditions. I read anything I could get my hands on — Buddhist, Taoist, Hindu, Sufi, and no doubt a great many other, less reputable things.

This taught me in short order how to distinguish a religion from an authentic tradition. I came to see clearly that authentic traditions always have a firm ontological basis. On the other hand, the tradition I came from—liberal protestantism—showed all the sure signs associated with the loss of ontological consciousness: mind-body dualism, juridical worldview, superficial moralizing, and lack of results. From there I went on my journey through Roman Catholicism to Sufism and into Far Eastern traditions. At this point I despaired that real Christianity had survived — if indeed it had ever existed.

But then one day at the end of my undergraduate studies, a friend of mine took me to an Orthodox service and put a book or two in my hand. The significance of what stood before me dawned on me rather quickly. Here was an ontological understanding of reality that could trace its lineage back to the earliest times and could prove that at all times up to the present it has gotten and continues to get results. Of course, this was Orthodoxy in books, whereas the incarnate version here in North America left a great deal to be desired. Like any tradition spread worldwide with millions of adherents, Orthodoxy presents many faces, and not all of these are pretty. But it nevertheless conceals an unspeakable treasure within.

When I returned to Canada after studying Orthodoxy, I began to seek out the best examples of contemporary Orthodoxy and some of its transformed people. I had the good fortune of being able to meet with some remarkable men and women around the world. My particular good fortune was to stumble into a relationship with the man who would later become my guide — a very old Russian priest who passed away in 1999. My nine years or so with him were a great gift to me, though it took me a while to realize that. I made the mistake initially of assuming he was just a rather poorly educated ethnic priest with not much knowledge of Orthodoxy, like so many others I had met. In fact, he was well educated (both as a professional engineer and as a theologian), came from a long priestly lineage, and had grown up in

Russia before the revolution. His formation in this authentic tradition was so strong and unshakable that even the phenomenal sufferings of his life – typical of those who lived under Stalin or who fought on the "Russian front"—were unable to undermine it. Though utterly humble and living in meager circumstances, he was indeed a prince among men and had a deep knowledge of the human condition.

Over my years of giving spiritual guidance to all kinds of people, I've noticed that life in the modern Western world has presented Orthodoxy and other authentic traditions with some entirely new challenges that are going to require a more systematic and tailored approach than the one initially imported from abroad. The present volume is an attempt to provide a fresh approach, and one that is can be used profitably by anyone, no matter what his or her background.

Please note also: None of the teachings in this book are mine. They are the teachings of transformed men and women from all over the world and it is to them, our most precious ancestors in the human race, that we owe an unpayable debt. But they have no interest in payment; they only want us to put their teachings into practice so that we can share in their joy.

Each chapter gives you a combination of the theory and practical exercises. You'll notice that there are a number of main points, called Miraculous Ancient Formulas, Inner Principles, and Paradoxes so you don't miss the main ideas. Finally, each chapter concludes with one key point that sums up the "trick" to understanding and implementing that chapter's contents in your daily life. Though they may appear simple, the Keys are very deep, in fact too deep to elaborate on in this book; but you can always find more information at www.RockSolidLife.com.

The one thing I can promise you is this:

If you follow the teachings in this book and put them into practice diligently, you will be astounded at the difference they make in your life within a matter of months, if not weeks. So if you have the desire, the commitment, and the love of truth, let's start training right now.

Chapter Two

THE PROGRAM: RECLAIMING YOUR TIME, ENERGY, and LIFE

Other than using flawed methods, the most frequent cause of failure in transforming any aspect of our lives is lack of focus. In today's culture, our energy is dispersed in a thousand peripheral activities, and we find ourselves quickly exhausted, our mental attention seized hundreds of times a day by the demands of others from the outside and our own passions from the inside.

All this, coupled with the frenetic pace of activity in our society, a pace that goes a long way toward keeping us blind, exhausted, and enslaved to the ego, contributes greatly to our inability to keep on any given path for any length of time. People have lots of energy, but unless they can plug the leaks and channel it, this energy is not available to them. "Without attention," wrote Joseph the Hesychast, "both the *nous* and the powers of the soul are diffused in vain and ordinary things, like useless water running down the street."[1] The danger here is that we will continue to fritter away vast amounts of

> ### MIRACULOUS ANCIENT FORMULA
> ﴾﴾﴾﴾﴾﴾ 1 ﴿﴿﴿﴿﴿﴿
>
> Program and Training: A carefully worked out program combined with correct and consistent training cannot fail.

time and energy, that our good purpose will be hijacked by our own weaknesses and/or the agendas of other people.

Our task now is to show you how to plug the leaks and harness your energy and your will so that you make steady progress toward your goals and objectives. The key to this harnessing of your resources is the Program.

The word *program* comes from the Greek word *programma* and means basically a schedule or regime that you follow. The Program is normally set up as a weekly schedule, and it encompasses all the twenty-four hours of your day and all of your activities during that time.

Your Program is the framework on which effective training depends. So your success depends on your training, but your training won't work without a Program. Virtually no one has ever succeeded at this greatest of all endeavours without a plan, and that's what your Program is. Think of it this way: In the vast arsenal of self-transformation, your training is an artillery shell, but your Program is the gun that fires it. What good is a shell if you can't fire it? Well, I suppose you could use it as a doorstop or a fence post, but in reality it's useless. And it doesn't matter how powerful a shell it is — it could have a nuclear warhead and still be equally useless in war. Without a Program, training has no effect.

Once you put your Program in place and work out the major bugs, you have to stick to it relentlessly; in a certain sense you have to treat it as a god. I know this sounds fanatical, but believe me, it's the only way to win. Later I'll add a bit of nuance to all this, because you can afford to be flexible with some elements of your Program and not with others. Why the fanatical approach? Because, unless you stick to your Program, you will be like an artillery unit that only fires a shell or two every day if they feel like it, and those rounds are duds that don't explode or cause damage even if they land on target. And just as no army could win a war this way, you won't ever find the happiness you

THE 5 PILLARS OF LIFE

seek without consistent effort. Succinctly put: The training must be carried out during every moment, because training that is limited to certain times of the day or week has insufficient force to effect deep existential change.

Your Program must:

- Reflect your goals
- Be based on an accurate assessment of your life circumstances
- Be feasible for you within the framework of these circumstances
- Cover twenty-four hours a day, seven days a week.
- Contain carefully chosen training activities

Let me ask you this. Assuming that a good many of you have played basketball in your life, how did you learn to dribble the ball? No doubt by doing it over and over again. So how did you learn to play the game as a whole? Was it just by sitting around watching NBA games and drinking beer? I rather doubt it! But let's take those NBA players for a moment, or anyone else who has developed high level skills in basketball. How did they achieve this?

- Well, first you probably realize it involved constantly drilling individual skills like dribbling, layups, jump shots, and so on.

- Then they had to get used to working with others, which involves passing, strategy, and teamwork.

- Then, of course, they had to get used to using these skills in a hostile context, first by going one-on-one against an opponent, and then in the larger game context.

- Then they had to learn to use all these skills in the complex environment of a real game, thus developing situational awareness.

- And finally, they had to train all these skills until they became second nature.

Western culture has no problem with the idea that learning a physical skill requires constant and repetitive training to assimilate the skills on a physical level. Unfortunately, when it comes to skills that go beyond the physical plane, Westerners do not readily make the same assumptions.

Western culture easily recognizes two planes of being: the physical and the mental or intellectual. You can learn a new physical skill, in which case the kind of training I've just talked about is necessary, or you can learn a new intellectual skill, like macroeconomics, for example. The first requires programming physical responses into your muscle memory, whereas the second requires the intellectual manipulation of abstract concepts.

What totally escapes the grasp of modern man, however, is the very existence of a third plane of being, which has its own skills and unique training methods. Whereas the reasoning mind can give you only indirect knowledge, authentic traditions insist that every human person has a largely forgotten faculty of unmediated direct knowledge. It is through the development of this and only this faculty that your life can be transformed in a profound way. As noted in the introduction, Orthodoxy calls this faculty the *nous*.

Now, in terms of training, whereas physical skill requires one type of training and intellectual skill another, "noetic skill," the skill of the *nous*, requires yet a third. All ancient traditions agree that noetic training requires:

- Bodily participation, because the body helps train the *nous*, and
- Consistent and repetitive effort, similar to that found in physical training

Authentic traditions have already noticed that Westerners don't readily understand how to do noetic training. Most Westerners coming to Orthodoxy, for example, unconsciously approach conversion as if it were a matter of changing ideological affiliation. Of course, you can change ideologies as easily as you can change your coat. (Have you noticed all those ex-Communists who are still running many of the countries in Eastern Europe? The ones who were proclaiming world revolution one day and then trying to join the World Trade Organization the next...?) But Orthodoxy and other ancient systems are trying to introduce you to a new plane of being, and that requires not so much the transmission of certain facts, as the effort to assimilate deeper principles, something the body and the *nous* must struggle together to achieve.

I started the discussion of training with the example of basketball, which resides on the physical plane of being. Yes, someone may have written a book called "The Zen of Basketball" or something, but most basketball players don't approach it that way. Now let's look at a more profound example, at a task that combines both physical and noetic elements: the Oriental martial arts (Although most Westerners and some Orientals in fact limit their own martial arts practices to the physical plane).

The Oriental martial arts have been woven into the fabric of Buddhist and Taoist life for centuries and are often considered in that cultural context as vehicles of self-transformation. This certainly does not mean you have to practise a martial art to make spiritual progress — this is not so even in the Shaolin Temple, the ancestral home of much of Chinese martial tradition. What matters for us is that in the martial arts, physical and noetic work are closely integrated.

The following chart outlines the approximate stages of development in the study of an authentic Oriental martial art as traditionally presented.

The would-be martial artist:

1. Learns basic conditioning to prevent injury.

2. Learns basic stances as a foundation.

3.   Learns to move from one stance to another, giving mobility to the foundation.

4.   Learns basic combat techniques (e.g., blocks and strikes, punches and kicks, throws, locks).

5.   Drills these endlessly, both alone and with a partner.

6.   Strings these together as a pre-arranged solo set.

7.   Strings these together as a pre-arranged dual set.

8.   Practices mock combat with a training partner (low threat scenario).

9.   Does the same in a tournament setting (higher threat scenario).

10. Assimilates these techniques until they become second nature. At this point he or she still thinks and strategizes, and the art is still perceived as "complex."

11. "Disappears" and the art becomes utterly simple, requiring no thought at all. This is true spontaneity and creativity, beyond all fixed structure and technique.

12. No longer requires physical contact to win. No longer thinks about "winning" and "losing," but only about benefiting the opponent. At this stage life becomes a work of art.

Notice that the training proceeds in a methodical, step-by-step manner, where each new step is introduced only after the previous one has been very well assimilated. In fact, each of the first three items would take months, without any other distracting material being introduced. This is the traditional way of teaching many Oriental martial arts, but it is almost never seen in North America, because Westerners have no patience. Needless to say, the disregard for the traditional syllabus almost inevitably leads to mediocre results.

In the martial arts, as in every authentic ancient tradition, the following inner principle applies: If you seek to learn a new step on the syllabus without having mastered the previous one, and especially the foundational practices, you will sabotage any possibility of reaching a high level of accomplishment.

> ## INNER PRINCIPLE
> ### ⋘⋘⋘2.2⋘⋘⋘
>
> If you seek to learn a new step on the syllabus without having mastered the previous one, and especially the foundational practices, you will sabotage any possibility of reaching a high level of accomplishment.
>
> ⋘⋘⋘⋘⋘⋘⋘⋘⋘

When contemporary Taoist master Wang Liping was being trained in China a few decades ago by his three aged mentors, the foundational practice of sitting meditation was drilled ruthlessly for long periods. But unless the foundation had been stabilized in this way, all the subsequent practices would not have had their proper effect on the whole transformational process. As Wang Liping's biographers note: "Later in life, his [Wang Liping's] eyes would fill with tears as he spoke with gratitude of the unsparing efforts, relentless severity and spiritual kindness of his Taoist teachers."[2] Likewise, when the German professor Eugen Herrigel apprenticed himself to a Zen archery master in Japan of the 1930s, he was forced to undergo a long and seemingly hopeless training in drawing the bow. And then came the endless months and years just learning to release the arrow. Can you imagine the average Westerner signing up for an archery course where the instructor refuses even to discuss the idea of hitting the target? Yet, at the end of it all, Herrigel noted:

> ...I passed through the hardest schooling of my life, and though the discipline was not always easy for me to accept, I gradually came to see how much I was indebted to it. It destroyed the last traces of any preoccupation with myself and the fluctuations of my mood.[3]

Notice as well that all of the first nine steps—which would normally take many years of training—are utterly devoid of individual creativity and originality. It is pure rote learning, the kind that our contemporary educational systems so abhor. You do nothing but copy what you are shown until you get it right. End of story!

You'll find the same dynamic in the traditional method of learning Orthodox icon painting. To become an icon painter yourself, you would apprentice yourself to a master and do nothing but copy the traditional models for each given subject you are painting, be it a saint, a feast, or some other person or event. You are not allowed to depart from the ancient prototypes for years.

These methods would be incomprehensible and probably dismissed as archaic and backward by our radically individualist culture. But since western culture has no real experience of the noetic plane of existence, there is no way to explain the ancient approach in a way that would be understandable on the basis of shared experience. And yet, this approach has been shared by ancient traditions the world over, and its inner principle is: Encouraging individual creativity blocks the manifestation of transcendent creativity.

The marrow of traditional culture—on which our whole project of real self-transformation is totally dependent—can be assimilated only in proportion to the destruction of the egocentric consciousness. Herrigel is a case in point: When he finally let loose a correct shot, he was no longer the one shooting:

> "Do you now understand," the Master asked me one day after a particularly good shot, "what I mean by 'it shoots and it hits'?" "I'm afraid I don't understand anything at all anymore," I answered, "even the simplest things have got in a muddle. Is it 'I' who draw the bow, or is it the bow that draws me into the state of highest tension? Do 'I' hit the

goal, or does the goal hit me? Is 'It' spiritual when seen by the eyes of the body, or corporeal when seen by the eyes of the spirit – or both or neither? Bow, arrow, goal and ego, all melt into one another, so that I can no longer separate them. And even the need to separate has gone. For as soon as I take the bow and shoot, everything becomes so clear and straightforward and so ridiculously simple..." "Now at last," the Master broke in, "the bowstring has cut right through you."[4]

Morihei Ueshiba, the founder of the modern Japanese martial art of Aikido, attained to the highest possible levels of martial ability, a stage which seemed to come out of nowhere, almost as a gift. Only after this point was he truly spontaneous and free from bondage to set techniques, and this to such an extent that when his students would ask him to demonstrate a particular technique for a second time, Ueshiba was virtually incapable of reproducing it exactly!

With all this discussion of the arduous demands of traditional training, I don't want you to get the mistaken idea that you're in for nothing but hard slogging. Nothing could be further from the truth! As you can see, the Program is the container for your training and holds it, much like a jug holds water. Before you start pouring water into your jug – which is the subject of the rest of the book –I'll share with you some ancient secrets to make your training vastly more effective. Hard slogging happens only when these secrets are not understood.

THE KEYS TO SUCCESS:
CASHING IN BIG ON THE TIME YOU INVEST

In any ancient system of self-transformation based on noetic work, there is something very curious you may notice. The masters of these systems discovered that by concentrating their training on key areas they could progress much faster with less effort, and even arrive at their goals much sooner than they would have, had they concentrated on other areas or foolishly tried to train all aspects at once.

These key aspects are what I call *levers*. Levers actually exist in almost any new task you would like to learn, be it a sport, a foreign language or a new piece of software. A lever is a skill that, if mastered, will quickly lead you to a high level of accomplishment in the entire system.

By contrast, every system has many other subsidiary skills which, no matter how much time and effort you put in to them, will not get you much further ahead in mastering the whole system. I call these subsidiary skills boulders. Boulders are entirely legitimate and necessary elements of any system. You can't build a castle without boulders. But if you try to move the boulders by hand instead of using levers to do it, you'll only multiply your pain, effort, and time needlessly. It's work without pay. It is an important inner principle of ancient tradition to identify those skills that, according to tradition, give the quickest and most comprehensive results and train them, though without neglecting other necessary skills.

So you must learn to discriminate levers from boulders. Levers will give you 80 percent of your results for 20 percent of the effort. Boulders are the reverse. The problem, of course, is that it's not always easy to tell levers from boulders in any given task. But in the context of self-transformation you don't need to worry too much — this whole book is about levers!

One of the traps in any system is trying to do it all. The result is that you spread yourself too thin, fail to discriminate levers from boulders, and end up with a mediocre result. In any authentic system of self-transformation, and even in most other human endeavours, you can reach a very high level while training only a few elements of the whole system. As with Herrigel and archery, when you really "get it" in the context of this one small skill you're training, you've understood the whole thing. But again, this "getting it" is not an intellectual trick —

LEARNING LANGUAGES BY THE LEVERS

I have always been fascinated by languages. My mother was a French and Latin teacher, and I can always remember even as a kid having an insatiable desire to understand foreigners and to be able to communicate with them. When I was about fourteen, I decided to learn Russian – on my own. Now I certainly made quite a lot of mistakes in my learning methods when it came to Russian and to many other languages. You might say I learned about boulders by knocking my head against them. But thanks to that, I can now teach anyone how to learn any modern language in the shortest and most painless way.

LEVERS

The first lever is building your own dialogues and imagining yourself in conversational situations. You need to learn basic grammar and vocabulary first, but this never takes long at all. "Dialoguing" phenomenally improves vocabulary retention, your understanding of the spoken language and, most importantly, your feeling of ease with the language. This feeling of ease is a tremendous motivator.

The second lever is finding an educated native speaker that you can spend at least a couple of hours a week with. This will multiply the already impressive results from the first lever several times over.

BOULDERS

The biggest boulder, and the reason most language courses in North America are a waste of time, involves endlessly drilling grammar and vocabulary without integrating it into the oral and aural use of the language.

Reading, in and of itself, is a boulder. Reading only helps you if you do it aloud and force yourself to speak the language at every opportunity. It's much harder to speak and understand a foreign language than to read it, in most cases. I've worked with other multilinguists, and we can all read more languages than we can speak – it's just an easier skill to acquire.

as poor Herrigel thought for a considerable time! It resides on the noetic plane of being.

So to achieve your goals, you must find the levers and pour your energy in that direction. The example on page 45 shows how the principle of discriminating levers from boulders can be applied to almost any learning situation.

Orthodoxy, to take one authentic ancient tradition, is a highly developed system of self-transformation, and therefore has its own levers and boulders. But when Orthodox life goes wrong in a given culture, it degenerates from lever training into mere boulder pushing.

Probably the most widespread deviation has been the reduction of life to difficult physical labours like fasting and endless liturgical services. There is nothing wrong with fasting itself. In fact it is an indispensable support for refining the *nous* and the body, and anyone who has fasted properly knows what an incomparable tool it is. And yet, for all that, fasting is still a boulder. Like many boulders, it is just a tool, and it won't lead by itself to the essentials, which are the levers; it will merely help you to get to the essentials. When practised in an exaggerated manner, fasting is even harmful — rather than clarifying the *nous*, it will produce noetic confusion. And when the artist begins to boast of his tools, instead of his work of art, then there is a big problem.

The real lever in any authentic tradition is the practice of unceasing noetic refinement. It is only through noetic work that you can aim at the real heart of the system, which is to resuscitate the *nous*, dethrone the ego and reorient the dysfunctioning psychosomatic drives in order to go beyond the self in love for the Absolute and for all other beings. So the traditional training syllabus is to assign the body the disciplines necessary to it in terms of food, drink and sleep, and then, in the context of a well-thought out Program, to turn all our attention to unceasing noetic work. There are other levers as well, but subsequent chapters deal with them.

Yet even noetic work can be transformed into a boulder, as has happened historically in two ways. One occurs when the "how to" is lost or perverted, as has happened with prayer in Western Christianity, where the ancient practice of unceasing noetic prayer has been lost for many centuries. Prayer, like meditation, is an exact science: there are right and wrong ways to do either, and the wrong ways can lead to noetic and psychological damage. The second perversion is to exaggerate noetic work to such proportions that you neglect other elements of the tradition, like fasting, which are the indispensable supports to noetic refinement itself. It's really quite amazing, but the old saying is absolutely true: no system is foolproof because fools are so ingenious. And if there is one area where we humans excel, this is it.

ROCK SOLID LIFE PRACTICE 2.1: BUILDING A PROGRAM

At this point, you're finally ready to begin building the Program itself. This exercise is the key to gaining control of your time and your life. So please, do yourself a favour and give it your undivided attention:

This exercise takes four weeks to complete. For each week you'll need a sheet of 8 H x 11 graph paper,

Week 1

All you need to do this week is to log all your activities. You'll need at least two copies of the form for this week. One copy you'll carry with you and write on during the day. The second copy will be your good copy which you'll fill out at the end of the week.

You will write down each of your activities and how long they take, including sleep, work or school and their associated sub-activities, television time, chance conversations, playing with the kids, going out with friends, and anything else that comes up. But don't drown in the details, since the purpose is to get the big picture.

Try to pick a "normal" week for this, one without any unusual activities planned. And don't try to influence the outcome of the exercise by changing your schedule; it's best to continue your usual routine for now. You can't fix your life unless you understand it.

Once you've finished Week 1 and transferred all your data to the good copy, make a few copies of your final version and then get out three coloured pens, green, red and blue. Mark off your time in the following way:

- Green: Free time (time you more or less know you'll have to yourself)
- Red: Time you do not control, but which is predictable (like work or school)
- Blue: Time you have only limited control over, like dealing with spouse, children or others

Week 2
This week you'll begin to create a little more space and definition.

- Using your final results from the first week, get out a new form and draw in the same green areas you discovered last week. Your goal this week is to enforce the boundaries of the green no matter what.

- Draw in the red areas from last week. You probably noticed that there are some green patches contained within the red (a lunch break at work or school for example). Draw these in and enforce their boundaries as well.

- Draw in the blue areas from last week. Make sure that you are allotting enough time to these activities. Your third task for the week is to keep the blue within these reasonable limits. This calls for great discretion, of course, since transforming your life implies service to others who, like yourself, have needs and demands that are not always predictable.

At the end of Week 2, take stock of your efforts. If you succeeded, don't get too impressed with yourself. If you failed at any point, try to understand the causes; was it your own lack of resolve, or unexpected and unavoidable circumstances?

Week 3

Take the results of your first two weeks of work and have a look at the green areas. What activities did you fill them with? Did you find yourself filling your free time with necessary things that you couldn't find time for anywhere else? Paying the monthly bills, for instance? Cleaning out the backyard shed?

If so, this week's activity is to anticipate and plan activities like this and make absolutely sure that they do not impinge on your green time. Stick them in the red or blue spaces where they belong.

The next step is vital: analyze all your activities from Week 1 and ask yourself these hard questions: "Is there any activity that I can simply eliminate?" Your first reaction will probably be "no," but if you really force yourself to look at your own situation objectively, you'll realize that there are probably lots of time-wasting habitual activities that you could simply chop out of your life with little consequence. Then ask yourself" "Is there any activity that I could delegate to someone else?" This may sound selfish, but it really isn't. I'm frequently astounded, for instance, at parents who do all the household chores while their spoiled and lazy offspring vegetate in front of the television. So if you find yourself compensating for other people's laziness, stop! You'll be doing both of you a favour!

Week 4

Try to enforce everything you've done up to this point, and make sure this time that you have at least $\frac{1}{2}$ hour of green time first thing in the morning and then the same sometime between supper and bed.

Taking Stock
Make time to sit down and consider the last four weeks. You've probably made some interesting discoveries about your time and how it can be used more profitably. You'll find yourself tinkering with your Program as this book outlines the kinds of training you'll need to insert into it. But make it a rule that after you have set up your Program at the beginning of each week, you attempt to stick to it, not modifying it until the next week.

THE FOUR P'S OF SUCCESS

I've already talked about *Program*, which is the carefully worked out schedule or regime you're going to be putting in place. *Principles* are the content of that Program, correct training in other words. But together with these *Persistence* and *Patience* are essential to success. And if you can put these four P's together in your life, you'll be on your way to a whole new world of possibilities.

There is a Taoist saying that water is the softest of substances, and yet it if you give it the time it can eat through solid rock. So persistence in your practice is like the water that will, given a little time, crush most of the obstacles in your path. The basic idea behind persistence is that the work has to be continuous throughout the day and not just confined to specific times you have set aside to work on the exercises in this book or any of our other materials.

This does not mean, though, that the intensity of your efforts will be or should be the same every moment of every day. Humanly speaking, that is just not feasible. Perhaps the classic illustration of this is the story about St. Anthony the Great, a fourth century Orthodox monk from Egypt:

A hunter in the desert saw Abba Anthony having a good time with the brethren and he was shocked. Wanting to show him that it was sometimes necessary to meet the needs of the brethren, the old man said to him, "Put an arrow in your bow and shoot." So he did. The old man then said, "Shoot another." And he did so. Then the old man said, "Shoot yet again," and the hunter replied, "If I bend the bow so much I will break it." Then the old man said to him: "It is the same with the work of God. If we stretch the brethren beyond measure, they will soon break. Sometimes it is necessary to come down to meet their needs." When he heard these words, the hunter was pierced by compunction and, greatly edified by the old man, he went away. As for the brethren, they went home strengthened.[5]

And, in fact, every traditional system recognizes this and has built its training syllabus around the idea that particular times of the day and seasons of the year will be characterized by either a moderate and stable effort or a more intense all-out effort. This is easy to see in Orthodoxy, where the four annual periods of extended fasting, and especially the seven weeks preceding Pascha (Easter) are given over to particularly intense spiritual striving at a pace that simply could not be sustained indefinitely.

Another way of describing persistence in your Program is to say that the Program is something you stick to ruthlessly, come hell or high water. The reasons for insisting on this are several. First, there is the unstable nature of the human person in the fallen world. On this plane of existence, the powers of our psychosomatic organism are in chaos and only this kind of persistence can reintegrate our being internally. This basic attitude gets us around the great trap of only training when we "feel like it." We forge ahead, paying no attention to how we feel physically, emotionally, or mentally. In short, we become determined and decisive. As one Orthodox elder has written, "By making the decision to maintain an invariable regime, man acquires resolve and bravery, something very important and essential in our life, since our contest is a struggle and, indeed, a fierce one."[6] And, as a Taoist master of long ago put it:

> If you do not arouse a determined will and sharpen a resolute, decisive attitude but merely pass the days at leisure just as you are, even if you say you are practising the Way, you cannot wake up and get free.[7]

The final P required is Patience. We are perhaps the most impatient people in the world and getting more so all the time thanks to our obsession with instant results and gratification. In fact, even before I started writing this book, I was told by a marketing expert that "easy and quick outsells difficult and slow all the time," so I would do well to make promises to the potential reader like "30 days to self-transformation." Instead, the first exercise takes 30 days! I can't lie you, the reader. You can't achieve perfection in 30 days. But I will also tell you this: you shouldn't care — relax and enjoy the journey!

On the noetic plane, the old saying that "Rome wasn't built in a day" holds true in spades. Whatever is easily and quickly gained can be lost even more quickly. But whatever you have to work for, whatever victories you gain by good planning, right method and plain hard work, those victories no one can take from you.

I'd like to stand up on the housetops and shout this out! It isn't effort that people of today are afraid of so much as psychological stress, that great plague of our times. If you put into practice what's in this book in a moderate and consistent way, you'll find yourself dealing with a lot less stress on a daily basis. One of the chief sources of stress is our neurotic tendency to tell ourselves "there's work to do, so you can't slack off." Some experts in the area of stress management have referred to this as "shoulding" or "*must*erbation." It's that not so small voice that is constantly pushing us to do more on the endless treadmill of things that just "have to be done."

The beauty of the Program is that it short circuits this wretched habit! That's right; once you start living by your Program, you will know what you will be doing at any given time of day, so you can't "should" yourself any more. It's simply not allowed and you'll find yourself doing it less and less. So you can say a final good riddance to that source of stress!

We are sometimes so goal-oriented in our lives that we can't stop and smell the roses. The fact is, though, that "journey" is a fundamental fact of human existence. The way our universe is structured ontologically means that temporal succession or "time" is essential to the process of change. We are in a process of becoming while we are here. And in the quest for self-transformation, all traditions agree that time is an essential part of assimilating the truths we encounter. Things gained too easily don't have the same depth. Witness the Apostle Peter, who was granted the vision of Christ as he truly was at the Transfiguration on Mount Tabor, but who then lost this gift and denied his master. And St. Symeon the New Theologian (949-1022) likewise received the divine mercy quickly, by the prayers of his spiritual father, but then fell back into a dissolute life. In both cases, what was gained without effort was lost quickly by inexperience and only regained after protracted and arduous exertion. So whatever system we happen to be attached to, we ought not to become results junkies, but rather give the journey its due respect.

Modern man is paranoid. He is afraid of everything. And in his fear he has built civilization to protect him from everything that threatens his biological existence. He has constructed cities where humanity is safe from wild animals and where the unpredictable nature of the seasons and the food supply scarcely makes any impact on his life.[8] But in all his striving to make life safe and predictable, he has ended up with *boredom*. Yes, there's no other word for it, modern man's life is the ultimate in tedium. In the Warrior's way of life that you're about to embark upon, boredom has been banished. It is a life of great contrasts compared to what secular humanity experiences, and where even learning to deal with boredom (which most people refuse to do – they drown it in so-called entertainment instead) is an exciting affair.

A life of high contrasts necessarily has ups and downs, and there will be periods of frustration, of hard slogging, and even of doubt. But don't worry – many thousands of people have come this way before. And they have told us that the invincible weapon against all these unwelcome changes is patience.

If you have ever watched *Star Trek*, you've probably seen the "Borg Collective" — an alien race that combines biological and artificial life and which thinks and acts as a single collective consciousness. When the Enterprise-D first encountered the Borg, thanks to an unwelcome entity called "Q," the latter said to Captain Picard: "You can't outrun them. You can't destroy them. If you damage them, the essence of what they are remains: they regenerate and keep coming. Eventually you will weaken — your reserves will be gone. They are relentless!" You see, the Borg have no morale, so they can't even get discouraged. They know only their goal.

In your new way of life, you don't want to have morale (morals, yes, but that's another story). You want to cultivate patience to such a degree that the ups and downs of daily life and of your training will be like water off the duck's back.

Now that you've begun to get a grip on your use of time and how to manipulate it to accommodate your goals, let's get started on making some big changes in your life. So hang on for what may be the most remarkable five weeks you have ever experienced....

Key to the Program: decisiveness — just do it! But continually strive to simplify your life; don't try to pack more and more into the same hours — that is the sure road to frustration and disaster.

Chapter Three

THE CLEANUP: RECLAIMING YOUR HEALTH, RELATIONSHIPS and FINANCES

It is impossible to add a few minutes of meditation or prayer to a blundering and disastrous life and expect results. The externals of life have to be set in order first.

It is true that some people can grow spiritually in the midst of horrendous external circumstances. For most people in North America today, however, these "horrendous circumstances" are largely of their own making and are intimately related to the inner illnesses they need to overcome. So to ignore or otherwise perpetuate the adverse circumstances will only make transforming the deeper levels of your life all the more difficult.

After years of counseling people I began to realize this: To the extent that a person's life is a disaster on the outside, it is impossible to address the real underlying problems on the inside. First you have to deal with some of the external symptoms of that disastrous life.

In most authentic traditions monasticism is the healing model par

MIRACULOUS
ANSCIENT FORMULA
⟪⟪⟪⟪⟪⟪ 2 ⟪⟪⟪⟪⟪⟪

Always Begin from the Outside In.

⟪⟪⟪⟪⟪⟪⟪⟪⟪⟪⟪⟪⟪⟪⟪⟪

excellence. Monasticism works on the following basis: it takes us out of the matrix of our previous life and puts us into its own matrix. In the monastic life the usage of time is regulated. Relationships, what a person eats, everything about the externals of life is fit into a prearranged pattern — a prearranged healthy pattern that works and has been proven to work over thousands of years.

The problem is that in living "in the world" as we do, we don't have the luxury of plugging ourselves into the life of such a community. But although we cannot leave our current matrix, we can change it, and change it profoundly. People in difficult life circumstances often see only two alternatives — stay or get out. But there are other changes you can make, changes that are less obvious but much more powerful and far reaching. These changes will demand more knowledge, commitment and energy on your part than simply walking away from a difficult marriage, finding a better job or adopting the latest fad diet, but there is a very large payoff. Whereas giving up on the marriage, finding the better job, or adopting the fad diet will leave your own inner state unchanged, so that you take those same inner problems with you into the new situation, the changes I'll show you will have a considerable therapeutic effect on many aspects of your life.

By beginning from the outside, you will learn that you can actually change your life. You may feel totally defeated in life, that you really are trapped and that there is very little you can do. But once you realize that's not the case, you will be filled with a wonderful rush of enthusiasm and want to go on, thinking, "If I can do this much, maybe I can do more." And you can!

Ultimately, it's impossible to make headway until the circumstances of life are put in order. On the other hand, sometimes the reverse is true: If there are external circumstances, you can sometimes even change them simply by undoing the mental and emotional knot that led to them, thus causing the entire situation to resolve itself.

UNTYING THE KNOT TO TIE THE KNOT

When I was in university and later on in seminary, I knew several young men and women who were totally obsessed with finding a mate. For these people their entire mental and emotional world was completely wrapped up in the search; everything was conditioned by this one task in life.

In seminary specifically, I can think of three or four cases — all, as it happens, were of men looking for women. And in each case, the outcome was rather amazing. Each one of these people independently came to an existential place in life where he realized the futility of what he was doing and each one independently fell down before God and said: "All right, I give my life over to you, whatever you want is fine with me. If I have not found a mate by such-and-such a date, I will go and become a monk." And in every case a mate miraculously appeared for them in the most startling way.

In other words, once they had dealt with the mental obstacle within, the external situation resolved itself in a completely natural way, because once they had removed the inner emotional knot, they were capable of accepting the reality that the Absolute wanted to give them. Before that, they would not been able to receive the gift in a healthy way — the gift itself would have fed the neurosis.

Ultimately, all this training is about recognizing and undoing inner obstacles — fears, cravings, aversions, obsessions, opinions and the rest of the ego structure — because that's the real source of all your misery. But because you cannot do that directly, you first need to create some space by dealing decisively with the externals of life. And what are these externals? They are your physical surroundings, your physical health, your relationships with other people, and your relationship with money and economic life in general.

PARADOX
3.1

People tend to implement changes that leave intact the very inner dynamics which have given rise to the life-situations they do not like. Consequently, they recreate similar life-situations over and over.

Now it's time to talk about setting up a "sacred space" for yourself. This space, which could be a room or just a small part of a room, will play a very important role in helping you to put into practice many of the practical exercises in this book. By setting up a defined physical space dedicated solely to self-transformation, you begin to create a small bit of order in your physical surroundings. You need to do two things: to create order out of chaos and to put in place a strategy for spreading order like a virus. The reasons are very simple: Disorder negatively affects your emotional level, even in ways that you don't usually suspect. You can't create inner order and outer disorder at the same time. One of the disciples of Joseph the Hesychast tells the following story:

> Elder Theophylaktos lived his whole life as an ascetic and hesychast, keeping a strict fast: he did not even eat [olive] oil. At one time he accepted a disciple — the future Father Arsenios — and told him laconically (because this blessed Father was temperate even in his speech): "Listen, my boy. If you are going to stay with me, I will want you to have order and discipline in your life, because without this you will never become a monk. Look around at the things I will show you. There's our jug, there's the cup, there are the bowls, there are the rusks and so forth, as you can see. I want them always to be in those places. If you happen to make a mistake, the first time I'll remind you of their proper place according to the rule, but I won't tolerate it a second time. If you continue this disorder a third time, I shall ask you to take your belongings and leave so that at least you won't trouble me, even if you yourself do not want to profit at all.[1]

This shows the extreme precision in the life of this spiritual warrior. And in fact, if we want to transform our lives, we all need this kind of precision in our own lives. We begin by creating in our living environment some small space where we can have peace and order, and we cannot have peace without order. Order and beauty belong to creation; everything that is disorder belongs to the fallen world and is linked to corruption and death. Everything in the fallen world tends toward maximum entropy (disorder), as science would say (and the state of my kids' bedrooms is proof of this).

The question is how you go about this. I am talking about creating a place of peace, harmony, and beauty, a place that is comfortable, that has no visual distractions unrelated to your greater purpose. In the beginning this can be just one room or part of a room.

Every tradition has its own suggestions about how to do this. In Orthodoxy this is usually called an "icon corner," typically in the corner of room and/or facing east. The icon corner usually has a cross on the wall and one or more icons (pictures related to the practice of the faith and painted in a particular style). It also usually has a candle or *lampada*. The *lampada* is a small glass candleholder filled with oil and with a wick holder floating on top. Often, there's also an incense burner.

In some traditions (like Orthodoxy or Tibetan Buddhism) you'll find a preference for sacred spaces that involve all the senses, with beautiful things to see, the elevating aromas of incense, and sacred music of whatever variety. You'll also find traditions that have a preference for a very sparse sacred space where there are few if any visual distractions, as, for example, in Japanese Zen Buddhism. You'll find the same thing within traditions, by the way, where some people prefer a complete absence of distraction and where others have sacred spaces that are extremely beautiful. To a certain extent that's a matter of personal preference. If you don't belong to any tradition at all for the moment, then I would suggest that you construct a sacred space that is very simple and sparse, so that when

Creating external order in your surroundings is of pivotal importance in gaining inner peace.

you're in your sacred space and facing forward there are no visual distractions.

The essence of the sacred space is that it has to be neat and functional. To participate in the Absolute you must conform to it. Otherwise, you block its manifestation, and this is part of the reason why it is essential to create external peace and order.

Creating order is not as difficult as you might think. In fact, it's really about localizing chaos, because there will be a certain amount of chaos in any place where human beings actually live. For instance, dirty clothes on the floor constitute chaos; however, if the same dirty clothes are put in a laundry basket that sits on the floor, suddenly that's no longer a mess. You localize chaos by providing a space for chaos to happen and by doing so you create order. It's not that you need to eliminate chaos; you just need to give it its place. And this makes it relatively easy to proceed to the next step, which is to spread order.

The basic principle is this: You want to create order in the public areas of the house, the areas everyone uses, and in your own private area as well, while leaving everyone else's private areas up to them. It's not as if the whole house has to be neat as a pin.

One way of approaching the problem is to analyze the system that's going on in each room so you can identify the source(s) of the chaotic mess. One of the greatest sources of disorder in most homes is the huge volume of incoming paper through the mail and through what people bring home from school or work. If you can find a way to handle the paper flow, then suddenly you localize the chaos and create order out of disorder in a relatively simple way. For instance, to deal with incoming paper you can devise a system composed of bins or boxes of some variety.

Let's be specific by taking one part of the incoming paper and devising a system for it: those unrelenting bills. If you're like most people, most of your bills will come in the mail. But the bill has a life cycle of its own, because you have to open the envelope, then process the contents in your financial system, eventually pay the bill, and then presumably file the bill in some place for your records. So your system for dealing with this has to take the entire procedure into account. If you don't take it all into account you may discover that bills end up randomly placed throughout the house in piles here and there, creating visual chaos and financial confusion. So to deal with this problem all you need to do is analyze the system and develop a particular path that the bill follows when it comes into your house, and then do the same with other types of mail. Next, you can examine the other systems in your house; the grocery system, the laundry system, the recycling system, the waste disposal (garbage) system, the "kids' stuff" system, and so on.

Of course, in a family situation you're always dealing with other people. I cannot emphasize enough that you must not use anger or lecturing to get your way in this matter. You must proceed in a calm and methodical way that mirrors the kind of peace and order that you want to create in your physical surroundings. But you will be surprised; you will realize that order is to a certain extent infectious, and that by creating this kind of external peace and order, you will be amazed at how much better you feel, how much more relaxed and more at peace — and all from this simple procedure.

ROCK SOLID LIFE PRACTICE 3.1: CREATING EXTERNAL PEACE AND ORDER

1. Take one week to build yourself a sacred space. Consider carefully which room to use: it should be a room where

you can be alone and undisturbed in the early morning hours or in the evening. Remember that you don't need the whole room, only a small area. That said, when you're standing or sitting in this space, there should be no distractions in your visual field, nothing inconsistent with your project of self transformation. When you're in this space, you should feel that the rest of the world doesn't exist; it should be an oasis of calm and peace.

2. Take one week to analyze your household's paper system — how you handle all of the incoming paper of every kind. Think through very carefully every element in the current system: who handles which kinds of paper, what path the paper follows, and where and why it ends up as clutter. Then simply design a system that is more streamlined and efficient and which ensures that at least the public areas of your house are entirely free from the "paper monster." After that, test your new system for a period of one week. The obvious criterion of success is no more mess!

3. Once you have defeated the paper monster, analyze the other systems in your household — the grocery system, the garbage and recycling system, the laundry system and any others that present problems. Implement your solutions one by one and then test them.

4. The final stage of creating external peace and order is to localize the chaos in your household so that it no longer lands in public areas, in your bedroom or — needless to say — in your sacred space. If you live with other people, much of Exercise 3.1 will depend on getting their cooperation, so work slowly and diplomatically!

THE 5 PILLARS OF LIFE

INTERPERSONAL RELATIONSHIPS:
FINDING FULFILMENT AND STABILITY

It is often in trying to find fulfillment through relationships that people make the unwise choices that sow the seeds of future unhappiness and instability. Once you understand why you take these wrong turns and start to undo the underlying emotional problems, you are on your way to finding joy and harmony in your relationships.

It is impossible to exaggerate the importance of interpersonal relationships. They are a vital component of your subjective feeling of happiness and fulfillment in life; much of the joy of life comes from your relationships with other people. And there are ontological reasons why this is so. Authentic ancient traditions understand clearly that human beings are meant for close interpersonal communion. We are not designed to be alone and isolated.

You might ask then why various forms of self-imposed isolation are found in most authentic ancient traditions, why hermits and small communities limited to one sex or the other exist. Well, it might surprise you to know that hermits of all traditions are deeply conscious of the needs of others. A disciple of Joseph the Hesychast wrote: "…we could see that such people felt everyone to be their neighbor and communed with each person in a very practical way, despite the fact that these men of prayer are virtually hidden and unknown. He (Elder Joseph) then gave us to understand in his own words the universality of prayer, the chief bearer of universality."[2]

I am now going to share with you some initial steps on the road to this joyous communion. Although these steps are at a basic and external level, the results can often be immediate and startling.

Authentic ancient traditions have an idea of interpersonal relationships that is different from our conventional one. In the West we often confuse familiarity with intimacy. Interpersonal relationships in the West are increasingly characterized by familiarity, an approach unknown in most other cultures.

When I was a young child beginning school in the mid-1960s, I remember that we always addressed our teachers and the friends of

> ## PARADOX
> ### ⟪⟪⟪⟪⟪⟪ 3.3 ⟪⟪⟪⟪⟪⟪
>
> Worldly people are surrounded by others but often they feel lonely, isolated and depressed, whereas transformed people enjoy a rich, deep and tremendously fulfilling communion with all humankind, whether or not others are physically present.
>
> ⟪⟪⟪⟪⟪⟪⟪⟪⟪⟪⟪⟪⟪⟪

our parents by their last names. Everyone was called Miss, Mrs. or Mr. So-and-So. In contrast to this, my own children often call their teachers by their first names. And they also tend to know other adults by their first names as well. Likewise, the workplace of today is a much more "familiar" environment than it was even a few decades ago. This is especially evident in the bilingual city of Ottawa, because the French language uses different forms of the word "you," depending on how formal or familiar the relationship is. Needless to say, the formal form of address – *vous* in French — is very seldom used these days.

The question is, has this created better interpersonal relationships? Well, that is debatable. Every ancient culture understood that familiarity easily brings with it a lack of respect. And yet, the tendency toward increased familiarity in Western interpersonal relationships in the last several decades can probably be attributed to the feeling that our social relationships were hampered by a kind of false distance and respect. And also, during these same years, there has been an ever greater recognition that much of the population feels a lack of fulfillment in interpersonal relationships. People crave intimacy and are not getting it. In such a situation, the assumption that familiarity will create intimacy is a relatively natural one — incorrect, but natural.

The greatest mentor and guide in my life was a very old Russian Orthodox priest. He did not speak English, and we had to communicate in Russian. My relationship with him was characterized by a certain "deference" and respect. I always addressed him using the more polite and respectful form of address in Russian — the equivalent of the French *vous*. So our relationship was not a familiar one, but it was an extraordinarily intimate one. It was characterized by a deep and abiding mutual respect in which there was no sense of distance to be traversed, no sense of alienation or lack of fulfillment. Rather, I can say

THE 5 PILLARS OF LIFE

quite truthfully that this relationship was one of the most intimate I have ever experienced.

On the other hand, I have never seen any evidence that the casual and offhand behaviors in vogue today produce the intimacy that we seem to expect them to.

People in the industrialized world have great material wealth, but suffer terribly from the lack of the one thing they crave the most — intimacy. And in whatever direction this craving takes the individual, whether healthy or destructive, this basic drive comes from the need to love and be loved.

> **PARADOX 3.4**
>
> You may strive for familiarity in your interpersonal relationships, thinking this will provide intimacy. And yet very often, it actually blocks intimacy instead.

A great many people in our society suffer from an inability to maintain positive and fulfilling relationships, with friends and colleagues, with family or with a romantic / sexual partner. For the most part, the reason we are incapable of maintaining satisfying interpersonal relationships is our own inner neuroses.

If you take the transformed person as a model, you'll see that he or she is typically capable of experiencing very fulfilling interpersonal relationships with a wide variety of people and personality types. If you look closely, you will notice the transformed person tends to inject into relationships a certain number of characteristics: love, forgiveness, seeing the good and the potential of others, acting for the good of the other, respect, and kindness.

If you experience this kind of love just once from one person, you're never going to forget it. As a contemporary Orthodox abbot put it about one of his spiritual mentors: "If you seek him, wherever you are, you will find him beside you. He lives only for you."[3] So yes, this amazing kind of love and affection and warmth in human relationships really does exist. But by the same token, I think almost all of us are well aware that our own relationships don't measure up to this standard at all. And that's why it's time for your next homework assignment:

▼ ▼ ▼ ▼

In this exercise you are going to take stock of all your primary relationships. When I say primary, I'm not talking about the most emotionally charged relationships of your life exclusively, nor am I talking about relationships that are voluntary as opposed to involuntary. First of all, there are family relationships: your parents, siblings, spouse or significant other, children, and other family members. Then you have your working relationships: your boss, colleagues, business partners, employees, clients and others. You also may have "spiritual" relationships — relationships that emanate from a shared vision of reality: you may have a spiritual guide, as well as spiritual brothers and sisters in whatever tradition you find yourself, if any. And then of course, there's a huge catch-all category called "friends."

Take a piece of paper and in each of these categories write down your main relationships. Of course, you're going to come up with a list that has rather a lot of people on it, so this will take time, and a lot of thought. Once you've done this, ask yourself the following questions and answer them with brutal honesty:

1. Do I feel real and genuine affection for this person?
2. Do I feel sympathy for this person?
3. Do I have anything against this person?
4. Do I maintain this relationship for:
   a. Self-protection — I would suffer in some way, economic or otherwise, by breaking it.
   b. Self-advancement — I am using this relationship to get what I want.
   c. Self-gratification: physical pleasure, emotional pleasure or both.
   d. Out of pure disinterested love for the other.

Transformed people can answer yes to questions 1 and 2 in

WORD OF CAUTION

By the way, beware of how you analyze your marriage. Many people start to feel guilty at this point because their marriage provides them with a degree of emotional and physical intimacy and perhaps with physical and financial security as well. But this is as it should be: marriage is a unique type of relationship, because reciprocity on many levels is part of what marriage is. You should never feel guilty that you enjoy any or every aspect of your relationship with your spouse! If you apply the criterion of "disinterested love" too strictly to your marriage, you'll finally end up with the absurd conclusion that the only kind of marriage you won't feel guilty about is one you hate!

every case; they can answer no to question 3 in every case, and they can answer yes to 4d in every case, even though they derive great pleasure and joy from these same relationships. And if you yourself are unable to do this, then every authentic ancient tradition says that you have some work to do.

My guess is that many of you will have to admit to having rather little affection for about one half the people on your list, and that almost none of you will honestly be able to say that you are maintaining even a single relationship out of pure disinterested love.

We are not born knowing how to maintain fulfilling and joyous relationships. But it is a skill that can be learned. Whenever I say this to an audience of people who belong to a spiritual tradition of some kind, I frequently meet with the objection that our relationships should come out of genuine feeling from the depths of our hearts. People will say to me that transformed people manifest their disinterested love spontaneously out of the purity of their inner being and that since we don't yet have this purity we cannot possibly manifest the same disinterested love.

This is simply mixed-up thinking. Then I ask them, how do you suppose it is that these holy people or "real people" (as they are sometimes called in both Taoism and Orthodoxy) acquired this disinterested love? Do you suppose they acquired it by acting with hostility, by acting out their passions? Obviously not. But, you know, there are a lot of people today who believe that if they act in any way that is contrary to their real feelings then they are somehow being hypocrites. This is complete nonsense. Hypocrisy involves an intention to deceive. But if I act for the good of the other in spite of my real feelings, this in no way constitutes hypocrisy; rather, it constitutes a wise and intelligent way of working on myself.

People who have the good fortune to grow up in loving homes have love and affection modeled for them. They grow up knowing that manifesting and showing love and affection is an appropriate and good thing to do. And so they themselves begin to do it, and the more they do it, the more automatic it becomes, and the more automatic it becomes the more this affection becomes part of their inner being. And soon without realizing it, they are not merely people who act affectionately, but they are people who have become affectionate. So in other words, acting the part is a very powerful method of self-transformation, and has nothing to do with hypocrisy.

The first thing you must do is to reverse your fallen default setting of tearing down others in order to build yourself up. This implies that you must stop judging and criticizing — the two greatest enemies of inner transformation. Every authentic ancient tradition says this. Tremendous energy is locked up and wasted in this useless habit of criticizing and judging others. As the old saying goes, we do not get to heaven by cursing hell. Passing judgment on others makes us feel good momentarily, but in the long run it is a cause of tremendous suffering. In all its forms, judging and criticizing simply reinforces the ego.

It's time to radically alter your approach to life. If anyone has offended you, abused you or hurt you, resolve right now to forgive him or her completely. Then get on with your life. Refuse to discuss the matter further with anyone, especially yourself (the ego is the one who is mainly interested in rehashing this stuff!). Do not sink your energies into what is already passed and what you cannot change. Move ahead with your life, create a clean slate, and resolve from this moment to treat your friends and your enemies equally well. St. Silouan of Athos considered love for your enemies to be the main criterion of the authenticity of your life.

Next, you must get out of the habit of arguing. Have you ever met anyone who loves to contradict, who loves to be right? I call this the spirit of contradiction. Experience will be quick to demonstrate that if you are constantly arguing and contradicting, you are going to have rather few friends because very few people enjoy being constantly argued with and contradicted. You can be right or you can be happy. Which would you prefer?

Now that you've begun to identify and eliminate some of your worst habits, you can learn some new ones to replace them. First, you must learn to warm the hearts of other people. What this means is that you are going to try in a very deliberate and methodical fashion to make everyone you come into contact with feel good about themselves, good about their lives, and glad that they talked to you. This takes a lot of work, but almost nothing pays off like this us, because the more affection you give up to others, the more you will receive in return. And the more you receive, the more you'll want to give them, so that the whole thing becomes a self-feeding cycle that has amazing consequences all around you.

When you have a hard time doing this with certain people — those people that are especially difficult or unpleasant — here's a tactic to use. Intentionally try to see the good in them. Make a list of their good qualities. If they do things that are wrong or hurtful to you or to others, or make mistakes of some variety, make excuses for them deliberately. Do this only in your own mind or perhaps in front of others when others attack them. Someone once said that everyone is doing the best they can with what they've got.

You also have to learn how to praise others, because there's nothing like praise to open the heart of someone else. So many people today are emotionally wounded, emotionally tired, tired of being abused, and tired of being ignored. So many people have low self-esteem. If you want to help people in any concrete way, the way to begin is by praising them, by telling them how much you respect them, how much you admire them for what they have done. St. Isaac the Syrian tells you how (some of the details of what he says are culture-specific, but you'll get the general idea):

> When you meet your fellow man, constrain yourself to pay him more honor than is his due. Kiss his hands and feet, often take his hands with deep respect, put them over your eyes, and praise him for what he does not even possess. And when he parts from you, say every good thing about him, and whatever it may be that commands respect. For by these and similar acts, you draw him to good and make him feel ashamed because of the gracious names by which you have called him, and you sow the seeds of virtue in him. From behavior such as this, *to which you accustom yourself* [emphasis mine], a good pattern is also imprinted in you; and you gain much humility for yourself, and achieve great things without toil. And not only this, but if he has any faults or voluntary imperfections, he will readily accept correction from you when he is honored by you, being ashamed because of the respect which you have shown him and the proof of love he continually sees in you. Let this always be the aim of your conduct: to be courteous and respectful to all. And do not provoke any man or vie zealously with him,

either for the sake of the faith, or on account of his evil deeds; but watch over yourself so as not to blame or accuse any man in any matter.... For love does not know how to be angry, or provoked, or passionately to reproach anyone. The proof of love and knowledge is profound humility...[4]

But for our praise to sound genuine, it has to be sincere. What helps our praise sound sincere is not only that it be sincerely felt from our heart, but also that it be specific, rather than general, and that it be timely. In other words, if your employee does an exceptional job at something, tell him or her right then and there and not a month later.

You know the person who always hijacks the conversation, who turns it into a conversation about him or herself? This kind of person fundamentally never listens to others, and that is his tragedy. Listening is one of the greatest relationship builders that there is. It is also in a sense one of the easiest, and yet many people find it very, very difficult, because strong egocentrism prevents them from caring about the other. If you want to acquire genuine affection for others and if you want them to believe that your affection is real, there is no better and more effective way to do this than to listen attentively to their cares and concerns.

And finally, you have to learn to show gratitude to others. Showing gratitude is an extremely powerful relationship builder. This has immense transformative power in our life, because it takes you out of your preoccupation with yourself and acknowledges that everything you have and everything you are is by and large something that has been given to you as a gift. The worst enemy of humankind is what the Orthodox tradition calls pride — not in the sense of being boastful, but rather in the sense of feeling autonomous and therefore not needing others. It goes without saying that if you constantly show gratitude to others, you will destroy this false autonomy and create superb relationships with others, killing two birds with one stone, as it were.

Once you begin to implement all these strategies in your dealings with other people, you begin to give them space to be themselves. Once you accept a person truly and openly, you give that person room to express him or herself freely. And just as flowers open to the sun, people will begin to open up to you automatically and spontaneously because they will feel love, warmth and acceptance. This acceptance is very critical because everyone needs to feel cared about and valued as they are and not as others want them to be.

Accepting people where they are does not mean you cannot suggest to them a higher standard or different ways of doing things. But their openness to any of your suggestions depends on being first accepted as they are. And yet this acceptance does not imply that you consider them to be perfect in every way.

The Orthodox monastic literature provides many startling examples of this. One of the disciples of Joseph the Hesychast writes that the old man seldom had a kind word for any of his disciples. These disciples knew, though, that beneath this outward harshness was a warm and loving paternal care and acceptance. But this acceptance contained within it the challenge to move on and make progress. The disciples were well aware that Father Joseph's outward harshness was a standard monastic technique to lead the apprentice toward humility, which itself is the wellspring of imperishable joy and riches.

ROCK SOLID LIFE PRACTICE 3.3: STOP JUDGING

Go through one full week with the goal of never judging or criticizing anyone for anything, no matter how blatant or obvious the infraction may be. You'll need a small notebook to keep track of your successes and failures.

Success is defined the following way: you have the urge to judge or criticize someone and refrain from acting on the urge — that is to say, you actually oppose and defeat it. A failure means verbalizing your critical feelings, usually in the presence of other people, or simply indulging the critical thoughts in your mind.

I have to clarify, though, that merely having a critical thought go through your head is not failure. Ancient traditions say over and over again that you are not responsible for what

LEARN TO "SHUT UP AND LISTEN"

People love to feel supported in expressing their opinions, concerns and fears. I can remember one incident in seminary that really underlined this fact in a rather humorous way. One of my professors liked to give oral examinations at the end of a course. As students, we soon realized that if at the beginning of the examination we could turn the topic of conversation to one that he was especially interested in, then he himself would take over talking and go on and on for several minutes. And because he liked what he heard, he would give us a good mark! Of course, our own practice of listening attentively to others should not be based on such shameless manipulation of the circumstances, but the story does nevertheless underline the basic principle.

I am personally very grateful to my parents, both of whom departed this life in 2002 within three months of each other. If there is one thing that their passing brought to the fore, it was the number of lives they had touched, the number of people who would rely on them, who felt themselves somehow indebted to them emotionally and spiritually. And to a great extent, this was because they were good listeners and supportive, loving people.

I always liked going to visit my parents, because they listened. And not only that, but they actually wanted to hear all the details of my life, so the conversation was mainly about me (people love to talk about themselves!).

When I was young I remember asking my mother why Dad was often out at evening meetings. Her answer was this: "He likes to help various groups of people and organizations because he feels that not to do so would be selfish." And he himself actually told me that most people who feel weighed down by their own problems would easily find relief from their sufferings by losing themselves in service to others.

My father was a lawyer by profession and eventually a judge. At his funeral one of his younger colleagues came up to me and told me this story: "I always tended to come down harshly on lawyers who screwed up in the courtroom — the ones who showed up ill-prepared or with incoherent arguments. Once, after I had raked a lawyer over the coals, your dad pulled me aside and said: 'I appreciate what you're trying to do, but you will achieve far more with honey than you ever will with vinegar.'"

thoughts come to you; however, you are responsible for what you do with them.

At the end of the week take stock of where you are. It will give you a very good idea of how far you are from being able to begin inner refinement in a profitable way. It is impossible to exaggerate the extent to which you must master this one exercise in order to proceed with the rest of the material in this book.

Although I have allotted you a week to do this exercise, you will have to keep returning to it over and over again until you get it right. But when you do get it right, when you can go several days at a time without judging and criticizing, or even better, when you feel in your innermost being that the urge to criticize itself has gone, then it is time to really celebrate. And you will feel like celebrating — your entire being will feel light and lively and joyous. You will feel like you have shed a 100-pound weight off your shoulders, a weight you didn't even know about before.

ROCK SOLID LIFE PRACTICE 3.4: REFUSE TO CONTRADICT

You're going to take one week during which you will refuse to contradict anyone. You will not argue your own point of view about politics, sports, religion or anything else for that matter. The only exception to this rule is a situation where failing to give your opinion could result in direct harm to yourself or someone else. And again, you will have to use your notebook to keep track of your successes and failures. It is vital that you see a record of your performance with your physical eyes; it is useless to arrive at the end of a week of hard struggle with nothing more than a vague impression about how it went.

When you have defeated the urge to contradict, you'll probably notice that your social relationships begin to improve. That's because very few people like to be contradicted. And you yourself will begin to feel much better as you begin to tear down that monstrous ego that has tormented you for so many years.

ROCK SOLID LIFE PRACTICE 3.5: WARMING THE HEARTS OF OTHERS

In the previous two exercises your goal was to stop inflicting harm on others and on yourself. Now it's time to start building others up. For a period of one week, make sure that all the people you come into contact with leave your presence feeling better about themselves than they did before the conversation began.

You may prefer to concentrate on a single person or a small group of people, rather than trying to warm the hearts of absolutely everyone you come in contact with. You're free to experiment with this in order to find out what works best for you.

As to how you warm the hearts of others, that really doesn't matter. There are no set techniques. In the end, nothing beats a sincere desire to act for the good of the other person. In other words, the more pure and sincere your desire to benefit the other person, the more likely it is that he or she will leave your presence having been touched deeply.

Don't forget to track in your notebook whether or not you remembered your objective of warming the heart of the other person when you should have.

Once you have mastered this, you will belong to that incredibly small percentage of the population that loves freely, and in a disinterested way, that small percentage for the sake of whom the world continues to exist.

ROCK SOLID LIFE PRACTICE 3.6: TREATING YOUR ENEMY WELL

This a one-day exercise. Choose an unpleasant person with whom you have frequent contact, someone with a difficult personality, someone you don't particularly care for or respect, but with whom you have to interact whether you like it or not. Choose a day on which you will have considerable interaction with this person. Ahead of time, make up a list of all of that person's good points. Then, believe it or not, you're to make a list of that person's bad points — as you see them. Try to consider these faults or bad points as if they belonged to someone else with whom you have no emotional involvement whatsoever. Then try to imagine the circumstances which may have led to the development of these negative character traits. In other words, you are using your analysis to start making excuses for this person.

The next part of the assignment begins the night before the date chosen. If you are a praying person, then pray for this person. If you happen to be in a non-theistic tradition, you can still dedicate the fruits of your meditation to this person. Or at the very least, try to maintain some positive thoughts about him or her.

On the date chosen, try to maintain a positive relationship with this person no matter how difficult that may be. Go over in your head all those good points that you jotted down and constantly try to see them in his or her behavior. Likewise, when you see negative traits arise, try to remember the reasons why such things might be there. This exercise has a twofold purpose: First, you begin to see positive traits, which you were unaware of before, and secondly, you begin to see negative traits in a more objective way. And by maintaining equanimity in the presence of this person, you may be able to influence these negative traits in a positive way.

ROCK SOLID LIFE PRACTICE 3.7: PRAISING OTHERS

This is another one-week exercise. Every day this week, find one person to praise. It does not really matter who it is — it

THE 5 PILLARS OF LIFE

could be a spouse or child or colleague or nearly anyone else. Prepare yourself ahead of time by finding one person who has done something worthy of praise, preferably something done very recently.

So when you have found the person of the day, all you have to do is to tell him or her how much you appreciated what he or she did. Try to do it in a calm and forthright manner, without any exaggeration or embellishment and with complete sincerity.

ROCK SOLID LIFE PRACTICE 3.8: SHUT UP AND LISTEN!

Find someone who wants to get something off his chest, in other words, someone who wants a sympathetic ear. And you are that ear. Many people find it difficult to be good listeners because the listener by definition is not the center of the universe. Suddenly, it's all about someone else and his or her problems and not me with my problems. The ego doesn't particularly like this situation and puts up a great deal of fuss. The good listener doesn't interrupt, except to seek clarification or to give positive feedback. It's important to listen attentively, to ask thoughtful questions, and to paraphrase back to the person what you think he or she is trying to say. All of these are traits of good listeners, and they will give the person talking to you the feeling of having been heard and understood on an emotional level.

ROCK SOLID LIFE PRACTICE 3.9: SHOWING GRATITUDE

The final exercise for this part of chapter 3 is to show gratitude. Always be on the lookout for opportunities, for instances of kindness shown toward you or similar things. Alternatively, think of someone who has done something for you or perhaps who has given you a gift and whom you have forgotten to thank. In any event, once you found this person, immediately go and see him or get in touch somehow to communicate your gratitude.

With these simple exercises, you have begun to uproot from yourself some of your most destructive and self-destructive habits. And even better, you have now begun to play a positive role in the lives of others and in the world in general. Although these actions on your part may seem very simple and insignificant, they are based on the deepest ontological principles behind the world's existence, as you will begin to understand in later chapters.

CARE FOR THE BODY:
CREATING INTERNAL PEACE AND ORDER

St. Basil the Great said:

> I think it is proper to take care not to undermine the body's strength by excessive abstinence and thus render it useless and ineffective for profitable activity. The body should be active and by no means disabled by excess. Had it been beneficial for us that our body be disabled and prostrate, as if it were scarcely breathing, then surely God would have created us this way in the beginning. But since he did not create us in this way, then those people sin who do not preserve intact what was created good.[5]

Many people involved in authentic ancient traditions end up quite confused with respect to what these traditions really say about physical health and care for the body. It's an unavoidable fact that each of these traditions contains statements on physical health that seem to be contradictory. And Orthodoxy is no exception to this. Just take a look at the following examples:

- St. Isaac (the Syrian) persuades a monk to relax his extreme fasting so as not to die young.
- St. Isaac says it is better to die in striving than to live in laziness.
- Joseph the Hesychast tells a monk concerned with his own physical condition that the purpose of coming to a monastery is to face death, so he shouldn't be such a coward.
- Joseph the Hesychast says medicines and doctors are important.
- St. Onuphrios the Great says God heals those who struggle (i.e. directly and miraculously, without the need for human medical intervention).
- St. Isaac calls good health a temptation.

So there is an apparent contradiction within the tradition itself on the importance of bodily health. On the one hand, you pray for the sick and anoint them for healing. On the other you "care not for the flesh for it passes away." So it's hardly any wonder that people within the tradition are somewhat at a loss.

It is often said that Far Eastern traditions like Buddhism and Taoism are much more accepting toward the physical body than is the "Judeo-Christian" tradition. This is misleading in at least two ways. First, all authentic ancient traditions totally exclude a dualistic approach to the mind-body composite, an approach that is largely unique to Western Christianity. Anyone brought up within Western civilization in general has a mind-body dualism deeply ingrained from childhood, and it's very hard to erase this conditioning. You can become a Marxist tomorrow if you wish, but you can't stop being a dualist.

Westerners react to Western Christianity's disdain for the body by seeking a tradition that seems to lavish care on the body and to accept all its demands. All authentic traditions are candidates because they see body and mind/soul as inseparable manifestations of one another, and therefore make use of the body in the process of self-transformation. The problem arises when Westerners see only the body-affirming aspects of these traditions and neglect, unconsciously or otherwise, the other side of the coin, which is equally present. So a Western Taoist may enthusiastically practice Tai Chi, but then gloss over texts like: "You should realize that this body is in impermanent thing, a painful material object with no owner, a bag of pus and blood, urine and feces. The whole body, inside and out, has nothing good about it at all."[6]

And that's the second point — the false notion that Far Eastern traditions are completely accepting of the body in the usual Western sense of the term. Buddhism and Taoism, like all authentic ancient traditions, have an extremely nuanced understanding of the nexus between the physical and mental.

So everywhere you turn you are confronted with ambiguity. And this is the hallmark of ancient traditions — that they do not try to simplify reality. Reality is by nature extremely complex and you simplify it at your peril. So how do you resolve the tension between these two currents — care for the body and ignoring the body? Guess what? You don't! That's right; you just have to live with this tension every minute of every day.

The temptation to seek some rational solution always leads to disaster. This is one of those damned *antinomies*, or paradoxes. The rational mind despises these antinomies, because they shatter its limited linear thinking. As you go along you'll notice that many aspects of the real world have a very mysterious and antinomic quality and cause the rational mind quite a bit of indigestion.

This is why Western civilization — the rationalist empire — has resolved all apparent contradictions by taking one side or the other of every antinomy. And when the suppressed side of the antinomy rears its head, as it always does, then all hell breaks loose. The suppressed side of an antinomy will resurface, usually with considerable violence, in the life of an individual or even a civilization. Take sexuality for example: long repressed in Western civilization, it has come to the fore with extreme "violence" in recent years, and not always in a healthy way.

You can gain more insight into this problem by looking at the thousands of Christian lay people who left the civilized world of Egypt and Palestine and went off into the desert from the fourth century onward. These desert fathers and mothers conducted what were in essence large-scale experiments on how care for the body affects the mind. Since their primary purpose was to maintain inner, noetic prayer, they had a very great interest in how other elements of their particular lifestyle would affect noetic prayer. Naturally, one such element is eating. They discovered that prayer is most easily maintained and intrusive thoughts most easily minimized if the body follows a particular nutritional régime. They realized that heavier foods such as meat actually weigh down the thought processes and increase the quantity of intrusive thoughts. So in their search for inner mental stability, they realized that a lighter diet was far more conducive to their way of life. They also realized that simply eating too much of any kind of food had more or less the same effect as eating food that is too heavy. On the other hand, experience also proved that excessive fasting led to exactly the same problem of intrusive thoughts as eating too much. So they developed a régime of extreme balance where the body is given exactly what it needs — not what it wants, but what it needs, which are always two different things — and where, generally speaking, it is given food in moderate quantities every day.

> ### PARADOX
> (((((((**3.5** (((((((
>
> Progress in self transformation involves the ability to care for the body and to ignore the body — each in precise balance.
>
> ((((((((((((((((((

Even today, Orthodox monastics are fed a very healthy, "Mediterranean" diet. And the intended consequence of combining an excellent diet and moderate fasting is to stabilize the mind.

The unintended consequence is described by Daniel Reid, an expert in Chinese medicine:

> One of the most effective of all immune system boosters turns out to be fasting, which all animals do naturally whenever they are ill. When properly conducted, fasting

can cure virtually all diseases, including cancer, and completely rebuild the immune system. Fasting is the most effective of all methods for stimulating elevated secretions of growth hormone, detoxifying the blood and all other bodily fluids and tissues, excreting accumulated wastes from the colon and other organs, dissolving tumors and cysts, repairing tissues, and healing internal and external injuries.[7]

The second and third stages of monastic training may involve the more isolated form of life — typically called hermit life or "life in the desert." At this point health has been built up and noetic life has been stabilized. This stage involves a complete renunciation of worldly preoccupations, to the point of ignoring bodily health and survival. But this turning away from the body has nothing to do with a disdain for the body itself, nor is it a kind of self-inflicted punishment for sins. Instead, it is based on deep and compelling spiritual evidence which pulls the person who is undergoing transformation in a particular direction, as Father Sophrony explains:

> When, moved by great love, a man prays for the world he reaches a state in which he is utterly unsparing of himself, and when this interior sacrifice is consummated, his soul accedes to a profound peace that comprehends all things… Back from prayer into the opacity of psychosomatic life, the soul feels a certain melancholy at the inadequacy of her sacrifice… So, gradually, there arises in his soul the need to overcome the mendacity of his life and take his prayer to its ultimate truth, which is only to be obtained in death.[8]

At the highest stage of training, the Orthodox Christian may go beyond natural laws without any harm. One Russian saint, Paul of Obnora, lived out in the forest all year round, spending the winter inside a hollow linden tree, without any fire. In the Russian far north it is physiologically impossible to survive under such conditions and yet he did so year after year. And many others have gone where "the flesh cannot follow." St. Varsanuphios the Great had reached the stage where he no longer needed to eat physical sustenance at all.

So if you distill the knowledge in authentic ancient traditions on bodily health, you come to the following basic inner principle: In the beginning, building bodily health is a prerequisite for inner refinement in self-transformation.

"See to it that you get well," writes Joseph the Hesychast, "Fix your nerves in any way you can, and you will find your prayer and peace again. See to it that you help yourself as much as you can. Take control of your appetite: don't eat things that you know are harmful to your health: fried foods, salty foods, sauces, pork, meats, salted fish, alcoholic beverages in general. Avoid all these things, and it will be considered to be fasting in the eyes of the Lord."[9]

So this refinement of the physical aspect of life is extremely important because it enables you to endure the disciplines necessary to transform your life. "Repair the alchemical workshop," writes a Taoist master, "Nourish the temporal; strengthen the physical body. To nourish the temporal is the point of departure; when vitality, energy, and spirit are vigorous, one can bear hunger and cold. Having cultivated the physical body until it is firm and strong, giving shelter from the rain and wind, it is good for refining the elixir."[10]

However much practitioners of authentic ancient traditions appear to care for the body, their mental attitude is that they are ready to die at any moment. After all, it's ridiculous to be attached to something you have to lose anyway. So from this point of view, you can understand that both the so-called health nut and the potbellied couch-potato are equally deluded in their approach to life. One is deluded by exaggerating a laudable approach, while the other is deluded by a reprehensible one. And while the results they get on the physical plane will be very different, neither one can make any progress in the real transformation of his or her life. So the real problem is not so much what you do, but the mind set with which you approach it.

For one thing, bodily training and building health are necessary so that you will be able to stick to your Program of self-transformation. This process takes physical energy, so I'll begin by teaching you how to get plenty of it.

Many Orthodox Christians today believe that following the tradition means neglecting their health. For the most part, this is quite false. Most of them have a lifestyle which indulges their passions, so they gain absolutely nothing from ignoring their health and in fact harm themselves on every level. This is completely and totally different from someone dedicated to self-refinement who has reached the stage of neglecting the body, whose "neglect" of bodily health actually serves to undercut the passions and ego. So despite the superficial resemblance between the two, the results are completely different on both physical and noetic levels.

Traditional Versus Allopathic Medicine

There have been numerous medical paradigms over the course of human history. Needless to say, our interest here is in medical paradigms that have proven over centuries and preferably millennia that they provide amazing results. Typically, these traditions, which I call traditional medicine, have been associated with authentic ancient traditions in general: the Taoist and Buddhist inspired medicine in Tibet, China, Japan and Korea, together with the Ayurveda tradition of India, the traditions of the Mediterranean world inspired by both Orthodoxy and Islam, traditions indigenous to the Americas, and several shamanistic traditions scattered throughout the world.

These traditions are deeply aware of the spiritual roots of illness, of the availability of transcendent knowledge to help with difficult cases, and of the importance of the spiritual state of the healer. Fr. Porphyrios (d. 1991) in Greece could diagnose hidden illnesses in others, even at great

WE CREATE HEALTH OR DISEASE

As a priest and spiritual father I'd say that one in every two people over the age of twenty-five who comes to me has a major physical challenge. Having misunderstood what the tradition says about physical health, many of them cast the blame for their condition on God. This doesn't mean necessarily that they're angry at God; it just means that they interpret their illness as a "cross to bear" that God has put on their shoulders.

However, in almost every case, the physical illness is transparently the result of their own lifestyle choices, and has nothing to do with God or karma or the devil or anything else out of the ordinary. If you send your child out on Halloween night, and he comes back with bags full of candy and then proceeds to eat most of it right then and there, will you be terribly surprised if he is sick and unable to go to school the next day? I don't think so. Still less will you blame it on God. If a case like this seems obvious, then why is it that very few people can apply a similar analysis to their own situation?

We create most of our own illnesses. This means on one hand, we can no longer take comfort in blaming external circumstances or God for our own problems. But on the other hand, it also means that we have, in most cases, the possibility of reversing our condition by undoing the causes we have set in motion.

distances. The Native American healer, Fools Crow, claimed to receive the appropriate healing method for each case directly from Wakan-Tanka (God).[11] Wang Liping's mentors taught him that without a pragmatic basis in inner work, the physician is limited to conventional techniques and would not be able to receive super-human guidance for difficult cases. I myself know an herbal master from the Mediterranean who openly admits that the herbal science he inherited is so complex that it would have been completely impossible for humanity to have invented it without help from on high.

These traditions treat disease as an imbalance. They consider man

INNER PRINCIPLE
)))))))) 3.8 ((((((((

It is grossly mistaken to conclude that because noetic
refinement is the central
issue in self-transformation,
bodily health is irrelevant.

in relation to the cosmos and in relation to all the subtle forces in his environment.

Over against this stands medicine of the modern West, which considers itself the apex of medical knowledge. Although Western medicine has proven itself very competent in matters of acute-care - that means if you get in a car accident, Western doctors can patch you up quite efficiently — this kind of medicine has proven uniquely ineffective in chronic care — that is, in dealing with internal disease conditions.

Nearly twenty years ago, I was trained as a nursing orderly and worked in a hospital for several months. Essentially, we did nearly everything the nursing staff did except that we were not allowed to dispense medications. This experience was a revelation, because I soon realized that if you know basic human anatomy and if you have an idea of the patient's symptoms, your diagnosis is likely to be just as accurate as that of the medical doctors. I was deeply shocked by the inability of the Western medical tradition to treat serious chronic conditions in a meaningful way. And, in many cases, their "cure" was worse than disease. Despite the fact that this was a very modern, well-equipped hospital, patients were kept in conditions that were psychologically appalling and physically unpleasant.

I will never forget the orderly who trained me. One day during our training, he warned us that if we happened to feel ill on the job and were to go to the emergency room to be checked out by a physician there, we should be very careful about accepting the diagnosis. He recounted the story of how he himself as a young orderly had once felt rather ill during his shift and had done just that. The physician on call gave him a thorough physical examination and told him, "Your appendix is acting up." The orderly looked at physician stonefaced and said, "Didn't you see the scar? I had my appendix removed when I was nine years old." The embarrassed doctor examined him again and this time he said, "Well, you know, it could be your tonsils." The orderly replied, "I had my tonsils removed at the age of 12."

This is not meant to slam all Western medical doctors, nearly all of whom are more competent than this particular one! But it is an interesting counterpoint to the almost universal Western idolization of the medical doctor, in which I grew up. My parents' generation, which grew up in the twenties and thirties, believed the doctor was next to God. The doctor could do no wrong, his diagnosis was infallible and his treatment not to be questioned. And I would say that my parents persisted in this belief until the end of their lives despite the massive amount of evidence to the contrary.

And it is precisely this evidence which is bringing about slowly but inexorably the health revolution of our times, the revolution spearheaded by those who have learned from bitter experience the dangers of entrusting one's life or the lives of one's loved ones to Western medical science.

When my son was in grade six, he suddenly became seriously ill. He lost all his energy, he could barely hold himself up, and he appeared for all intents and purposes to be on his last legs. He continued in this condition for several weeks. We knew that he had had a minor neck injury in gym class about two weeks before the onset of symptoms, but we were not sure if this had anything to do with his symptoms. And we were assured by medical doctors at the local hospital that this was not possible. The doctors believed that he had a virus and gave him a powerful sedative to put him to sleep for over twenty-four hours so as to give his body the ability to overcome the virus. Instead, this made him more miserable.

Although we were skeptical about the virus theory, knowing that Western doctors revert to it when they do not know what they're dealing with, we allowed them to try it. When this failed, I took my son to a Chinese doctor I know. She said to me, "I can treat the symptoms easily, but what bothers me is that I do not know the cause. From what you have told me about his accident in gym class, I think you should go and see an osteopath."

When we eventually found an osteopath — these were not easy to find in Canada at that time — and explained the problem, the osteopath said, "I know exactly what's happening." He took a model skeleton of the head and spinal cord and proceeded to show us how the accident in gym class had caused the soft tissue around the injured area to seize up. This had forced to top two vertebrae together and thereby cut off some of the blood supply to the brain by putting pressure on the arteries that run between the two vertebrae. The osteopath showed us some simple massage therapy, which in a matter of a few days restored my son to full health.

I've included this as only one of the hundreds of similar horror stories from my own experience and from people I know personally.

What is now called "Western medicine" is technically known as allopathic medicine. The word *allopathic* comes from two Greek words, *allos* and *pathos*, the first meaning "other" and the second meaning "suffering." In other words, suffering and therefore disease comes from other sources, sources external to the human body. This underlines the basic precept in Western medicine that disease is caused by external pathogens; bacteria, viruses or parasites. Daniel Reid explains:

> Ever since Louis Pasteur discovered the existence of bacteria, Western medicine has subscribed increasingly to the germ theory of disease. According to this theory, human diseases are caused by germs, which enter the body through contaminated food, water, or air, or from physical contact with infected persons... While there is no doubt that certain germs can cause specific diseases, certain conditions must prevail in order for any particular germ to invade the human system and multiply sufficiently to cause disease. Pasteur himself noted in his journals that each particular strain of bacteria he studied required a very specific and narrow range of temperature, moisture, light, pH balance, and other conditions in order to survive and multiply. If any of those conditions were altered or eliminated, the germ automatically perished... This aspect of Pasteur's

work has been played down by the Western medical and pharmaceutical industries in favor of the assumption that the same germ causes the same disease in all patients under all conditions. Consequently, modern Western medical practice relies entirely on powerful antibiotics, antifungals, antivirals, antihistamines, and other toxic chemicals to bludgeon various germs into submission, often without success and without the slightest regard for the damage such poisons do to the sensitive essences and energies of the human body. This chemical warfare approach to the treatment of disease severely disturbs the subtle mechanisms which regulate vital functions and disrupts the delicate balance of energies upon which human health and vitality depend.[12]

The modern Western medical tradition is based on the discredited mechanistic worldview of Newtonian physics: the body is essentially treated as machine and you deal with it the same way you deal with a broken-down car. Very little thought has been given to the physical or emotional causes of illness, such as nutrition or stress. This is why Western medicine so often mistakes the symptom for the disease and then tries to suppress the symptoms, an approach which never works for long. More problematic from a public policy angle is that this system of technologically and drug dependent health care is leading even the world's richest nations into a financial impasse.

In other parts of the world, this relatively new Western medical tradition has been integrated admirably into the pre-existing health tradition to form a synergistic whole for the benefit of patients. I have often heard this from both Russian and Chinese medical doctors, for example, who have expressed to me their shock and concern about Western treatment methods they witnessed here in Canada. And in general, they would both the readily agree with the following critique:

Chinese medicine does not cause the patient more pain and suffering, but can diagnose, prescribe, and give treatment based on external manifestations. Western medicine, in contrast, can hardly take a step without instruments; when it comes to afflictions of the internal organs or ailments below the surface of the skin, Western medicine needs to perform biopsies or exploratory surgery to make accurate diagnoses, thus bringing the patient even more pain and suffering. Western medicine also lacks a consciousness of the totality and cannot practice dialectical treatment: when the head hurts, the head is treated; when the feet hurt, the feet are treated — regardless of what side effects medicines employed may have. Often it happens that when one illness has been eliminated, another ailment arises. This way of going about things may seem advanced, but in reality it is primitive.[13]

Western medicine has not always been like this. Prior to the pharmaceutical revolution of the 1920s and 1930s, there was a widespread recognition that the disease process in the human body was not simply the result of external pathogens and could not efficiently be dealt with by trying to wage a chemical war on the pathogens once they are in the body. Health pioneers like Dr. Norman Walker and Dr. Bernard Jensen propounded a vastly different and more successful approach that is discussed in more detail later in this chapter.

Allopathic medicine in general is blind to certain internal dynamics. It acknowledges the presence of bioelectric energy, for example, but believes this energy to be a secondary result of physical processes. This is in stark contrast to traditional medicines, which see the body as a congealed form of energy itself. In other words, the body is a solidified form of energy and is subtended by energy. This may seem like a radical statement, but to all authentic ancient traditions it seems as obvious as saying the sky is blue and the grass is green. Moreover, it seems to accord very closely with what modern physics is now telling us about matter — that the existence of matter is merely apparent to our senses, while in itself it is simply a matrix of energy.

If this is true, as traditional medical systems suggest, then health and healing are possible on an entirely different basis — that of energy. This explains the documented successes over the centuries of such healing modalities as yoga, Qi Gong, acupuncture and similar related practices. If this is true, as the evidence suggests, then health is more a matter of internal physical, psychological and emotional balance than anything else, and less a question of external pathogens. The

pathogens, of course, exist anyway, and surround us all the time. The only issue is whether our immune systems are strong enough to fight them off or not. This traditional approach gives rise to healing modalities that are:

1. Comparatively non-invasive and painless
2. Far more effective against chronic conditions
3. Independent of or less reliant on expensive technology
4. Holistic in the true sense

So the question is, "How do I acquire this superior health, immunity and longevity?" Well, if you are really serious about your health, then pay very close attention to the following Inner Principles 3.10 and 3.11.

Cancer now routinely claims one quarter to one third of the population. And the majority of those who do not succumb to cancer succumb instead to cardiovascular disease or stroke. Yet however appalling these trends are, the fact that these degenerative diseases were very rare in pre-industrial societies and that the risk factors for them are increasingly understood proves one thing:

There are specific lifestyle choices that you can make that will in all probability result in continued health, immunity, and longevity for many years to come. The most important factor in your health is what you do. Every other factor has less influence than this.

This is the single most important principle in all the material presented on health here. Traditional medical systems succeed because they deliberately adopt a strategy of creating health. Everything they do from morning till night creates better health. This is the implicit and never stated basic principle behind the success of these systems.

To create health means that you deliberately adopt strategies that lead to optimal physical and mental function in every area of your life. The opposite strategy, fighting disease, is what 99 percent of Westerners do. We bumble through in our chosen lifestyle –often one chosen unconsciously — without any particular regard for health. When something goes wrong and symptoms emerge, we rush off to the medical authorities for drugs to mask symptoms, but make very few if any adjustments to our lifestyles. Even if successful, the underlying disease condition will eventually manifest itself again, and with greater force. And if we do not change our strategy, the disease condition will at some point become irreversible. The incredible advantages of adopting a strategy of creating health are these:

1. You have the initiative; you are no longer passively awaiting your fate. You are not constantly trying to put out fires.
2. Many symptoms and their underlying disease conditions can be cured without being addressed directly. By adopting a strategy of creating health many illnesses will disappear on their own.
3. Your energy level and health will improve day by day, reversing the steady decline that you will experience if you merely fight disease.

Incredible immune boosting changes to your lifestyle are within your grasp, and these changes just coincidentally happen to be central to very process of self-transformation itself, because they optimize your mental, emotional and physical function.

Here is a brief description of the plan I recommend. And a plan is absolutely essential because, as you realize from having read chapter 2, only what is put into your Program is likely to get done. Without a plan, you have absolutely no chance of improving your health and gaining superior immunity and longevity. In general, people are overwhelmed today by health information and really don't know where to

turn. It's precisely this information overload that paralyzes many people who otherwise are quite serious about their health.

This remarkable health plan addresses all aspects of your health. It is a simple step-by-step plan that anyone can use. It takes all the guesswork out of improving your health, because you have the distilled wisdom of ancient health traditions all translated into an easy to use, step-by-step method. Because it is based on ancient methodologies, this plan is essentially future proof — it is not going to be invalidated by this or that study that appears in the next few months.

Where to Begin Building Health, Immunity, and Longevity

Acquiring superior health, immunity and longevity depends in no small part upon where you're at right now. You may have a serious chronic condition like asthma, diabetes or arthritis. You may suffer from weight problems. All of these and many other conditions certainly require special handling. But in general there are steps that we all can take radically improve our health, to acquire a first-class immune system, and to give ourselves a very good chance of living to a ripe old age in good health.

Right now there are millions of people in North America who would very much like to improve their health, or at the very least who would like to stop feeling like helpless victims of the epidemic of degenerative diseases that they face, waiting for their number to come up in this macabre lottery. In my parents' generation it was assumed the lottery was simply a part of life, that there is nothing anyone could do about it. Nothing could be more false. You can get out of the lottery. The risk factors are relatively well-known and understood for all types of degenerative disease. And incredible immune boosting changes to your diet and lifestyle are easily possible — all you have to do is take the responsibility to put these changes into practice.

The Rock Solid Health Program

Like everything else in this book, the Health Program itself is based largely on ancient authentic traditions, on what I've learned in Orthodoxy, Buddhism and Taoism. These strategies have produced amazing results for many centuries and continue to produce those same results even today, in many parts of the world. However, the Program also takes into account the latest research, and also the unique circumstances that pertain to us who live in the industrialized West. That is to say, as Westerners, we usually have very specific ideas about health. We tend to suffer the same health problems and have very similar starting points in our quest. We also tend to have very similar health resources at hand that we can draw on.

Go to www.rocksolidlife.com as soon as you can. There you will find most of the information you need to make a radical difference in your health starting today. But please take your time and try to assimilate the information — learn as much as you can before you begin. We also offer the works of a number of famous authors in the field so that you have a basis for comparison. Don't just take my word for it — learn about your health! And don't start buying haphazardly the products we offer — learn what they are for and how they fit in to an optimal health maintenance plan. Start at the beginning and work slowly and methodically.

The www.rocksolidlife.com website will provide most of the necessary products, tools and information you would need to accomplish your goals, all contained in a series of home study units. These units are designed to make acquiring health, immunity and longevity as simple and clear as possible. Each course can be broken down into a number of very definite steps for you to take, so that you always know where you are and where you're going next.

For the sake of convenience I've divided health into five separate areas or pillars. The pillars of health encompass every facet of your health, both mental and physical, as well as the nexus between the two. The description of the Program that follows is necessarily brief, but I've tried to include enough detail so that you can at least get started.

Health Pillar 1: Cleansing

Cleansing in this context means cleansing the body of accumulated toxins in order to establish perfect internal equilibrium and boost your immune system. This course will explain why bowel health is the key to overall health and why it is urgently necessary for most people who've grown up on a "Standard American Diet" to undertake a bowel cleanse. You will be introduced to some simple bowel cleansing methods, and then later on to some more sophisticated methods. You'll learn how to incorporate cleansing and rebuilding programs into your life, and how to take advantage of the miracle of fasting — one of the ultimate curative exercises.

Health Pillar 2: Fueling

In this unit you'll learn why your diet today bears virtually no resemblance to the diet your ancestors, so that it's no wonder your body is having a difficult time coping. You'll learn what foods to eliminate immediately from your diet and exactly what you can replace them with. Many of you probably would like to adopt a better diet. The first thing you absolutely must do is to eliminate what is harmful. Many ingredients in modern processed foods are known to cause degenerative disease. You will then be introduced to a high-performance diet and to the best supplementation program and products available. Proper nutritional supplements are indispensable for boosting your immunity and energy level, and for protecting the body from the increasing threat posed by our polluted environment. To implement this can be a major transition in life and certainly requires both time and determination. But it is an unavoidable fact that self-transformation demands that you eat in order to live, not that you live in order to eat. You must learn to give the body what it needs and not necessarily what it wants.

Health Pillar 3: Energizing

Energizing is all about circulating energy throughout the body, and to a certain extent this does involve what is commonly called "exercise"! Few people are aware that there are two radically different kinds of exercise, internal and external. The exercise most Westerners are familiar with is external: it involves things like running, stretching or weightlifting. In other words, it is exercise for aerobic fitness, flexibility or muscular performance. These external forms of exercise certainly have their value when used in moderation as part of an overall fitness plan.

But there's another form of exercise — internal exercise — which produces even more startling results, but which is more dimly understood in West. Westerners have for the most part at least heard of such exercise systems as Yoga, Qi Gong or Tai Chi. These are classic examples of internal exercise and I highly recommend that you learn the basics of one of these systems.

"Yoga" actually refers to Indian *Hatha yoga* — a system of physical postures designed in part to optimize health by toning the body's internal organs and energy pathways. One advantage to the "health consumer" is that yoga training in general tends to be relatively standardized.

Qi Gong (Chi Kung) is a recent name for Taoist and some Buddhist energy arts in China. Like yoga, it provides phenomenal immune-boosting benefits, but unlike yoga, it does not rely on unusual physical flexibility and complex postures, and is therefore more accessible to a wider range of people. On the downside, Qi Gong is also less standardized — the quality of teaching here in North America varies widely, and the quality of the systems taught is also a mixed bag.

Although most people in the West assume it is a form of health exercise, Tai Chi (or Taiji) is one of the most sophisticated and deadly martial arts ever devised. Of mixed Taoist and Buddhist heritage, its exact origins are shrouded in legend. Four major styles exist today, any one of which, if properly taught, can provide you with enormous health benefits.

Tai Chi is much easier to find than Qi Gong. And most Tai Chi schools also teach a certain amount of Qi Gong. Unfortunately, though, they sometimes teach only a smattering of Qi Gong without really understanding it. The practice of the Tai Chi form itself is a kind of Qi Gong, and has similar curative potential to many Qi Gong systems, but only if the form is done with its internal content. The external physical moves themselves are only about ten percent of the health equation. So yes, Tai Chi will do as your primary internal exercise, provided that the instructor understands the internal aspects of the art and is willing to teach them to you. I have met instructors who teach nothing but the external, mechanical movements and call this Tai Chi — it's just a waste of time and money. Once you learn the inner principles of Tai Chi, you can practice them constantly and everywhere, while walking, standing at a bus stop or brushing your teeth! And the Health Pillar 3 course will teach you exactly how to do this.

This leads us to the question of qi (Pronounced CHEE): almost everyone with any background, even slight, in Oriental culture has ideas about qi, but many of these ideas are mistaken. Some treat it like "the force" in George Lucas's *Star Wars* movies. Whatever Lucas had in mind with his "force," what I can definitely say about qi is the following:

Chinese medicine divides the human energetic structure into three realities: Jing (sometimes translated as vitality or essence), Qi (usually translated as energy), and Shen (usually translated as mind or spirit). These three realities are actually three different manifestations of the same thing, and each manifests itself in the body as a form of bioelectricity. The body's electromagnetic field can be brought under conscious control and used for health purposes, to heal others, to achieve certain goals in the martial arts, and for numerous other purposes. The first goal in Qi Gong is therefore to stabilize the Jing, Qi and Shen.

The remaining chapters of this book focus very heavily on stabilizing shen — basically the equivalent of the *nous* — because this is the one essential and indispensable criterion for stabilizing jing and qi, and it is also the one step that many modern Qi Gong teachers, and even teachers of Taoism, leave out. Many Qi Gong teachers are ready to teach energy circulation as a deliberate practice, but few understand that in the long run this is completely ineffective unless Shen is stabilized as well. In other words, they're willing to teach secondary and ancillary techniques, all the time telling you they are the essence of the art, when in fact they are not. And it is often the case that these teachers themselves do not understand the essence of Qi Gong or the traditions of self-transformation that gave rise to it.

The Health Pillar 3 course at www.rocksolidlife.com/health is a simple yet powerful Qi Gong program for beginners and advanced students alike. It refines jing and qi to stabilize the central nervous system, enhance energy circulation, improve organ health and boost the secretions of the immune system. Moreover, it also provides more information on how Qi Gong works than most Qi Gong classes will give you.

Health Pillar 4: Stabilizing

Chapter 4 of this book deals with nothing but stabilizing the *nous*. And www.rocksolidlife.com/health also has a home study course that goes into greater detail about practical application than chapter 4 does. Stabilizing means stabilizing first of all your central nervous system. You'll learn methods that allow you to switch from the sympathetic circuit of your central nervous system to the parasympathetic circuit. This induces a deep relaxation in your entire being and is a precursor to removing the energy blockages that are compromising the function of your internal organs. And only by stabilizing the central nervous system can the immune system itself be radically improved, because as long as excessive stress is taxing it, it is functioning at a very low level.

Moreover, it's impossible to make progress in self-transformation without refining thought on a deep level, and that cannot be dealt with as long as the central nervous system is in complete disarray. So stabilizing the mind becomes a primary objective. But first you must understand what the mind is, the difference between the rational mind and the *nous*, and how to bring the mind back to its natural state. The methods to do this are outlined in the next chapter, and these methods are absolutely and unequivocally the key to self- transformation, as taught by all authentic ancient traditions.

Health Pillar 5: Programming

Your entire being, from your personality to your physical body, has been deeply conditioned by everything you have experienced up to this point in your life. The birth process, family relationships, early childhood experiences, friendships, traumatic events, peer pressure, diet, and innumerable other factors have gone into making you who you are. The purpose of self-transformation is to find the real you under all of this conditioning, because only then is it possible to achieve a radically expanded consciousness, to turn life into love, and to conquer death itself.

Much of this conditioning has affected not only your personality, but also your physical body. And in fact, there is a very close connection between your emotional makeup and your physical health. This is one of the central propositions of traditional health systems. It is well known that stress has a direct impact on the immune system, though the mechanism of interaction between the two is not yet totally understood by science. Nevertheless, the new field of psychoneuroimmunology is dedicated to mapping out precisely this and has made some amazing discoveries.

The Health Pillar 5 course will help you to examine your physical and psychological makeup in order to discover what programming already exists within your psycho-physical being. Many of our health outcomes have been programmed into us by our interactions with the world of persons, events and things. And many of these outcomes can be modified or prevented by understanding the mechanism which put them in place and then undoing the process. In this sense, programming builds on stabilizing, but makes use of it for a specific purpose.

There was a man named George (not his real name) who came to me at the age of 37 and told me the following story. George had suffered with chronic anxiety for most of his life, the main symptom of which over the previous fourteen years had been heart palpitations. The palpitations began when George was a university student, finishing off his bachelor's degree. But the anxiety problem predated that by many years.

George had been deeply affected by an incident that took place when he was age four and was playing with his playmates. They were playing doctor and one of his playmates mentioned that a previous patient had died from high blood pressure. This trivial and insignificant piece of information had been stored in George's subconscious, and added to other bits of information which came his way in the years that followed. From his upbringing in the modern industrialized West, George had the feeling that health was something out of his control, and that everyone around him was waiting as a kind of passive victim in the macabre lottery of health. The attitudes of his parents and the attitudes of people around him further reinforced this notion. His parents, for example, did not take particular care of their health.

As George got older, a kind of internal paranoia ensued. George felt himself a passive victim waiting to become the next heart disease statistic. So by the time he was 13 years old, George was already having severe bouts of anxiety and thoughts were beginning to oppress him telling him that he was going to die of a heart attack. Of course, to die at age 13 of heart attack is highly unlikely, but you must remember that in the world of programming perception is everything. As George went through his teenage years he had frequent bouts with thoughts of this kind: His heart would begin to pound, he would experience shortness of breath, and yet the doctors would tell him that he was fine. Whenever he believed them his symptoms would abate, but eventually they could no longer convince him and the symptoms became more frequent.

When George entered university, the added stress of academic life only exacerbated his symptoms. For one thing, George did not know how to deal with psychological stress, and certainly no one had taught him (It's amazing how much stress the educational system callously puts on students, without ever teaching them how to deal with it). At that time, in the late 1970s, there was not much help to be found in the public domain. So George struggled on, though rather ineffectively.

George had been brought up in an Orthodox Christian home, but his parents' observance of Orthodoxy was rather nominal and they knew next to nothing about the spiritual tradition of the Church and its therapeutic value. Although George became a committed Orthodox

Christian himself, he was a loss to deal with his psychological symptoms and found no help within Orthodoxy. He prayed, but his prayer brought little help. As he later learned, the answers were actually there in the tradition and right under his nose, but there was no one competent enough to point this out to him! His practice of prayer was superficial and largely incorrect, but he did not know this. Unaware of all this, George learned Taoist meditation, and only then began to find significant relief from his symptoms. In fact, the change was so significant that it was a revolution in his life. When I introduced George to some of the deeper aspects of Orthodoxy, he began to see that the cure for his condition had been there all along, but that he had been ignorant of its existence and no one was there to tell him otherwise. Now, by practicing noetic prayer in the context of Orthodoxy, George has gone on to deepen his practice and to further improve his physical and psychological health.

ROCK SOLID LIFE PRACTICE 3.10: BUILDING HEALTH, IMMUNITY, AND LONGEVITY

1. Take the online health test at www.rocksolidlife. com/health and score your results as instructed
2. Then use the online Rock Solid Health Plan Builder to develop personalized health goals and find the methods to accomplish them efficiently

Whether you decide to use all or part of the Rock Solid Health tools, always proceed slowly and step-by-step. Making meaningful changes to your lifestyle will take time, so don't get obsessed with doing everything at once. Remember that only changes that you have thoroughly assimilated into your life will bear fruit. It is better to do one thing thoroughly than ten things poorly.

SEXUALITY:
LIVING WITH THE DOUBLE-EDGED SWORD

We live in a truly sex-obsessed society — it's impossible to go to a store, to turn on the television, or to open a newspaper or magazine, without being hit with some explicit reference to sexuality. This is in stark contrast to half a century ago, when the total lack of reference to human sexuality was virtually a conspiracy of silence. Each of these extremes represents an imbalance in the life of society as a whole; hence the current confusion throughout the Western world about all things sexual.

Our goal in this section is threefold:

1. To acquaint you with a radically different vision of sexuality than any you are accustomed to — the vision of authentic ancient traditions. This understanding of sexuality has an entirely different frame of reference from that found in the West, whether among puritans or playboys.
2. To help you evaluate your sexual situation in terms of this vision, and
3. To show you how you can transform sexuality from an obstacle into an element of the transformational process

Origins and Consequences of
the Western Religious View of Sexuality

The Western world alternates between extremes of sexual repression and indulgence, a kind of pendulum effect indicative of a deep-seated heresy or wrong assumption about life. Authentic ancient traditions, however, see reality as antinomic — as full of apparent contradictions, where you must find your way between two or more rationally under-standable extremes.

The key sexual extreme in the West comes through the fifth century theology of Augustine of Hippo, whose very negative view of human sexuality, juridical worldview, and concept of God as the external cosmic authority who punishes transgressions laid the groundwork for an exceptionally oppressive moralism. The subtext to this view of sexual sin is that if you commit one, God will punish you. Although moralism is extremely useful for social control, it controls society at the expense of the quality of life of the person.

The key fact, though, is that moralism is possible only if you have long since lost any sense of the real ontological meaning of the moral prohibitions. In a moralistic environment, fundamental questions about sexuality — how it relates to the essence of the human person, to the human psychosomatic structure, to the very being of the universe itself, or even to the being of God — these questions are seldom asked and certainly never answered. Unlike their moralistic counterparts, the cautions about sexual sin in authentic traditions are there not because God will harm you if you fall into sexual temptation, but rather because you will harm yourself. Misuse of the potent energies of sexuality invariably results in harm to the person misusing them, and possibly to others as well.

Unfortunately, the Western moralistic version gave rise to centuries of sexual repression, based largely on the Roman Catholic Church's Augustinian notion that sexuality within marriage serves only to perpetuate the species, and is little more than a necessary evil. Under this relentless logic, you could only really escape sin by having sexual intercourse in order to get pregnant, and even then as fast as possible, and preferably in total darkness while trying desperately not to enjoy it. There would be no justification for sexual relations during pregnancy, between times of trying to conceive, or after childbearing years. And for that matter, sexual intimacy not involving intercourse would logically be excluded. The whole position is a reductio ad absurdum, which is the invariable result of the rational mind's trying desperately to ignore the antinomic nature of reality in favor of an artificial intel-

> ## INNER PRINCIPLE
> (((((3.12 (((((
>
> The principles of sexual morality outlined by authentic ancient traditions were intended to prevent people from harming themselves. "Religions" have misappropriated them and used them to cause severe emotional harm.
>
> (((((((((((((((

lectual schematization. In the words of the well-known Orthodox writer, Philip Sherrard:

> [In the traditional Roman Catholic teaching] Man and woman are reduced in marriage to the role of instruments serving to populate the void of a monstrous materialized space-time future and to do this in a way that is explicitly identified as a serving the divine plan itself. This conception, by displacing the purpose and fulfillment of the relationship between man and woman from the center of their respective beings and projecting this purpose and fulfillment into an external, nonexistent, cold and impersonal space-time continuum stretching into an entirely false infinity, adulterates the conjugal principle at its very heart. Man in this conception merely perpetuates his condition of slavery to a process in which his own personal created dignity is sacrificed to the abstract common good of a hypothetical future human society.
>
> It is worth noting that what is here proposed as Christian teaching differs in this respect but little from Communist teaching, which likewise claims that the purpose and fulfillment of the lives of individual men and women are to be found in serving the abstract good of the future human society.[14]

The Protestant Reformation wisely rejected a church run by celibate males, but made the mistake of eradicating consecrated celibacy as well — a hallmark of nearly every authentic ancient tradition. Moreover, Protestantism never questioned the real theological problems at the basis of the Western understanding of sexuality, and therefore its own Puritanism was equally oppressive.

The traditional Western Christian view of the past one thousand years or more can be summarized as follows:

- The sexual relationship between husband and wife is reduced to the narrow category of genital intercourse.

- Sexual intercourse itself is tainted with sin.

- Children are therefore conceived in sin (Orthodoxy regards this is a false interpretation of Psalm 50/51).

- The act of conception transmits sin to the child (this is Augustine's theory of "original sin," based on St. Jerome's mistranslation of St. Paul's words in Romans 5:12. The theory says that we are all born guilty of Adam's sin. Orthodoxy considers this whole theory fanciful and absurd — we inherit mortality but not personal guilt).

- St. Paul's symbolic parallel of the marital relationship with the relationship between Christ and the church is understood in a purely external way and has no practical consequences.

- Because of this, the purpose of marriage is reduced to reproduction.

- Because the Western idea of the Holy Trinity is devoid of any real concept of communion among the three divine persons, there can be no concept of the marital relationship as mirroring the divine communion of persons.

- Therefore, the role of the woman is reduced to that of a factory through which God populates the world. Secondarily, she is also a sexual safety valve to keep the all-powerful male sex drive in check.

- It is the marital couple's duty to have children, because this is the will of God, but the means for accomplishing God's will in this case are inherently evil.

Authentic Ancient Traditions on Sexuality

The picture presented to us by traditions of self-transformation, however, is radically different. The following synthesizes the main points:

1. In the highest states of self-transformation, carnal attraction or desire is left behind. St. Isaac the Syrian knew this from his own experience and said that if everyone were suddenly to attain this state, the world would be deprived of succeeding generations.

2. Sexuality connects all levels of the human person: its energy is basic and is related to all types of energy in the human psychosomatic composite. I have heard both Orthodox monks and Taoists say that sexual energy is basic to their prayer or meditation practices. Philip Sherrard explains:

    > The energy which manifests itself as the sexual energy in man and woman has its source in the deepest strata of their life. It is rooted in the ultimate mystery of their being. It is the source and generator of all human creativeness, whatever form this may take. It is the radiating, magnetizing, vibratory current which courses through the whole living fabric of human life, and beyond human life. It is the energy of life itself, divine in its origin and sacred in its nature, and not ceasing to be sacred even where its use, through ignorance or malice, is perverted or abused.[15]

3. The power of sexuality is related directly to the Absolute Reality. Sexuality is, therefore, an unfathomable mystery emanating from the creative power within the universe and the Uncreated power behind the universe.

4. The sexual union of a man and woman touches the deepest ontological levels of their beings and of the universe. It also brings them into a particular relationship with the Absolute. The more the union approximates the conditions of unconditional and disinterested love, and of enduring commitment undertaken for the good of the other, the more the act brings the couple into an ontological participation with the Absolute reality. This is why St. Paul himself referred to marriage as a mystery that mirrors the relationship between God and man (Eph.5:31-32).

5. Sexual activity undertaken simply for personal gratification does not correspond to its ontological prototype and results in harm. Instead of destroying the false self, the sexual act in this case will strengthen it. Instead of giving yourself to your partner, you are taking something from him or her. Essentially, the ego is using sexuality for its own purposes.

6. The task that confronts the human person is to personalize the blind urge toward sexuality in one of two ways. Either by (a) placing it in the context of a committed and loving relationship, or (b) sublimating and converting the sexual drive, preferably in a life of deliberate and dedicated celibacy such as monasticism.

In the fallen world, the power of sexuality has become a blind and impersonal urge, the biological imperative of indiscriminate procreation. Our task is to transform the blind sexual urge into a personal expression of disinterested love, and this transformed sexual energy may or may not have a "sexual" expression in the conventional sense.

Although ancient traditions often give the impression that celibacy is the best possible choice (most of their higher level spiritual literature comes from a monastic milieu), their real position is more nuanced. St. Silouan, for example, considered all discussions about which form of life is the "highest" or "best" to be abstract and irrelevant. Everything depends on what is more suited to bringing about the transformation of the person in question.

When you fail to place your sexual expression within the framework of a committed and loving relationship and instead reduce it to a means of ego-gratification, it then ceases to be a manifestation of the Absolute, or even of real love, and is reduced to physical lust–the crudest form of sexual energy. When progressively refined, it becomes warmth, tenderness, compassion, loyalty, and fidelity. And finally it is transmuted into love for the Absolute, a total and erotic devotion to the Truth. And, while this erotic love for the Absolute in no way excludes a human sexual relationship, it does imply an elevation of sexual energy to the point where sexual expression is under complete and voluntary control, and where the incredible energy of lust or "sex drive" has lost its power to coerce and control the human person. As for unbridled lust, authentic traditions know from experience that it gives rise to severe psychic abnormalities, compromises physical health and shortens the lifespan. This is especially true of males and has been well documented in the Oriental medical tradition:

> Like a strong appetite for food, strong sexual drive has always been regarded as a fundamental sign of good health and flourishing vitality in Taoist tradition. How this drive is expressed in practice can make all the difference between health and disease, regeneration and degeneration, even life and death. The same principle applies to food... Like nutritional needs, there are right ways and wrong ways to manage sexual needs, and the choice has nothing whatsoever to do with morality.
>
> According to the Taoist view, overt sexual drive stems from the expansive wood energy of the liver, an energy associated with the spring season, while sexual essence comes from the potent condensed water energy of the kidneys. While sexual activity releases and relaxes tension caused by the pent-up liver/wood energy of the sexual drive, it can also exhaust or stagnate the kidney/water

energy that supplies the hormones for such activity. For men, the problem is depletion of kidney energy due to excessive ejaculation. For women, the problem can be stagnation of kidney energy due to insufficient or incomplete orgasm.[16]

It is quite common these days for converts to Oriental traditions in the West to claim that their teachings are much more open and accepting of sexuality and realistic about it than is Christianity. Since they mean Western Christianity, this is an understandable claim and true as far as it goes. The problem, however, is not so much that this ignores Orthodoxy, as that it distorts or oversimplifies the Far Eastern traditions. The real truth of the matter is that both Buddhism and Taoism — the authentic versions, that is — are well aware of the antinomic nature of sexuality. It's especially important to emphasize this point today, because of the increasing popularity of "sexual yoga" practices, based or allegedly based on either Hindu or Buddhist Tantra or on Taoist practices.

At the beginning of the nineteenth century, Taoist master Liu I-Ming described how pseudo-Taoist practices had completely misinterpreted the original symbolism of classical Taoist texts: "The ignorant think that 'the merging of yin and yang'... means the intercourse of man and woman. This is wrong. The gold elixir is made by the crystallization of the energy of primordial nothingness; it cannot be formed by temporal, physical substances." He also noted, "The ignorant think... the 'gate of the birth of the self' is the female birth canal. This is wrong. The birth canal gives birth to humans — how can it give birth to immortals?" Much earlier, the Preserver of the Truth had been even more explicit in slamming some of the very same techniques that you will find today in New Age presentations of Taoist sexual yoga:

> So if you want to build up basic energy, first you should stop debauchery and lustfulness; this work must be done with a clean mind free from thoughts. Worldly people ignorant of this use physical pressure to stop the emission of

> ## INNER PRINCIPLE
> ### ❮❮❮❮❮❮ 3.13 ❮❮❮❮❮❮
>
> Sexual energy is the basic created energy of the human psychosomatic composite.
>
> ❮❮❮❮❮❮❮❮❮❮❮❮❮❮❮❮

semen in sexual intercourse, thinking that to be prevention of leakage. They do not know that vitality is to be stabilized before it has created a concrete substance. If you wait till it has made a substance and then try to stop it, the semen may not be emitted but the spiritual energy is long gone. How ignorant is it to keep deteriorating, stagnant matter accumulating in the pelvic region, thus producing bizarre ailments! Even more in error are blind teachers who go on to fool people by saying they should draw their semen up their spine, calling this 'restoration of vitality to repair the brain'.[18]

From my own experience and research, I would say this: while I believe it is premature to consign all Taoist and Tantric sexual yoga practices to the dustbin of pseudo-self transformation (some of it may be useful for improving both health and relationships), please exercise extreme caution if you ever become involved with this kind of thing.

As a general conclusion on sexuality, it must be stated clearly and for the record that there is no basis whatever within authentic ancient traditions for thinking of sexual union per se as "dirty" or somehow a "necessary evil". In its proper context, it is a marvelous and positive thing and an inexpressible mystery. Orthodox canon law from as far back as the fourth century has reserved extremely harsh penalties for anyone who would condemn sexual relations within marriage as in any way evil or suspect.

So now the question is: "How does this affect me and my life?" Well, with regard to sexual relationships, nearly everybody is in one of five different scenarios, as explained in the following sections.

Celibate and Happy

To be celibate and content at the same time is a wonderful thing. The only qualification that Orthodoxy or other traditions would add to this is that the celibacy must have been chosen for the right reasons. If it is simply because of the inability to relate to the opposite sex, disappointment with personal relationships, from neurotic childhood conditioning, or fear of rejection, then these are not good reasons for celibacy. Self-transformation is about facing and overcoming conditioning, and not letting it run your life. The perceived inability to relate is an egotistical manifestation. As you begin to use the training program in the next chapter,

> ## INNER PRINCIPLE
> ### (((((((3.14 (((((((
>
> In its crude, unrefined form in the fallen world, sexual energy expresses itself as lust. In its most refined form, it becomes an "erotic" love of the Absolute and universal love and compassion toward all people, creatures and things.
>
> (((((((((((((((((

your whole being will be more calm and at peace, and you will experience a progressive release from the bonds of prior conditioning, allowing you to form and manage relationships more easily.

Celibate and Unhappy: Looking for a Mate

The search for a mate can become obsessive and fear-driven, especially with the age twenty-plus crowd. Now the good news: all authentic traditions believe that, unless you feel called to a life of consecrated celibacy, your appropriate mate does exist and is waiting to meet you. In other words, you really don't need to frequent the bars or post ads on the Internet in a desperate search for Mr. or Ms. Right. You just need to purify yourself from your own egocentrism so that when this person is put in front of you — and yes, it will happen — you will have the clarity and perception needed to recognize him or her.

Likewise, there is no magical set of criteria to consider when deciding whether a particular person is right for you. Perhaps the one indisputable condition is that there has to be a shared vision of reality, because in the sea of life you can only stay on course if you are both rowing in the same direction.

Married and Content

Your training in self-transformation can only help improve your rela-

In the fallen world, this energy has but one direction and "purpose," which is to ensure the perpetuation of the species, even though it expresses itself as a desire for sexual gratification. It becomes a blind, impersonal urge that attempts to dominate your mind and will.

⟨⟨⟨⟨⟨⟨⟨⟨⟨⟨⟨⟨⟨⟨⟨

tionship. As you begin the apparently "selfish" task of working on yourself, you will become actually less self-absorbed, and more attentive to the real needs of your mate, warmer and more compassionate.

If you have a spouse who opposes what you're trying to do, you should proceed straight ahead nevertheless, but slowly and carefully. Opposition may be a natural reaction to something not understood — and this describes most cases I know of. You must not only reassure your mate that your efforts in self-transformation will benefit him or her, but you must also prove it in action. And over time, this shouldn't be difficult — as you become more calm and centered, warm and compassionate, the results will speak for themselves.

Married, but with Relationship or Sexual Problems

In this case, there are two possibilities. The first is what's called a "relationship problem." These are problems of a more deep-seated nature, and it goes beyond our scope to go into all of the possibilities. If you believe you have blundered into an ill-advised relationship, you may be torn between trying to make it work or just getting out. If there is any ambiguity in your mind, it is better to opt for the former, since it is often difficult to determine whether a relationship should never have happened. If the relationship has to be ended, all efforts should be made to do it amicably, especially if children are involved (few things cause more damage to a child than an acrimonious divorce).

From what I've seen, the most common way that young couples bumble into an ill-advised relationship is this: they "sexualize" the relationship far too soon. By introducing the incredible energy of intimate sexual activity into their relationship prematurely, they blind themselves to the reality of the situation. If you are looking for a mate, you'll save yourself a whole lot of grief by taking an extended period of time to get to know the other person first as a person. This will give you the distance and perspective you need to make an accurate assessment and decision. But once sexual activity is introduced, this kind of objectivity inevitably goes out the window!

> ## INNER PRINCIPLE
> ((((((3.16 (((((
>
> One of the principle tasks of self-transformation is to free you from this kind of biological determinism by "personalizing" your sexual energy, refining it, and bringing it under conscious control.
>
> (((((((((((((((

On the other hand, the fact that you have relationship problems should not be construed as meaning you have blundered into an ill-advised relationship. Very few marriages that I know of have consisted of smooth sailing — in fact, virtually none. Problems in a relationship are almost inevitable. What matters is whether or not they can be fixed, and most relationship problems can, as long as goodwill is present on both sides.

Or, you may have sexual problems. Many couples run into sexual problems at some point in a relationship. The bad news is that there are numerous kinds (e.g., desire differences, sexual dysfunction), they are widespread, and they can easily put a relationship in jeopardy if they are not addressed and resolved. The good news is that most of these problems can be resolved rather easily. Quite often this requires the presence of a trained sexual therapist. I have seen numerous people helped by professional sexual therapists, so don't be shy: such services are not hard to find, they are confidential and well worthwhile. The only criterion is that the therapist must be someone that each of you can relate to easily, because you must be willing to open up to this person. I have seen cases where this kind of therapy has been able to uproot sexual neuroses entrenched from childhood.

Living Together/Cohabitation

This actually covers quite a range of situations. Some people who "live together" do it for reasons not far different from marriage: that is, they feel a serious, long-term commitment to the other party. There are oth-

You can personalize, refine, and control sexual energy either by using it within a loving relationship of enduring commitment that is freely entered into, or by sublimating and refining the energy directly in a life of celibacy.

ers, of course, who live together temporarily or because it's convenient or pleasant. Still others decide to live with their "significant other" as a trial period prior to marriage in order to be sure that the relationship will work out in the long-term. This is typical of people who have been through long-term relationships that did not work out, who often have both a fear of commitment and of making a wrong choice the second time around. And, strange as it may seem, there is a certain logic to this position: in earlier times, traditional societies typically had much better mate pools: you could be reasonably sure about the cultural expectations and psychological stability of any potential mate, whereas in the modern industrialized West, many people are not what they seem to be.

It is true that authentic ancient traditions do not believe that casual relationships are advisable. On the other hand, there's a big difference between a casual sexual relationship and the sincere dedication and commitment felt by many people who are living together. So to paint them all with the same brush of "fornication" is rather inaccurate from an ontological point of view. On the other hand, there is no doubt that practitioners of these ancient traditions of self-transformation would advise committed couples to consecrate their commitment explicitly as soon as they feel able to do so.

It's impossible to talk about sexuality without talking about birth control. Orthodoxy has never made any blanket pronouncements on birth control, at least none that is universally recognized as valid.[19] Rather, it is usually left up to the couple to decide, in consultation with their spiritual guides. Prohibiting all birth control can cause uncontrollable pressures within a marriage. For example, many women reach a stage in their lives where they are petrified of becoming pregnant. If unable to use birth control, their only recourse is to refuse relations with their mate, who is then put into an untenable position. Now alienated from each other, feeling isolated and alone with nowhere to turn, the couple has virtually no way out. If such a situation runs its course, breakdown in the marriage is nearly inevitable.

The blind and legalistic prohibition of birth control in Roman Catholicism (decided upon and enforced by those least qualified to understand the realities of the situation — a celibate clergy claiming to represent the will of God) is bound to lead to disaster. And it frequently has. As an Orthodox priest and spiritual father I am constantly cleaning up the mess created by moralistic Western sexual ethics, as well as by Western ecclesiastical authorities. I can only thank God that when it comes to the absurd ban against contraception in the Roman Catholic Church, most Catholics simply ignore it.

There are, of course, good and bad reasons for deciding not to have children. My experience indicates that most young couples go through periods of using birth control for rather specific reasons. These reasons may be related to health, psychological preparedness, the economic situation, or to other factors, but usually the intention of the couple is to have children. Authentic ancient traditions consider having children to be a good, blessed, wonderful thing.

Some couples decide not to have children for valid reasons. Some women would be putting themselves at severe health risk were they to become pregnant. But there are also couples whose sole reason is to remain free and unencumbered so they can pursue their own agendas unobstructed. This is a kind of egotism-for-two, and a decision like this can make progress in self-transformation impossible.

As Westerners, we have to get over our "either/or" mentality. We implicitly give ourselves a choice of saying sexuality is bad, but won't go away, so therefore we hedge it in and try to repress it socially. Or we decide it is good, and therefore all of its manifestations deserve to be

> **INNER PRINCIPLE**
> ((((((3.18 ((((((
>
> Use of the sexual energy for pure self-gratification has destructive side effects on the personality and increases the grip of the false self or "ego," the source of all torment.
>
> (((((((((((((((

flaunted. Unfortunately, as with many of the realities of the universe confronts us with, sexuality is neither completely good nor completely bad. It simply is what it is in all of its unfathomable complexity. Our refusal to admit the existence of nuance in the universe and in our own lives is our undoing.

In the fallen world, sexual drive is on autopilot. To follow its promptings blindly is the equivalent of "going along" in Taoist terms. To exert conscious control over it, avoiding its harmful manifestations, is "reversing the natural process." Here you can see the wisdom of this Taoist terminology; in our current condition, the indiscriminate use of sexual drive really does seem "natural." And to a certain extent, it is. The only problem is that in the fallen world, "natural" processes lead to disintegration and death. So the strange paradox is that in order to achieve self-transformation you must defy what appears to be normal and natural. And this really does require effort and determination. As Joseph the Hesychast wrote to one of his spiritual children living in the world, if you don't force yourself to be chaste (which does not mean "celibate" in this context), then you'll certainly fall victim to lust.

ROCK SOLID LIFE PRACTICE 3.11: EVALUATING YOUR SEXUALITY

1. Looking at Inner Principles 3.13 – 3.20, evaluate how well you handle your own sexual energy. Is your use of sexual energy perfectly in line with what authentic ancient traditions have taught?

2. Look over the five sexual scenarios discussed previously. Are you currently in the one you would freely choose?

If you answered no to either question, you probably have some work to do. The tools in this book and in the Rock Solid Life system in general will help you gradually to take control of your sexual drive and find a sexual lifestyle where you can thrive and make progress. If you are looking for a compatible mate, you will attract one into your life. If you are over-powered by lustful thoughts, you will learn how to render them harmless and control your sex drive as easily as you turn a tap on or off.

If you answered yes to both questions, you must be one of the blessed few for whom sexual lifestyle and energy are not even issues. If that's really the case, count your blessings and move on. Always remember the ancient wisdom: "If it ain't broken, don't fix it!"

There is almost no one who goes through life untroubled emotionally and physically by the seemingly all-powerful human sex drive. That's why it's imperative to find peace in this area of your life so that your efforts at inner refinement can proceed undisturbed (because you are either in a workable relationship or are happily celibate) and so that you will have the reserves of energy to carry out the refining process (because you manage your sexual energy carefully).

MONEY: RETHINKING YOUR ECONOMIC FOUNDATION

Chances are that unless you live alone in a cabin in the woods, your economic and financial well-being is a prime concern for you, and this

INNER PRINCIPLE
𝕮𝕮𝕮𝕮𝕮 3.21 𝕮𝕮𝕮𝕮𝕮

Whatever career path you choose in life, your over-riding goal is to free yourself from worldly cares and distractions.

is especially true if you have a spouse or children who depend on you economically. Money is a source of great stress for much of the population and a source of great temptation for many as well.

This short section will not solve all your financial problems overnight, but it will (1) show you how authentic ancient traditions understand both economic life in general and the nexus between your life purpose and career in particular, (2) give you a framework for understanding your own situation, and (3) give you the tools you need to make meaningful changes.

A lot of books today claim that if you are not making your living — and a really good living — by working at your major passionate interest or "life purpose," then there's something wrong. Authentic traditions are not so categorical. They have a point of view you won't find among the wealth coaches who are trying to sell you their wealth-creation systems.

Authentic traditions are unanimous that the only life purpose for every human being is self-transformation — outside of this, any other achievement in life has little meaning and no lasting positive effect. Your career will inevitably help or hinder this effort, and that's the major concern here, hence the Buddhist concept of right livelihood. It's obvious you can't find enlightenment through a career as a mercenary or an organized crime czar. But on a more subtle level, you're also sabotaging yourself by working in any capacity that causes harm to others or the environment in the name of individual, corporate or national self-interest. Humanity is a single whole, and we all win or we all lose together.

Do you have to make your living by working at your major passionate interest? No. After he had made considerable progress at self-transformation, St. Anthony the Great was sent to a cobbler in Alexandria who was even more advanced than Anthony himself. Was making shoes the cobbler's "life purpose" and greatest passion? Probably not. More likely he had just inherited the family business. The important point, though, was that making shoes did not hinder his transformation and, in fact, he turned it into a tool on the path.

By "life purpose," I mean a natural talent, something you are really interested in and something which you feel compelled to give expression to in your life or you will only feel half alive. Discovering what this is amidst your various talents and interests in not always easy, but if you come to www.rocksolidlife.com/lifepurpose, you will find some resources to help you clarify your own situation. If you can make a living at your life purpose, that is wonderful, but if not, know that ancient traditions don't insist that you must.

The Warrior's task is to arrange his or her economic life to support rather than hinder the overriding goal of self-transformation. That may entail working at a job that appeals to some of your interests, while finding some other expression for your "life purpose" in your spare time. Many people do this and achieve a degree of financial stability that allows them to focus on self-transformation. This is a perfectly acceptable pattern if it works for you, because, if you truly wish to practice inner refinement and transform your entire life, then you have one primary mission with regard to money: Whatever career path you choose in life, your overriding goal is to free yourself from worldly cares and distractions.

This doesn't mean that money is evil in itself and that you have to distance yourself from it to make any progress. It is equally possible to be in business or investing, to handle money all the time, but not to be a slave to it. Both the rich and poor can be enslaved to money or free from it — everything depends on your interior attitude. Needless to say, the Warrior's intention is to be internally free from the power that money can exert so as to maximize inner peace. This also implies that the imperative to become financially free (i.e. so you no

To change your financial circumstances, you must not only learn more about financial matters than you do now (i.e., acquire factual information), but you must principally find a way to process the inner, emotional "knots" that would prevent you from using new information constructively.

《《《《《《《《《《《《《《《

longer have to work to earn money) — which all of today's wealth coaches are pushing at you — does not necessarily apply to you personally. Nevertheless, working to achieve financial freedom as quickly as possible for the sake of your dependants and to facilitate your efforts at self-transformation is one possibility. In the Warrior's world, there are no patterns that apply to everyone and no dogmas about the externals of your life. There are only basic principles to follow, and within those bounds, the ancient traditions leave you free to find your own way.

The essence of Warriorship is to have a plan for life and it is an absolute necessity for you to have a plan for your economic and financial future, as far as this lies within your power. It does not matter whether that plan includes attaining financial independence and freedom or whether it includes working at the same job you're working at now indefinitely. What does matter is that you are deeply convicted that this is the way you should go and that it is financially viable so that you are as untroubled as possible by financial affairs.

On the other hand, there have never been so many possibilities for making a living from you major passionate interest as there are now. To find out more about this, come see the resources available at www.rocksolidlife.com. Because I don't have space here to go into all the background knowledge you would need to make an informed decision and build a plan, I have outsourced that task to professionals. Although the advice you will get from modern financial gurus and wealth coaches is not always compatible with the general tenor of authentic ancient traditions, you will still find a lots and lots of useful information and even inspiration. Academic studies and ordinary observation will easily confirm that most people's socioeconomic levels are largely determined by what they themselves have experienced as children. Our parents' attitudes toward money and our own experiences with it will largely determine what money represents to us — opportunity, pleasure, security, fear or other things — and this conditioning will often determine our level of economic well-being.

So the first step on the road to this is to face honestly and openly your own attitudes about money. Some people are ruled by fear of losing money, and will hardly ever spend it, while others can't keep money in their hands for more than a few seconds! The fundamental truth, though, is that for many if not most people, repressed emotional factors have a significant impact on their financial well-being. The logical conclusion is that unless you want to remain forever trapped in your current financial paradigm, you may have to deal with some deep-seated emotional issues that you may be barely conscious of.

Come to www.rocksolidlife.com to see what psychological prejudices you have inherited. This will give you some concrete material to work on once you have mastered the work in chapter 4. And, in fact, the art of stillness and dealing with the emotional content of the mind is the only way to deal with these kinds of barriers in a truly effective, permanent way. As mentioned previously, the purpose of self-transformation is to free us from all determinism, including inherited cultural biases about money and wealth in general.

I leave you with one principle on the subject of money that would be universally supported by authentic ancient traditions and has been frequently expressed by modern authors: If you make serving others your goal, you will never lack for money.

ROCK SOLID LIFE PRACTICE 3.12: YOUR LIFE'S WORK AND FINANCIAL WELLBEING

1. If you haven't yet chosen your life's work or you are planning a change of career but are not sure where to

go next, come to www.rocksolidlife.com/life purpose/ for some amazing resources to help you in your quest.

2. Take the Money-Mindset test online to find out how you relate to money emotionally. This is one of the most important voyages of self-discovery you can take if you are dissatisfied with your financial situation.

Strictly speaking, self-transformation doesn't depend on external circumstances, but millennia of experience have proven that a stable external environment makes the whole process much easier. And that's why settling into a career and a financial situation that is stable and workable for you is of prime importance. If you happen to be blessed with this already, then the same principle mentioned in the previous section applies: "If it ain't broken, don't fix it!"

SUMMARY

By having followed the directions in this chapter over the past six weeks you will have put yourself well on the way to accomplishing the following critical goals:

1. You will have begun to integrate many of the major facets of your life into your Program.
2. By adjusting your physical surroundings to facilitate self-transformation, you will have created external peace and order.
3. By analyzing your interpersonal relationships and taking positive action you have begun to find fulfillment and stability in your dealings with others.
4. By embarking on a comprehensive health program that includes both internal and external exercise, and that includes

all five pillars of health, you are on your way to creating internal peace and order.

5. By reexamining your sexual nature within the context of ancient authentic traditions you have begun to establish peace and harmony in this area of your life.

6. By dealing directly with your inherited attitudes toward money and by determining your life purpose, you have laid the groundwork for a financial plan for your life.

Key to cleaning up: Begin with the end in mind. Picture how your health, relationships, living space and finances could best help you in your quest and then move steadily toward this ideal.

Chapter Four

STILLNESS: RECLAIMING YOUR STRESS-FREE LIFE

Many years ago in my high school French class, the teacher asked for a list of adjectives describing character traits and divided the list on the blackboard into positive and negative qualities. I was fascinated that one of the girls in the class suggested "extrovert" for the positive list and "introvert" for the negative.

We live in a very extroverted society that values noise, activity, and busy-ness, while looking down on calm, quiet, and reflection. We admire "people of action," not deep thinkers. Even our ideas of religious community and spiritual life are tinged with this activist perspective, so "religion" in the popular mind is little more than a socially comfortable morality combined with social service. Religion is seen as a way to "do good." And so we forget the axiom of all authentic traditions — before doing, one must be.

All authentic traditions exist solely to transform human life on the ontological level, to actualize its unbelievable potential here and now.

"Doing good" in the conventional sense is only an external by-product of this true state of being. Your primary task, though, is to develop the inner qualities of disinterested love for others, because without this inner transformation your ability to help others will be quite limited. Worse still, if you use a socially active approach to doing good as a way to avoid facing your inner demons or for selfish motives, you may end up heading toward existential disaster.

That is why you'll find St. Isaac the Syrian giving this warning to monks who were tempted by the thought that they should go and minister to the physical and spiritual needs of others:

> Do not compare those who work signs and wonders and mighty acts in the world with those who practise stillness with knowledge. Love the idleness of stillness more than providing for the world's starving and the conversion of a multitude of heathen to the worship of God. ...It is better for you to make peace with your soul, causing concord to reign over the trinity within you (I mean the body, the soul and the spirit), than by your teaching to bring peace among men at variance."[1]

Let's review where you've been so far: By setting up your Program you've acquired more control of your time and a modicum of self-discipline. Having then gone through all the main "compartments" of life, you've begun to uproot destructive habits and replace them. The real purpose of all of these actions is the creation of space — you are reducing the destructive influence of the outside world. You are giving yourself some breathing space and the peace in which to turn to more important things.

You may remember that the Second Miraculous Ancient Formula was that change must be created from the outside in. Well, now that you've taken measures to deal with externals, it's time to look within, because all real and lasting change takes place there, in the domain of mind-consciousness. The external changes you've begun to put into place are really only there to facilitate your internal changes. And internal change, the refining of the self, is all based on the work of the mind.

STEP 1: SITTING STILL AND DOING NOTHING

What we desperately need is a method of inner transformation that is so powerful that it can uproot our deeply ingrained phobias and complexes anchored in the subconscious. These inner parasites are too numerous to mention in a complete way, but the most common phobias are the fear of sickness and physical suffering (e.g., you may be terrified of the prospect of getting cancer), fear of emotional suffering (e.g., the fear of the loss of a loved one, as when a parent is overprotective of a child — but it is not only the child that the parent is protecting), fear of what others will think and say (a crippling condition that robs us completely of spiritual independence), and last, the fear of death, which is the real root of all fears. Whoever overcomes this is free.

Linked to fears are complexes, those self-limiting ideas that I am inadequate to a particular task (so I can't possibly succeed and therefore I subconsciously make sure that I don't); that I don't deserve this happy romantic relationship (so I subconsciously sabotage it); that I'm undesirable (so I feel, act, and project undesirable qualities, even though I may be very attractive in many ways). And there are many, many more.

All of these phobias and complexes are learned. Not one of them is the truth. To leave them in control of your life is to live a lie. Does that sound pleasant and fulfilling to you? Of course not. Happily, these things can be overthrown. They are part of the "yin," the slavery to the environment that you are going to learn to put a stop to. All of these phobias and complexes are learned from the surrounding culture or are the result of how you have internalized the actions of

A "spirituality" of external
good deeds that is not solidly
based on inner refinement
may benefit others, but only
in a limited way, and will
harm you in the long run.

others, often the actions of those closest to you.

The method powerful enough to uproot all this is one I have named after the Chinese word for meditation: Sitting Still and Doing Nothing (SSDN for short). This chapter covers the specifics of the method and how you can start practicing very soon, but first let's fill in some gaps.

Ancient Traditions of Stillness

All authentic ancient traditions are schools for learning stillness, because stillness is the universal method for reconstituting the true human personality. Even the original Christian tradition was based on this, and in fact Orthodoxy's spiritual path is called *Hesychasm* or "stillness." This is a living tradition that efficiently transforms life on every level, eventually granting the human person direct participation in the uncreated life of the Absolute. Fr. John Romanides explains:

> Having faith in Christ without undergoing healing in Christ is not faith at all. Here is the same contradiction that you find when a sick person who has confidence in his or her doctor never carries out the treatment which he recommends. If Judaism and its successor, [Orthodox] Christianity, had appeared in the twentieth century for the first time, they would most likely have been characterized not as religions but as medical sciences related to psychiatry. They would have a wide influence on society owing to their considerable successes in healing the ills of the partially functioning personality. In no way can prophetic Judaism or Christianity be construed as religions that use various magical methods and beliefs to promise escape from a supposed world of matter and evil or hypocrisy into a supposed spiritual world of security and success.

The patristic tradition is neither a social philosophy nor an ethical system, nor is it religious dogmatism: it is a therapeutic treatment. In this respect it closely resembles medicine, especially psychiatry. The spiritual energy of the soul that prays unceasingly in the heart is a physiological instrument which everyone has and which requires healing. Neither philosophy, nor any of the known positive or social sciences is capable of healing this instrument. That can only be done through the Fathers' neptic and ascetic teaching.[2] Therefore those who are not healed usually do not even know of the existence of this instrument.

The Fathers do not categorize people as moral and immoral or good and bad on the basis of moral laws. This division is superficial. At depth humanity is differentiated into the sick in soul, those being healed and those healed. All who are not in a state of illumination are sick in soul... It is not only good will, good resolve, moral practice and devotion to the Orthodox tradition that make one Orthodox, but also purification, illumination and deification [the three stages of self-transformation in Orthodoxy]. These stages are the purpose of the mystical life in the Church, as all of the ancient liturgical texts bear witness.[3]

Hesychia works by keeping the *nous* free from form and undistracted by "intrusive thoughts" (Greek: *logismoi*). By this process, writes Fr. Sophrony, "...the imagination is curtailed and the mind is released from all the mental images that have invaded it."[4] "If you wish to engage in spiritual warfare," counsels St. Hesychios, "let that little animal, the spider, always be your example for stillness of heart, otherwise you will not be as still in your *nous* as you should be."[5]

According to the Orthodox tradition, the *nous* enables you to transcend yourself and touch the Absolute directly. Although you cannot isolate the *nous* in this or that physical space, its "home" is in the human heart, and not merely the physical heart, but the deep layers of the heart that go beyond the physical level. And the heart is the centre and access point of all real wealth: "The heart directs the entire organism, and when grace gains possession of the heart, it reigns over all the thoughts and all the members; for it is there, in the heart, that the *nous* and all the thoughts of the soul have their seat."[6]

When your *nous* is healthy, it remains within and guards the heart, but in its current decrepit state, the *nous* is scattered externally through the physical senses and it scoops up indiscriminately everything it comes into contact with — stimulation without and passions within — and sends it unfiltered to the very centre of your psychosomatic organism — the heart. Now there's a recipe for disaster! In this case the *nous*, to use Joseph the Hesychast's expression, "is diffused in vain and ordinary things, like useless water running down the streets."[7] And this is why the Taoists say, "The arising of thoughts is sickness. Not continuing in them is medicine."[8]

When you send everything that you encounter to the heart unfiltered, your reason runs amok, thoughts are multiplied exponentially, and you are over-stimulated and off balance. In other words, your reason comes to dominate and eventually suppress your *nous*. But ironically, when reason dethrones the *nous*, what you get is not the rule of reason in the sense of true rationality and logic — no, you don't become *Star Trek*'s Mr. Spock — but the very opposite; you end up ruled by passions and emotions. Or, to be more exact, the rule of perceptions (sensory impressions from the external environment), cognitions (thought forms and concepts about these impressions), and feelings (attachment, aversion, or indifference to these impressions).

So to end your slavery to the environment, the yin condition of your being, you must overcome perception, cognition, and feeling. Since these are longstanding mental habits, you will need a very powerful method to reverse your condition, to subjugate the rational mind, which currently is using the beleaguered *nous* to run errands for the ego.

The basic sequence for accomplishing this miraculous transformation is the following:

1. Still the rational mind.
2. Detach the self from the thoughts and create inner order.
3. Allow the *nous* to resurface.

How Stillness Relates to Meditation and Prayer

Stillness is the fundamental building block for the noetic prayer of Orthodox Hesychasm, for any other form of true prayer and for the authentic meditation systems of the Far East. This chapter describes the simplest, safest, and most effective methods for entering stillness, and you will be able to use what you learn here as a stepping stone to the further practices of whichever authentic ancient tradition you like. This book does not teach noetic prayer itself, both because it has been written for a wide audience and because even among the Orthodox Christians who read this book, very few are ready to begin such a work.

If you are a Christian, Jew, Muslim, or other "theist," you're probably wondering how all this relates to prayer and why you should follow this advice. Well, here's why:

I am not telling you to stop praying. But most people, even the vast majority of Orthodox Christians in North America, have seriously misunderstood prayer and how it works. Having little grasp of the key concepts of attentiveness (*prosoche*) and watchfulness (*nepsis*), and having cultivated neither, their prayer lacks foundation, strength, and resilience. Their prayer does not have depth because the *nous* is still enslaved to the environment and is incapable of remaining in its place. This means that inner noetic power lacks "critical mass" and is insufficient to undermine the passions and neuroses that chain the *nous* to the environment and support the rule of the ego. As Fr. Damascene writes, "The vast majority of people never reach deep levels of interior noetic prayer simply because they have not followed the first half of Christ's injunction to 'Keep Watch and Pray.'"[9] This ineffective prayer is still part of "going along," not "reversal." As Philoxenos of Mabbugh, writing in the sixth century, pointed out,

Pure prayer such as is worthy of God... is not uttered by means of words... (It) consists in this: that one gather one's mind from the entire world, and not let it be secretly bound to anything; that one place it entirely at God's disposal and forget, during the time of prayer, everything that is material, including one's own self and the place where one is standing.[10]

Here you see the extent to which stillness is integral to the proper practice of prayer or any inner work. Philoxenos is referring to the cultivation and refinement of the *nous*. The Taoist equivalent of the *nous* is *shen* – the higher intuitive mind capable of apprehending the Tao or Ultimate Reality of the universe. "Followers of Lao Tzu's teaching in China came to call it 'the spirit of man,' 'the original spirit,' or yuan-shen, while the ancient Christian ascetics called it the *nous*, a Greek word which may be translated as 'spirit' or 'higher mind.'"[11]

The presuppositions and basic practices of stillness are essential to mastering your thoughts and emotions and allowing you to work directly with your inner world. Are you tired of being a victim of your inner world and would rather be its master? Then read on, because I am about to share with you the most effective and proven methods ever devised for this purpose.

Sadly, most Western people are no more aware of the *nous* than they are of the radio waves that surround them. Rational thought, with its multitudinous doubts, cares, concerns, fears, and deliberations, has so buried the poor beleaguered *nous* that it might as well not exist. Westerners only briefly experience the *nous* at moments of extreme and desperate concentration (like the intense prayer of a parent for a child undergoing a serious operation), or in a rare moment of heightened awareness (as sometimes happens in the case of accident or illness), or in the form of an unexplained inner prompting (e.g., you may have a sudden urge to contact someone you've hardly thought about in years, and then this person phones you moments later).

The Rational Mind and Inner Chaos

I must underline that reason, the ability to think logically, to analyse and reflect, is not evil in itself. None of our faculties is. The real problem is the balance among them.

"Reason," says Fr. Sophrony, "functioning impersonally, is by nature only one of the manifestations of life in the human personality, one of the energies of the personality. When it is allotted priority in the spiritual being of man, it begins to fight against its source — that is, its personal origin.... And it is a fact that when man's spiritual being is concentrated on and in the (rational) mind, reason takes over and he becomes blind to anything that surpasses him and ends by seeing himself as the divine principle."[12]

In other words, a culture that believes reason to be the highest human faculty will inevitably produce almost nothing but noetically and emotionally ill people. Ancient Taoist tradition came to a very similar conclusion. Noting that reason is always a slave to the world of phenomena and appearances, one Taoist commentator admonishes: "See through the things of the world. If you cannot see through the things of the world, you will sink into an ocean of suffering."[13]

In fact, every single authentic tradition is based on the experience of the *nous* / shen / higher mind, and each has described in detail the dangers of uncontrolled discursive thought.

But you yourself can verify the dangers of a rationalistic approach to life. Do you know any neurotic people? (In the Western world, that is rather like asking if you know anyone at all!) Have you ever noticed how full of thoughts they are? How the internal debate never ceases?

INNER PRINCIPLE
ᙅᙅᙅᙅᙅᙅ**4.4**ᙅᙅᙅᙅᙅᙅ

When this inner balance is lost and reason is given free reign, it wreaks mental, emotional, and spiritual havoc.

ᙅᙅᙅᙅᙅᙅᙅᙅᙅᙅᙅᙅᙅ

How every stimulus from the outside is like another log on their mental fire? And lest you think that when I say "neurotic people" I am referring to some tiny percentage of mentally ill people among the general population, quite the contrary! Based on my own counseling experience with a wide spectrum of people from all ages, ethnic backgrounds, and social strata, I am convinced that at least 90 percent of the population is or has been afflicted by some crippling neurotic condition. Westerners are trained from an early age to hide these undesirable elements of the personality behind a socially acceptable exterior, so the truth only becomes evident when you get to know the person well or deal with him or her in the context of some form of guidance or counseling. And every time neurotic people concoct a solution to this or that personal problem, it just makes things worse. Why? Because, on the one hand, reason always seeks a synthesis, to construct a complete and watertight view of any problem. And on the other, its synthesis always appears incredibly compelling.[14] So it's with good reason that Fr. Damascene refers to the rational mind as "the problem solver."[15]

Contrary to this is the traditional approach to life, in which decisions are based on the inner prompting of oneself or of a trusted guide. "When you want to find out the will of God," explains Joseph the Hesychast, "abandon your own will completely, together with every other thought or plan, and with great humility, ask for this knowledge in prayer. And whatever takes shape or carries weight in your heart, do it and it will be according to God's will."[16]

The link between rational thought and neurosis is universally acknowledged in ancient culture. Even St. Isaac the Syrian, a seventh-century desert-dwelling ascetic in the Persian Empire, commented on this:

> (Rational) knowledge keeps within the boundaries of nature
> in all its paths. But faith makes its journey above nature.

THE GODS MUST BE CRAZY

I was once in the company of an experienced Orthodox monk and a Hindu woman of his acquaintance. He told me that she was from a small village in India and grew up in nearly complete ignorance of the world outside her village. To her even New Delhi was like an extraterrestrial civilization! Then he said to me: "Do you see that woman, Father? There is not a neurotic bone in her body. She is completely childlike, completely calm and undisturbed by anything around her."

This is a typical result of having grown up in a traditional culture, whether Orthodox Christian, Hindu, Buddhist, or other. The contrast between this naïve and uneducated Indian woman and her contemporaries here could not be more stark. It reminds me of the first few minutes of that great comedy film *The Gods Must Be Crazy* and its hilarious comparison of the Kalahari bushmen with the white South African society a few hundred kilometers to the south. If you have never seen this film, go and rent it — consider it your homework assignment!

(...) Fear accompanies knowledge, but confidence accompanies faith. The more a man journeys in the pathways of knowledge, the more he is shackled by fear and cannot be found worthy of freedom from it.[17]

Plus ça change? Did you ever stop to consider the extent to which the Western educational system is exclusively centered on the rational mind? It is an endless stream of facts to fill the brain, but virtually nothing to fill the heart. So it is not surprising that if you analyze this educational system more closely, you will also discover that it is largely based on fear: it is all about making this world a safe and ordered place, while excluding all that is wild, mysterious, or unpredictable — the same fruitless dynamic that the ancient traditions tell us is responsible for all human suffering. "If we consider carefully all aspects of the educational process," writes Matthew the Poor, "from the alphabet to the building of a rocket, we find that education is basically an attempt to avoid pain and weariness and need."[18]

Why Western Peoples Are "Noetically Challenged"

Noetic stillness is inculcated in a certain measure by the cultures associated with authentic traditions. Most Westerners, though, lack any noetic stillness at all. They have been brought up with a constant bombardment of noise, sensory stimulation, confused moral input and ingrained anxiety. It is absurd even to suppose that you can begin to transform your life in a meaningful way without first cutting away all the worldly anxieties, all the effects of external sensory bombardment, and reaching a state of inner stillness. St. Hesychios alludes to this when he says: "If we have not attained to prayer that is free from thoughts, we have no weapon to fight with."[19]

No doubt you will protest that there is no way for you to remove yourself from the constant sensory bombardment of daily life. But you don't have to. Only apply what is in this chapter and you won't need to stop the bombardment from the outside, because you will have stopped it from penetrating into your inner world. A tank commander in battle doesn't have to care about all the weapons his enemy has, only about the ones that can penetrate his armour.

It's true, though, that Westerners face major obstacles in inner work. For one thing, they are often unaware that their own inner world even exists, so they must first refine themselves in order to find it.

Every authentic tradition affirms that human intelligence is not confined to the brain. You know all those common expressions linking mental processes to physical organs, such as "a compassionate heart," "a broken heart," "butterflies in the stomach," "the gall to say such a thing," "the guts (or a certain part of male anatomy) to make a decision"? There was a truth to them that was much more keenly felt by less cerebral civilizations and less "sophisticated" people. Oriental medical systems, in fact, have a detailed map linking positive and negative emo-

LIVING IN YOUR HEAD

When I was attending seminary in New York, some of us went off to a three-day course at a center for recovering alcoholics, where we were thrown straight into a support group. We were more than a little dumbfounded at their claim that they themselves were in no way responsible for their alcoholism. They were merely victims of a "primary disease," they said, as if it were a virus like the common cold. (Starting with this kind of delusion–denying all personal responsibility — is a sure way to end badly. Chapter 6 explains why it is only by accepting personal responsibility for everything in our lives that we can possibly be free).

What really struck me, though, was that these people lived completely in their heads. They had no conception of intelligent life below the neck. The ancient Taoist maxim that "Thoughts are sickness; not continuing in them is medicine," was there in living color before us. Not surprisingly, their therapeutic approach hinged on trying to "put them in touch with their feelings." Well, their feelings were as deluded and as cloudy as their unceasing and tormented thought processes, so the outcome looked pretty dubious.

tional states to particular organs, and it should come as no surprise that Orthodox writings on inner work often make similar references.

Of course, if you believe that discursive thought is the sum total of true intelligence, then Descartes' "I think, therefore I am" becomes your motto, whether you're aware of it or not. Constantly focused on external realities, you may develop impressive technical skill, but as an individual you will lose access to vast areas of your potential, and as a society you are doomed to a neurotic state, falsely believing that all intelligence resides in the brain.

Our conscious thinking brain relates to persons, events, and things only indirectly. You think about them. You don't really touch them.

The result is that life becomes a series of mental concepts, and truth itself is reduced to a proposition. Hence all the wonderful western ideologies have so tormented mankind: fascism, communism, capitalism, nationalism, and the like. But you will ask: Is not religion itself just another ideology? . Yes, in fact, because there are only two possibilities: You have either a system of self-transformation or a religious dogmatism. It's always one or the other. But if you look at all authentic traditions, you will notice that even though they are expressed in conceptual frameworks, their goal is to liberate you from enslavement to concepts by introducing you directly to the reality behind the necessary verbal or written formulation. So they are systems of ontological transformation and not ideological dogmatisms.

Traditional cultures inculcated a blessed mental simplicity, a childlike and straightforward approach to life. In Orthodox countries, for example, this allowed people to proceed directly to the life of inner prayer with few impediments. To try to do so in the modern Western world, though, is often a recipe for disaster, because all the underlying neuroses remain untouched. "What?" you will ask, "If I pray to God will He not take them away?"

Think for a moment about the absurdity of this idea. Is it not like asking the Absolute to cure you from obesity while you continue to gorge yourself? Neuroses and all passionate conditions can only be cured if you stop living them out. This is again why monasticism works: It imposes a healthy lifestyle on body and mind, immediately cutting off all the fuel for the grosser physical passions like lust and gluttony, and imposing a healing regime for the rest. Experience has shown that adding a smattering of prayer or meditation to a neurotic life does very little; the inner work must be carried out consistently and correctly, allowing it to penetrate deeply and then become habitual before it has the power to uproot destructive thought patterns.

Of all the claims made for noetic prayer in the Orthodox tradition, the ultimate is "deification" (Greek *Theosis*) — when the small, weak, mortal, and insignificant human being becomes totally suffused with the divine energies, going beyond the power of death to a total integration into the Absolute. So even before death, a person

THE 5 PILLARS OF LIFE

UPROOTING NEGATIVE EMOTIONS

The following true story recently came to my attention. A French Protestant woman had been mortally offended by someone close to her over a decade previously, and despite all her attempts to remove the hostility in her heart through prayer — as she understood it — she was unsuccessful and still bore a grudge the size of Mount Everest. Very distressed by the strength of the passion, she began meditation work with a Tibetan Lama, and was the able to overcome her anger within a couple of months.

To me as an Orthodox Christian, this is not the least bit surprising. For one thing, Protestantism has no knowledge whatsoever of the *hesychast* tradition, so its understanding of prayer is necessarily shallow and limited: If you do not know what the *nous* is, how to develop it, how it is related to the heart, and how to use it in prayer, you will never be able to use "prayer" to accomplish much at all. You will be limited to a shallow and cerebral prayer that will never develop enough power to uproot deeply ingrained emotional states. The Lama, on the other hand–who may never have heard of Orthodoxy but certainly understood the presuppositions of *hesychasm*–was able to guide the poor woman into noetic stillness and teach her how to separate herself from her thoughts. And this story underlines again the extreme importance of following authentic traditions, and of using correct methods.

can become everything by participation that the Absolute is by nature. He or she can become "supracosmic" and be filled with a burning compassion for everyone and everything, receiving a joy that defies all description. And such people continue to exist.[20]

But long before all this magnificence can take place, *hesychasm* and its equivalents in other authentic traditions allow the practitioner to gain control of his or her own inner world. This involves slowing down and observing in minute detail mental processes that previously went unnoticed. At the very least, these practices will bring you deep calm and inner peace; a release from the power that other people, events, and things hold over your mind; great clarity of thought; a feeling of inner solidity; and much improved physical health.

How Our Inner World Falls Apart

First, you must deal with a concept that presents a great problem for the Western consciousness — the problem of "sin." In the West the whole concept of sin has been tainted with a juridical theology and what one Orthodox theologian understandably called its "terrorist God of juridical ethics."[21] So the Western concept no longer bears any resemblance to the original Christian understanding of the word. In practical terms, this means that the mere mention of the word conjures up ideas of oppressive social taboos, of fear used as a means of social control by religious institutions, and of a puritanical approach to life in general.

In the Orthodox tradition, sin is not the violation of some external commandment issued imperiously from on high, nor a transgression against socially accepted codes of morality. Sin is the existential misdirection of our powers and faculties in a way that causes us harm, hence the biblical word for sin (Greek *hamartia*), which literally means "missing the mark." In other words, it is a kind of self-inflicted violence because it goes against the way our psycho-physical organism is constructed. In other words, when you sin, you are harming yourself. This is not always evident, except to those whose inward attentiveness has been trained to a high level.

The process of existential error or sin goes through several stages of development before it results in adopting a self-destructive thought or course of action on our part. The task of stillness is in part to slow this process down and bring it under continuous scrutiny. Here is what the process looks like:

1. *Provocation:* An energy or suggestion from the outside enters our mental universe. The suggestion is called an "intrusive thought" (Greek: logismos) and it attempts to gain the attention of the *nous,* either seductively (e.g., as with a thought of physical lust) or violently (e.g., as with a thought of fear or anxiety).

THE 5 PILLARS OF LIFE

DRIVEN TO ATHEISM

If you have ever had any exposure to the most oppressive strains of Western Christianity, you will understand what I mean. In his youth, long before he became a famous Christian writer, C.S. Lewis abandoned his strict Calvinist upbringing to become an atheist. Looking back on that period, he later remarked what a great weight had been lifted off his shoulders by that decision! The case of Quebec is also very apropos. The French speaking province gradually divorced itself from the Catholic Church during the "Quiet Revolution" of the 1960s, but the deep subconscious of the Quebecois as a people is still in rebellion against anything that smacks of Christianity or organized religion. My mother, brought up in a Presbyterian home in Southwestern Ontario, went to Quebec in the early 1940s as part of her training to become a French teacher. She was quite shaken by the degree of social control held by the Catholic clergy, which went as far as using the pulpit to instruct the flock how to vote in upcoming elections. The women had to wear gloves half way up their arms in church and no one was allowed to "have fun" on Sunday. What does all this mean? Only this: Authentic traditions leave you free, refreshed, and comforted. False ones leave you oppressed.

Although you can't free yourself entirely from intrusive thoughts, you can learn to free yourself from their power.

2. *Momentary disturbance*: The *nous* is very briefly distracted by the thought, though without actively participating in its development. Eventually, after much inner refinement, it is possible to avoid this stage.

3. *Coupling:* Here the *nous* begins to participate willingly in the development of the intrusive thought, allowing itself to be controlled by the energy behind the thought. No matter what

the external appearance of the thought, the energy behind it may be very harmful, and by assenting to it, the human person compromises his or her spiritual and emotional freedom. This is the beginning of sin and self-inflicted harm.

4. *Assent:* The *nous* actively plays with, believes, and identifies with the intrusive thought, and resolves to act upon it. Whether or not the person can or does act upon it in the physical world, or merely in the form of mental images, is irrelevant, hence the words of Christ: "You have heard it said, 'You shall not commit adultery.' But I say to you that everyone who looks at a woman lustfully has already committed adultery with her in his heart (Matt. 5:28; translation mine). "

5. *Prepossession:* Once the coupling with intrusive thoughts of a certain kind has been repeated many times, the person develops a natural affinity and identification with the energy behind them. This inner habit makes it more and more difficult to break with the thought in question. The person has lost a considerable measure of noetic freedom and is partially enslaved to the corrupt energies of the fallen world. In Orthodox terms, he is developing his fallen nature and destroying himself. The Buddhist would say he is immersed in *samsara*, the world of appearances and endless suffering. To the Taoist, he is becoming more and more "yin," controlled by temporal conditioning and losing his true and original nature.

6. *Passion:* This is the final stage, at which one identifies so closely with the sin that it develops into a passionate condition. The real meaning of the word *passion* is "suffering," and it carries the idea of passively undergoing something — again the idea of becoming "yin," or controlled by outside forces. Here the energy behind the thought is so familiar that it gains entrance and proceeds through all these stages of development instantaneously.

Unless the person resolves to fight against the passion, he or she will become possessed by it in a very real sense.

How Stillness Reverses Inner Disintegration

Through stillness you can learn to cut off the process in its early stages, you can stop being a victim of the numerous destructive influences around you and regain your psychological and spiritual independence. The practice of stillness is so powerful in fact that it can uproot deeply ingrained neurotic behavior patterns learned through years of cultural and environmental conditioning.

The importance of stillness can readily be seen in Wang Liping's biography, where it is clear that the stabilization of his inner world at the beginning of his training became the basis for all the other exercises undertaken within the vast and complex training syllabus of Dragon Gate Taoism. This stabilization was far more critical than the work with inner energy (qi), something undertaken only later.[22] As long as the *nous* is refined, the body's energy system will spontaneously revert to functioning properly: "Similarly, the true energy in the body rises and descends... naturally having its own place of abode; what need is there for people to visualize it in order to arrange it?"[23]

Wrong Practices Are Lethal

Now comes the most misunderstood point in the whole enterprise: It really does matter exactly how you do your practice. We have been culturally conditioned to believe that how we pray or meditate or think or move has no bearing on our quality of life. When it comes to prayer, 99 percent of the population assumes that one kind of prayer is as good as another. After all, the God who hears them is the same God, is He not? And with meditation, people tend to think that if it "works for them" or gives them what they think they're looking for, then it must be good.

Because of the divorce between theory and practice in Western Christianity a millennium ago, and the total loss of the correct practice, Western man today has a syncretistic, anti-theoretical mentality. So he is also incredibly inexperienced in matters demanding a deep existential exploration of life. The juridical and moralizing focus of Western Christianity has bequeathed to us an attitude and approach to life that affords us very little intuitive understanding of subtle mental and physical processes. In fact, the whole genesis of psychoanalysis in the West came about to fill the void left by the vacuity and ineffectiveness of the Western Christian spirituality of the time.

So learn this phrase and repeat it over and over until you believe it. Post it on your fridge, write it on your lunch bag, or put it on your email signature block: *Some types of inner work are healthy and fruitful while others can cause great and irreparable psychological and/or physical damage.* You can shorten this to the following: *The details matter!* You will know what it means.

Surprising? Is it really that difficult to imagine that what you do with your mind affects your mental equilibrium as well as your physical processes? In the 1950s and 1960s the medical establishment would not hear of the very idea that physical ailments could be psychologically caused. Now the reality of psychological stress is acknowledged everywhere and how it degrades physical health is well known.

The practices offered in all authentic traditions are extremely powerful and are not to be trifled with. In his famous book *The Arena*, the nineteenth-century Russian ascetic Ignaty Brianchaninov warns of the dangers of reading the traditional works on inner life in the wrong order, or of using certain practices prematurely, or of taking the book out of context. The results are, in the best case scenario, a simple lack of progress, and in the worst, demonic delusion.[24]

And it's not only that certain practices are dangerous if you get into them too soon, but that there really are methods that are just plain dangerous in themselves. The Orthodox Tradition has a detailed knowledge of many forms of prayer, for instance, and can even tell you why some are sound and some are downright dangerous.[25]

So how do you tell what is dangerous and what isn't? There are several criteria, the most important of which is that methods which actively seek "spiritual" or "mystical" experiences are condemned the world over as leading to demonic delusion. As one Taoist authority has written, "When beginners polish and refine their minds, as they attain a state of stillness, extraordinary experiences or visions may occur. If they take these experiences seriously, they will become attached to falsehoods; if this is not eliminated, it will develop into incurable mental illness."[26]

Understanding Today's Spiritual Smorgasbord

Let's talk for the moment about what usually comes under the heading of "meditation" rather than "prayer"; there are things you need to know about what's on the market today. The three types outlined here are all proven commodities in themselves, but that does not mean that any particular example of each type you run across is either authentic or safe.

1. *Pure stillness*: "See that you never have a single thought in your heart, whether accompanied by an image or not" writes St. Hesychios, "then you can easily recognize that alien tribe, the first-born sons of the Egyptians."[27] In this type of exercise, you observe the inner world with detachment, avoiding entanglement in thoughts. The thoughts eventually subside and profound stillness ensues. This is the most basic and vital task in most authentic traditions. You see this with Wang Liping's training, where the grueling first stage, called "repentance," involved intensive "sitting still doing nothing" until random thoughts were cleared away and the young apprentice was anchored in stillness. As mentioned previously, the failure to respect this element of the traditional syllabus is one of the chief characteristics of the New Age versions of Taoism and Buddhism. Ignorance of this principle among the Orthodox reduces Orthodoxy to a religion.

2. *Thematic*: In this kind of meditation you consider a certain theme and meditate on it in ways that a particular tradition may specify in greater or lesser detail. This allows you to co-opt your rational mind, to put conscious thought at the service of self-transformation rather than at the service of the ego.[28] The tradition often uses this kind of meditation as inspiration for noetic prayer. A visitor to Mount Athos once came upon an old monk sitting on a lofty crag overlooking the sea and asked him what he was doing. *"Mazevo ili,"* he replied in Greek, which means, "I'm gathering fuel." The old monk was using thought to create a state of mind conducive to noetic prayer. Similar to this, but more formalized in its method, is the classic Tibetan Buddhist *Lamrim* meditation. And this is not just an exercise for beginners, but something to use continually. In the Tibetan system, the *Lamrim* is acknowledged as the safest and most reliable way to eliminate egocentric grasping and develop *bodhicitta* (loving kindness), even though one tends to hear less about it in Western Buddhism than about the "sexier" Tantric practices. Thematic meditations form an indispensable foundation. Why?

Imagine that your inner being is like a garden that has been left at the mercy of nature, so that it's infested with the weeds of cultural conditioning, phobias, and complexes. The function of pure stillness is to weed the garden. But once the garden has been returned to a virginal state, it won't bear fruit until you sow some seeds. Thematic meditation contains the seeds and subsequent chapters deal with it extensively.

3. *Energy meditation*: These methods allow you to manipulate the bio-electric energy of the human body (Chinese *qi / chi*, Japanese *ki*, Sanskrit *kundalini*) through various energy pathways and centers. The simplest and safest is the "body scan" type, in which you move your attention slowly down your body from the crown of the head, intentionally relaxing areas of tension. At least, this is a very simple description of a complex

process.[29] This kind is in fact so easy, safe, and fruitful that it is frequently integrated into stillness meditation systems. One example is the Theravada Buddhist Vipassana system. Various Chinese Qi Gong methods use this type of meditation for health-related purposes, and practiced properly, it can be quite effective. Other energy methods, particularly the Tantric methods found in some Hindu schools, Tibetan Buddhism, and some strands of Taoism, can be far more dangerous. The danger resides less in the methods themselves than in practicing them without the guidance of an experienced teacher or in practicing them before having acquired a solid basis in pure stillness. A few centuries ago, a great Taoist master had this to say about people who thought they could achieve real self-transformation solely by using energy meditations:

> If you want to operate yin and yang and the five elements in your own body, do not by any means focus your effort on yin and yang and the five elements. You must concentrate on the Absolute, practising being unborn [achieved using a combination of stillness and thematic meditations]; then yin and yang and the five elements will operate spontaneously and naturally without your having to seek to operate them... [If you seek to operate them consciously] the slightest deviation in your practice can produce a hundred bizarre changes; you may go to your death without turning back, ultimately unable to operate yin and yang and the five elements."[30]

The Health Benefits of "Sitting Still and Doing Nothing":

Stillness even has numerous physical benefits. It is no accident that in Taoism stillness is one of the most important factors in the scientific cultivation of longevity. You see this in Orthodoxy as well: St. Anthony the Great (c.250-357 AD), the Egyptian Copt who founded organized desert monasticism, once walked twelve miles through the

PARADOX
4.2
《《《《《《　《《《《《《《

Our obsessive self protection is the chief cause of all
our suffering. The more we
flee physical and emotional
pain, the more we become
vulnerable to it.

《《《《《《《《《《《《《《《

desert one night after supper at the age
of about 84 and with no ill effects. Then
there was Elder Melchizedek of
Yaroslavl Forest, who started his solitary
ascetic life at age 80 and lived to 125
years of age. Likewise, the Native American holy man and healer, Fools Crow
(1890-1989), contended that faithfulness
to the will of Wakan-Tanka (God) was
the basis of his continuing physical
health.

Your aim, though, is personal transformation, not a simple exten-
sion of physical life. As long as we protect ourselves at every turn, we
remain slaves, because our overdeveloped sense of self-preservation is
a function of our egocentrism. In reality it is just the "biological and
psychological self-defense of the ego," a phrase that the contemporary
Orthodox theologian Christos Yanarras uses to define the process of sin
itself.[31] In other words, it is existential suicide.

The practice of inner stillness does have incomparable health benefits, though. There is no better way to protect your physical health
and well-being than inner stillness. The ancient Taoist sage Sima
Chengzhen writes: "After a long time of calm stabilization, illnesses
dissolve and life is restored." And he cites another sage who says, "It
is possible to live long by virtue of the unification of body and
spirit"[32] In the words of Daniel Reid:

> Spiritual practices such as meditation also help fortify the
> Four Foundations (of health, according to Chinese medi-
> cine: blood, energy, nourishment and resistance) and
> should always be included in any program of preventative
> health care. Chronic stress severely strains the adrenals and
> nerves, and meditation is a quick and effective way to
> switch the autonomic nervous system from the stressful
> sympathetic circuit over to the restful, restorative parasym-
> pathetic circuit. Meditation permits the entire body to relax

and the energy channels to open up, so that energy as well as blood may circulate freely throughout the system, invigorating organs, stimulating glands and tonifying other vital tissues... Meditation cultivates the emotional equanimity and positive outlook which are so essential to maintaining health and promoting longevity.[33]

Dangers on the Road

Make no mistake — your whole attitude can make or break your inner work. There are certain strands of Western Christian spirituality, for example, that encourage you to see and appreciate your own virtues and moral superiority, to acknowledge before yourself and others that your relationship with God is solid and your postmortem happiness assured. This kind of ego-building and self-deception is the opposite of what the real tradition is trying to achieve. Every authentic tradition is built on the bedrock of confronting and acknowledging our existential errors, character flaws and neuroses. "If one is sick of sickness," says Lao Tzu, "then one is not sick."[34] However, this sickness is only revealed to us in the measure to which we open ourselves to see the truth about ourselves, and we cannot do this if we are really just trying to make ourselves feel more complacent. Note that the traditional Orthodox word for "repentance" is the Greek *metanoia*, which literally signifies a change in the orientation of one's mind. Fr. Damascene has a most compelling description of this:

> Metanoia begins with the realignment of all our powers away from our former loves — for ourselves and for created things — and toward the Tao, the Way of the Universe, the wordless Word from whom we have been fleeing. With this occurs, in the words of Lao Tzu, a reversal or return. We are no longer giving the lower soul mastery, for we are starving to death the ego or false identity that has made a home in it. Now the spirit [*nous*] is allowed to get out from under the ego and resume its rightful place.[35]

Here are the three safety precautions that will ensure no harm will ever come to you during practice. Ignore them at your peril:

1. While striving in your inner work, let go of striving. Take what comes calmly and consider yourself unworthy of anything better.
2. Ignore all unusual physical and psychic sensations. Let them pass and don't try to get them back. In any event, most of them are caused by subtle, inner physiological adjustments and have no importance at all.
3. Although wrong methods are harmful, remember that even right methods are not ends in themselves. They are just tools to help us uproot self-obsession. An artist does not pay much attention to the paint brush and certainly doesn't boast about it. He cares about and builds his reputation on the final product. So it should be with us. Force yourself to think humble thoughts and all will be well.

Sitting Still and Doing Nothing: Preparation

This is the most universal, safest and yet the most effective method of cutting through thoughts and achieving inner stillness. Its basic technique exists in Orthodoxy and in the Far East, and similar techniques exist among Native Americans as well. It has the great virtue of being equally suitable for the beginner and the more advanced, and with diligent practice, it never fails to deliver.

Posture

Sit! This work is done sitting. Eventually you'll learn to do it everywhere and at all times during any type of activity, but even then you will never abandon your sitting practice. Any number of sitting postures is possible. When most people think of Far Eastern meditation, of course, they tend to think of the full lotus posture (sitting cross-legged with each foot resting on top of the opposite thigh). Although many have expounded the obvious virtues of this posture — and it superbly anchors the whole body and supports the lower back exceptionally well — the good news is that you do not have to sit this way. In fact, if you force the full lotus too much without enough preparation, you can seriously damage your knees over time. Here's the "full-lotus litmus test": If, after stretching for a few minutes, you can get into the full lotus and maintain it painlessly for fifteen to twenty minutes, then your legs are probably flexible enough for it and your knees can handle the strain. If you can't do this, then use another posture for now.

And, in fact, there are other postures used, even in the Orient, like the half-lotus or the ankle-lock, or the Japanese Zen kneeling posture. Some Taoists prefer to sit on a chair. So all things are acceptable if they meet the following criteria:

1. Your back must be straight. This promotes blood and energy circulation to the inner organs and calms the nervous system, thus minimizing the impact of physiological processes on your state of mind.
2. The blood circulation to your legs should not be inhibited. After all, you want to be able to sit for long periods without the inconvenience of your legs going numb.

So experiment with your body and see what works best. Remember, even the best posture for you may not feel comfortable in the beginning.

Tips

Try putting a cushion or two under your buttocks, especially if using any cross-legged position. This is a traditional means of taking the strain off the lower back by tilting you slightly forward and will allow you to remain comfortable for a much longer period. If you are on a chair, one cushion will usually do, and although it does help support the back, its main function in this case is to facilitate blood flow to the legs. And here it will be important to move your buttocks relatively far forward on the chair to prevent the legs from going numb. Experiment! If you are sitting in a kneeling posture, you can use cushions to take some of the strain off your ankles and knees.

Ambiance

Remember that sacred space you've prepared? Now is the time to use it. Ideally you want a location that is dimly lit; candlelight or complete darkness are often the best. This does not mean you can't do inner work during the day, only that it can be more of a challenge. As Joseph the Hesychast noted, the *nous* tends to scatter more easily during the daylight hours. In any case, do not try doing your inner work under bright lights if you can help it — they have a stimulating effect on the sympathetic nervous system that will conflict with what you're trying to achieve. When it comes to sacred images of any variety, or candles, you will not be using them as objects of concentration during this type of inner work. Incense is quite useful in moderation, as it creates a mental association of calm with your inner work. Inner work involves the paradox of integrating body and mind while at the same time forgetting both one and the other.

STEP 2: PUTTING "NOTHING" INTO YOUR PROGRAM

When you set out to practice inner work, distractions can easily defeat you. Knowing this, it's best to practice in the early morning or later evening, when the chances of interruption are lessened. Moreover, there are certain natural rhythms at play, too, because the predawn period, for instance, does have its own special ambiance, a kind of pervasive quiet that easily penetrates into the soul.

As for duration, I recommend starting with about 20 minutes and then slowly and gradually working up to one hour. It may take a while for you to find the best position and for your muscles and joints to get used to it, so don't be discouraged if you run into real physical difficulties in the beginning. The good news is that, as long as you pay close attention to your posture and persevere even a little, these difficulties will generally dissolve of themselves quite quickly.

Now for the bad news... This is not some kind of Californian, new-age, namby-pamby, feel-good and bliss-out pseudo-mysticism. There is going to be discomfort, and if you want to make any progress, you have to bulldoze your way through it. Unless you take the attitude that you are going to succeed and you disdain the physical discomfort, that discomfort will grow rather than retreat and you will end up frustrated and defeated. And even if you do not, you will never actually accomplish your goal of undermining the ego — instead you will just be catering to it yet again with your search for pleasant and restful sensations.

Joseph the Hesychast worked so hard at prayer that "sweat poured from my body as if from a faucet."[36] Wang Liping's early training was, as mentioned previously, so demanding that he would pass out from the physical pain of sitting for so long in a full lotus position: "Sitting cross legged to practice inner work is most painful; sitting until you pass out is the limit. *Essentials of Attainment* says that even iron men find it hard to endure, for it is more painful than any other pain. The pain doesn't kill you, and yet it doesn't let you live."[37] (I do not recommend that you push yourself this far without the direct supervision of a qualified master).

What I do recommend is that (1) you be rather strict with yourself about the time you are going to remain sitting, and (2) once a week you give yourself a little extra time and sit about 10 to 25 percent past your usual limit. You will find the results very educational.

But please remember to use common sense: If you have recently injured your knee, for example, and your knee starts to give you trouble while sitting, this is probably not the time to bulldoze through and

> ## INNER PRINCIPLE
> ### 4.6
>
> Unless you push through the barriers of physical discomfort and boredom, you will never succeed at refining the mind and undermining the ego; you will be merely "going along with the natural process" and will never find the "way of return."

ignore the pain. You obviously need to adopt a different position for the time being. If you are foolish enough to ignore this kind of pain, you may find yourself in surgery as a result.

How to Sit Still and Do Nothing

1. Having decided on the place for your practice and the physical position you plan to use, prepare everything calmly and spend a few minutes doing some light stretching of the whole body.

2. Once in your sitting position, let your hands rest on your knees; whether palms are up or down is a matter of choice.

3. Gently arch your back, pulling the vertebrae apart. Then relax the spine again so the vertebrae come back together in a relaxed fashion.

4. Gently turn your head three times to the right and left as if to look over your shoulders, and then bring the head back to the center while leaving the back straight (I do not mean totally straight, because the back's natural S-curve shape is maintained. The idea is not to slouch, because slouching impedes the body's natural energy flow up the spine and puts excess pressure on the internal organs.)

5. You should have cushions under your buttocks so that your torso is leaning ever so slightly forward. The test is this: If it requires effort to keep the small of your back from collapsing outward to the rear, then your buttocks must be raised a little more. If you are sitting correctly, it is your skeletal structure, and not your muscles, that keep you erect. If you use muscles, the pain will become very distracting within a few minutes.

6. Gently close your eyes either part way or all the way.

7. Let the tongue rest on the hard palate (roof of the mouth) or behind the upper teeth.

8. Breathe through your nose in a slow and rhythmic way. The breathing should feel very comfortable and relaxing. Make sure that when you inhale, your abdomen (not your chest!) expands, and that it contracts with the exhalation.

9. Spend a few minutes imagining that as you inhale and the abdomen expands, energy is rushing in and filling the abdomen, and that as you exhale, this energy is dispersing outward around you in all directions.

10. Once the mind is relatively calm and quiet, you can loosen your concentration on the breath somewhat. You should still be consciously aware of every breath, though.

11. When thoughts arise, your task is to find the middle ground between identifying with them so that they take over your attention, and directly resisting them with force. Both identifying and resisting strengthen the energy of intrusive thoughts and are dead ends. Merely make a mental note of thoughts that arise and return your attention to your breath.

12. Once you have sat for the prearranged time, get up very slowly and stretch your muscles. Try to carry with you the mental calm you experienced.

There you have it. Simplicity itself! But by now you are probably wondering why it so important to concentrate on the breath.

Every authentic tradition knows that the *nous* and the breath are linked. You experience this daily when you find yourself in various moods. When you're angry, your breathing becomes faster and rougher. "If thoughts arise, the breathing is rough."[38] Here the *nous* is influencing the breath. The genius of ancient cultures was to realize how profoundly this same connection could be made to work in reverse.

When you "tune" the breathing deliberately, you switch the body to the parasympathetic nervous system, which reduces the quantity and energy of intrusive thoughts and heightens, paradoxically, both relaxation and concentration.

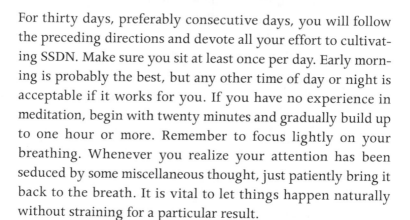

ROCK SOLID LIFE PRACTICE 4.1: PRACTICING SSDN

For thirty days, preferably consecutive days, you will follow the preceding directions and devote all your effort to cultivating SSDN. Make sure you sit at least once per day. Early morning is probably the best, but any other time of day or night is acceptable if it works for you. If you have no experience in meditation, begin with twenty minutes and gradually build up to one hour or more. Remember to focus lightly on your breathing. Whenever you realize your attention has been seduced by some miscellaneous thought, just patiently bring it back to the breath. It is vital to let things happen naturally without straining for a particular result.

But no matter what I say, you're going to run into the same three walls that everyone else does.

1. "But there's nothing to do!"
   Precisely! You've got it! In all types of inner work the *nous* has what I would call, for lack of a better term, an object. In Orthodoxy a common object is the Jesus Prayer, sometimes in conjunction with the breathing. Other traditions use all kinds of different objects. But the one object that every authentic tradition uses is the breath. This is the easiest, fastest and safest way to stabilize your inner world.

2. "I just can't keep my mind free from thoughts!"
   That's okay. Perhaps there is too much of you in the process? Take your self and what you want out of the equation. Just keep practicing and never give up. And remember that inner work is process-oriented, not goal-oriented. Just acknowledge what you are experiencing in your practice and don't worry about it.

3. "Sometimes I have really good sessions, but there are even more bad ones, where I just can't concentrate or sit still." This is called the Law of Changes, and chapter 8 deals with it in more detail. What it really means is that there are a number of internal and external factors influencing your sessions and you don't control them. Just be patient and persistent and their power over you will gradually fade away.

STEP 3: SEPARATING FROM THOUGHT

Many ancient cultures throughout the world made three incredible discoveries about humanity and the universe, and used very similar methods to arrive at their conclusions. Many of these cultures gave rise to particular groups of people dedicated to the exploration of reality, and despite the widely differing cultures in question, all used the human psychosomatic organism as the instrument for their research and all used the practice of inner silence as the principal method. Their conclusions about the human condition were astonishingly similar.

The first discovery was what Orthodoxy calls the "consubstantiality" of the human race. In other words, we are not the separate individuals that we think we are. Rather, we are all organically connected, ontologically linked with each other and with the rest of the cosmos at levels much more profound than the physical. The human race is

> ## INNER PRINCIPLE
> ### 4.7
>
> Just as your state of mind influences your breathing pattern, so modifying your breathing can alter your state of mind.

one vast being. Yes, the personal elements really are distinct and will remain so, but we are nevertheless far more connected than our fallen perceptions would lead us to believe.

The second discovery was that everything that is real, permanent, and eternal is somehow related to unity and oneness. Unity tends toward wholeness and completeness and the origin of things, whereas multiplicity appears to be linked to the whole process of disintegration and death — to what is temporal and impermanent.

The third discovery, and the one that concerns us in this chapter, is the fact that when most people use the word *I* — "*I* want, *I* think, *I* love, *I* hate," and so on - the "I" they are referring to is an illusion; this "I" does not really exist. There is an "I" that does, but this isn't it.

The methodology of using your own body and mind as instruments to explore the nature of reality has been in use for millennia and is the basis of every authentic tradition. The West, though, sees the results as "invalid" and, since there is no "impartial observer," it is impossible to demonstrate the results to an independent third party. It's also difficult to reproduce the experiments on demand. Western science has typically labeled these endeavors as "subjective" and derided them as "mysticism." Authentic traditions, in contrast, teach that this method is perfectly valid, extremely reliable, and time-tested, and using it followers of these traditions made astonishing discoveries.

With regard to the third discovery, how is it possible that when most people say "I," the "I" they are referring to has no concrete existence? Most people's minds are so overlaid with layers of historical and social conditioning from family, friends, the surrounding culture and incidents from the past interpreted in a certain way, that they have lost all spiritual independence. They have become totally "yin," totally susceptible to energies from the external environment and to the powers of soul and body run amok — the passions. Such people identify themselves totally with their own thoughts, their

THE 5 PILLARS OF LIFE

SCIENCE: MODERN AND ANCIENT

The modern scientific viewpoint comes directly from the so-called scholastic theology of the Franco-Latin tradition of the middle ages, which itself was based on the erroneous views of Augustine of Hippo, a fifth century bishop in North Africa. Augustine taught that the Bible was itself, as a text, as words on a page, God's revelation to man, and that God gave man the rational mind as the instrument for correctly interpreting the text. So the supreme irony is that modern science comes directly from religion.

Contrary to this, the original tradition claims that the Bible is not God's revelation. Rather, it is *about* God's revelation. The real revelation is what took place in the lives of the prophets, apostles, and saints who followed the path of inner transformation and reached the stage of participating in the divine energies, of having an organic and "physical" communion with the Absolute while still in this world. In other words, the text describes how the process of deification works and how to apply it as a healing remedy to one's own life. It describes how to heal the malfunctioning noetic faculty and unite it to the heart. Anyone who applies the methods used by the apostles, prophets and saints to his or her own life will inevitably get results proportionate to the faithfulness with which he or she has replicated the experiment.[39]

So neither Orthodoxy nor the real traditions of Judaism, Buddhism, Taoism, Hinduism, and much of "shamanism" the world over, including several Native American traditions, can be called religions. This has nothing to do with the relative accuracy or inaccuracy of these traditions. It is simply a question of method and goal. All of these "authentic" traditions have aimed at the transformation of the human person on the ontological level and his or her integration into the Absolute. Religion does not — it remains stuck on the level of external moralism and juridical categories, and in fact explicitly denies that direct communion with the Absolute is even possible in this life. Authentic traditions possess a scientific methodology linked to a realignment of the powers of the soul, which necessitates subjugating the rational mind to the higher mind or *nous*. Religion, however, does the reverse: it subjugates all other faculties to the rational mind, thereby perpetuating the neurobiological illness that keeps people enslaved to their environment.

own opinions, prejudices, preconceived notions, whims, desires, aversions, and are unconsciously manipulated by powerful forces they may be only vaguely aware of and do not control — everything from hormonal shifts to the phase of the moon. So when most people in their fallen condition use the term "I," they are not referring to something concrete and permanent, but to what Taoism calls "emotional consciousness" and to what Orthodoxy calls the "passions" or the bondage to the "world." This bondage is the very thing we are trying to overcome.

The best known formulation that the "I" is unreal comes from the Shakyamuni Buddha himself. His analysis of human consciousness into the five aggregates or *skandhas* shows definitively that whatever this "I" is, it is not what most people assume.[40] Whereas in the holy person, the overlap between the superficial personality and the real, eternal person is very large or complete, for a great many people there is very little overlap. So, while you obviously have superficial character traits conditioned by history, you have a real personal identity or *hypostasis* (to use the Orthodox technical term) that persists within you, although you may have thoroughly obscured it. As one Orthodox theologian put it:

> Our temporal characteristics and our history in life depend on many superficial things which vanish with death, but our real personality is not superficial and does not depend on changing and vanishing things. It is our real self. It remains with us when we sleep in the grave and will be our real face in the resurrection. It is eternal.[41]

So what people are referring to when they use the word *I* is simply an inner state of disintegration. It's quite interesting to read ancient historical documents; you notice that people in several ancient cultures — and you see this among the Coptic desert fathers of the fourth and fifth centuries–instinctively referred to themselves in the third person. You cannot help wondering if some profound psychological insight was behind this.

You might say that the real purpose of self-transformation is to rediscover the real "I" – and yes, the real "I" really does exist! The genius of Orthodoxy and of all authentic traditions lies in showing you how to go within and see for yourself all the layers of conditioning that have been laid on you. And then they show you how to expose and eliminate these layers one by one—how to eliminate your bondage to the energies of this world, your yin state, and to become yang again, the master of creation rather than its slave. All authentic traditions realized that this inner disintegration takes place mainly through the neurotic overuse of the rational mind, and its reduction of reality to conceptual thought. So the first step toward health is to accept the fact, at least on an intellectual level, that your thoughts are not you.

The sheer magnitude of this discovery can hardly be overstated. Think about it. Were you not brought up to believe implicitly that the thoughts you have are your own creations? Is it not assumed in Western culture that the continual production of thoughts is the most important indication of intelligence? Do we not measure intelligence by the infamous "IQ," by how adept the person is at linear thinking and manipulating concepts? Is not our entire educational system based on teaching endless abstract concepts and how to play with them?

Authentic traditions teach that thoughts may come from a number of sources, both external and internal. Some are products of the disordered drives or "passions" we find within us. Memory is another source, one that can be helpful or harmful depending on how it's used. For now you need to know that when thoughts from all these sources come to you, they are intermingled and difficult to separate. In a state of deep inner concentration like noetic prayer or meditation, it's easy to see that these thoughts approach the *nous*, the inner attention, as rather undefined "shapes" or energies. And only after that do they take the shape of a conceptual thought or image.

The purpose of doing SSDN is to develop unceasing inner attention (Greek *prosoche*) and awareness. The use of this attention in the pursuit of inner freedom is called "watchfulness" (Greek *nepsis*). St. Hesychios tells us that, while this inner attention is, "the heart's stillness, unbroken by any thought," watchfulness is, "a continual fixing and halting of thought at the entrance to the heart. In this way predatory and murderous thoughts are marked down as they approach and what they say and do is noted."[42] (By "murderous thoughts," Hesychios means any thoughts that forcefully attempt to take over our inner attention.)

To maintain constant inner attention in the midst of daily occupations may seem like an impossible task. But, like all other skills, it can be learned through practice. When this is accomplished, our noetic attention is stabilized inside the body and becomes the true guardian of our real self. Once refined and clarified, it becomes able to detect the arising of thought-energy from whatever source.

At this point you'll be able to watch thoughts approach and attempt to gain admittance to the mind, at the same time separating yourself from them and preserving your inner integrity. Then you'll see that the thoughts themselves will begin to fade over time and lose their power over you.

Have you ever had a crush on anyone — been romantically obsessed with someone — but it didn't work out? Well, the dynamic is similar: When you indulge thoughts and identify with them (which is what happens during a crush), they become extraordinarily powerful and take over your whole inner world forcefully. But when you cease to give them attention (as when you have been separated from the object of your affection for months or years), the thoughts are gradually reduced to bare ideas devoid of real emotional power. "If not a single thought occurs," writes the Preserver of the Truth, "then you shed birth and death. Therefore enlightened people cultivate their behaviour, detaching from emotion, breaking down obstinacy and blunting sharpness, working to overcome and eliminate unwholesome states of mind in order to see the original face before birth."[43]

As your freedom expands, so will your pleasure at being alive. Your creativity and mental acuity will improve vastly. Your fears, your sense of loss at unfulfilled desires, your deeply rooted complexes, all these will actually vanish. Your whole being will become a unified whole, and you will be able once again, perhaps for the first time, to use with perfect accuracy, the word *I*.

"Little by little," writes St. Theophan the Recluse, "you will separate from your thoughts. Then you will find that you have strayed far away from your first created image."[44]

STEP 4: ACHIEVING PERPETUAL INNER STILLNESS

If the benefits of your inner work are to be preserved and multiplied, you must cultivate them literally twenty-four hours a day, otherwise what you gain in SSDN you will quickly scatter once you are at work, school, or any other situation that demands your attention. The inner stillness that you have begun to taste has to be extended beyond your sessions of SSDN to penetrate into every waking moment and, eventually, the sleeping moments too. Needless to say, all this is easier said than done.

Once you have tasted the delight of inner peace and order, you begin to pursue it almost automatically. Then you discover that the whole world of persons, events, and things seems to be conspiring against you. On the one hand, you should not allow yourself to be too easily discouraged — this is a long-term project. On the other, you do need a plan. No army goes into battle without a plan. And the plan needs to be continuously adapted to your circumstances because, as a great military strategist once observed, no plan survives first contact with the enemy. And yours won't either.

Achieving continuous inner stillness was somewhat easier in traditional cultures, where most daily occupations were more physical than mental, where direct contact with nature was the norm, and where the pace of life was much slower. That's one reason why Orthodox monastics have always preferred simple and rote tasks, because that kind of work has much less potential to disrupt the inner attention on which inner work depends. Nevertheless, there are ways to deal with the increased distraction of our cerebrally oriented workplaces. Here are the three most powerful foundational strategies to help you get started.

Three Winning Strategies

Co-opt the Thinking Process

Inner work tends to sideline the use of the rational mind, to tame it and keep it in its place. But the most effective strategy to use against discursive thoughts is not to bludgeon them into submission, but to co-opt them. It's nearly impossible to keep the mind free from thoughts, especially in the beginning. So part of our task then becomes changing the quality of the thoughts the mind dwells on. The mind, says Orthodoxy, is like a mill — if you give it suitable grain, it will give you quality flour in return. And Wang Liping's old mentors gave him specific strategies for working with thoughts at the outset of his training. You need to develop your own individual ways to keep your mind focused during your busy days. Traditional reading materials, especially theme meditations like the *Lamrim*, can give you lots of ideas in this regard. It takes time to build up the habit of using thoughts constructively, but it can be done and will help you to return your *nous* to stillness after it has been distracted. Later chapters will give you lots of food for the rational mind to work on. Chew it well!

Uniting Energy and Spirit

The second part of the method is perhaps the most powerful and, not surprisingly, hinges on the breath. I have already explained the significance of using the breathing and uniting the mind to it. Taoism refers to this practice as "the union of energy (qi) and spirit (shen)." According to an ancient Taoist source, "When mind and breath stay together and work in unison, this keeps the mind from leaping about and prevents attention from running off."[45] To use an Orthodox example, a disciple of Joseph the Hesychast has this to say about the cultivation of the breath, albeit in the context of noetic prayer:

> Controlled breathing (along with attentiveness) is necessary
> to keep the *nous* from escaping. In this way we shall be able
> to cut off distraction, which bleeds the essence out of

prayer… By eliminating distraction, we give the *nous* the ease to pay attention to the heart…

This method of prayer is very effective. First, it will bring undistracted prayer; it will bring joy and peace. Simultaneously it will bring clarity of the *nous* and tears of joy. The *nous* will become receptive to *theoria*. Afterwards, it will create absolute stillness of the heart. One will not hear anything at all. He will think he is in the Sahara Desert.[46]

The method itself is very simple: During daily activities you strive to pay attention to your breathing. This tunes the breathing almost automatically and without effort. You don't therefore try to impose a breathing pattern, but simply follow the natural rhythm in an unconstrained way. Your attention will be seduced by countless other things, but you patiently bring your attention back and put it on the breath. Over a long period of time your attention stabilizes more or less permanently so that you are no longer even conscious of the breath anymore.

There is no more efficient way to overcome stress than this. Uniting energy and spirit (i.e., paying attention to your breathing) is nature's built-in tranquilizer. But unlike the chemical tranquilizers that numb your mind and kill your ability to focus, this method magnifies your mental powers. And instead of making you drowsy, you'll get more and more energy for your daily activities. And, as if that weren't enough, it will even break the downward spiral of neurotic thinking that produces the physical symptoms of stress.

Living in a Dream
The third method is a simple psychological technique of extraordinary power. It reminds me of a text from the Orthodox funeral service: "Life is but a shadow and a dream." In its original context, this reminds the living how fleeting life is and that you should be constantly preparing yourself for what awaits you (more about this in chapter 6). There is, however, another dimension to this that you need to consider: the fact that the supposedly solid, tangible, material reality around you is much less solid, tangible and real than you think.

As Westerners we have no idea just how unique our worldview really is. The average Westerner is a materialist on a very deep level, whatever his purported belief system. He sees the material world as absolutely real and solid, as an objectively existing reality outside of and separate from himself. He is, to put it bluntly, a Newtonian. The mechanistic worldview of Newtonian physics is deeply ingrained in the Western psyche. This is all the more ironic because modern science and particularly quantum physics has proven this view to be deeply erroneous.[47] Actually, it pretty much proved this over half a century ago, but the cultural conditioning every Westerner is subjected to is very difficult to defeat.

We now know that material reality is not at all solid; all of what we see is energy in one form or another. And our perceptions of it are arranged by the senses, which act as filters, allowing us to see only a very narrow spectrum of reality. We see very little of the electromagnetic spectrum, for example. We perceive objects as solid, although they are mostly composed of empty space. We naively believe that we are independent from the natural world, yet we remain tied to it in a thousand ways we don't see or understand. According to all authentic traditions, we are quite blind in our current state: We do not see reality as it is. The Orthodox tradition takes for granted that there are levels of reality inaccessible to ordinary sensory perception, and that even on the level of material reality, we see very little of what's around us.

One startling example of this in recent times is the life of Fr. Porphyrios, an Orthodox monk who spent most of his life in Athens, Greece. He could recognize and understand the language of animals, see into the depths of the earth or the far reaches of space, find petroleum deposits, buried monuments, lost icons, subterranean springs; see great distances, radioactivity, the human soul itself.[48]

As for Taoism, it has made a detailed examination over the centuries of the forces at work in the universe and, in the words of Wang Liping's biographers: "Modern science has made minute analyses of those forces that can be perceived, but it does not recognize the existence of countless imperceptible forces. Yet the effects of these forces on the human body and human life are even greater than those of the perceptible forces."[49]

People in traditional and even primitive cultures may inhabit the same physical space we do, but they tend to perceive it in a vastly different way: as something not so solid and immutable, but as porous, as a world of appearance hiding a different and greater reality. Is this naïve? Well, if it's based on actual experience that we have blocked out from our own consciousness, then who is naïve, they or we? And now science has not only dealt the Newtonian worldview a coup de grâce, but it has also gone a long way toward validating the traditional or primitive worldview.

From the point of view of self-transformation, though, what matters is not your philosophical opinions about material reality, but how you relate to it psychologically. There is an old Christian spiritual text from the medieval West called the *Cloud of Unknowing*, in which the author, basing himself on the writings attributed to St. Dionysios the Areopagite, talks about the need to fashion a "cloud of forgetting" between ourselves and the doings and activities of worldly life.[50] In Taoist terms, it means transcending the plane of "persons, events and things." In some Tibetan practices, this approach is called "changing the karmic traces." Here is how you do it:

> Upon waking in the morning, think to yourself, *I am awake in a dream*. When you enter the kitchen, recognize it as a dream kitchen. Pour dream milk into dream coffee. *It's all a dream*, you think to yourself, *this is a dream*. Remind yourself of this constantly throughout the day.[51]

The hidden principle behind this practice is this: "As phenomena are seen to be fleeting and essenceless, grasping decreases. Every sensory encounter and mental event becomes a reminder of the dream-like nature of experience. ...By changing habitual and largely unconscious reactions to phenomena, the qualities of life and dream change. When we think of an experience as 'only a dream' it is less 'real' to us. It loses power over us — power that it only had because we gave it power — and can no longer disturb us and drive us into negative emotional states."[52]

In other words, at its most basic level, this practice enables us to neutralize what Fr. Sophrony so eloquently called, "the persistently destructive influence of the outside world."[53] Without such a practice, your noetic energy will be bled out of you by the trivialities of life, your inner state will remain yin and governed by the energies acting on you from our environment, you will never achieve spiritual independence, and your sitting practice, no matter how intensive, will fail to bear the fruit it could.

ROCK SOLID LIFE PRACTICE 4.2: PRACTICING PERPETUAL INNER STILLNESS

You are going to spend one week working with each of the three strategies for assimilating stillness into your everyday activities. You will find this an exhilarating challenge, but also very difficult. In fact, maintaining the continuity of stillness in the face of outside pressures is incredibly difficult, so don't be disheartened by your apparent lack of success. Treat it as a learning experience.

1. Find suitable reading material to inspire you and keep it with you during the day. The material must be from an authentic ancient tradition. Read a little bit whenever you can and try to pick out one key idea at a time — whatever idea speaks to you. Dwell on the idea in silence for a moment and then try to keep the idea central to your consciousness for the next hour or so. And whenever your mind becomes restless and refuses to be quiet, just say to it: "Fine. If you insist on thinking, here's what you're going to think about!" and give it a topic from your reading. Try this for at least five days in a row. Note your results in your journal.

THE 5 PILLARS OF LIFE

2. During the following week, you will spend five days in a row paying attention to your breathing on a constant basis. Your concentration must find that fine balance between ineffective laxness on the one hand, and obsessive straining on the other. Straining your concentration too much will strain the muscles and cause harm. If you're doing this correctly, you'll start to feel very relaxed. Note your results in your journal.

3. During the final week of the exercise, you will practise the fine art of seeing the world as a shadow and a dream. Whatever you are doing, tell yourself it is an illusion, that none of the visible reality of this world is really the way it seems. If you're doing this correctly, you'll begin to notice that what other people consider to be very important in life seems rather trivial to you. Write down your results.

So these three practices — co-opting the thinking process, joining energy and spirit, and living in a dream — jointly facilitate achieving perpetual inner stillness. There are lots of other practices that will have a similar effect, but all of them depend on a firm foundation in the basics have presented here, so I will leave them until later chapters.

When you have begun to practice SSDN on a regular basis, and made efforts to continue this stillness throughout the hours of your busy life, you will find both fantastic results and more than a few challenges. I cannot promise you this will be easy, but I can certainly promise that it will be exhilarating! A good foundation in inner work is the key to integrating into your life all the elements discussed from here on.

Key to stillness: Persistence with no thought of success or failure.

Chapter Five

INTENT: RECLAIMING YOUR INVINCIBLE WILLPOWER

"I have no willpower!" True or False?

"I can't quit smoking — I've tried a hundred times!"

"I can't keep weight off — weight loss programs don't work for me."

"My New Year's resolution to keep in shape seems to have fizzled out."

How often have you heard all this? How often have you said it yourself? All of us have things we can't let go of — our daily addictions like chocolate, coffee, or soft drinks, our comfort-loving habit of taking the daily hot shower, our rich fantasy life where everything is just as we would want it... And then there are the things we just can't seem to accomplish: sticking to an exercise regime, learning a new skill, managing our money. In short, persevering on any one course of action for a long enough time with enough determination to achieve our goals.

This chapter will help you solve all this, more easily than you might have thought possible. It will help you understand what willpower is, the laws for using it effectively, and the reasons why you often fail. Once you learn these basic laws and how to access your willpower using a process called "intent," you will never fail again in the conventional sense. You may occasionally be defeated, but you will never again fail.

The average person trying to use willpower to accomplish something is usually sabotaged by two internal forces:

1. Lower desires: the pursuit of pleasure and comfort on the emotional or physical level in all its forms
2. Fear and unbelief: doubting in one's own ability to succeed

When we fail because of these internal enemies, it is a sure sign that we're still in the realm of "going along," that we have not yet begun to "reverse" the natural process. We are still yin to the environment and under its control. "Going along with the usual course of conditioning makes one an ordinary person; going against it makes one an immortal."[1] Any goal that takes you toward self-transformation defies the "natural" process and that's why attaining it seems difficult.

So a prerequisite for success in remaking your life is to begin to leave the fruitless world of "going along" and to become more yang or impermeable to your environment. Fortunately, if you have begun to integrate the practice of SSDN into your Program, you have already taken by far the most important step in that direction. No other tool is as powerful or indispensable as perseverance in inner refinement of the mind. From now on, everything you undertake in this course will depend to a greater or lesser extent on this practice. This is because, "When practitioners respond to events, they must have inner autonomy and inner peace, and then they will hit the mark every time."[2]

FEAR, DOUBT, AND UNBELIEF: THE UNHOLY TRINITY

When you examine all of your past failures in life, you not uncommonly discover that most of them can be traced back to a fear of suffering, a fear of failure, an unbelief in your ability to succeed, or a deep-seated feeling of unworthiness to succeed. Fear, doubt, and unbelief: the unholy trinity of the emotional world and the causes of untold pain and suffering. There is also one other factor — the lack of burning desire — which is covered subsequently. When we fail, we do so because:

- We *fear* the suffering involved in changing our self-destructive lifestyles — the pain of giving up our cigarettes, our junk-food or our five cups of coffee per day. And the pain of facing up to inner emotional obstacles can be even more daunting.
- We *doubt* our ability to succeed. We see ourselves as incompetent in math and so we do badly in our math course — a self-fulfilling prophecy. Experience in any human endeavor is quick to prove that if you don't think you can succeed, you won't.
- We don't *believe* enough in our goal and persevere when the going gets tough, so we don't follow through with the disciplines of self-transformation in a consistent way. We compromise our way of life, lose our faith in "reversal" and settle for the pseudo-happiness of "going along."

These are the primary reasons that it seems to us that we have no willpower.

Now the good news! You really do have the willpower, and more than enough to do anything you desire to do; you only need to discover that willpower, how to use it, and how to rid yourself of the emotional parasites of fear, doubt and unbelief that are holding you back from the only adventure truly worthy of a human person.

THE PARADOX OF POWER AND HELPLESSNESS

In all authentic traditions we live constantly with the insoluble paradox that "on our own, we can do nothing," and yet there is no power in heaven or on earth that constrains our free will and predetermines our outcomes. We are impotent and all-powerful at the same time.

Unfortunately, we tend to latch onto the first part of the equation and use it as an excuse for our lack of progress. St. Isaac the Syrian once addressed this problem by telling the following true story:

> A certain philosopher set a rule in his mind to keep silence for a period of time. The king of the Romans was amazed on hearing this, and wished to put him to the test. He therefore ordered that the philosopher be brought before him; but when he saw that he remained silent to every question which he asked him, and gave no answer, the king was enraged, and commanded that he be put to death, since he did not reverence the throne and crown of his glory. But this man was not afraid and held fast to his resolution, and quietly prepared himself for death. The king, however, instructed the executioners saying: "If he fears the sword and breaks his resolution, slay him; but if he remains constant to his purpose, return him to me alive." When, therefore, he drew nigh to the appointed place of execution, those to whom he was committed harassed him, constraining him to abandon his resolve and live. But he thought to himself, "It is better for me to die in the course of one hour and so hold fast to my purpose on account of which I have struggled so long, rather than be vanquished by the fear of death and outrage my wisdom and incur the reproach of cowardice upon myself due to the necessity of the moment." Thus he calmly laid himself out to receive the blow of the sword. Thereupon he was delivered and lived, according to the command. The king, being told this, marveled together with all his subjects, and released the philosopher with honours.[3]

Isaac the Syrian knew from his own experience that once burning desire has been aroused, it overcomes any and all obstacles, including our deep seated doubts and fears. So in reality, there are no barriers to us, except in our minds. When we falter, it is always from a lack of burning desire, whatever the other factors. (This is not to discount the possibility that wrong methods had something to do with it, but that is not the concern in this chapter.) We can achieve much more than we sometimes believe, and every athlete knows this. If you have ever been involved in sports or athletic endeavors of any kind, you

probably know the feeling of looking back on an important game or race or contest and wondering how you ever managed to push yourself that far out of your comfort zone.

SO JUST WHAT IS WILLPOWER?

Before you can tap into your willpower, you must know what it is and how it's related to your entire psychosomatic structure. If your ideas on this matter are not correct, you will inevitably get off track when you try to apply them to your practice.

Orthodoxy sees the human person as a dynamic reality: We have within us a kind of natural impulse and energy to grow and evolve in the direction of the goal for which we were created in the first place — union with the Absolute in the process of deification. Just as we evolve physically in a certain direction in the years after birth, so it is spiritually. The difference is that, while we can't stop the physical growth process, it's unfortunately rather simple for us to move ourselves off course in our existential approach to life.

This has amazing implications. It means that at a very deep level, nature is on your side. The way you have been constructed is actually helping you along. It also means that once the external and internal forces sabotaging you have been neutralized, you will naturally head in the right direction. This is why Isaac the Syrian said: "When life's concerns do not incur into the soul from without, and she abides in her nature, then she does not require prolonged toil to penetrate into and understand the wisdom of God."[4] You will go from knowledge to knowledge, strength to strength and accomplishment to accomplishment.

The process of SSDN is the ultimate lever in neutralizing and clearing away the debris of these forces that have held you back all your life, and which continue to hold sway over the masses of humanity. These forces literally keep the whole world locked up in undesirable ways of thinking and acting, on an endless and unproductive treadmill, obscuring the true human will. But through perseverance in the practice of SSDN, you will identify and eliminate these forces from your own life, one by one, and gain access to your own true natural will and the incredible power that flows from it.

So, how do you define willpower? Willpower is our ability to harness the innate tendency of our psychosomatic being to move toward its highest potential.

There are several classic scenarios in which people put their willpower to the test and fail:

- Losing weight
- Quitting smoking
- New Year's resolutions
- Managing money
- Learning a new skill
- Improving relationships
- Physical fitness
- Self-transformation

Chances are that you're keenly aware of having failed in the past at several of these. And I'd be willing to bet that you've failed for one of the following seven reasons:

1. You did not define the goal in a measurable way

2. You defined the goal in a negative way
3. You did not develop sufficient desire
4. You did not develop sufficient revulsion
5. Your preparation was not sufficient
6 Your plan was unworkable
7. You decided to "go it alone"

Let's see how each of these factors can sabotage even the best of intentions, using the ever-so-common scenario of trying to lose weight:

1. Not defining the goal in a measurable way: Maybe you did not have a clear idea of how much you wanted to lose and by what date. Perhaps your motivation was only to "look better." To accomplish any goal you must know precisely what it is and how to determine when or if you have attained it, or at least how far along the road toward it you are.

2. Defining the goal in a negative way: To "lose weight" is a self-defeating goal in the first place. The sub-conscious mind has a great deal of difficulty helping you on your way to any goal that is expressed in negative terms. Why not restate the goal in a positive way? Say to yourself: "I want to achieve optimum physical and emotional health." The moment you say this, your subconscious will sign up.

3. Not developing sufficient desire: Strange as it may seem, many people really are not all that enthused or "properly obsessed" with the goals they allegedly want to achieve. With weight loss, many just feel it's something they "have to do." But experience proves that unless you want to do it, unless you have a burning desire, you are unlikely to persevere when the going gets tough — as it always does with any worthwhile goal. Reversing the natural process says, "When the going gets tough, the tough get going." Going along with the natural process says, "When the going gets tough, the tough go shopping" (also known as "retail

therapy"!). Burning desire is the key because it will give you the strength and determination you need to persevere, and whoever perseveres will always win.

4. Not developing sufficient revulsion: One very powerful way to increase that desire is by doing the opposite — considering everything that is totally unacceptable about the present situation. For example, we know that if we lose weight we will have a more positive self-image, we'll be physically much more attractive, we'll function far better on the mental, emotional and physical levels, and, of course, our health will improve. On the other hand, if we don't lose weight, we'll be forever saddled with the feelings of inadequacy and failure, thinking others find us unattractive, and knowing that we are harming ourselves on a daily basis. Developing revulsion for our current state is a very powerful motivator. As Isaac the Syrian put it, there's nothing more powerful than desperation.[5]

5. Insufficient preparation: For many of us, the New Years' resolutions of the past — the ones we have failed at — were just vaguely formulated ideas. And even when we were serious about them in our own minds, we did not think through the whole process or plan it in advance. It never ceases to amaze me that so many people who come to me for counseling seem to think that they can attain this or that result in their lives on the basis of little more than a vague intention. They are often stunned when I ask them what their plan is for achieving a given result. If you want to lose weight, but you keep on buying all the same fattening foods you are still addicted to so that they are still under your nose at home, how do you think that will impact on your success? What exactly do you plan to eat and how do you plan to avoid your bad eating habits and replace them with better ones? Planning is everything! That's what this whole book is about. If you want to succeed at anything, you must plan down to the last detail.

6. An unworkable plan: You won't lose weight and keep it off without a method, and one that works. Some commercially popularized diets, unfortunately, are based on a scanty knowledge of nutrition (to say the least), and because they are so unnatural the body actually rebels against them physiologically. So not only do you need a plan, you need one that works, which brings us to the next point.

7. Going it alone: Don't reinvent the wheel. Whatever your goal is, find a plan that has demonstrated success to back it up and adapt it to your own situation. Then find someone who can show you how to put it into action — there is a huge difference between having the world's greatest plan and knowing how to apply that plan to your life. And just as important is having other people working on the same or similar projects — nothing motivates like shared adversity. The famous Weight Watchers' program owes its success to the principles in this paragraph!

As you may have guessed by now, not one of these strategies is anything new — every authentic tradition has used them for millennia and has warned its followers about the dangers of ignoring them. Using the example of Joseph the Hesychast, note that:

- He defined his goal in a measurable way: to implement a program of self-transformation in a consistent way without giving in to compromise.

- He defined his goal in a positive way: to love God with his whole being and to enter into a real communion of being with Him. He didn't enter monastic life to punish himself for some past transgression or from some feeling of being unable to relate to women, or because he couldn't make a go of economic life in the world (actually, he had been a successful young entrepreneur in the world).

- Joseph knew the power of desire and fueled his longing both by reading the lives of people who had already achieved what he wanted and by actively seeking out such people.

- He understood the power of revulsion and constantly rehearsed in his mind the undesirable consequences of a life wasted in *philautia* (self-love). He had read St. Hesychios, who warned him that failure to refine the inner world of the mind and thereby free himself from evil thoughts, words and actions in this life would mean continued slavery to them after death.[6] Joseph prepared himself well, both by rehearsing his way of life before he left for the Holy Mountain to become a monk (he would spend nights praying in the wilderness), and by meticulous planning once he became a monk.

- The young monk knew his plan of action — his program — was workable, since it came largely from someone who had already refined and used it successfully himself, the hermit-elder Daniel, who lived in the cave of Peter the Athonite.

- Joseph did not make the mistake of trying to figure out this new life and apply it all by himself. He sought out the best and most reliable advisors and also a companion of like mind with whom to share the journey: Fr. Arsenios.

One of our hidden problems as Westerners is our totally unfounded belief that we can change our lives by using our reason alone, that change made on the basis of our most superficial mental faculty can somehow accomplish whatever we want. Well, most of our apparent failures of will in all the areas mentioned previously are related to this idea. People today think that they can make progress and achieve their goals simply by adopting some new ideological outlook. Every authentic tradition testifies to the fact that you will never get very far unless you reevaluate every area of your life and bring it into congruence with your goal — so your diet, your use of time, your relationships,

THE 5 PILLARS OF LIFE

your work, and every other element that comprises your life as you know it will necessarily change.

Real transformation is based on what you do. Your life today is the sum total of your previous actions, what you have been doing. So if you don't change what you do in every area of our life, where will you end up? Right back where you started. Simple as that.

We also don't take seriously enough the problem of competing priorities and lack of time. Unfortunately, not everything can be a priority at the same time. Adopting new priorities in order to transform your life means that some of your current priorities will have to be dropped, at least for a time. I learned this the hard way: my own temptation is to try to do it all at the same time. But years of experience have taught me that in the end, self-transformation or any other project moves along much faster if you do *one* thing at a time and do it well. This approach will save you from endless frustration!

In the West we have been brought up as rugged individualists, and while that does tend to build certain virtues into our character—self-reliance, toughness, perseverance, and so on—it also means that we overestimate what we can achieve on our own and underestimate one of the greatest levers of self-transformation: the help of others.

Just look at the phenomenal success of all the modern day support groups: Alcoholics Anonymous, Weight Watchers and many more: all of them use this leverage to help their clients achieve results that they would never have been able to on their own. Look at John Stanton's Running Room™ chain; while it may look like any other running shoe supply store, it actually offers classes to teach people how to learn distance running, and regular times when runners at differing levels of experience can run together, for free. It's an amazing concept, to be sure, but one that's as old as the hills. So why is it that we almost invariably get better results when our efforts are part of a group?

- We can push ourselves much harder when we are surrounded by others that are doing the same. The momentum of the group almost pulls us along and undermines our tendency to do the minimum, to take it easy and in general, to slack off.
- The experience of the group acts as a check on our own practice, keeping us from drifting into sidetracks that lead either nowhere or into danger.
- Group enthusiasm is contagious. Experience shows that if you try to embark on something without direct involvement in a group, your chances of persisting and completing your project drop very sharply.

Almost no one has ever succeeded at self-transformation by going it alone. Wang Liping had both expert guidance and a community of support in the form of his three old mentors. Joseph the Hesychast had both Fr. Daniel for guidance and Fr. Arsenios for sharing the perils of the path. Both the monastery and the parish are intended to provide both of these essential elements. The same can be said for the Sangha, or community of believers, in Buddhism. The fact that it is one of the three realities in which the Buddhist "takes refuge" attests to its overriding importance.[7]

Even in secular endeavors the principles of peer support and expert advice are well-known and considered indispensable. You will never find a success guru or wealth coach who will do otherwise than insist that you find a mentor and a network of contacts to fulfill these two roles. In the words of two such people who have built their remarkable success on this principle: "Incredible power can be released when people work together. Associating with like-minded, success-oriented, joyful individuals — a Dream Team — is one of the most amazing success tools that exists. Anyone who achieves great success — anyone — must have a Dream Team"[8] In every human endeavor, success is a team effort, and the input from the team, both its guidance and its support, are factors in your success that you cannot make up for by sheer willpower.

The bottom line is to never underestimate the power of the other. Someone else who shares your vision and your practice is a very

powerful lever, a true "force multi-
plier." While your willpower, once you
uncover it and learn to use it, will seem
like some new and incredible force in
your life, it is vastly more effective
when buoyed up by another human
being. The truth of the consubstantiality of the human race, discussed previously, has this corollary: You were not
meant to "go it alone"!

DISCOURAGEMENT: THE MALICIOUS SABOTEUR

How often have you begun some project or activity full of enthusiasm,
convinced for the first few weeks or months that this was for you and
was something you would stick with your whole life long, only to
waver and finally give up altogether? Maybe a particular sport or
hobby was not as enjoyable as you had thought. Or perhaps the
demands on your time were too great.

Discouragement in a sport or hobby is one thing, because the stakes
are relatively unimportant, but in the world of self-transformation
where the stakes are life and death, it is entirely another matter. Discouragement — which I define as giving up in the face of adversity —
is the most serious danger to your willpower because it saps it right at
its very root. Willpower — the ability to persist on a given course —
depends largely on the promise of the good things to be gained by
enduring the pain, inconvenience and discomfort of the path. Every
serious athlete knows this dynamic all too well. You only achieve great
things in any human endeavor by your will to persist in the face of
adversity: that's just the way it is, whether in sports or education or
business or self-transformation. A Taoist master of old tells us:

> In this endeavor, unless you concentrate on develop-
> ing your will, you are highly likely to give up along

the way. Therefore, you must have unbending determination, persistent thought and unflagging energy. First, let go of yourself, then let go of your holdings, and be unfazed by sickness or even death. Only then have you any hope of success.[9]

The path of self-transformation is incredibly exhilarating and fulfilling in itself, but there is no shortage of difficulties and obstacles en route. If we are not masters of delayed gratification, we will probably lose our inspiration at some point and give up. There is a kind of "honeymoon" period where everything seems relatively easy, interesting and even fun. But it never lasts. As Joseph the Hesychast warned one of his disciples: "The war of the enemy begins after three or four years, because grace withdraws to test a person, and your torch goes out. Things that seem beautiful now — which are truly beautiful — will then seem repulsive, black and dark."[10]

Aside from ordinary discouragement, there is a more subtle, dangerous and widespread kind of giving up — a situation I call "compromise." This happens when we fail to acquire self-discipline and willingness to pay the price of victory.[11] At this point we are readily deluded by love of comfort, and settle into a practice that keeps us prisoners inside our comfort zone. We settle for "going along with the natural process" and turning our practice into a religion.

If you examine the words of Fr. Joseph, you will notice another key principle: Extending the honeymoon is not to our advantage because real progress happens in the midst of difficulties. It is very much like a marital relationship — the romantic love, the tantalizing newness of the other, fades with time and is overtaken by the challenges of daily life, but it is only in the midst of the life's challenges that real love can mature.

So, when the path confronts you with problems and obstacles that are discouraging, remember these two points. Post them on your fridge, make them into a screen saver on your computer or do what-

ever else you have to do to keep them
fresh in your awareness at all times:

1. Difficulties are inevitable: the ego
    will not give up without a fight.
    It takes time to reverse years and
    even decades of the "noetic self-
    abuse" you have put yourself
    through.
2. Difficulties are an indication
    you are on the right path. If
there were none, you'd certainly be wasting your time in some
kind of imaginary la-la land. So whether you are dealing with
the physical discomfort of SSDN, the battle against negative
emotional states or a general "dryness" during practice, know
that you are probably doing things *right*!

Courtesy of Abba Isaac the Syrian, here is a story to boost flagging
morale.

It begins with am embattled young monk going to see an Elder and
telling the old man that he is being hit with terrible trials. The latter
calms him down and says:

> Know, child, that for thirty years I have made war with the
> demons, and until the time when I had completed the
> course of twenty years, I had not received any help what-
> ever. But thereafter, when another five had also gone by, I
> began to find rest. And as time continued slowly on its way,
> it increased. The seventh year slipped by, and after that,
> when I was in the eighth, it was intensified to a much
> greater degree. And now that the thirtieth year is running
> past, and has already reached its end, rest has prevailed to
> such an extent that I do not even know to what measure it
> has advanced. When I wish to get up for my rule of prayer,
> I am permitted to say a single "glory" [i.e., the first words

INNER PRINCIPLE
⟨⟨⟨⟨⟨⟨⟨5.5⟩⟨⟨⟨⟨⟨⟨⟨

Because our very being is
communal by nature, it is
unnatural and counterpro-
ductive to travel the path of
self-transformation without
the guidance and support of
others.

⟨⟨⟨⟨⟨⟨⟨⟨⟨⟨⟨⟨⟨⟨⟨⟨

of the first prayer], but as for the rest, if I stand for three days, I am in awestruck wonder with God and feel no weariness at all. Behold that labour of many years and what limitless rest it bore![12]

STRATEGY IN THE FACE OF DISCOURAGEMENT:

Here is a five part strategy to help you get through the worst of it.

1. Read! The preceding story by Isaac the Syrian is one he deliberately included in his *Ascetical Homilies* for the precise purpose of helping the less experienced ward off the dangers of discouragement. You must find literature on self-transformation that gives you the immediate zeal to work right now and unshakable resolve in the face of adversity. Our website can supply some suggestions, so visit www.RockSolidLife.com.

2. Go back over our previous discussions about morale in chapter 2. Remember the axiom: "Winners never quit and quitters never win."[13] It is a basic axiom of Orthodoxy that the only defeat is to give up. Even if you slog through to the end, apparently losing the struggle, the mere fact that you have not quit guarantees success! What could be better than a guarantee of progress and success? This is why Abba Isaac tells us that it is better to die in striving than to live in our fall.[14] Remember: persistence and correct practice always demolish all obstacles and overthrow all opposition.

3. Know this too: The process of self-transformation can be working at a deep and unseen level even though for the moment you do not see visible results. All authentic traditions are agreed: the fact that you don't sense any progress is irrelevant, as difficult as that may be in our climate of instant gratification. Remind yourself that a lack of obvious results doesn't matter.

4. The consubstantiality of the human race also gives rise to this curious fact: all of your sweat and hard work also goes to help others all over the world in unseen ways that they do not, for the most part, suspect. That's why authentic traditions everywhere put such emphasis on the power of prayer for the other. To pray for others is to love and cherish them, and to live for them: "If we think clearly we shall realize that all our present and future happiness depends upon our cherishing others," writes Kelsang Gyatso.[15] Remind yourself that as long as you are working toward this, you are making progress, no matter what you "feel."

5. Look at the chart in Appendix C. It describes the stages of the plan of self-transformation laid down in this book. This will show you concretely where to go and what to do. This will enable you to maintain your sense of direction and progress even when the going gets tough. An essential condition for success in any endeavor is a path made up of measurable milestones and accomplishments. While the results of self-transformation depend on the Absolute and are out of your hands to some extent, whatever does depend on you — and that is an awful lot at the beginning — should be made to serve as a continuous and steady stream of motivators.

YOU CAN HAVE ONLY ONE REAL PURPOSE

The problem is not that we allow worldly concerns and the cares of everyday life into our lives — if that were the case we would all be doomed — but that we subconsciously ascribe the same value to them as we do to self-transformation.

Even a quick logical analysis will show you the folly of treating self-transformation as just one element in your busy life. Because it is the basis of the only true and lasting happiness you can attain and because it makes your success in worldly pursuits much more likely, it clearly has to be the first priority. If your psychosomatic being is not functioning properly, how do you expect to be happy?

If you don't hold the practice of refining and harmonizing your inner being at the center of your attention, you will be unable to maintain your mental focus during the day, to incorporate the spirit of your SSDN practice into daily activities, and to preserve your inner integrity when other people confront you with stimulation toward the passions or with various demands. Here is a method for maintaining your focus that is so powerful that I would advise you to try it for only one part of your day in the beginning, and then to expand it gradually so that you use it always and everywhere. And at the same time, this method is ludicrously simple:

ROCK SOLID LIFE PRACTICE 5.1: TRANSFORMING THE BODY

1. Divide your day into various time periods and then sub-periods organized around your activities, not around the clock. This also means that you may have more or fewer sub-periods on any given day.
2. Color code each subperiod: Red for activities where you will interact with others; Yellow for subperiods where you will be working on a specific project, but working largely alone; Purple for sub-periods that may be dangerous to your inner calm, such as a confrontation with someone, contact with an annoying person or the presence of food you like but shouldn't eat, etc. Green is Disposable Time, time you can use any way you wish;

Blue indicates sub-periods either left deliberately open or not yet determined.

3. Choose the major, definite focus of your day (Much more material on this follows in chapters 6-8). For the moment, simply preserving conscious awareness of your breath would do. Note: This focus is about preserving inner noetic integrity and has nothing to do with accomplishing any particular goal or project. Your ability to accomplish this or that task during the day will be magnified exponentially once you can preserve your inner world intact.

4. Fill in each subperiod with a separate focus. The focus of each subperiod has to be a variation on the overall focus and each "sub-focus" takes account of the likely circumstances of that part of the day. For example:

   • Major Focus for the day: Generating compassion for others

   • Green Focus: On the way to and from work, read about or think about related practices, such as the Orthodox practice of saying the Jesus Prayer for others, or the Tibetan Buddhist practice of "Exchanging Self with Others." In other Green opportunities, pray for those who need help.

   • Red Focus: Set the real happiness of the other as your highest goal and do everything to fulfill it. This works best for one-on-one encounters. For group encounters or meetings, simply try to generate compassion for all present.

   • Purple Focus: Cultivate a more intense desire for the

other to receive mercy and to overcome his or her inner and outer obstacles.

- Yellow Focus: Focus on following the breath with the mind to preserve inner calm.

- Blue Focus: Remains to be seen. In sub-periods where you are hopping back and forth between solitude and interacting with others without warning or breaks, you have to learn flexibility and how to change focus instantly.

This method is extraordinarily powerful. It will get you past the great trap of viewing each day as a single whole. If you treat your day as a single whole, despite all its many and varied circumstances and encounters, you will never be able to maintain your inner focus and integrity. Yes, it may work for a short time, but then the cares, concerns, demands of others and your own intellectual tasks will crowd it right out. You will travel through large parts of the day in a mental fog, on automatic pilot, and will arrive at the end of the day burned out because the *nous* will have spent much of the day diffused out in the world through the five senses. You will experience defeat after defeat, every day bringing further frustration until you finally quit. You will then conclude that you have no willpower.

But you will be wrong. Your previous failures were not failures of willpower in the strict sense, but occurred because you set yourself impossibly high standards using wrong assumptions and approaches.

I can't tell you how much time I personally wasted over the years until I discovered this approach. It is implicit in authentic traditions, but is seldom made explicit because these traditions developed their techniques of self-transformation in simpler and less demanding noetic circumstances. Life in the modern Western world is really quite unique in human history, and requires very particular approaches.

This method also overcomes one great trap that lots of people who want to transform their lives readily fall into headlong — the trap of believing that their worldly responsibilities are an obstacle to their inner refinement. The Orthodox Christian who dreams of living in a cave on Mount Athos while doing the weekly grocery shopping, or the Buddhist who dreams of a pilgrimage to Lhasa while changing diapers are typical examples. As St. Theophan the Recluse said, we have to find a way to make daily occupations a part of our path, to leverage their content for our own benefit. The beauty of the method just described is that it allows you to maintain your inner integrity even when the energies of the outside world of persons, events, and things collide with you and threaten your course. Once you realize that you can stay focused in the midst of these opposing energies, you will no longer be tempted to think of your worldly responsibilities as obstacles and annoyances to be gotten rid of or avoided.

SURROUNDED BY TEMPTATIONS

We often fail because we are surrounded by temptations that we seem powerless to resist. In fact, this failure is more often one of tactics than willpower.

By "temptations" I mean persons, events, and things that have an enticing or seductive quality, rather than difficult or trying situations. Temptations are major obstacles to your progress, and you must deal with them swiftly and decisively from the outset. And that's not as hard as you think. "When you start to practice refining your mind ground," writes the Preserver of the Truth, "you must take your previous subjectivity, attachments, schemes, evaluations, hopes, calculations, antagonisms and rivalries and cut right through them. Also take your previous obsessions with alcohol, sex, money, power, competition, judgment, clinging, craving, selfishness, perversity, ambition and greed, and stop each one of them."[16]

Alcohol, food, sex, money, and power are not evils in themselves, of course. It's only when you allow them to control your inner world through competition, judgment, clinging, craving, selfishness, lust, ambition, and greed that they can harm you and others. And not everyone is vulnerable to any given temptation.

For example, the chocolate chip cookie jar is neither evil in itself, nor a temptation to me personally, but I know lots of people who would succumb to it. Likewise, the temptations that would lure me in might not affect someone else.

Succumbing to temptation actually drains your noetic and even physical energy, enslaves your mind, shortens your life and leaves you empty, drained, dead and addicted — in short, it prevents the Absolute from shining through you and transforming your life.

Addiction is slavery to the environment — it robs you of your noetic independence and leaves you more and more "yin." The *nous* then ceases to function properly, and it is dethroned by those strange bedfellows, the rational mind and emotional consciousness, which set up a corrupt regime to make your life miserable. Sounds pretty awful, doesn't it? So why do we choose it again and again? Part of the reason was described by St. Paul when he said, "The flesh lusts against the spirit and the spirit against the flesh" (Gal. 5:17; translation mine). At this point we are still caught up in the pleasure-pain dynamic of the fallen world, on that merry-go-round that goes nowhere, and it's high time we got off!

The second aspect is temptations that entice us to relax our Program and our discipline. Whereas the first group of temptations mentioned sap our will by leading us into the world of addiction, the second group leads us straight into negligence. Negligence is a great vice. "Negligence," said Joseph the Hesychast, "is like a drought in which nothing grows… it does not permit the fallen to get up. In general, negligence spells destruction for those it holds captive."[17] You cannot succeed without persistent effort, which negligence makes

THE 5 PILLARS OF LIFE

impossible. In the words of an ancient Taoist master: "Make determination endure. If you want to accomplish something that endures unchanging, it requires work that endures unceasingly. Don't be afraid of hard work. With strength of mind one will climb to the summit; *if you are afraid of hard work, you will never enter the real.*"[18] [emphasis mine]

This kind of temptation could be nothing more than the presence of an easier alternative to what your Program tells you you should be doing: It might be just the television, or a chair in the sunshine with a good book and a cold beer. Now, there is nothing wrong with relaxing. The question is, is this relaxation part of the Program and is it replenishing your energy or is it a temptation that will sap your energy?

One thing is for sure: "If you work hard only when you are in the mood, but then get distracted by things and slack off when this mood wanes, then your spirit is influenced and your energy is taken away when you are not practicing, just like someone who has no accomplishment at all."[19]

Chapter 8 deals with methods for confronting various temptations, and I won't repeat them here in detail. For now I present you with a single example of how to overcome one simple temptation so that you can see how willpower fits into the equation:

The scenario is as follows: You are hopelessly addicted to cookies. You eat several every day and you now realize that you are harming yourself physically and have become addicted mentally. Here is a gradual, step-by-step method for reversing your downfall:

1. Minimize the damage: Get a supply of healthy cookies containing no harmful ingredients. Eat these for one week with no other restrictions.

2. Confine and limit your consumption by a fixed number per day and only at prearranged times. The parameters you set should be slightly uncomfortable but feasible. Continue this for one week.

THE RULES TRAP

A young Orthodox woman in her early twenties once came to me and asked if going to movies was a sin. She was rather startled when I told her the real question was the effect of the movie on her inner world. She never came back. Some people are actually looking for rules, for some external authority to absolve them of the responsibility of using their freedom constructively. The tragedy is that we can never have a true encounter with the Absolute outside of love, and love demands freedom. This is why a life lived by abstract moral rules is a trap. Dostoevsky graphically illustrated this point in his story of the Grand Inquisitor in *The Brothers Karamazov*. The Grand Inquisitor would legislate morality and force everyone to "be good," and yet winds up actually opposing God!

3. The third and fourth weeks, plan it so that you run out of cookies for the last two days of the week. Taste the battle that arises inside you and get used to it. Make sure that no one offers you any cookies either. You must be 100 percent committed to going without for the two days. Prefer death to surrender.

4. Plan to go through the fifth week without cookies. Don't even buy them. And don't buy any other sweets to substitute for them. Continue this on alternate weeks for one month. At the end of each week of abstaining from cookies, ask yourself how you feel. In fact, keep a journal for the duration of the project. The results will convince you that you feel better and function better without the cookies.

Does this mean you can never eat cookies again? No, I didn't say that. The important thing is not to fall back into the addiction again. With cookies, it's easy to see that you may be able to have them now and again without falling back into your old habit pattern. With substances that are physically addictive, like alcohol, there is no going back ever for the ex-alcoholic — it is just too dangerous. As for tobacco, there can be no compromise at all. Smoking is incompatible with self-transformation and that's all there is to it. End of story.

MIRACULOUS
ANCIENT FORMULA
‹‹‹‹‹‹‹ 4 ‹‹‹‹‹‹‹

Harnessing the Power of Intent

‹‹‹‹‹‹‹‹‹‹‹‹‹‹‹‹

As a basic principle, you have to train yourself not to evaluate situations according to abstract moral rules, like "cookies are sinful." The real question is whether or not you are addicted, whether your inner noetic independence has been compromised. And yes, there are always people who try desperately to fool themselves and who use the freedom from social convention offered by every authentic tradition as a cover for their own vice. But that is not a reason to prefer a regime of moral rules, because moral rules obscure the reality of the situation. Moreover, they are poor motivators because they are usually expressed negatively.

The human willpower is incredibly powerful, as shown by St. Isaac's true story of the philosopher who had resolved to keep silent. If we find ourselves unable to harness it at the moment, this does not mean the power does not exist within us, only that we have not yet understood the rules of its use. When we focus our willpower on a limited goal, we are using what I call "intent." Only by learning the use and rules of intent can we harness the vast resources of willpower that lie dormant within us.

Life in the post-industrial age is characterized by widespread discontent, by the feeling of being trapped by the circumstances of life, hemmed in by them on all sides and unable to escape. This feeling is pervasive in our society and results in untold stress, illness and depression in the lives of millions of human beings.

Brian Tracy, a leading authority on success and personal achievement, summarizes this perfectly in what he calls the "Law of Control": "The Law of Control says that you feel positive about yourself to the degree to which you feel you are in control of your life."[20] So one of the main symptoms of the malaise of our times is this gnawing feeling of a loss of control. We exist, but we don't live; we survive, but we don't triumph.

In fact, this feeling is only a symptom, not the problem itself. The real problems are beneath the surface and are twofold. First, the feeling that life is out of control is grounded in a lack of time — we are so busy that we have very little "disposable time" left.

By this point in the program, you will have discovered that you have much more disposable time than you originally thought, simply because you fritter away less of it and are more focused. And the more you refine your Program, the more disposable time you will have.

The second problem hiding behind the feeling of the loss of control is our belief in our own powerlessness. There are two kinds of belief in our own powerlessness, one healthy and one destructive. The healthy one is experiential knowledge that all real power comes from the Absolute. Joseph the Hesychast once said that if he could write a book, he would call it "Man is Nothing!"[21] Over against this there is the neurotic belief that "no matter what I do, I can't change my life." This, too, is a conclusion based on experience. It's a false conclusion, to be sure, but those who say this are going on the evidence they've seen. Fr. Joseph, on the other hand, would never agree. He changed his own life radically, adopted a program of self-transformation and knew all too well the centrality and indispensability of the human will in effecting the transformation he sought.

These two problems, the feelings of lack of time and our own powerlessness, have persistently sabotaged all the best efforts of many of us for years. We become habituated to failure and convinced nothing will make a difference. This is how we have ended up where we are now – beaten and demoralized.

The ancient traditions of self-transformation are about to give you your morale back. If you will apply what follows in the rest of this chapter, you will be astounded at your ability to make meaningful change in your life.

THE USE OF INTENT

What is intent? It is the ability to apply your willpower to a specific situation in order to obtain the desired outcome. As stated previously, our problem is that we have so often tasted defeat in the realm of self-transformation that we scarcely believe we have any hope of winning. The most important objective in this chapter is to teach you how to reverse this situation, because it is absolutely imperative to your progress that you taste victory, and repeatedly at that. In the words of Elder Joseph, "We must win."[22] This will only happen when you clearly understand how to create victories and avoid defeats.

Carlos Castaneda's mentor, Don Juan, summed up the use of intent like this: "[It] begins with a single act that has to be deliberate, precise and sustained. If the act is repeated long enough, one acquires a sense of unbending intent, which can be applied to anything else."[23]

The key is this: Your victories start off very small. Each victory must be a struggle so you know you have won in a battle. And yet each can be small enough to make the victory feasible. Once the dynamic of victory, which I have called here the Rules of Intent, are mastered, there will be no stopping you.

The following two examples demonstrate how the Rules of Intent determine success and failure (yes, it's playing by these rules, and not your "willpower," that determines whether you will succeed or fail at any endeavor!). The examples are simplistic but deliberately so in order to show the stark contrast between life according to the Rules of Intent and life against them.

- Example One: Susan decides that because it's New Year's Day she is going to start a new health program of improved diet and regular exercise. She has a vague sense of discomfort about her fitness level and believes she has gained a few pounds. Susan has a book describing exactly the program she wants to use and, although her daily schedule is already busy, she is confident she can spare an hour or so three times a week to go to the gym nearby. She also plans to resume her old favorite of going for an early morning run every day or two.

- Example Two: Janet has decided that she absolutely must see the season finale of her favorite television show, a two-hour special airing in a week's time. She immediately talks it over with her husband, who agrees not only to support her, but to watch it with her. Then she lines up her sister to take care of the kids at the sister's house. She then decides that she will unplug the telephone while the show is on, keeping her cell phone on in case of an emergency with the kids. She won't answer the door either, which should take care of any possible interruptions. But just in case, she will also tape the program as she watches it.

Now, which of these two has the greater chance of success? You're probably going to object that the answer is too obvious for words, that this whole section is just a setup that uses examples that are too ridiculous to be helpful. If so, I understand, but bear with me. Let's look at the scenarios individually:

- Example One:

  1. Susan has obviously decided to go it alone. She doesn't have a coach at the gym or a support group for her running. As for the diet, she's taking that from a book. She may have shared her New Year's resolution with a friend or two, but they are in no position to help her. Has she even asked for expert opinions about the worth of the book she is pinning all her hopes on?

  2. The gym sessions and the running are just two more

THE 5 PILLARS OF LIFE

Table 5.1: Susan's Mathematical Chances of Success

	Yes	No
Goal positively defined?		X
Goal measurably defined?		X
Adequate mentor/group support?		X
Integrated into program/schedule?		X
Obstacles anticipated?		X
Sufficient desire generated?		X
Sufficient revulsion generated?		X

things to cram into her already packed schedule. None of the other elements of her schedule has been moved or adjusted to make room for the new plan.

3. The three disciplines she has decided to adopt — the gym, the running and the dietary changes — are all uncomfortable to some extent, so she will need a very strong motivation to succeed.

4. But since she is operating on a vague feeling that she's a bit out of shape and may have gained some weight, it's unlikely that she has generated either the desire or the revulsion needed to succeed. Worse still, she has defined her goals in a negative way — losing weight and becoming less unfit.

5. And without having measured the problem, she can't

measure the solution either. She can't measure the fitness level she wants or the weight she wants or, for that matter, how she will know when she has attained a sufficiently healthy diet, even according to the book she is going by. Her only target is a vague and indefinite idea of sticking indefinitely to her new regime.

6. Susan hasn't planned what to do when her schedule interferes with her gym dates or her running. Rather than scheduling the gym sessions, she has the vague idea of getting there three times a week. Will she persevere when she starts to worry during her exercise sessions about other things she should be doing? Will she go running in the morning if it's raining or snowing? She hasn't taken these obstacles into account and is about to find that out the hard way.

Susan's plan conforms perfectly to the seven reasons for failure outlined at the beginning of this chapter. Personally, I would give her no more than a 5 to 10 percent chance of success. In fact, I'd be willing to bet that her efforts have collapsed by the end of February! It's not surprising that every major health club "bulges at the seams" every January, yet their classes have tapered off to "the regulars" by March.

- Example Two:

    1. Janet, on the other hand, is not going it alone. She has already leveraged the help she needs to ensure her plan can work: of the three other people in the house, one (her husband) supports her and the other two (the kids) will be removed for the duration of the event.

    2. Janet's existing schedule won't interfere. At that time in the evening she would normally be putting the kids to

Table 5.2: Janet's Mathematical Chances of Success

	Yes	No
Goal positively defined?	X	
Goal measurably defined?	X	
Adequate mentor/group support?	X	
Integrated into program/schedule?	X	
Obstacles anticipated?	X	
Sufficient desire generated?	X	
Sufficient revulsion generated?	N/A	

bed anyway, so she has effectively altered her existing schedule to give adequate room to this one-time event.

3. Her goal is a pleasurable one, and something she is eagerly anticipating.

4. She defines the goal positively and by constantly looking forward to the event in her mind — seeing what promises to be a good program — and also sharing the experience with her husband without interference from young children — she is generating a very strong desire several times per day.

5. Her goal is easily measurable in time and space. She will have no doubt about having achieved it or not. And more importantly, she will experience the immediate gratification of achieving it.

6. She has anticipated the likely obstacles and planned around them. And if all else fails, she has a back-up plan — to tape the program.

Janet will almost certainly succeed. Even in the unlikely event that something goes seriously awry — suppose one of the kids gets the flu — her backup plan will probably work. The chances of a confluence of circumstances overwhelming her plan are minimal. I would give her a 95 percent+ chance of success.

There it is. Do you see how we have so often made our own successes and failures? Susan violated all of the Rules of Intent and so she set herself up for failure. Janet inadvertently followed them and is almost guaranteed to succeed. It's true that Example Two seems incomparably easier, but the fact is that no matter how easy or difficult a goal is, you can achieve it if you respect the Rules of Intent.

The most basic principle of using intent is this: It is better to take one small and measurable objective at a time, no matter how small it may be, and to do it thoroughly and successfully, than to take on larger or more numerous goals or objectives and fail miserably across the board. Susan violated this basic principle by choosing a goal with no definable end in time, making it overwhelmingly large. She set herself up for the "agony of defeat," not the thrill of victory.

After a lifetime of perceived failure, you may not even understand what a thrill it is to experience success, knowing that you planned it and made it happen, and that you can repeat the experience at will in any area of your life!

This is the basis of belief, because your success feeds your belief in what is possible. The more you succeed, the more you believe you can succeed. That's why you should always start small, with an objective that you believe you can achieve, even though it may be somewhat challenging. From there, your belief in the possible grows and grows, and you begin to experience a feeling of power. Then finally, after you have experienced many victories, you enter into new realms of human existence hitherto unsuspected, where all you can do is prepare yourself and the results are out of your hands. And this is where you experience that

OVERWHELMING FORCE

During the Cold War, the Soviet Union anticipated a war against NATO in the heart of Europe, and to that end maintained huge armored formations totaling six thousand battle tanks and over a quarter of a million men in East Germany. These would have attempted to break through NATO lines, penetrate into the relatively unprotected rear areas, and bring about the collapse of Allied Forces in short order.

Although the war never came, we can learn some useful lessons from Soviet military strategy. To engineer the crucial breakthrough, the Soviets determined that only the offensive thrusts making headway would be reinforced. Those that stalled would be left to their fate. Once a thrust started to push through enemy lines, it would be quickly and automatically reinforced by special formations held at the regiment, division and army levels for just this purpose. So the longer Soviet prospects appeared promising, the more Soviet forces would mass at the potential breakthrough point, changing what initially may have been only a two to one superiority in the Soviets' favor into a local superiority of up to twenty to one!

Now consider this from the **NATO** side: The worse your situation becomes, the worse it is about to become.

From the Soviet perspective, once a hole in the enemy line appears, a huge crescendo of brute force descends on that hole in an incredibly concentrated fashion and with a single objective; to keep the hole open, to widen it, and to pour more and more forces through it. It becomes like the mythical pin-sized hole in the dam that begins as a drip and ends as an unstoppable flood.

The use of intent is exactly like this — a huge concentration of force is focused on a very small key point, forcing it to collapse. This method is nearly foolproof — a good thing, since we are all such ingenious fools much of the time. You will taste victory this way, and then you will know by experience that you have the power to change your life.

genuine and healthy sense of human powerlessness that Joseph the Hesychast alluded to earlier. But for now you must learn and master the secrets of success.

THE RULES OF INTENT

Once you learn and apply the following rules in your life, you will be well on your way to mastering your willpower.

1. Your overarching purposes or objectives must be broken down into numerous smaller and measurable stepping stones or goals. We often fail because we insist on taking on so much that our efforts are hopelessly diffused. The correct use of intent involves concentrating all of our powers and resources on a single point.

2. You must work smarter, not harder, to quote a current cliché. That is, you must apply intent to levers and very selectively. When the anonymous pilgrim of nineteenth-century Russia wanted to learn real Christianity, his elder didn't tell him to go and master church music. Beautiful as it is, church music is a boulder — it is a tool, not a goal (see chapter 2). And the more single-mindedly you pursue it, the more it will actually impede your inner progress. This is why his elder told him to concentrate on noetic prayer, the ultimate lever. So make sure your effort uses levers!

3. Your goals must be measurable. "I want to stop judging other people" is a laudable goal but it's not measurable. "From ten to eleven tomorrow I will be in a situation that often leads me to judge other people. But for that one hour I will prepare myself and will think only good of everyone I encounter." That is a measurable goal. It's limited in time and is easily verified.

4. The limited subgoal you are focusing your intent on must be part of your overall strategy so that all your efforts are congruent and you don't work against yourself. For example, on a day when you want to practice obedience, don't set sticking to your own agenda and fending off the demands of others as a priority. Both have their place, but they don't mix too well.

5. Your subgoals must be within your power to accomplish. The pilgrim's elder, for example, didn't tell him to "achieve unceasing prayer of the heart within a month," but rather told him to do a certain number of repetitions of the Jesus Prayer per day. Unceasing prayer isn't something you can "achieve" in the usual sense; all you can do is prepare yourself to receive it, and it's this preparation that the elder directed the pilgrim to do.

6. Your preparation must be meticulous. Nothing that lies within your control must be left to chance either physically or mentally.

7. Your motivation must reach the point of burning desire. To you it must become a matter of life and death. "What can you not accomplish," writes a Taoist master, "if you do it in deadly earnest?"[24]

8. You must believe on every level of your being that the goal is attainable. If you think you will fail, you are probably quite right. Likewise, if you think you will succeed, you likely will. What you think and believe becomes reality, and your thinking can be changed deliberately and by you. Chapter 6

PARADOX
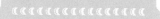
5.3

The true Warrior can never lose, because he or she has learned how to win even in defeat.

explains more about that. My experience in the martial arts always showed me that if you believed you could beat your opponent in a tournament situation, you almost always would. The loser was almost always the one who either lost this belief first, or didn't have it to start with.

A Word on Failure

We are such as success-driven culture that we are often afraid to fail. And so this fear holds us back from ever trying, absolving us even of the responsibility of trying. Part of the wisdom of this traditional path of self-transformation is that success is built on failure — we learn from our mistakes and become wiser and more experienced.

When I said, "You must taste victory," I did not mean that you should never taste defeat. Even in worldly pursuits, those who succeed are those who are most willing to fail, and those who have the longest string of failures behind them. Failure is like the manure in your garden: it may smell bad, but without it you will never see the beautiful flowers you want. Robert Kiyosaki's "rich dad" put it quite elegantly: "Losers are people who think that losing is bad."[25]

Studies in the field of education have shown that if a child is put into a supportive school environment that encourages risk-taking and supports failure, the child will be much more willing to take appropriate risks in later life. Unfortunately, too many of us have been traumatized by home and school environments more built on the 'fail-blame-shame' paradigm than on real education.

In the world of self-transformation though, there is another dynamic going on. When you apply all the Rules of Intent to any particular goal, when your preparation is thorough and you give it all you've got until you finally collapse in defeat despite a 100 percent effort, you still have not failed. If you really gave it all you had and were defeated nevertheless, you will find no sense of failure in your heart afterwards, no sense of guilt. Yes, you will know intellectually that you failed to attain your goal, and yet you'll still have a strange sense of gain. This is why the Warrior never loses, even when he or she is defeated. As St. Theophan the Recluse puts it: "Asceticism is ceaseless triumph."[26]

Our sense of failure usually comes from a failure of determination on our part, when our will to win flags during the last and most difficult part of the execution phase, when we give up before giving it everything we've got. This always leaves us with the vague consciousness that our loss was due to ourselves. Essentially, we withdraw from the battlefield to avoid further discomfort.

The dynamics of inner warfare and the externally visible wars of this world differ on this point. The military commander wisely withdraws from a battle he cannot win in order to protect his resources. The practitioner of inner transformation, on the other hand, knows that staying on the battlefield and taking a pounding will actually increase his power. "Do not lose your nerve;" writes Fr. Ephraim, "Our objective is not to turn our backs to the enemy in despair."[27] He is willing to accept both pain and defeat in order to come out stronger and demoralize his enemies. "Cursed is the man who does the works of the Lord carelessly, keeping back his sword from blood" (Jer. 48:10; translation mine).

So the real key to self-transformation in general and to mastering intent in particular is to literally prefer death to surrender. Chapter 6 explains more about this principle.

You have already seen that Wang Liping had to repeatedly endure sitting in a full lotus position for a grueling four hours at a stretch and that his only choices were to win or to pass out from the pain. Note that either outcome was acceptable to his old masters who, knowing full well the dynamics of self-transformation, sought to keep their young apprentice from failure, but not from defeat.

In the world of self-transformation, this stage is absolutely critical.

Literally everything depends on this: that you fix a goal, that you apply the Rules of Intent to it, and that once you put your plan into effect, you go for it with all the resources of your entire being, and that you push forward until you either win or collapse.

The deep reason this process works so well is that the ego is built on the fear of death, on the "deification" of biological survival above all else. So when we accept death in the pursuit of self-transformation — the real goal of which is to attain perfect love — we actualize life on a totally different basis. In a concrete and "incarnate" way (i.e., a way that is not merely abstract and intellectual) we are saying that life depends on love and truth, and not on biological survival. This also explains why authentic traditions have extolled martyrdom.[28]

The "bloodless martyrdom" of self-refinement is a practical and incarnate acknowledgement that the universe is a mystery, that there is an Absolute, that to follow this Absolute and to pattern one's life after it is the ultimate good, no matter what the temporal and biological outcome may be.

On this level, intent overcomes all obstacles. We taste victory in our pursuit of transforming our lives, perhaps for the first time, and this taste becomes the basis for the growing certainty of continuous victories in the future. Now we know that we really can change our lives because we have seen the proof with our own eyes.

When we understand and apply the Rules of Intent our lives change forever. We are like a lumberjack who, after years of using an axe to cut down trees, is suddenly given a chain saw, so that every tree no matter how large falls quickly and easily. If you have ever tried to cut down a good-sized tree with nothing but an axe, you can appreciate the vast difference between the two.

The following is your "graduation exercise" for this chapter, in a series of four short assignments. Once you put these exercises into practice, your very ideas about "willpower" will change forever. Never again will your willpower fail you and never again will you question your own ability to change your life.

ROCK SOLID LIFE PRACTICE 5.2: APPLYING INTENT

For each of these assignments you will be applying the methods explained in this chapter. In other words, you will have to:

1. Define your goal in a measurable way
2. Define your goal in a positive way
3. Develop sufficient desire
4. Develop sufficient revulsion
5. Prepare meticulously
6. Devise a workable plan
7. Find adequate support and guidance

Assignment 5.2.1: The Body

This assignment will help you prove to yourself that you really can modify your world in a substantial way. Your objective is to choose a physical goal that you would like to accomplish in any one of several areas. It could be to lose weight, to gain a centimeter of muscle around your bicep, to do ten push-ups, or anything similar. The main point is that whatever you chose as a goal, it must be:

1. Meaningful for you, something your really want to accomplish
2. Something that is limited enough that you can accomplish it in relatively short order
3. Large enough to measure so that when you do accomplish it there will be no doubt you have done so. For example, don't set losing one pound as a goal, because it's too small an amount to measure accurately
4. A goal that fits in with your overall plan of self-transformation

Assignment 5.2.2: Addiction

Choose something that you are "addicted" to, that is, something that you would be hard pressed to give up. But do not use any of the true physical addictions like smoking and drinking — these are bio-chemical problems as well, and are not suitable for this assignment. The kind of "addiction" you're looking for could be food, like our chocolate-chip cookie example, or just the habit of turning on the television at a particular time every day, or taking a hot bath, or any number of other things. Just make sure that whatever you choose corresponds to the same criteria as those in Assignment 5.2.1.

Assignment 5.2.3: Relationships

Here you are going to choose a relationship with another person, but it must be a relationship that has been troublesome for you — an impatient boss or an ungrateful teenager, perhaps. However, do not pick a relationship where the emotional content is overwhelming, as in the case of someone who has abused you as a child, for example. Your goal is to deliberately engage in this relationship for a definite time period and to control your own thoughts and actions with respect to the other person. Start small — go for an hour, then work up to a day. You will have to decide on a definite plan of action designed to show good will to the other, and to keep the welfare of the other in mind throughout the period. Your goal, I repeat, is only to act perfectly in the relationship, and not to have the relationship turn out in a particular way. If you try to make it go a certain way, you fall into the trap of setting up as a goal something you don't control — the reactions of the other person.

Assignment 5.2.4: Your Program

Here your assignment is to go for one week without deviating from your Program. When you accomplish every element in it without giving in to laziness, negligence, temptations or the energies of others that are constantly side-swiping you, then you can say with assurance that you have

1. understood the process of setting up the program, and
2. developed the power of intent necessary to apply it.

When this happens there is no stopping you — you have found and internalized an essential part of the path toward a new life full of undreamt-of possibilities. Chapter 6 introduces you into this new life in more detail, so read on...

Key to harnessing Intent: Intent is pure action. It is an action, not a concept. And it is pure because it is utterly selfless. It is not defiled by thoughts of success or failure, victory or defeat, nor even of life and death.

Chapter Six

the WARRIOR'S WORLD: RECLAIMING YOUR TRUE HUMAN LIFE

"The Kingdom of Heaven suffers violence and the violent take it by force," said Christ. In the Orthodox Church, a person about to be baptized is referred to as a "newly enlisted Warrior." And when someone becomes a monk or nun, he or she is handed a prayer rope and told: "Take, brother (or sister), the sword of the spirit." According to St. Ignaty Brianchaninov, a former army officer, our life is a war that has many of the same features as the wars of this world. It lacks only a declaration of war.[1] In the words of St. Silouan of Athos, our war rages every moment of every day.[2] Joseph the Hesychast wrote to a disciple of his who was suffering from the violence of this war, "So, at the time of battle, when you are firing shots and bullets, don't expect them (passions and demons) to throw marshmallows and chocolates!"[3]

Lama Chögyam Trungpa says that warriorship is the key to the Tibetan Buddhism in which he was raised, and correctly notes that the

Warrior's approach to life also belongs to traditions in India, China, Japan, Korea, to the indigenous peoples of North and South America and even the Judeo-Christian tradition. Warriorship, he says, is an approach to life, and is the opposite of violence against others.[4]

Taoist sources call the road to self-transformation a battle, meaning it necessitates "vigorous and intense refinement" and that "the whole body flows with sweat" during the struggle.[5]

So everywhere and at all times, the search for perfection and self-transformation has been likened to a war. All authentic traditions talk about it in these terms. It means that any attempt on our part to change our life demands considerable struggle. After all, if you take the path of least resistance, you'll simply vegetate in front of the television.

You may find the Warrior paradigm unattractive at first. Perhaps you equate inner transformation and spirituality with peace. The great paradox, though, is that the only way to find perfect peace is through war. This is why the New Age pursuit of ease and feel-good pseudo-mysticism is such a waste of time and why it can never fulfill its promise of bringing you lasting peace and happiness.

Life in this world is like a hurricane. Most people live on the outer rim, where the storm rages. Our path takes us through the storm and into the center, where perfect peace reigns. So, yes, there is a state when the violence and struggle come to an end. Once we've actually achieved our goal, the inner struggle and conflict that characterize our beginning stages disappear, and while trials coming from external circumstances (e.g., illness, torture, poverty, hunger) may continue, they no longer bother us. After a certain point in his training, Wang Liping was no longer affected internally by outer events. One of his teachers said to him: "Now you are not the same as other people. Now all you need in this world is a bowl of food to eat. The rest is extra. Understand?"[6] In the words of Varsanuphios the Great, "...the sailor has crossed the sea."[7] As for ourselves, we haven't yet crossed it, and perhaps we're just packing our bags to head down to the sea shore, so we need to be prepared for the fact that this journey is not always easy.

Success in our endeavor depends very greatly on adopting certain attitudes and perspectives. These attitudes and perspectives comprise the Warrior's way of life, and anyone who strives to adopt them and live by them is a Warrior, irrespective of gender, age, background, or occupation. It is a life of great contrasts, of great joy and incomparable benefit to you and to those around you.

Some people are put off by the Warrior paradigm because they equate the word with gratuitous violence, aggression, haughtiness, or similar evils. This is simply a wrong interpretation. Warriorship is not an expression of male dominance, and still less of aggressiveness or arrogance. Warriorship is what you have just finished learning part of in chapter 5: It is a deliberate and purposeful approach to every aspect of life. There I developed the notion of the will and explained how to use Intent to prove to yourself that you really can change your life. This chapter discusses in more general terms the overall "atmosphere" and strategies necessary for success. But again, all of this depends totally on two things: (1) You have already laid a firm foundation of regular sitting practice, and (2) You have learned how to apply the Rules of Intent correctly, on however small a scale.

Warriorship as a paradigm for approaching life has gained more currency in recent years, partly through the works of Carlos Castaneda, Dan Millman and others. Many of these strands are well summarized in Robert L. Spencer's book *The Craft of the Warrior*. Despite the New Age bent of some of these sources, I believe the Warrior paradigm is still worth using, partly in order to reclaim it from any such connotations, because it is far too precious a thing to lose. The Warrior paradigm has a long history all over the world and it would be a shame, if not a disaster, to let it fall uncontested into the hands of the misinformed.

Ancient sources take for granted that their Warrior approach is built upon and depends upon the inner refinement of the mind, and so unfortunately they have no need to explain this refinement and how to do it. The modern sources are often ignorant of this dimension and so either ignore it or underestimate its importance or, worst of all, present it in a totally secularized context and with incorrect practices.

Here you have, for the first time, a step-by-step training program with clear guidelines solidly based on authentic traditions. In other words, these are strategies that have been "clinically tested" by countless people for millennia. They work, but only if you put them into practice. Ah, there's the rub!

THE FEMALE WARRIOR:
WARRIORSHIP IS NOT A MACHO THING

Warriorship is a set of attitudes and an approach to life that produce great self-mastery, incredible subtlety of perception and a self-forgetting heart burning with compassion. It is therefore not a Rambo-like approach to life. It does not correspond to any of Hollywood's macho icons. Perhaps the only Hollywood icon it does correspond to in many ways is Kwai-Chang Kaine, the hero of the movie *Kung Fu* and its two offshoot television series. Kwai-Chang is a true Warrior: He is modest, gentle, and compassionate, while very skilled, very disciplined, and very powerful. He knows what he seeks, he knows how to get there and no one and nothing is able to knock him off his path. And yet, for all that, he remains humble and loving.

Not all Warriors are martial artists, though — far from it. Warriorship is an internal affair and its external manifestations vary greatly. In fact, the association of the martial arts with self-transformation is a particularly oriental phenomenon, and one not universal even there, despite what the entertainment industry would have you believe. One Taoist source even lists martial arts among the distractions to be avoided for those who want to make serious headway![8]

Arrogance, hatred, aggression, and violence against others — all these things come easily to us. This is our default setting in the fallen world, a simple, easy and seductive path leading straight to the disintegration of our inner world and therefore to death on every level. In other words, it is the very opposite of Warriorship. But to be

TABLE 6.1: Advantages and Disadvantages of Women

Advantages of Women	Disadvantages of Women
Meticulous at organization and planning	Can lose sight of the "big picture"
Sensitive to feelings; intuitive	Vulnerable to mood swings and emotional storms
Less enslaved to reason	Judgment impaired by emotions
Nurturing, mothering	Indecisive and vacillating
Practical, down to earth	Comfort loving

patient in trials, to be self-sacrificing, to be humble in the face of arrogance, loving in the face of hatred, unconcerned with oneself in times of danger; these are some of the universally recognized measures of true humanity. There are many aspects of violence in the Warrior's way of life: decisiveness, tenacity, an uncompromising will to win. But unlike the violence associated with evil, this is not the product of a passionate sickness of the soul. And, it is never directed against others, except in the most rare and unusual circumstances. True Warriors are extraordinarily warm and kind, because they, and only they, are free from themselves, from the ego that so torments everyone else.

Women are just as well suited to the Warrior's path as men. Although the Warrior image would be interpreted by most people as a masculine one, that's not the real intent, and a woman should not let herself be put off by it. There have been many peerless female Warriors in Orthodoxy and in other traditions because, not surprisingly, women have many advantages over men in their pursuit of self-transformation.

The fact is that each sex has its own stereotypic advantages and disadvantages. Here are some of them. But remember, these are generalizations. They are generally true but they may not be true for you.

TABLE 6.2: Advantages and Disadvantages of Men

Advantages of Men	Disadvantages of Men
Can approach problems without undue emotional bias	Fails to develop and use intuition; seduced by what seems "logical"
Decisive	"Shoot first, ask questions later" approach
Can see the big picture	Impulsive: Loses sight of details

I've used masculine pronouns in this chapter when talking about the Warrior, but only because it's standard English usage — English is unfortunately much more gender specific than some of Orthodoxy's native languages, such as Greek and Russian/Slavonic. But if you're a woman, I would encourage you to substitute "she" for "he" so that you give yourself a feeling for what the life of the female Warrior is like and to encourage yourself on the path. Otherwise, you may end up unintentionally giving your subconscious the wrong message, the message that you can't succeed at self-transformation, that it's a "men only" club. Nothing could be further from the truth. And, in relation to the Absolute we seek, we are all equally yin or "feminine" in a very profound way, as every authentic tradition maintains.

The history of self-transformation shows that the two sexes tend to "converge" on the path: the more progress a person makes, the more he or she develops those traits traditionally ascribed to the opposite sex. Men tend to become more gentle, peaceful and compassionate: "Staretz Silouan," writes Fr. Sophrony, "had an astonishingly tender, loving heart [and a great]... sensitivity and swift response to any kind of sorrow,"[9] although he was above average in height and very strong physically. Women become more determined and decisive. A fourth-century desert hermit, Mother Sarah, once chided her male counterparts that she was more of a man than any of them.[10] She meant by this that she was outdoing them on the path of self-transformation. As we progress, we overcome the fallen default settings typical of our own sex.

THE 5 PILLARS OF LIFE

WOMEN UNDER CHRISTIANITY

There is a general belief in Western culture that Christianity, and perhaps all "Semitic religions," are innately oppressive to women. And certainly present day Islam tends only to reinforce that notion. But the notion is wrong: It is very specific to the later "Christian" experience of the West European/North American civilization in particular and is based on a number of historical trends. The first was the confusion in the Western Church between clergy and monasticism. The enforced celibacy of the clergy meant a Church run by people who did not and could not understand women or sympathize with them, or with family life in general. If you add to this the innately chauvinistic tendencies of the Frankish (i.e., Germanic) culture that came to dominate the West from the ninth century on, then you have a real problem. It's quite interesting that during the first exchanges between the East Roman Empire and the pubescent Frankish Empire in the eighth century, Frankish Emperor Charlemagne was scandalized by the fact that the East Romans were ruled at the time by a woman!

A fascinating example from the fifth century is found in the life of St. Mary of Egypt. Mary was a repentant harlot who had been living alone in the foreboding Transjordanian Desert for some forty years before her existence was discovered by a wandering priest-monk, Fr. Zosima. When this woman (whom he had never met) spoke his name, Zosima realized that she must be holy, a completely transformed person. So despite the fact that he was a priest, he prostrated to the ground before her and asked her blessing — a complete reversal of the usual situation. She in turn did the same to him, saying it was up to him to bless her, since he was a priest. He insisted that she was holy and should therefore bless him. Eventually, after several minutes of standoff, the holy woman relented and gave the blessing. So each sex finds its fulfillment on the Warrior's path.

In every tradition of self-transformation there are examples of women of extraordinary achievement.[11] One legendary Taoist master, Sun Pu-erh, actually outdid her husband on the road to perfection, even though the same teacher had taught them both. After attaining the Tao she returned to give her spouse some pointers.[12]

Authentic traditions have been the great equalizer between the sexes throughout history, strange as that may seem to the Western reader, who has been brainwashed into believing that nothing good ever happened to women before the modern feminist movement. Authentic traditions consider the struggle for self-transformation to be life's only worthwhile quest, and in this one and only worthy endeavor, men and women have an equal playing field.

On the Warrior path, your sexual identity attains its true meaning and finds its place in the yin and yang balance of the universe. Unfortunately, Western people at the moment have very little feel for the subtle interplay of yin and yang in creation. This makes it nearly impossible for us as Westerners to understand the real nature of the roles of the sexes in any traditional society, whether Orthodox, Oriental, or whatever else.

ATTITUDES AND MOODS OF THE WARRIOR

Most people's worldviews are a mishmash of the attitudes current in the surrounding culture in general, combined with or modified by prior conditioning, specifically by family, friends and peer group.

Attitude, as I use the word here, means the basic presuppositions about the nature of existence — i.e. the worldview. *Mood*, in contrast, is the atmosphere or ethos that you adopt internally. Whereas ordinary people accept their own attitude without question and make little effort to control their mood, the Warrior works hard to bring both under conscious control.

Western man has a very particular existential stance, very different from that of any other culture that has ever existed. Cultures associated with authentic traditions had a clear sense of the human person as the "microcosm and mediator" of creation, as deeply and organically connected to the natural world on every level, yet somehow above it. For the West, though, this is no longer the case. For centuries now Western man has viewed the natural world as a neutral backdrop, a stage on which the drama of his life is played out. He sees the natural world as hostile, an enemy to protect himself from on the one hand, and as a source of raw material on the other. So

INNER PRINCIPLE
6.1

The primary difference between the Warrior and the ordinary person is precisely this: the Warrior chooses his cultural paradigm, and chooses his attitudes, all quite deliberately.

it's hardly surprising that he has developed a medical science obsessed with protecting the body from external pathogens, while largely ignoring the body's real connection with both the mind and the natural world, and that he has developed an economy based on the rape of natural resources, an economy which has polluted the water, air and food supply to the point of endangering his very survival.

So, strange as it may seem, the radical conformist in the business suit and the scruffy deviant whose life is "sex, drugs, and rock 'n roll" actually do share most cultural values. They may express them very differently, but their attitudes and reactions to external stimuli are largely identical, and are quite different from the attitudes and reactions of non-Western people. In other words, Western culture, and probably any other culture for that matter, inculcates a relatively narrow range of attitudes into its people. The culture does this in ways that are hidden but very thorough. The main question to ask then is "How accurate and therefore how useful is the cultural paradigm that I have been fed since childhood?" And also, "Have I been fed the same cultural paradigm in the context of family life as out in society?"

The Warrior constantly re-examines his cultural paradigm, and he chooses his moods based on the attitudes he has adopted. And by aligning his attitudes, his moods and his objectives, he develops strategies and tactics for attaining his objectives. This allows the Warrior to evaluate every day what he is up against and how to deal with it. He treats reality in an open-ended way, which demands detachment from earthly reality and from conventional evaluations of reality based on society's perceptions.

As mentioned previously, the attitude is the general existential stance, the worldview and all the presuppositions behind it. The Table 6.3 compares the existential view of Western people with that of a typical traditional society.

There is a huge gulf, by the way, between the Warrior's group identification and that of an ordinary person. Most human group identifications cater to the fallen psychological need to be right and to be superior to others, who are, of course, wrong. Nationalism is typical of this: a mindless identification with an accident of birth, a sometimes boundless devotion to fallen cultural traditions that often have very little redeeming value.

This psychological need to be right and to have others be wrong is really a neurosis based on fear. Authentic traditions are not immune to it — they too sometimes attract people who try to use the "rightness" of the tradition to prove the "wrongness" of others. These people often become purveyors of a kind of pseudo-conservatism that, unlike the real tradition, tries to bury its head in the sand and resist any engagement with contemporary culture and any suggestion that new terminology might be necessary to convey the essence of the tradition in new cultural circumstances.

The Warrior's goal is to free himself from determinism of any kind, part of which involves freeing himself from cultural conditioning. He is always trying to distinguish between values and thought patterns he has picked up by "osmosis" from society in general, and thought patterns congruent with his goal of self-transformation. He wants to gradually weed the garden of the mind from all hidden prejudices and replace them with values reflecting transcendent truth. While many human laws and customs are related to transcendent truth, this truth seldom avoids a certain amount of mutilation when it is expressed as law and custom. In traditional societies there tends to be more congruence between the two than you find here and now.

TABLE 6.3: Existential View of Western and Traditional Society

WESTERN	TRADITIONAL
The individual is the ultimate point of reference	The Absolute is the ultimate point of reference
Society is based on ethnic association	Society is based on a shared tradition, often across ethnic boundaries
Society is a conglomeration of individuals	Society is a communion of persons
The law exists to serve social order by regulating competing demands	The law seeks to express the ontological truth of the universe on the human plane
The natural world is separate from man; a neutral stage on which life takes place. It is a hostile reality to be exploited and subdued	The natural world is an icon of the Absolute, organically and ontologically connected to man
The Absolute cannot be known or experienced directly in this life	The Absolute is open to participation here and now
Earthly life is an autonomous, secular reality. This is a mechanistic worldview	Earthly life has an illusory, holographic quality; it is a "porous" reality open to the Absolute and to other levels of being
"Religious convictions" are unconnected with daily life	Belief and action are interdependent and inseparable
The "fallen" experience of life is taken as normal; real ontological transformation is excluded	Only the purified and transformed person — the holy person — is considered normal

TURNING ATTITUDES INTO STRATEGIES

As I said before, if the attitude is your general perception of reality, then the mood is your inner stance related to this perception. If life

THE WARRIOR'S IDENTITY PARADOX

One of the most fascinating culturo-political studies on the modern world around these days is Benjamin R. Barber's Jihad vs. McWorld (Ballantine Books, 1995). Subtitled "How Globalism and Tribalism are Reshaping the Modern World," the book discusses two opposite but interrelated tendencies. The first, McWorld, "paints the world in shimmering pastels, a busy portrait of onrushing economic, technological and ecological forces that demand integration and uniformity and that mesmerize peoples everywhere with fast music, fast computers and fast food... pressing nations into one homogenous global theme park."/‹ In contrast, Jihad—a word Barber borrows from Islam to describe the search for any kind of self-identification and meaning — is ultimately "the will to hold out against the numbing and neutering uniformities of industrial modernization and the colonizing culture of McWorld."/›

The Warrior is deeply antithetical to McWorld, which represents the triumph of mediocrity, of the mundane; man's self-condemnation to the pseudo-happiness of the passions. It is an insult to the dignity of the human person, and his imprisonment in the world of the senses. The Warrior spends much time turning his life into a whole. So he is working against the very secularism that McWorld represents and demands of its followers. On the other hand, the Warrior is deeply opposed to both extremism and violence.

What Warriors seek to avoid and to root out of themselves is the neurosis of identification — the psychological need to belong, to be validated, and to identify with one's own culture, which is the matrix of opinions, attitudes and values comprising the worldview of those around you. But as for the inability or unwillingness to understand others, the psychological need to be right and have others be wrong — the Warrior's life is directly opposed to all this.

The identification that the Warrior is against is not the conscious and deliberate adherence to an authentic tradition. He is only against a semi-conscious, neurotic, ego-driven and insecure identification of self with any given set of values, attitudes and opinions, however "right" it may be.

THE 5 PILLARS OF LIFE

were a game of soccer, for instance, you could say that each player's perception of the overall situation, including the game of soccer in general with its rules and conventions, together with his evaluation of this particular match would correspond to the attitude, while the mood is the inner stance adopted by each player, consciously or otherwise, at any given moment.

At the start of each day the Warrior considers his ultimate objective: what goals to pursue that day and how to get there. He considers the methods he will use, what opposition he is likely to run into and how to handle these opposing energies. Each tradition of self-transformation has its own attitudes and these differ somewhat from tradition to tradition. The overall attitudes within each tradition give a particular atmosphere or "ethos" to the group of practitioners and this ethos is a very palpable reality.

This overall ethos is an extraordinarily important ingredient for success and it cannot be underestimated. Without it, you as the individual practitioner are left to reinvent the wheel, to supply 90 percent or more of your own motivation — a very difficult situation! This is why the authenticity of your peer group of practitioners is so important. This doesn't mean, by the way, that every representative of the tradition of your choice has to be a superb role model, but it does mean that you should find an authentic representative of that tradition whom you can have regular contact with.

There are certain fundamental attitudes of the Warrior, and this chapter explains them one by one. And it shows you exactly how to integrate each one into your life. To those who are familiar with the works of Carlos Castaneda, you will note that I have employed similar categories. The fact is that, when I compiled and systematized the traditional material I have been studying and using for the last three decades, I came to the inescapable conclusion that no one could beat Castaneda's categories. But beware; much of the content is quite different!

THE WARRIOR LIVES STRATEGICALLY

Strategy is a long-term, macro-level plan geared toward accomplishing your overall objectives. If you look at Wang Liping's training, for example, you can see that quite easily; his fifteen years of training were divided into three levels, somewhat enigmatically named:

1. Persons, events, and things
2. Heaven, earth, and humanity
3. Universe, time, and space

Each of these in turn was subdivided into a further three levels, with numerous sub-levels, forming a detailed training syllabus. Orthodoxy also envisions three levels of accomplishment, and these have had various names throughout history:

1. Praxis or practice /Purification/ Repentance
2. Illumination of the *nous* / Theoria (vision) / Gnosis (knowledge)
3. Deification / Mystical Theology/ Perfection

The tactical and the strategic levels are very different, though related. The tactical comes from the strategic and embodies the precise details of how to accomplish those individual steps — in other words, the goals — on the way to the overall objectives. A famous illustration of the difference can be found in the late fourth century dialogue that a young man named John Cassian and his friend, Germanos, had with a great Orthodox ascetic in Egypt known as Abba Moses the Black (sometimes called Moses the Ethiopian or Moses the Robber— because of his previous career choice):

> "The soldier," said Abba Moses "ignores the dangers of war and the miseries of service abroad. His purpose is to gain a higher rank by using his ability and skill, while his objective is to enjoy the advantages of this rank. Now, our profession [self-transformation, in this case in the context of

an Orthodox monastic life] also has its own immediate purpose and its own ultimate objective, for the sake of which we willingly endure all manner of toil and suffering. You have given up your country, your families and everything worldly in order to embrace a life in a foreign land among rude and uncultured people like us. Tell me, what was your purpose and what objective did you set before yourselves in doing all this?"

We replied, "We did it for the Kingdom of Heaven." Abba Moses replied: "As for the objective, you have answered well, but what is the purpose we set before ourselves unwaveringly so as to reach the Kingdom of Heaven?"

When we confessed we did not know, the old man said: "The objective of our profession, as you have said, is the Kingdom of God. Its immediate purpose, however, is purity of heart, for without this we cannot reach our objective. We should always have this purpose in mind, guiding our life according to it as if it were a carpenter's rule."[15]

Inner work and the refinement of the mind is one "sphere" of life, the others being relationships, economic life and health. However, inner refinement is the most important one because it permeates all the others and, for the Warrior, makes success in other areas possible. Without inner refinement, whatever results you get elsewhere in life are unstable, shallow and irrelevant. It is inner refinement that knits all these spheres of life together into one whole.

So how do you go about applying this in a concrete way? You adopt a focus. Chapter 4 explains how to create inner silence and take charge of your inner, noetic world. Chapter 5 builds on that foundation by demonstrating how to apply your intent in a specific direction in order to prove to yourself that you really do have the power to revolutionize your life. Those skills are the two indispensable preconditions of focusing. Focusing is an extraordinarily powerful transformational practice and is the key to integrating the tactical and strategic levels and making every moment of your life count. Focus is really the Warrior's offensive or attack strategy. It's what he uses to refine himself most efficiently and to have the most beneficial impact on others as well.

I suggest you use Appendix A. Please respect the time lines and do not rush; it is far better to accomplish one focus and integrate it successfully into your life than to dabble in all of them and end up with nothing! This goes back to the basic principle of all ancient training methods: The foundation must be drilled constantly until it is rock-solid — irrespective of how long that takes.

A Tai Chi master from China once addressed this very principle while talking to a group of his Western students, of whom I was one. He told us:

> "I'm afraid your whole approach to Tai Chi is badly mistaken, and it is the same mistake I see everywhere in the West. You think that Tai Chi, any style of Tai Chi, consists of a slow form, a fast form, some drills, some Qi Gong, as well as push-hands practice and the martial applications. So you push your teachers to teach you the 'whole system' as quickly as possible. You think that to know Tai Chi, to be able to claim that you are an expert or that you are qualified to teach, you need to know each of these elements.
>
> "This approach is in your culture, in your blood. And perhaps it serves you well in other fields of endeavour. But here it does not work. Tai Chi is not a collection of techniques which you can learn and then say, 'I know it, so I can teach it.' Tai Chi is an

inner knowledge, a manifestation of the great Tao. And even as a martial art, it is not just techniques. It is the grasping of the inner principles of energy and movement, and not intellectually, but in real life.

"In my country, there are people just like you studying our system, but who do not learn any of the forms for years. In fact, we don't even let them see the forms in use, so they will not be distracted by what looks more flashy and interesting than what they are doing. They may drill nothing but the horse stance for months on end, one or more hours per day. And after that they may just practice issuing power (*fa jing* — this refers to delivering force against an opponent), repeating the same one or two drills endlessly, day after day, month after month. And the fruit of this "boring" training is real Tai Chi. In combat you cannot move them with your force, nor can you resist theirs.

"By your criteria, they are ignorant and haven't learned even the basics of Tai Chi. But in reality, they could throw any of you through a wall without ever tensing a muscle. So who is ignorant of the essence of Tai Chi?

"Stop thinking in terms of breadth of learning and think instead of depth. Be willing to put up with boredom and pain, and you will make real progress."

Now it's time to plan the other areas of your life using Appendix B, and then to determine the small steps needed to attain your goals in those areas. Then try to do just one step this week. This goes back to the basic principle of using intent stated in chapter 5: Using intent involves utilizing your willpower to accomplish one very small thing at a time.

By now the main difference between the Warrior and the bulk of the population should be evident: most people bumble through life in a semi-conscious state. Unable to control their internal world, they cannot seriously modify their external circumstances, nor can they positively affect the world at large. The Warrior, on the other hand, acts deliberately and with intent at all times. Changing his inner world, he controls the general direction of his life whatever the outward circumstances may be, and this is why he alone can bring about deep and meaningful change in the lives of others and in the world at large.

THE WARRIOR LIVES BY FAITH

This may sound very strange to modern secular ears. Doesn't this contradict everything that's been said up to this point? Isn't Warriorship about taking life into your own hands and becoming entirely self-reliant? The Warrior is self-reliant, but not at all in the conventional sense.

He knows that there are ontological forces pulling us in the direction of union with the Absolute and it is these forces that the Warrior relies on. The Warrior does not rely on his own ego, which is the conventional meaning of "self-reliance." Since all self-transformation undercuts the ego, we are not practicing the kind of individualistic, macho self-reliance that is so often touted as a great virtue in contemporary society. Although our own efforts make self-transformation possible, by themselves they are incapable of bringing this transformation about.

Even if you don't belong to a tradition of self-transformation and just want to use these directions to vastly improve the quality of your life, faith is still very important. The dynamic of faith in an authentic tradition functions much the same way as faith does in achieving worldly goals.

If you are put off by the word *faith*, because your childhood experience linked it to some seemingly dead religious dogmas that apparently couldn't be verified, or because it was used by a religious

RESOLVING TO BECOME AN ACE

During the horrendous violence on the Russian Front of World War II, the Germans destroyed about forty thousand Soviet aircraft. Fully thirty thousand of these were destroyed by only one hundred German fighter aces. In stark military terms, this shows the incredible value of the ace, the master fighter pilot, compared to the thousands of other average pilots.

Well, the same dynamic applies to the world of self-transformation: St. Seraphim the wonder-worker of Sarov once said: "Acquire a peaceful spirit and thousands around you will be saved."[16] A similar idea can be found in a letter of St. Varsanuphios the Great to the Elders of his monastery in sixth century Gaza, where he notes that in his time disaster on a civilization-wide scale was staved off by the prayers of only three people, "John in Rome, Elias in Corinth and one in the Jerusalem Eparchy."[17] Along the same lines, one Taoist text says: "If you can keep mindful of the spirit, even if locked in death energy, you can cause the dry bones of seven generations of ancestors to have living energy."[18] The concept of the Bodhisattva in Mahayana Buddhism is based on a similar experience. Nor is this positive effect limited in time to this short life: every single authentic tradition insists that the transformed person can affect the world dramatically even after death. Wang Liping speaks of receiving the medical information on a difficult case from a departed immortal.[19] Joseph the Hesychast tells of seeing the patron saint of his skete, John the Baptist, coming by night to fill up the grain containers in difficult times.[20] There is no end of stories like this.

Resolving to become such an "ace" at transforming your life is not egomania, as some would say. It's really the only thing you can do to bring real, profound and imperishable benefit to those you love. So resolve right now to become such a person. And then repeat that resolution every day the moment you get up in the morning. Soon you will begin to see the fruits of it, and then your subconscious will begin to believe it too, and then even more victories will come, and you will know indisputably that everything our ancient traditions have promised us is true. And then you will love your life, you will love everyone and everything around you, and you will be endlessly grateful that the Absolute put you in this blessed time and this blessed place.

Faith grows in direct proportion to knowledge — the more you experience the truths of an authentic tradition in your life, the more your faith increases. Therefore, how much faith you have depends on the depth of your practice.

institution as a none-too-subtle means of social control, don't despair! Real faith has nothing to do with all this. It is a relationship of trust with the Absolute, a conviction that the transformation promised is true and attainable. In traditional societies this conviction was based, not surprisingly, on having met transformed people. You know beyond any serious doubt because the evidence is right in front of you.

When I was at seminary in the early 1980s, one of my acquaintances in first year — let's call him John — decided to take the second year off for personal reasons and, in fact, he never did return to complete his studies, as far as I know. However, he did come to visit in the autumn of my second year. I ran into him in the cafeteria and I immediately noticed that he seemed quite shaken. "You look like you've seen a ghost," I said. "You might well say that," he replied cryptically.

After a little prodding, he told me the whole story: "Two days ago, when I was back home, an abbot from the Holy Mountain came through town and was hearing confessions at the local Greek (Orthodox) parish, so I decided to go. After all, it's not every day that you get a chance like that here in America. As I was approaching the old man, I had a very peculiar feeling that I've never had before. I could sense — I don't know how — that this little old man loved me. He had never met me, and didn't know who I was, but he loved me. I've never felt such warmth before. And when I began to speak with him, through an interpreter because he doesn't speak English, he proved me wrong. He does know me, but not in the usual sense. He had never heard of me and had no second-hand knowledge of me or my life. But he told me things about my life that no one else knows. No one! There were no secrets from him. It was like the Last Judgment at the end of all things. There I was, surrounded by a love I don't deserve, and from which nothing could be hidden."

Fr. Vasileios, a different Athonite abbot, has written about this kind of experience in reference to a monk he knew (not the same one "John" met):

> "Such monks, unknown and anonymous, but full of light, exist. I know one. He literally overflows. This is an expression which gives some idea of the truth about him… He has a treasure of inexpressible joy hidden in an earthen vessel, small and fragile. And this joy overflows and spreads all around him, filling his surroundings with its fragrance… He is a man who has won paradise with his blood. He has torn himself to shreds, broken open his own person, and now he offers himself. Now he moves untroubled in the midst of all things, in a way unlike that of other people. Everywhere he finds himself at home, since he has always burnt his own hut for the love of others. Wherever he places his foot he finds a rock, because everywhere he has humbled himself and let the other pass over him. In all his words he speaks clearly, he finds the image he desires, because he has never mocked anyone, has wounded no one, and never hurt any creature. He has assuaged the pain of the whole world… All confess to the bearer of this light and he confesses to all. No one hesitates to reveal the secrets of his heart to him. On the contrary, everyone opens his heart to him with confidence, as a flower opens toward the sun."[21]

Encountering a transformed person generates what we call "introductory faith." This is really vital in giving you the inspiration to undertake a discipline of self-transformation and in allowing you to graduate to other kinds of faith. Because eventually you will reach the level of direct experience of realities beyond anything you have encountered before. In Orthodoxy this implies a direct experience of the Absolute. Here the Orthodox Warrior enters into what is called "faith of *theoria* (vision)," which means faith based on what you have seen or experi-

Unless you believe you can succeed, you will certainly fail! But this in no way implies believing that you don't need "outside" help.

enced. At this point faith no longer involves believing in something you've never seen, or just taking the tradition's word for it. Now you know and all traces of doubt go out the window.

Western presentations of Far Eastern systems often downplay the whole idea of faith, usually because Western converts to these traditions have been traumatized by Western Christianity's concept of faith. But in fact, both Taoism and Buddhism are totally dependent on faith. Lama Kelsang Gyatso writes: "Faith is the root of all virtuous qualities and spiritual realizations. In particular, our ability to enter the spiritual path depends upon our having the faith that believes that spiritual realizations directly protect us from suffering and fear. Since faith is the root of all attainments, it should be our main practice."[22] "When faith in the Tao is insufficient," says the Tang dynasty Taoist sage, Sima Cheng Zhen, "then one is touched by the calamity of disbelief. How can one then hope for the Tao?"[23]

Living by faith means we are back at the same paradox explained in chapter 5 — our usual paradigm of self-esteem and self-confidence simply doesn't fit. The Warrior has absolute confidence that it is possible to attain his goals and objectives — as long as right method and consistent effort are used. He also has the certainty that, although he himself does not have the resources and fortitude he needs to do this, these will be supplied by the Absolute when necessary.

The dynamic of faith is very similar in self-transformation and in worldly endeavours. Suppose you're a reasonably good amateur hockey player. You see what a really good professional player can achieve and so you know it is at least theoretically possible for you to do the same. After all, the professional is a human being like you, with very similar abilities and limitations to your own. So the logical thing to do is to go and ask the professional how to reach his level of accomplishment. He tells you what you have to do to get there. You go and do it, and then with time you too eventually reach that level of skill.

It all has to do with right method and right effort. And it's all based on faith — faith that the results you want are possible because you've seen them in someone else, and faith that if you replicate the conditions of success and achievement in your own life, you will get the same results.

It's so easy for us to be held back by our inner lack of belief in ourselves. There is a lot of confusion on this point because people often mistakenly assume that the total humility of the holy person excludes any self-confidence. Even Orthodox people often assume that if they believe they can accomplish something, this must be pride and ego. This is a complete misunderstanding. The saint, the bodhisattva, the immortal, the "real person," all succeeded in self-transformation because they believed they could.

When Joseph the Hesychast arrived on the Holy Mountain, did he think he would fail? Was he tortured by self-doubt? No. He knew that if he simply applied with due diligence the principles he had learned, he would be victorious. Self-transformation is about winning the ultimate prize in life. His disciple, Fr. Ephraim, writes: "Let us not say we are unable to do anything, because then we shall not succeed..."[24] Do you like to win? Of

BELIEF CREATES REALITY

When I was in Grade 7, I was certainly no model of athletic prowess. I was often one of the last to be picked for a team and I only earned a bronze medallion on the Canada Fitness Test. But in Grade 8, I won gold, could run faster than almost anyone else in the school and gained considerable respect for my athletic abilities. How did this amazing change come about? To tell you the truth, I really don't know. I do know that the *only* real change was that I started to believe that I could be a winner in sports. It was not a matter of training or exercise; there was no real physical difference in my abilities from the one grade to the next. I rose to the top because I believed I could. What changed my belief is still a mystery to me, but it happened. What you believe about your possibilities is the greatest factor in your ability to transform your life. This is why cultivating faith is one of the most powerful levers of meaningful change.

course, everyone does. But the fact is that we often lose, and usually because of some inner doubt.

So what's the secret? Faith. And faith can be trained. That's right. Faith is not some sort of inborn quality. You have to grow it and nurture it. Faith is opposed to doubt and to fear. Doubt itself is based on fear and fear on ego.

How do you grow and nurture it? Well, to take Orthodoxy as an example, all the beautiful and profound liturgical rites of the Church exist in part to grow the faith and trust of the Orthodox Christian. When we assemble liturgically, we retell the stories that Orthodoxy is based on. We consider them in great depth and from many different angles. We hear about those who have put these principles into practice and the results they achieved. And every authentic tradition does the same. So if you want to be inspired on your journey of self-transformation, you must feed yourself with inspiring and instructive material and you must do it constantly, day in and day out.

Now, all of this serves to feed introductory faith. From there you eventually come to faith of *theoria*, but if and only if you consistently apply the principles of self-transformation in your life. Every time you persist and follow through in your practice, every time you win a battle (that is, every time you use intent successfully, no matter how small the target), something in you grows. Your whole being seems to expand. Your belief in what you can achieve increases. You feel inside you the beneficial effects and are drawn toward further inner work. But if you continue to feed yourself a diet of doubt, you will get nowhere.

The subconscious mind believes whatever you dwell on, whether or not it is true, and once it has thoroughly digested the concepts of self-doubt and failure, it will work to align objective reality to itself. In other words, no matter what you actually do, if deep down you doubt it will turn out well, it won't. You see, fear and doubt are strongly emotional thoughts, and the greater the emotional content, the more easily the thought is processed by the subconscious. Eventually you begin to believe these thoughts so strongly that you work to make them come true, even if you are not self-aware enough to notice. This is why people who worry about getting sick usually do.

On the other hand, a person who is convinced he can accomplish a given task probably will.

Now that you have become much more aware of the importance of your noetic diet, you are in a position to improve it dramatically. This means feeding yourself on thoughts of success and faith, rather than on failure and fear.

ROCK SOLID LIFE PRACTICE 6.2: DETERMINING YOUR BELIEF STRUCTURE

Sit for SSDN and, after quieting the mind, repeat the following three affirmations aloud in a low voice:

- Self-transformation is absolutely for real
- I can attain self-transformation
- I know this to be true because [choose one] I have met a transformed person / I have read many accounts by and about transformed people / I just know that it must be so.

Consider the impact each statement had on you. What emotional undercurrents were stirred up by the affirmations? Search deeply within and see if you find any of the following inner saboteurs:

- Doubts about your ability to succeed
- Fear of the consequences of failure
- Doubts about the existence of self-transformation
- The feeling that no project you undertake will succeed
- The feeling that you deserve your miserable lot in life
- Fear of surrendering your own will
- Fear of entrusting your fate to the Absolute

Each of these inner obstacles is a doubt or fear. In almost every case I know of personally, each and every doubt or fear is the

INNER PRINCIPLE
❀❀❀❀❀❀ 6.5 ❀❀❀❀❀❀

In every sphere of our lives
we all have a certain amount
of prior conditioning that
has to be acknowledged and
uprooted if we are to become
inwardly free enough to
pursue a productive course
of action.

❀❀❀❀❀❀❀❀❀❀❀❀❀❀

result of some previous experience in life, and very often during the formative years.

Know this: If your subconscious has internalized previous experiences and interpreted them to mean that you are a failure, or that you deserve to suffer, or that you are unattractive, or that you cannot make money or hang on to it, or that you have poor health, then you will fail at everything, have a miserable life, without meaningful relationships, being financially broke and chronically ill, unless you take a few simple steps to uproot these poisons from your life. The choice is yours.

And perhaps you secretly harbour some of the following unhelpful attitudes:

- The Absolute is judgmental and demanding, and will punish me unless I do what He wants.
- Spiritual people are lazy do-nothings.
- Spiritual people are fanatical and dangerous.
- Organized religion is not for me.

None of these ideas reflects reality, by the way. Each is an interpretation based on experience. But in almost every case, you will find that the experience was someone else's and not yours. Once you accept an idea or attitude though, your mind will interpret everything you experience in such a way as to justify your ideological perspective. In some cases these conventional attitudes are just part of the surrounding culture — they are in the air. You have a choice — you can live as a Warrior, which means deliberately choosing attitudes based on whether they are useful or not, or you can run your life according to the current version of the shifting values of your cultural milieu. There are no other choices.

You may notice that up until recently you were doing the latter. But presumably you are reading this book because you were not satisfied with the life built on those premises. If that's the case, you should go on to the next exercise and start wrapping up and taking out your noetic trash.

ROCK SOLID LIFE PRACTICE 6.3: TOSSING OUT THE GARBAGE

Proceed through the following steps to clean your noetic house:

1. Begin SSDN.

2. Find one of the previously mentioned factors or any similar self-limiting belief and call it to mind.

3 Consider the belief from every angle. Try to feel all its emotional content and intensity. Confront it by acknowledging its existence, while neither agreeing with it nor fearing it. Remain a neutral observer. This can be very hard for some people; I have literally seen people run screaming from the room at this point, so traumatic was the confrontation with inner reality.

4. Examine the belief, considering its impact on your life to date, its probable impact on your attempts at self-transformation, and its effect on your whole life in general, if left unchecked.

5. Clearly list in your mind the reasons why this belief is undesirable.

6. Notice whether the belief elicits an emotional response that results in a physical sensation. Do you feel it in

the belly, in the chest, in the back or elsewhere? If so, visualize it as a mass of black vaporous energy at this location.

7. Hold up your right hand, palm up, in front of you at a comfortable height and distance, and then exhale this black energetic mass onto your palm. Feel the negative energy sitting on your palm and notice how much better your feel inside.

8. With a flick of your wrist, disperse the negative energy back into the universe for recycling.

9. At the same or another SSDN session, redo steps 4 and 5, but imagining that this same noetic poison is in someone else's life. This will give you some more objectivity and is especially useful in cases in which the emotional content associated with the belief is overwhelming.

10. At the same or another session, go through steps 1 to 5 and then try to see all the ridiculous aspects of the belief, how silly it is, how unproven it is, and how stupid you would have to be to believe it in the first place. Laugh out loud at it; force yourself to laugh at it and mock it, even if you don't feel like doing so at first. Continue doing so for at least a full minute.

Follow these steps faithfully, going through each of the limiting beliefs in your life. This will definitely loosen some of that encrusted noetic sludge.

Some people come and say: "I'm not really into this visualization stuff. That black smoke, that doesn't really exist, does it? I mean, it's just a game, isn't it?" The answer is simple: Who cares? The Warrior does not care whether the cat is brown or grey, so long as it catches mice. Even if the exercise is based only on a convenient verbal description, if it helps you to undo years of conditioning and dramatically changes your life, why does it matter? It's time to practice a technique in real life that you use constantly when you watch television, go to movies or read novels: Suspend your disbelief.

ROCK SOLID LIFE PRACTICE 6.4: REPLACING THE JUNK
▼ ▼ ▼ ▼ ▼

1. Consider one of the self-limiting beliefs you have begun to uproot. Construct a belief that contradicts it and better reflects reality.
2. Consider what your life could have been like until now, if only you had held this particular point of view. Consider what the results might have been in your relationships, for your career, for your health. Make a mental list of all the advantages. Some people start to sob at this point, when they realize how much damage they have done to themselves and others.
3. Now imagine yourself as someone totally convinced that this new belief is true. What would it mean for the decisions you make in every area of your life? Imagine all the beneficial results you are going to have as a result of adopting this belief.
4. Repeat the belief aloud several times.
5. For best results, deal with only one self-limiting belief per SSDN session.

ROCK SOLID LIFE PRACTICE 6.5: BUILDING A NOETIC DIET
▼ ▼ ▼ ▼ ▼

A noetic diet is a reading list but may also include audio or video reproductions of any type. You are to make a list of works from the authentic tradition of your choice, and only the works which deal directly with self-transformation. Come visit www.rocksolidlife.com. for suggestions, or consult the bibliography. For Orthodox Christians, for example, this means works on the ascetic life, or works about those who have succeeded at it. It does not include works on theology that are of a theoretical or philosophical nature, church history, liturgical practice, or ethnic cooking during the Great Fast. Not that these are bad — not at all — but they do not count as part of your noetic diet.

The noetic diet is extraordinarily important for us in the West today precisely because we are surrounded by a culture that is antithetical to our overriding purpose. In our traditional cultures this was not a problem because the world around us acted as a support, its energies pushing us toward our goal. Here the energies around us sap our strength and distract us from the only important thing in life.

Here are the rules for making your noetic diet effective:

1. Read slowly and carefully, trying to ingrain in your mind a particular passage that has struck you, and how you might apply it to your own life.
2. A slow, in-depth reading is better than a quick, superficial one.
3. Do your reading at the same time every day, without fail — make it part of your Program.
4. Have a small notebook with you, even pocket-sized if you wish, where you can note down the main themes to jog your memory during the day.
5. Keep this notebook easily accessible for a quick glance at several prearranged moments during your day.

To be sure, the key to your self-transformation strategy is the inner refinement of the *nous*. But your plan may well include other areas of life as well: health and exercise, relationships, finances, and so on. In these areas, too, you need to find reading material, peers, and mentors if you hope to succeed. Remember, building the ethos of your new life depends on you because no one else can do it for you. It is up to you to make sure you get inspired and stay inspired. To do so, you have to think, breathe, and become this new ethos by constant repetition of thought and action!

THE WARRIOR ACCEPTS DEATH

You could say that since we all know we are going to die, we all accept death. Of course, this is only an intellectual acceptance, and if we look at the behaviour of modern people, we see that they deny and resist death on a very deep level: they shut the terminally ill away in institutions, pay others to prepare corpses for burial, close caskets if at all possible, surround themselves with entertainment and advertising that preach that life is a carefree joyride, and in general try to forget about death.

The Warrior takes the opposite tack. He thinks about death all the time and finally reaches the point where he no longer fears it, rejects it or pushes it away. You see, yet another paradox discovered by every authentic tradition is that true life can only be found by accepting death on every plane of your being.

Joseph the Hesychast says that to succeed, you must not be intimidated by death. A Taoist sage writes: "Practitioners should view this body as an ox being led to slaughter, every step taking it closer to death. Thus, death is what is on your mind; everything else is cast off."[25] And meditation on death and impermanence is one of the foundational practices of Tibetan Buddhism.[26]

This acceptance of death is a mortal blow to the ego, to the false self, whose goal is biological survival. So when you use the acceptance of death as a weapon to undercut our drive for biological survival in this world, you begin to demolish the ego, the real source of all your difficulties, and this is why the acceptance of death has such a powerful effect.

We are conditioned to believe that thinking about death is somehow morbid. The truth is that it grounds us in the reality of our situation. Ordinary Western people live as if death did not exist, as if they had unlimited time ahead of them in this world, as if they were immortal. The Warrior knows that there are no survivors on the earth, so his time is precious. The acceptance of death also puts an end to worldly fear, since this ordinary, neurotic fear is really the fear of death in many different disguises. The whole complex of the ego then begins to wobble, as one of its principle supports crumbles.

When Argentina launched its surprise invasion of the Falkland Islands in 1982, the British outpost was defended only by a very small garrison, ill-equipped to repel any serious attack. One of the British soldiers later said that, when he saw the Argentinean ships off the coast, the landing craft heading toward him and the aircraft streaking overhead, a terrible dread seized his whole being. But after a few minutes he said to himself that today he would be killed in the line of duty. And the moment he did so the dread disappeared. By accepting his death he had destroyed the fear of death and was free from the egocentric panic that had initially prevented him from taking constructive action in a desperate situation.

It is impossible to make significant progress in inner refinement, to break free from inner bondage, if bodily welfare is your top priority. The acceptance of your departure from this world is a measure, a litmus test, of your connection with the Absolute. To accept death is also part of humility, the most vital of all virtues and the ultimate shortcut to self-transformation. Acceptance of death also teaches you to forget the past, the years of wasted time, and to concentrate on making the best use of the time you have left. St. Paul called this approach "forgetting what lies behind and straining forward to what lies ahead" (Phil. 3:13; RSV). In the words of an ancient Taoist master: "What you must do is bury your past: cut off the time that has gone by and don't ask about it."[27]

The remembrance of death plays an even more vital role; it lifts your inner vision and focus above and beyond all the cares of the material world. The range of your thought begins to expand, to consider the whole mystery of existence, your place in this universe, where you have come from and where you are going. You cease to be centered totally on your own individual "problems" and desires. Remembering death gradually cures you of that most disastrous and foolish disease of soul — the search for individual contentment in this world. The search for permanent happiness in an impermanent world ruled by time and death is one of the greatest sources of human unhappiness. It is a widespread and almost unquestioned delusion in Western civilization, yet ironically it does not even stand up to any rational examination.

So the more you accept death as a reality, the more you remember it, the more you accept change and impermanence, the less real all your previous attachments will seem to you. Likewise, your negative emotional states will seem less real to you and their ability to control your mind and behavior will weaken and fade. Anger, fear, desire, and every passion linked to this transitory reality will wither away. As you begin to understand the transitory nature of the phenomena of this world, you take them less seriously and they lose their power over you.

Another result of the unceasing remembrance of death is that every single thought, every single act, and each moment of time becomes incredibly significant and imbued with great power, force, and meaning. Nothing is trivial anymore. There is no such thing as boredom. Most people wander through life with their eyes closed, their behavior and reactions controlled largely by habit. Life is wasted on an automatic pilot headed for a crash landing. But the more you dwell on your final end, the less habitual your actions become. An ever growing percentage of your daily actions becomes deliberate and therefore filled with great power and potential. Try it and you will see for yourself! Only experience can teach you the truth of this statement. And it does not matter if the actions are the same ones you carried out previously on automatic pilot while daydreaming about nothing important. The Warrior and the ordinary person can both pour themselves some orange juice in the morning — but the qualitative difference between the two acts is infinite. If you train yourself to assume that you will not see another day in this world, everything you do becomes terribly important. This gives your life a feeling of exhilaration. It keeps you wide awake, aware, and living in the present moment — the only moment you can alter.

This helps to concentrate and renew all the powers of your psychosomatic organism, banishing random thoughts, keeping the *nous* stable and the noetic energy concentrated within. Strangely enough, this in turn is the most powerful way to strengthen the immune system. In the words of a Taoist master of long ago, "Ancient wizards knew that the preservation of life is a matter of keeping basic energy stable."[28]

By the way, when I say that you should train yourself to assume you have no more time in this world, I do not mean in any way that you should not plan for the future. Yet another paradox! To build a meaningful future, you have to assume you don't have one. If you look at the life of any transformed person, you will find that he or she has based that life from the outset on the remembrance of death in a very strong and forceful way.

How did they accomplish this? As mentioned before, Joseph the Hesychast would constantly defy death and do dangerous and seemingly reckless things, like putting on the clothes of those infected with tuberculosis. But, as he said, "Death fled away from me to those who feared it."[29] Consider also the desert fathers and mothers — that great exodus of people into the Egyptian desert of the fourth century and beyond. The Orthodox have a tendency to romanticize them somewhat, their life of quiet prayer, close to nature and far removed from the distractions of life in the world. What we often overlook is that to go out into the desert was, by worldly standards, a completely absurd and reckless thing to do. The desert is a terrible and foreboding place, filled with dangers of every kind. And the chances of human survival in that desert were not very heartening. Between the man-eating lions, the scorpions, the poisonous snakes, the crocodiles (if you were

PARADOX
6.4

To build a meaningful future, you must assume you have no future in this world.

foolish enough to get close to a water source), the dangers of dehydration (while avoiding the crocodiles), of starvation, of sunstroke by day and hypothermia by night, these people did not seem to have an impressive chance of survival. Good thing that life insurance policies hadn't been invented yet.

Yet this is precisely why these early Christian laypersons went out into the desert — to put their lives very directly into the hands of God. To face imminent death. To destroy the ego and all its games with a single stroke. Now that is living by faith. And by acknowledging in this concrete way that their lives depended only on communion with the Absolute, they ceased to base their existence on biology, the fortress of the ego.

The Coptic Orthodox monk known as Matthew the Poor, a wealthy pharmacist who gave everything up decades ago for a life of poverty in the desert, developed this remarkable schema about the relationship between acceptance of death and finding True Life:

- To find the divine love we are searching for requires self-renunciation to the point of self-destruction
- The destruction of the self [the ego] is achieved by the elimination of its will [to survive biologically]
- The degree to which we accept death is the measure of the extent to which self-will has been eliminated
- To eliminate self-will, we must practice "self-hatred" until we are no longer concerned with our survival or the things we used to hold dear
- Self-hatred is an inward attempt to deliver the personality

from the captivity of the self [ego], so that it can be united with the other (whether God or other people) through love

- Acceptance of death only takes concrete form when we set ourselves an ascetic contest, such as regular fasting, in which we prefer physical death to surrender. [Preferring physical death means saying with our whole being that our life depends on communion with the Absolute and not on biology. Surrender means gratifying the desires on which the ego structure is based][30]

ROCK SOLID LIFE PRACTICE 6.6: LIFE IS BUT A SHADOW AND A DREAM

This exercise requires both SSDN and a bit of preliminary work. First, pull out some old family photo albums, and look through photos of your parents' life before you were born, then of your own childhood and adolescence, working up to the present. Then:

1. Make a list of all the people in those pictures who have already died.

2. Choose at least a few of the ones whom you knew personally and consider their lives in detail: Did they have a happy and carefree childhood, or a difficult one marred by incompetent parents or by war, poverty, or tragic events? Did they have the benefit of a good education? Were their marriages filled with the joys of spouse and children or did the relationships end unsatisfactorily? Were they victims of war, poverty, or natural disaster in their adult lives? Did any of their children predecease them? Did they suffer from debilitating illness? Did they die young? Did they live to a ripe old age?

3. For one of these people, pull out all the photos you can

find. Take the photos and build an age progression for this one person. Try to find as many photos as you can from different periods of the person's life. Make sure you have at least one as a baby or toddler, one as a child, one as a teenager, one as a young man or woman, important dates like birthdays or graduations, wedding pictures, pictures of his or her children as babies, pictures right through life up until he or she became a grandparent. Then try to find a picture taken not long before death. If you have pictures of the funeral, even better.

4. Then sit down as you would to practice SSDN and arrange all the photos of this one person in chronological order on the floor in front of you, so that you have, as it were, the vast expanse of the person's life before your eyes. Look over the photos and consider how fleeting and transitory life really is. Put yourself in this person's place and try to imagine how it would feel. Remember your own interactions with the person, your shared experiences. Do this for about ten minutes, and then go into your normal SSDN practice. Note the thoughts that come to mind. Repeat this same procedure every day for five days, using the same photos of the same person.

5. Now consider the person's life and ask yourself: Did this person accomplish self-transformation? If not, why not? Did he or she use the time well? How would you like to use your time differently? How would your priorities differ from this person's? On your present course, will your life likely turn out significantly differently from this person's? All of this is to be done in an honest and analytical way. It has nothing to do with judging or condemning the other person. You are only trying to understand, given everything mentioned in this chapter, how the life of the Warrior and the life of the average person in Western soci-

ety (and statistically, the person you chose probably fell into the latter group) are quite opposite.

6. The following week, go to the Web site www.rock-solidlife.com. and download the audio file of the funeral *stichera* (verses) of St. John of Damascus (eighth century). The *stichera* are in English and sung to Russian melodies. The text is also available on the site to make the singing easier to follow. These *stichera* are still used at all Orthodox funeral services, and you may find their realism somewhere between graphic and brutal. Get used to it; ancient cultures were not hung up on political correctness or social nicety. They called a spade a spade. Listen to the *stichera* a few times just before practising SSDN. Then, while doing your inner work, just allow your mind to float through these themes, considering how brief, how false, and how deceptive life in this world really is. Ask yourself then, what is really important in life? What to you want out of life? Have you really taken the steps necessary to get there or are you wandering aimlessly? For purposes of this exercise it doesn't matter if you're an Orthodox Christian or a part-time tree-worshipper — the themes are universal. Remember, the time you have to take action is between this moment and the moment of death, because you too will share the common fate of all — in the proverbial pine box, six feet under.

ROCK SOLID LIFE PRACTICE 6.7: LIFE IN THE COSMIC CEMETERY

During the third week, take at least two walks through a local cemetery. Take your time and read some tombstones, some of which will tell tragic stories. See how long people typically lived and understand that there is no guarantee that the eighty years or so that we assume we have will actually be ours. Perhaps you will run into a burial while you are there — so much the better. Consider the grief of the loved ones left behind.

If you do these exercises attentively, your whole being will be filled with the conviction that this world stinks. It's an innately tragic and insufficient existence, full of suffering and disappointment. What most people pursue in this life as valuable are things they must eventually lose. This world is just a huge cosmic cemetery.[31] In the words of Lama Gyatso:

> People devote their lives to acquiring possessions and social standing, and building up a home, a family and a circle of friends; but when they die, they lose everything. All they have worked for suddenly disappears, and they enter their next life alone and empty-handed. They long to form deep and lasting friendships with others, but in *Samsara* this is impossible. The dearest lovers will eventually be torn apart... We may feel that those who have good relationships and have fulfilled their ambitions in life are truly happy, but in reality their happiness is as fragile as a water bubble. Impermanence spares nothing and no one; in *Samsara*, all our dreams are broken in the end.
>
> Buddha compared living in *Samsara* to sitting on top of a pin — no matter how much we try to adjust our position it is always painful, and no matter how hard we try to adjust our *Samsaric* situation it will always irritate us and give rise to pain.[32]

In conclusion, every authentic tradition maintains that:

1. You are not your body. This is not to say that your body is not "part" of you or that it is unrelated to you as if it were just a container to be tossed away. But you are far more than your visible, physical form.

2. To stop identifying yourself with your body and to stop protecting your physical existence in a paranoid or passionate way is a precondition of making real progress.

3. Everyone really does survive physical death.

4. The important thing is not how or when you die, but the inner progress and transformation you have achieved prior to death. It is the inner state of your being, the state of your heart, that will follow you beyond the grave, either as an imperishable treasure that no one can take from you, or as a millstone causing great suffering.

The Warrior trains himself to understand the impermanence of the phenomenal world on a very deep level, until it becomes an unshakeable inner conviction. Then he uses this conviction as a weapon to defeat his two greatest enemies: (1) anger aimed at other people or at circumstances and (2) desire for and grasping at the fleeting security and pleasure of this world. Chapters 7 and 8 cover this in more detail, but for now it is important to understand how this works. Grasping at the world, trying to hang on to persons, events, and things as if they were permanent, to seek to have them and "consume" them in isolation and for one's own self-satisfaction and contentment, is the greatest enemy of happiness. When this inevitably fails, as it does on a daily basis, you become angry and bolster the reign of the ego within you. But the Warrior meditates on death so strongly that he recognizes the absurdity of this dynamic and takes steps to undo it. In his deep heart he breaks with the world and determines to align his inner being with the Absolute, the only "permanence" that really exists. In so doing, he not only gets imperishable and true life, but even all the things he had abandoned return to him in a different form.

THE 5 PILLARS OF LIFE

THE WARRIOR ASSUMES RESPONSIBILITY

There are two ways to go through life, and only two. Either you can be a Warrior or you can be a victim. There is no third alternative. The victim is anyone who blames other people and circumstances for all misfortune. As you know from your own experience, this is a very widespread syndrome. In fact, when you adopt the stance of the Warrior and begin to free yourself from this, you will come to realize that almost everyone around you is reveling in victimization.

The victim syndrome can be very comfortable because it absolves you from accepting any responsibility for your own life or for the evils around you. It also absolves you from taking constructive action. This insidious syndrome leaves you with the ever-so-comfortable feeling of being morally right while, paradoxically, it does not oblige you to do anything whatsoever. The victim syndrome is a big ego game and nothing more.

The essence of being a victim is to abdicate power over one's own fate. The Warrior takes this power back. The Warrior assumes that all positive occurrences in life are manifestations of the mercy and bounty of the Absolute, whereas all negative occurrences are the effects of his own evils. If you adopt the Warrior's position, several conclusions will become obvious:

1. Since the Warrior accepts personal responsibility for everything that happens, he does not blame other people.
2. Since he does not blame others, he cannot judge them either.
3. Therefore, the entire ego game of exalting oneself while condemning others is wiped out.

And here is the great miracle: If I am responsible for what goes on around me, *I have the power to change it.*

The judgmental and self-righteous ego is undercut and the heart is humbled. If what you experience are only effects of which you're the main cause, then this means that all along you've had the power to build a wonderful future, but you've wasted your life and squandered this potential. So from now on it only makes sense to resolve to take your life in your hands in order to create a brighter tomorrow for yourself and others. This explains why the Warrior's life is vastly more fulfilling and exhilarating than the life of the victim.

This also means the Warrior can't be offended. If someone irritates or offends him, he simply assumes that he is responsible and so remains at peace and unruffled on the inside, and feels little if any impetus to lash out. In our fallen state, we react to the world of persons, events, and things in one of three ways: grasping, aversion, or indifference. This existential stance immediately puts your inner life under the strong influence of forces outside your control and is part of that process of becoming yin to your environment, of developing the fall within you. When you take back responsibility for what happens around you, you become yang again. "Rather than holding so tightly to our discriminations of the external world," writes Lama Gyatso, "it would be far more beneficial if we learned to discriminate between valuable and worthless states of mind."[33]

Through SSDN the Warrior gets so used to watching thoughts arise and disappear that the thoughts and feelings provoked by this or that incident during the day are easily observed. But he lends no power to these thoughts and feelings, and that is why persistence and right method in inner work are the keys to ending suffering and neurosis. In the beginning, of course, considerable effort is still necessary, so don't be alarmed if your life doesn't turn into a bed of roses the same day you decide to take responsibility for it. This, like any other aspect of the Warrior's life, must be trained.

By now your rational mind has probably developed a whole diatribe that goes something like this: "How can we possibly accept responsibility for all the evils around us when it's blatantly obvious that other people and other factors are often the cause? This is unacceptable! It will end up as some sort of neurotic guilt complex. This is

　　　　　　　　　　THE 5 PILLARS OF LIFE

nothing but a mind game and a form of self-deception! How can we carry out a process of self-transformation if we replace objective truth with outright fiction?"

You're partly right, of course. To deny the part played by the passions of other people in the misfortunes of the world would be foolish. However, if you accept the worldview of any authentic tradition, you cannot deny that you have some responsibility for the health and well-being of everyone and everything. And this is the truth that most interests the Warrior. He knows it is a simple matter for the rational mind to use "objective truth" to blind yourself to this fact and to convince yourself you should lay the blame squarely on the shoulders of others. In other words, "objective truth" is not only *not* the whole truth, but it drags you into the pits of pride, self-righteousness, and passing judgment. And that puts you right back in the victim syndrome.

Self-transformation means that you become more and more deeply conscious that you are linked to every other person in the universe, and indeed, to the very fabric of the universe itself. And this is not some airy-fairy New Age notion, but a deep conviction of organic unity expressed by highly developed persons all over the world for millennia on end. If these traditions are true, then the state of your innermost being reverberates throughout the entire creation, and it is this "inner influence" that means you are constantly playing a part, for good or for ill, in the unfolding of history. And if you are playing a part, then you are responsible. And if responsible, then you have power, however small it may seem to you, to affect the entire cosmos. So you are no longer a victim.

Throughout human history you will find that the transformed person can have an effect on others that is out of all proportion to his or her apparent abilities, charisma, or public exposure. Seraphim of Sarov, or more recently Fr. Porphyrios in Greece, made revolutionary changes in the lives of thousands of people. Only the consubstantiality of the human race explains this incredible phenomenon. Fr. Sophrony writes that God's self-revelation to the human soul, to any single soul, is incomparably more important than any other event that takes place in the universe.[34] It is more important than kings and conquests and empires and riches and technology and fame. This is the *real history* of humankind, the history of the union of transformed people with the Absolute, and this is incomparably more real than our conventional idea of history because it belongs to a different plane of being, one the Orthodox ascetic calls "eternity."[35]

So how do you put this principle of assuming responsibility into practice? Here is an example in the words of a recent holy Elder of the Orthodox tradition, Fr. Paissios:

> The Elder was asked, "But how can you consider yourself at fault if, for example, someone in Athens separates from his wife?"
>
> The Elder answered, "Well, I say within myself: 'If I were holy like the ancient fathers, I would ask God to grant that they agree and love each other, and God, who has promised to hear the saints, would help them. Therefore, because I am not a saint, God does not hear me. In consequence, I am at fault that this family is being broken up and for whatever evil happens.' And so, in this way I do not judge anyone, but accuse only myself for everything. *Then God helps*."[36] [emphasis mine]

None of this, by the way, is related to the neurotic guilt complex so widespread in Western religious culture. And in fact, this complex is unknown in any authentic tradition.

ROCK SOLID LIFE PRACTICE 6.8: TAKING RESPONSIBILITY FOR OTHERS

This is an exercise in observation. As you go through your week, watch the world around you. Observe all the evils and misfortunes you can, and using Fr. Paissios' example, consider in detail how you yourself are responsible for two or three of them. After you have laid the blame on yourself using your reason, spend one session of SSDN examining the matter. After you have tuned the breath and calmed the mind to some degree, allow yourself to consider the matter, noting all the thoughts that come to you.

For example, suppose you see a friend making obviously wrong decisions in her life, perhaps in the area of romantic relationships. (I pick this example because I see it so often!) Say to yourself, "It's my fault. If I had bothered to become an authentic human being, she would have been so taken with my example that she would have wanted to know what I know, would have opened herself to it, and would have realized that her misfortunes are her own doing. This would have given her the power to change her life. Moreover, if I were a real person, just my thoughts, prayers, and sincere wishes for her welfare would be enough to help and protect her, and avert further disaster for her."

ROCK SOLID LIFE PRACTICE 6.9: TAKING RESPONSIBILITY FOR YOURSELF

Do a short SSDN session. Once the mind is calm, and you have found and stabilized the natural mind of the observer, turn your mind back in time to some sort of interpersonal conflict you experienced—it could have been with your parent(s) or sibling(s) when you were growing up, or later with a friend, spouse, child, boss, colleague, and so on. Try to find a conflict in which you became passionately involved. By "passionately involved" I don't mean "enthusiastic," but rather immersed emotionally to the point where you were unable to rise above the situation, see all sides of the question objectively, and offer a constructive solution to bring about reconciliation and growth. During your SSDN session, frankly acknowledge your responsibility in a matter-of-fact way, considering how the conflict played itself out, and how you perhaps could have acted to bring about a more desirable outcome. This means that you will have to see yourself almost as a separate person involved in the drama and learn to evaluate your own past actions in a fair and objective way. As you replay the conflict in your mind, there is of course the danger that the same highly charged emotional atmosphere present in the original conflict will begin to take shape in your inner world and take over your mind. Simply note such thoughts as they arise and let them go. If past emotions trouble you, it may take several sessions to work through them. And, in fact, although it is a good idea to have some emotional content to work with in the beginning, it may not be wise to start with the most emotionally gripping conflict you have ever experienced!

THE WARRIOR ERASES THE SELF

In the wars of this world, the more effective the soldier is, the less he thinks about his own survival. Ideally, his only concern is to serve his country and complete the mission at hand. There is less and less thought of individual welfare and more thought of the collective welfare. Find any example of real heroism, and you are bound to see a similar dynamic–a low regard for individual survival and a high regard for the welfare of others.

Every authentic tradition discovered this fact. But they discovered other dimensions of it that are even more important. They learned that the constant obsession with your own individual safety and security in this world is responsible for most of your misery. And forgetting your individual welfare, ironically, actually causes your well-being!

As someone once said, the saints (people undergoing self-transformation) are the most perfectly selfish people, because they, and only they, act consistently in their own best interest at all times. Fallen man, who is selfish in the conventional sense of the word, tries to act in his own best interest, but is ignorant of what really causes well-being.

The saint's version of reality is far more realistic and fundamentally intelligent. He seeks what really is permanent. If you examine reality closely, you will see that the welfare of the other is the key. According to Orthodoxy, our excessive concern for ourselves produces a state called *philautia*, which literally means "self-love." In this state we remain isolated individuals and while

PARADOX
6.5

You acquire true well-being on every level by forgetting about your own individual biological ease, comfort, and even survival.

thinking to acquire happiness, we open ourselves to great suffering, becoming more and more yin — open to the forces of the external environment and under its control, completely conditioned by the deceptive world of appearances.

The Orthodox concept of *philautia* and the similar Mahayana Buddhist concept of self-cherishing must not be confused with the modern concept of self-esteem. The saints have defeated self-love but do not suffer from the neurotic lack of self-esteem. The latter is a psychological problem linked to the ego and produced by painful experiences in the past. In fact, it is very difficult to follow the path of the Warrior until this problem is dealt with.

When I say *individual* in an Orthodox context, I mean a mode of existence, a particular existential stance vis à vis others and the world in general. It's a self-destructive mode that seeks pleasure and runs from pain. But since our individual search for physical and emotional pleasure and comfort in the matrix of the fallen world always ends up causing us pain, we put ourselves on a kind of fruitless treadmill, doomed to repeat the same unsatisfactory experiences over and over. The individual sees himself as the center of the universe in a very subtle way and has no real knowledge of the inner, ontological connection he has with other people. The individual sees other people as "other" with a capital "O," as distinct and autonomous entities whom he judges as "good" or "bad" based on whether they improve or degrade his individual enjoyment. A society of individuals is inevitably a society based on conflict and competition.

The personal mode of existence brings you into a deep, ontological communion of being with others, while maintaining your personal distinctiveness.

The concept of the "person" is quite different. The person exists in communion. The person is totally and inextricably linked to others, while remaining totally distinct at the same time—an insoluble paradox. This paradoxical or "antinomical" aspect of the person is a sure sign that we are touching on the deepest realities of the universe. The only paradox of the individual, by contrast, is that while pursuing one objective (pleasure), he always gets the opposite (pain). But otherwise, the individual is flat, linear, and monochromatic.

So you can see that by erasing your obsessive self-concern, and by lavishing your concern upon others instead of on yourself, you can find the real source of permanent and imperishable peace and happiness for yourself. This and only this will undercut the entire ego process.

The power of love, desire, and concern is innately part of our psychophysical makeup. The desiring power of the soul (which chapters 7 and 8 cover in more depth) is always active. There is never a time when it's "turned off," when we're not preoccupied or concerned with something, when we're not loving someone or something. So the question at this level of inner work is not so much about how to acquire the power to love, but about where to direct the power we have. People often ask me how they can acquire love for others, but the real question for all of us is how can we take our already existing and vast reserves of cherishing love and transfer it to others.

All authentic traditions testify that when this power is directed toward our individual self, it becomes the cause of untold suffering. But when it is purified and then directed toward the Absolute, toward other people, and toward creation in general, it becomes a source of bliss. Fr. Sophrony put it this way: Human life oscillates between two poles: At one end of the continuum there is the love of self to the point of hating God, and at the other, the love of God to the point of "hating" oneself.[37] Of course, the "self" you hate here is only the false self

THE 5 PILLARS OF LIFE

of the ego, not the true self as the image of the Absolute and as microcosm and mediator of the universe. In this example, we are all, at any given moment, somewhere on this continuum, even if unconsciously. The tragedy is that people heading in both directions are seeking happiness, but only those heading toward the love of the Absolute to the point of "self-hatred" will find it. Lama

Gyatso notes that all the misery of disease, sickness, natural disasters and war can be traced back to human self-cherishing.[38] The loving power within us is incredibly potent and it is always directed toward something. If we consider the centrality of the human person in the cosmos, it follows that the use or misuse of this power causes huge reverberations affecting the very fabric of the world we inhabit.

ROCK SOLID LIFE PRACTICE 6.10: TOTAL OBEDIENCE

For one twenty-four-hour period, resolve to do everything that anyone asks of you, without hesitation or complaint. Make yourself 100 percent available to other people. The only limitation is that, of course, you should not do anything that is overtly contrary to the values you stand for. Don't rob a bank or give your kids an unlimited supply of chocolate ice cream just because they ask you.

ROCK SOLID LIFE PRACTICE 6.11: SEEING ENEMIES AS FRIENDS

For a second twenty-four-hour period, think nothing but good things about those who cause you pain or annoyance. Cultivate these thoughts deliberately; don't just wait for them to come to you, because they won't. The list of people may include children, spouses, friends, enemies, colleagues, bosses, self-interested bureaucrats, or nearly anyone else. Do this exercise conscientiously and it will seem as if you have truly entered into a different world.

ROCK SOLID LIFE PRACTICE 6.12: LIVING FOR THE OTHER

For a one-week period, adopt a different person for each day and dedicate all your thoughts and actions to his or her welfare. This means that not only calling this person to mind frequently and praying for his or her welfare, wishing him or her well, but also dedicating any sacrificial act–even following your Program, for example–to this person's welfare. Your concern for the person must be disinterested, though, without any ulterior motive of receiving something in return.

THE WARRIOR ADOPTS HIS OWN MOOD

One of the prices of self-cherishing is what the Taoists have aptly called "the descent into emotional consciousness." When the *nous* is properly enthroned and ruling over the interior world, outside forces have very little impact and emotional life functions on an even keel. In the opposite scenario, when the reason has usurped the throne of the *nous* and set itself up as king, it immediately appoints the emotions as its cabinet ministers. And these are not just emotions in the truly natural sense of the word, but disordered and powerful passions that can twist your perceptions of reality and ultimately destroy your life.

When I talk about *mood*, I am referring to our general subjective evaluation of how we "feel." What emotions or elements of emotional content are dominant in our inner world at the moment? There are, of course, many influences from the outside that can impinge upon our inner world: the actions of others, memories, the weather, our diet, hormones, and all the cultural baggage we have acquired since childhood, which act as a filter for all of the other influences. The inner world of most people is very heavily affected, if not controlled by all these factors. Because of all this external input, their moods fluctuate to a great degree and in ways that they cannot control, although most people cover this up in social situations with the mask of polite and socially acceptable behavior inculcated from a young age.

Needless to say, the Warrior has a different approach. The path of self-transformation is a path of becoming steadily more yang in relation to the surrounding environment and to all the conditioning that it throws at us. This increasing impermeability gives the Warrior the freedom to choose how he feels.

This lesson is one that Carlos Castaneda talks about in his books on Don Juan. Don Juan is trying to teach Carlos–the quintessential Westerner–that his mood does not have to depend on

CHOOSE YOUR MIND

Years ago I met an older woman from Russia who had lived through the unspeakable horror of life under the Stalin and World War II. At a very young age she made a most unusual and life-changing decision: She decided that since she could not control external events, and yet she wanted to be happy, all she could do was decide to be happy no matter what transpired. She *chose* her mood.

Without knowing it, she had decided to live her life by one of the central pillars of the Warrior's way of life. And in the twenty years I knew here up until her death, she really did remain one of the most infectiously optimistic people I've ever had the privilege of knowing. I never saw her sad, depressed, angry, or upset, despite some pretty challenging situations that came her way in that time. The power of the human will is quite remarkable!

the outside world, but that he can choose it. "One needs the mood of a Warrior for every single act. Otherwise one becomes distorted and ugly. There is no power in a life that lacks this mood. Look at yourself. Everyone offends and upsets you. You whine and complain and feel that everyone is making you dance to their tune. You are a leaf at the mercy of the wind. There is no power in your life. What an ugly feeling that must be!" When Carlos objected that it would be impossible not to feel offended if he were being harassed by a cruel and malicious person in a position of authority, Don Juan retorted: "A Warrior could be injured but not offended. For a Warrior there is nothing offensive about the acts of his fellow men as long as he himself is acting within the proper mood."[39]

In your daily life you have precious little control of the ethos around you—the ethos of the office, of friends, community, and sometimes even of your own family. But the one thing you can learn to determine is your own mood. And this is one of the Warrior's central tasks. Many of the failures in spiritual life come from not paying attention to this central point — your mood will determine the quality and integrity of your efforts toward self-transformation, and your success depends upon your increasing ability to define and maintain your mood.

For one week keep a journal of your mood. Note all the recurring situations that elicit a strong negative reaction. For example, when my children haven't cleaned off the counter by the time I have to make supper — one of their chores — that really gets to me. And I'm sure you have similar situations that get you riled up just as easily. The following week, designate a one-hour period during each of the five weekdays. For most people, an hour at home works best, although you can certainly experiment with that. Your only purpose during this one hour time slot is to hold on to one single thought. Not surprisingly, the one hour is to coincide with one of those recurring situations that drives you nuts. And you will do nothing to prevent the situation from arising, as it always does. In fact, it has to happen if you are going to learn. Just prepare yourself ahead of time, because you really are heading into a violent contest! And you'll learn that noetic violence is just as powerful as physical violence. Choose from one of the thoughts listed subsequently and be prepared to hang on to it when you are assaulted by the temptation of your habitual reaction. A tip: The secret is to focus intensely on the thought, rather than on fighting off your natural reaction to the annoyance. If you are successful, you will be pretty much oblivious to the stimulus that previously got you wound up like a rubber band. This works in part because the conscious mind, unlike the subconscious, can only hang on to one thought at a time. You will learn by direct experience that you can choose to replace a negative thought with a positive one and that with training, you can do this at will. Here is a list of possible thoughts:

1. Asking for mercy for yourself
2. Asking for mercy for someone else

3. Unquestioning obedience to those around you
4. Seeing the world as illusory, as a dream
5. Accepting your inevitable death
6. Seeing others as lacking real happiness
7. Cherishing others as valuable and irreplaceable
8. Imagining the world as it could be

THE WARRIOR ACTS DECISIVELY

The idea of acting decisively depends greatly on having a program that you adhere to faithfully, the Program you began to build in chapter 2. It also has to do with the constructive use of intent, which chapter 5 introduced. Now that you are quite familiar with these two elements, it is time to put them together.

The adherence to a Program does not imply some sort of mindless rigidity. But on the other hand (and here is one of those dread paradoxes again), unless you adhere strictly to your Program you can never break free of the slavery to your own desires and feelings of the moment and of your shifting passions.

So, in order to become free, you have to sell yourself temporarily into a kind of slavery to a set routine and carry it out regardless of how you "feel." Fr. Joseph of Vatopedi, biographer of Joseph the Hesychast, writes: "One of the main characteristics of these blessed spiritual Warriors was their strictness in keeping their rule of life. We could see this in the case of our own Elder, and he demanded the same of us. He told us that the beginning of acquiring character and personhood lies in insistence on following an ordered and systematic way of life."[40]

You are probably familiar with the concept of "escape velocity" when it comes to rockets trying to break free of the earth's gravitational pull. Likewise, in the world of inner refinement, there is a point at which you become sufficiently strong interiorly that you can make seri-

THE 5 PILLARS OF LIFE

ous progress. But unless you reach that point, there is a real danger of just "dabbling" and "spinning your wheels," unable to unleash your potential for self-transformation. In Taoist language, the concept of "reversal of the natural process" is related to achieving escape velocity, whereas "going along with the natural process" implies following the path of least resistance, of extreme yin.

To achieve your desired escape velocity you must follow your Program ruthlessly. This doesn't mean you should not modify a Program that is not working out; only that once you have made the necessary adjustments, you follow it continually without deviating. Working at something systematically, persistently, without regard for how you feel, is absolutely critical to your success. Fr. Joseph notes:

> By making a decision to maintain an invariable regime, you acquire resolve and bravery, something very important and essential in our life since our contest is a struggle, and indeed, a fierce one. ...There is another equally imperative reason for order in keeping to a regime: the mutability of man's unstable character since the Fall of Adam. Also, the general sinfulness which each of us carries with us dulls our courage and resolve. Equally, inexperience, ignorance, the unknown form of the invisible war and the inequality of this struggle naturally increase one's discouragement. No other human factor is such an aid to success as our firm and steady resolve and a carefully worked-out regime.[41]

In order to work at something with this kind of persistence, you must cultivate one particular trait of character: decisiveness. When you act decisively, you refuse to allow fears, doubts, and momentary mood swings to interfere with your progress.

For a period of two weeks, keep track of your adherence to your Program. Write it down in your journal. Tick off each element of your Program as you do it. Note any lapses that occurred and also, more importantly, why they occurred.

Let's assume that you lapsed a few times. The first question to ask yourself is whether the Program in its present form is realistic and feasible given the overall structure of your day-to-day commitments. When you first built your Program, you were probably full of enthusiasm and may not have taken all the practical problems into account. Perhaps you did not allow for the fact that one of your children seems to need to talk to you about the same time every night. Or maybe you are not giving yourself enough transition time from one activity to another.

What's important to note, though, is when you slipped up because of what the tradition calls *negligence*, a word that encompasses lack of focus, indifference, and plain laziness. It usually happens when you allow that feeling that says, "I don't really feel like doing this right now," to take over.

Were there times when external circumstances pushed you off track, but not so strongly that you could not have resisted them? This practice of developing resistance to energies from the outside is very important. It is the heart of developing decisive character and a major key to self-transformation.

Make a list of your lapses. Beside each one, write "N" for negligence or "P" for Program. Lapses that occurred because your Program is not as feasible as you thought or because domestic circumstances have changed are things you can readily make adjustments for, using the material in chapter 2. Lapses due to negligence you can only confront with better inner preparation. Go back to the exercise on "Putting on Noetic Armor" in the previous section and consider how to

WORD OF CAUTION

The corollary of being decisive is that your decisions have to be right. Otherwise you can easily head straight to disaster in a very decisive fashion. Fortunately, the program of self-transformation in any tradition makes it quite clear in most cases what direction you need to go. So the effort is not deciding between two or more alternatives, but deciding to pursue the one you know you have to in a decisive, persistent, and uncompromising way.

Decisiveness is actually one of the chief characteristics of a true human being. When you talk about a holy person, a "real" person, an authentic human being, you always find someone who is decisive, someone who sees, moves forward, and takes action.

Also, by allowing a lapse in your Program, you set yourself up for even more difficulty. It is much easier to maintain a given level of commitment and practice than it is to get there in the first place; you'll learn this by experience. Likewise, it is much more difficult to regain the level you have lost than to keep the one you have. Think of it in terms of mountain climbing: As every mountain climber knows, when you reach a plateau, it is easy to stay there. Ninety-nine percent of the work is in getting there. When you begin a Program, you go through an initial phase of difficulty during which you really do have to force yourself to accomplish it. And yet, within a relatively short time you discover that by simple force of habit and constant repetition, the Program becomes part of your mental and physical universe, and you can carry it out without great effort. But when you cease to be decisive and allow something to knock you off your course, you fall from your proverbial mountain and end up back at the base camp. This is why it is so important to maintain your regime, and even more, to maintain the zeal to maintain your regime.

apply it to these situations. If you need more help still, it's probably time to review chapter 5!

In the monastic tradition, the monastery's environment and schedule act as supports for the new monastics and help them to

KEY TO A POWERFUL LIFE

This approach explains one of the most astounding features of traditional Orthodox monastic life. A friend of mine, who had lived on the Holy Mountain for some time, once noted that even a professional athlete would be physically unable to follow the way of life practiced by some of the monastic Elders, and yet the latter follow their Programs with no difficulty at all. I noticed this myself when I was there. Where I was staying, the abbot was a little old man of almost ninety years, but he seemed to have no problem at following a schedule that allowed rather little sleep, demanded hours of standing at prayer, physical labor in the community, and did not supply very much food on which to carry this out. Although I was not yet forty, and was in good physical shape, I just could not keep up with him.

Fortunately, one of the factors on our side is that the whole process of self-refinement, however hard it may be, is addictive. The more you do it, the more you actually want to do it, both because you see the results and because many parts of the process are pleasant in themselves.

develop a decisive character. Then, later on when they choose a more isolated lifestyle, they will have already developed decisiveness. They will have become spiritually strong. And this is the goal of acting decisively.

As we all know, psychological stress is one of the great plagues of modern times. There are very few people in the industrialized world who go through life without experiencing some kind of acute psychological stress at some time, often resulting in severe psychological symptoms, emotional disturbances and even debilitating physical illness.

Many psychological components go into stress. There is the sense of constant anxiety, of constant busy-ness, of having a thousand things to do and no time to do them in, of being constantly in demand. Have you ever felt that everything depended on you and then doubted your ability to come through? Now that's a recipe for stress! Then there is the fear of danger, one widespread example being the fear of illness (hypochondria).

MIRACULOUS
ANCIENT FORMULA
))))))) 5 (((((((

Eliminate Stress by Embracing Struggle

)))))))))))))))

The common denominator among most of these ingredients is the feeling that life is out of control. And this is part of the key to unraveling stress: when you feel that your life is out of control, that you're going downhill on a train with no brakes, it's impossible to have a feeling of peace, of centered-ness, or to be satisfied with the direction of your life. Life itself becomes an unsupportable burden and stress at that point.

In all of this, "objective" reality does play a certain role, but experience is quick to prove that your subjective evaluation of a given situation is vastly more important than the external reality in itself. Our perceptions are heavily conditioned by what we have learned over the years since our childhood. This goes back to what has been mentioned previously about the awesome but unseen power of cultural conditioning, and the necessity for us to recognize our own cultural programming and to extricate ourselves from it.

There are many other elements of psychological stress that are largely overlooked, even by the most comprehensive sources on the matter. And it is quite natural to overlook one particular factor in the Western world, and that is the constant overuse of the rational mind. You have already seen that every ancient tradition believes that overuse of the rational mind is enough all on its own to cause an imbalance in the psycho-physical organism.

So our nonstop thinking and cogitating is itself a source of stress and anxiety. Ironic, isn't it, that by thinking about our problems in order to solve them and relieve ourselves of anxiety, we just end up causing more anxiety. Descartes said, "I think, therefore I am." He should have said, "I think, therefore I am a neurotic mess." When you take the secondary faculty of logical reason and enthrone it as the primary faculty and ruler of your inner kingdom, you are working against the way your organism is built. Can you think of a better way to cause illness? I can't. The Taoists couldn't either, and hence the immortal expression: "Freedom from thoughts is the normal experience: this is immovable."[42] And in Orthodoxy we pray, "Cleanse my soul and sanctify my reasonings,"[43] and "Grant me...a release from the slavery of my own reasoning."[44] Yet what medical authorities in the West will tell the stressed-out patient that he or she thinks too much? But this is far and away our chief underlying problem, and it all stems from our civilization's idolization of reason.

Psychological stress is intimately related to the structure of the ego and feeds on an inevitable egocentrism. So, to the extent that you have fallen into the trap of self-cherishing, you are vulnerable to stress. And stress then reinforces that constant dynamic, putting us on yet another treadmill of dreadful suffering.

Not surprisingly, many of those who suffer the most from psychological stress are highly intelligent and sensitive people. These are the people who are perhaps most vulnerable to the constant overuse of the rational mind. You can probably think of several people who fit this description; it is often the most gifted, the most creative, who suffer the most. Now, let's compare those people with representatives of the authentic traditions of self-transformation. Silouan of Athos, Joseph the Hesychast, the Native American healer Fool's Crow, Wang Liping, and the rest, all of whom lived through some of the darkest moments of the twentieth century, were strangers to psychological stress. Do any of them ever mention or even allude to stress? No. Do they exhibit its symptoms? No. Once you refine the mind, external events are no longer capable of causing you stress, however traumatic their effects may appear to be objectively. My own spiritual father went through unbelievable suffering (as did so many Russians who lived during the Bolshevik period); in fact, I habitually refuse to discuss it in detail with others for fear of frightening them. But by his own admission, he never suffered from stress in the contemporary sense of the word.

There are many physical results of stress. We know, for instance, that the "stress reaction," the so-called "fight or flight response," stimulates an overproduction of adrenaline and cortisone. "Stress causes the adrenals to secrete adrenaline and cortisone, the latter being a particularly powerful immunosuppressant, especially in the thymus, lymph nodes and spleen. Cortisone also impairs the production of interferon, one of the body's most potent immune agents. Diseases associated with high cortisone levels include cancer, hypertension, arthritis, stroke, chronic infections, skin diseases, Parkinson's disease and ulcers."[45] When these elements are being constantly pumped into the blood stream, they remain there longer than they should without being eliminated. Then they begin to break down and decay in the blood stream, actually forming toxins. So psychological stress results in major physical stress and sets up a cycle in which one starts to feed the other: you feel unable to cope, so you get sick (your organism's way of telling you to smarten up), which makes you feel even less able to cope. And so the cycle continues.

Stress can give rise to any number of symptoms. In fact, there are virtually no debilitating physical symptoms that stress cannot either cause or at least mimic. So stress causes two different kinds of physical problems: the apparent, when it mimics a certain physical condition, and the real, when it actually does cause the real thing. In either case, these symptoms can be digestive, cardiac, muscular, skeletal, neurological, and so on, and they may or may not give rise to a severe and life threatening condition.

I know a woman in her fifties who was undergoing a difficult emotional period in her life a few months ago. At one point she began to experience chest pains, and a friend whisked her off to hospital, where severe cardiac symptoms were diagnosed. In fact, the doctors were so concerned about her condition that they insisted she call her next of kin because she might not survive the night! But when all the test results finally came in two days later, the doctors realized the shocking truth:

There was nothing wrong! Physically, there was no cardiac blockage or damage whatsoever. Such is the ability of stress to imitate physical symptoms of real disease!

Unless you deal with the real causes of stress–the overuse of the rational mind and a self-cherishing mentality–no amount of rearranging your life, taking vacations, buying herbs, taking drugs, or doing yoga is going to help you in the long run. Believe me, I know. And I learned the hard way.

Stress relief absolutely has to be one of the first priorities for modern Western people interested in self-transformation. And for those few holdouts who think that stress, like some other forms of suffering, should be borne stoically and accepted as part of the path of self-transformation, know this: I state categorically that this view is totally mistaken. Stress indicates a noetic malfunction in the human person and is overcome naturally if the process of self-transformation is pursued correctly. Moreover (and here is the good news) stress is one of the first major adversaries you will defeat. Complete victory over it may take some time, even a few years, but a considerable amount of relief will come to you very quickly as a result of practising SSDN and refining the mind using the exercises described here.

All this may sound a bit paradoxical to some of you. You may have read up to this point and become convinced that applying this program of self-transformation will add exponentially to the stress in your life. Chances are, though, if you have suspended your doubts and begun to apply what we've shown you thus far, particularly the material from chapters 2-5, you have already noticed your life becoming less stressful. You see, although the Warrior sees life as a struggle and a war, this view eliminates stress, paradoxical as it may seem. For one thing, the Warrior is in charge of his life, and no one who is in charge can be stressed. *Stress is a by-product of feeling helpless.* But whoever lives strategically, lives by faith, assumes responsibility, accepts death, erases himself, chooses his own mood, and acts decisively cannot feel helpless, no matter what the external situation may be. So paradoxically, you eliminate stress by embracing struggle. It makes no apparent sense, and yet it is absolutely true.

Unlike most of the other stressors in our life, the struggle for self-transformation is something deliberately chosen, and chosen for our own good with the idea of moving toward a more satisfactory life. Second, because the entire program here, based on the ancient models, is grounded firmly in correct anthropological principles, it naturally creates balance and harmony within the psychosomatic system, calming the nervous system and the whole person. Whatever you undertake in life by way of "self-improvement" will stress you out and inevitably fail if it is not based on correct assumptions about how human nature really functions — not how fallen man *believes* it functions, but how thousands of years of deep existential research have *proven* that it functions! That is why so many people who try to beat stress without ending their enslavement to linear, discursive thought inevitably fail. Third, self-refinement radically changes your viewpoint on what is stressful and what is not. You will find that stimuli that previously elicited a stressful reaction have begun to lose their power. So not only is struggle for self-transformation not stressful, but it is the single most effective antidote to stress.

By constant attention to your inner world, learned in self-refinement, you learn to remain calm and centred at all times, until you begin to build up and actually collect energy and vitality during the day, rather than being constantly drained by the situations around you. Then you start to realize the degree to which you had allowed people and situations to control you, that you had unconsciously been giving power away to people and situations. When you learn subconsciously that people and situations are a drain, how does your system learn to react? You guessed it — stress! So when you refine the mind so that there is no more energy drain, you can uproot the

WARRIORSHIP KILLS STRESS

You may have a hard time believing that struggle does not lead to stress, and the truth is that you will not understand this unless you adopt the Warrior's way of life in a thorough-going manner. I have a friend who went on a ten-day meditation retreat a few years ago. Put on by a group of Theravada (i.e., Southern) Buddhists, this retreat was the farthest thing from a NAM retreat you can imagine. There were six hours of meditation per day, broken up into several periods, some of them quite long, two vegetarian meals per day, and no contact allowed with the outside world except in extreme emergency. There was also no talking, so he had no contact with his spouse—the men's and women's quarters were separate—and, in fact, he did not even learn the name of his male roommate until the last day!

So, all in all, this was a very challenging retreat physically, emotionally, and spiritually. Physically, the limited quantity and lighter quality of the food, with no snacking between meals, and the difficulty of maintaining a meditation posture for several long periods every day meant that he had to "argue with his flesh" on many occasions. ("The desires of the flesh are against the spirit and the desires of the spirit are against the flesh"–St. Paul in Gal.5:17; RSV).[46] Emotionally and psychologically, to be cut off from the entertainment that the Westerner has been trained to seek as a means of avoiding uncomfortable inner realities, to be unable to speak, to have very little interpersonal input, all this is even more difficult for many people to handle than the physical discomfort.

When I asked him if the retreat was stressful, he replied that it was not. And not only that, it was a great relief from stress. It was very hard on many levels, but it was not stressful. In fact, he said, "Stress simply flowed out of me and I became very, very calm." And to this day, my friend continues to meditate for an hour every morning before leaving for work and loves doing so.

The bottom line: the Warrior's struggle is not only not stressful, it eliminates stress!

ingrained stressful reactions that you have learned on a subconscious level since childhood. This is the beginning of your release from the world of "persons, events, and things."

> PARADOX
> ꗷꗷꗷꗷꗷ 6.10 ꗷꗷꗷꗷꗷ
>
> The Warrior's task is to learn not to defend himself on every level of his being, in order to collapse the ego.
>
> ꗷꗷꗷꗷꗷꗷꗷꗷꗷꗷꗷꗷꗷꗷ

"For whoever desires to save his life will lose it, but whoever loses his life for My sake will find it." (Christ speaking in Matt. 16:25)

"No one who has security can know God." [47]

Another paradox is that Warriorship has nothing to do with defeating other people or with defending yourself in the conventional sense. Quite the reverse: It is about learning *not* to defend yourself on every plane of your existence, because this and only this will lead to the collapse of the ego and the end of all suffering.

This may sound bizarre, because people usually equate the word *warrior* with organized, military violence. So they somehow assume that the Warrior is obsessed with self-defense. Instead, the Warrior goes beyond the need for self-defense. He has learned that self-defence in the usual sense is the path to disintegration and death. The Warrior recognizes that the way of violence against other people, be it verbal, physical, or any other kind of violence, is easy and seductive. It is part of the default setting of the fallen human being. It takes no real strength, no real guts to go this route. You find the energy to do it is readily at hand. But to do the opposite, to not return evil for evil, to not abuse those who abuse you, to cease to defend yourself — this takes incredible strength of character. In the words of the great nineteenth-century American philosopher Henry David Thoreau, "Cowards run away and enlist." In other words, the wars of this world, which are manifestations of collective passions, are easy to fight. The war of the inner world is vastly more difficult. The first produces death, and the second produces life eternal and indestructible.

So the Warrior is someone who neither blames nor criticizes anyone else for anything at all. Blame and criticism do nothing but reinforce the reign of the ego in both the person who blames and in his victim. The whole cycle of evil, of negative cause and effect, remains intact. Only the refusal to participate has the power to break the cycle. It will not only save your skin, but it has the power to reach the heart of the other as well and save that person too. It can never work, you say? Twenty centuries ago, a dozen fishermen from Galilee taught and lived this principle and by doing so conquered the world's largest empire. And only a few decades ago, a humble Indian man dressed in cotton robes overthrew the British occupation of his country by rejecting violence. Think about it.

There is no guarantee, of course, that if you return good for evil, the person who has done evil to you will see the error of his ways and change. But at least the possibility exists whereas, if you return evil for evil, the cycle of disintegration and death will continue unabated.

If the Warrior has to defend himself or others either verbally or even with physical violence, he'll do it calmly and dispassionately, based on an intuitive evaluation of the circumstances at hand. The process of dividing the world into friends and enemies — into those we have affection for and those we dislike or even detest — is a deluded state of mind. St. Maximos the Confessor tells us that we have not yet arrived at perfect love if our regard for people is still swayed by their characters.[48] Even if the Warrior has not yet arrived at this exalted point of development, he is still convinced that he, and only he, is responsible for his own world and circumstances. The corollary of all this is, paradoxically, that he has both the power and the obligation to change his situation. This is a vastly more powerful, more effective, and more fulfilling way of engaging life. This was a point made to the well-known Buddhist author, Lama Anagarika Govinda (a German convert to Buddhism) by his guru, Tomo Geshe Rinpoche, at a remote Tibetan monastery in the 1930s:

> As long as we regard ourselves as superior to others or look
> down upon the world, we cannot make any real progress.
> As soon, however, as we understand that we live in exactly
> that world which we deserve, we shall recognize the faults
> of others as our own — though they may appear in differ-

ent form. It is our own karma that we live in this 'imperfect' world, which in the ultimate sense is our own creation. This is the only attitude which can help us to overcome our difficulties, because it replaces fruitless negation by an impulse towards self-perfection, which not only makes us worthy of a better world, but partners in its creation.[49]

One of the purposes of the Warrior's way of life is to arrive at a direct experience of what the tradition calls the "consubstantiality of the human race," to know in a direct and indisputable way that our fallen "individualist" default setting is completely false. The experience of consubstantiality is to see that everyone is innately precious and is in fact part of your "self" while still being the "other"–another insoluble paradox. "Our life and death is with our neighbour," says St. Anthony the Great.[50] Once the Warrior arrives at this point, the true nature and value of the human person is revealed. He sees and understands why the tradition can go so far as to say that a single human soul is vastly more important than the rest of the created universe. Whoever attains this vision will recoil in horror at the mere idea of violence against others, and this is why Fr. Sophrony writes that those who are holy would much prefer to die than to take a life.[51] And this tenderness for the human person also extends to all other living things, and even to "inanimate" creation: "A merciful heart burns for the sake of the entire creation, for men, for birds, for animals, for demons, and for every created thing."[52] Likewise, Wang Liping was inconsolable when he thought he had accidentally killed some wolves in self-defense.[53]

This is why self-defense is the opposite of martyrdom. Did you ever wonder why so many Christians in the first three centuries of our era were willing to die rather than strike back at their persecutors? When the *nous* has been illumined by the divine energies, you no longer have any interest in doing so and regard all external events, such as torture and death, as fleeting and unimportant compared to the incredible reality in front of your inner vision. As Fr. Romanides explains:

> While in a state of noetic prayer or 'glory'... one attains to
> such physical resources that one resists the normal effects
> of the environment. This has nothing to do with self-tor-
> ment or an attempt to appease God. Noetic prayer is also
> the key to understanding the spiritual power by which
> Orthodox Christians persevered in martyrdom, and also
> why those who renounced Christ under torture were con-
> sidered to have fallen from the state of grace, also called
> 'Illumination' [of the *nous*] or 'noetic prayer'.[54]

Hence the word *martyr*, which simply means "witness." So the mar-
tyrs are those who not only believe in the Absolute but have seen It.

All that I can say is that when it comes to a decision to lay down
one's life or to preserve it, we stand at the brink of a mystery that goes
beyond ordinary perception and any of the criteria we normally use
to judge situations in the visible world. There is no rule you can put
to use here. The Orthodox tradition gives us many accounts that touch
on this mystery. St. Seraphim of Sarov, when already a God-bearer and
wonder-worker, once readily submitted to a severe beating at the
hands of two thieves. He was quite prepared to accept death at their
hands and in fact nearly died. Yet, he refused to press charges, and by
refusing he actually brought the thieves to repentance, completely
changing their lives and saving them not only from the imprisonment,
if not execution, that they "deserved" (according to rational justice),
but also from hellish sufferings beyond this world.

Every tradition agrees it is far better to die than to renounce the
truth. And this is the principle of martyrdom: the refusal to put one's
individual biological survival above the truth of existence. Truth is
not an abstract concept—as we are used to thinking — that we can
temporarily and conveniently pretend to renounce; it is participation
in true life. Followers of ancient traditions knew that to renounce the
truth for the sake of saving yourself from suffering was an inner disaster on the road to self-transformation. Although you're unlikely ever
to be faced with a clear-cut choice like this in your own life,[55] you will
face it a thousand times a day at a lower level. That is, every choice

that your free will confronts between following the Warrior's path on the one hand and serving the egotistical demand for individual survival and physical/psychological/emotional comfort on the other, every such decision is a true martyrdom. True, it is bloodless in the literal sense, but it will feel like you are shedding your blood!

The Warrior knows that the real source of all his suffering is the ego, and that the entire ego system is based on defending the false self. The ego blames others and circumstances for all unpleasantness and takes no responsibility for its own world. When you get right down to it, the ego believes wholeheartedly in this world — in the stability of the unstable, the immutability of what is in constant flux, the wholeness of what is in a state of corruption and decay. The ego is engaged in the vain struggle to make a permanent home in a place that is not permanent. But again this comes back to the concepts of "reversal" and "going along." The ego is going along with the apparently natural process, with what it perceives as the self-evident direction of human nature and the world, following the blind urges for survival, perpetuation of the species, and self-aggrandizement. The Warrior is following a far deeper current, the path of reversal or return that, while seeming to go against what is "natural" to the world, is actually engaging a much deeper and more fundamental natural process–the process that is at the very origin of the universe.

Through direct experience, the Warrior comes to the inescapable conclusion that what the majority of people think of as natural is a path that leads to destruction and death. Far from being natural, "going along" is in fact alien to the real fabric of human life. Yet we are seemingly trapped in a matrix that makes us believe that this is the way things should go. But in the deeper current of existence that the Warrior taps into, he finds vast stores of energy that enable him to continue on in the difficult path of "reversal."

The principle of forsaking self-defense in order to undercut the entire matrix of the ego is implicit in many of the Warrior strategies discussed here: accepting death, erasing yourself, taking responsibility, and so on. And even in the worst-case scenario of martyrdom or voluntary death, the Warrior is not a victim, because a victim is someone who has given away power or control over his inner world to the external world of persons, events and things. And this the Warrior never does.

On the stage of daily life, however, the principle of not defending yourself has many applications that surround you all the time. First, you must examine your daily actions carefully in order to realize that you are constantly defending yourself. In fact, every vestige of self-preoccupation and self-cherishing, the fact that much of our daily round is spent catering to our own desires and whims, all of this is really a form of self-defense. When you begin to hunt down and methodically eliminate these habits, many of the deeper neurotic self-defence patterns—and virtually all neurotic behaviours are fear-based behaviors aimed at protecting the ego—will disappear on their own.

So let's take the concrete example of someone who offends or insults you during the course of the day. What does the Warrior do in such a case? Chapter 8 explains more about the passion of anger and how to deal with it, but the short answer is that the Warrior would immediately put into practice these tried-and-true "anti-anger" strategies. The advanced Warrior may have already arrived at a spiritual level where he feels pity rather than anger for his antagonist. Once you've been purified, you can be abused up, down, and sideways by the whole universe and feel no anger or bitterness at all. But if some trace of egocentrism remains in the heart, a certain metaphysical pain arises within you, and your urge to lash out is really an urge to end this inner suffering.

In any case, the traditional methods of dealing with this passion accomplish several things: First, they begin to root the passion out of you. Second, they allow you to maintain your spiritual independence from the world of persons, events, and things. Third, they allow you freedom of action *because* your inner integrity remains intact, so that you are able to make constructive decisions even under pressure from such a violent passion, giving you a greater range of options to choose from. The Warrior's methods allow him to maintain inner health and peace while giving him the best possible chance of resolving the situation constructively. And they are also better for the abuser, because by refusing to lash out, you avoid feeding the passion that controls your assailant.

Millennia of experience in all traditions have proven that if you (1) refuse to lash out and (2) treat your assailant with equanimity and kindness, then you can actually reach his heart and cause repentance and regret to take shape in him. Recall Mahatma Ghandi's strategy of nonviolent resistance to the British Raj. Ghandi's strategy was based on the conviction that deep down in the human person is a notion of what is good, just, and right, and that no matter how deformed people may be in this *kali-yuga*–the age of spiritual darkness in which we live, according to Hinduism–this conscience of right and wrong has not been totally obscured.

ROCK SOLID LIFE PRACTICE 6.15: DEFENDING YOURSELF 24/7?

Keep a journal for three separate one-week periods. Do not use consecutive weeks. In the journal, note down all the instances and circumstances in which you tend to defend yourself. Keep an eye open for the following:

- When do you defend your own point of view, contradict, or correct others, or generally try to be right (I call this the Infallibility Syndrome)?
- Do you defend yourself when slighted, verbally attacked, or simply ignored? Do you worry about your reputation? Do you take advantage of opportunities for revenge?
- How much time and effort do you spend catering to

your own comfort–making sure that your favorite foods are in the house, that you will not miss your favorite television programs, that you can spend time with friends?

You will notice that these three points begin with the obvious and move to the more subtle, so you might want to spend your first week looking only at the first point. Ask yourself which situations that you noted were rare or "one-off" occurrences and which happen time and time again. Ask yourself and those who know you best how the principle of self-defense of the ego most often and easily manifests itself in your life. The opinion of family and friends can be very valuable in this case, although it may sting a little!

ROCK SOLID LIFE PRACTICE 6.16: STOP DEFENDING YOURSELF

Take one of the recurrent situations you noted–a situation that you know will inevitably come up in the week ahead–and develop a strategy for dealing with it in a dispassionate and constructive way. Here is where your practice of SSDN becomes the key. Once you have sat down to do your inner work, tuned the breathing, and calmed the rational mind somewhat, call this situation to mind. Note your emotional reactions while regarding them with indifference, as if you were watching a bad movie whose plot failed to engage you emotionally. Now calm the mind again. Call the situation to mind a second time, and this time, picture someone else in your place reacting in an ideal manner. This could be someone you know and greatly admire. It could be a holy person or bodhisattva you have only read about. What would this person say or do? How would he or she handle the attack? Note how your emotions did not bubble up so easily when you pictured someone else taking the flak. Now, calm the mind for a third time and start over, but this time you are the victim again. The difference is that now you will react exactly as did your "ideal" person in the last scenario.

Train this method for a week and see how it affects your handling of the real-life situation. Don't get discouraged if your performance on the mental field of inner work outstrips your finesse in the world of physical reality! In time the latter will become ever closer to the former, and finally they will be identical. Remember: The key to success is constant training in right methods. The method has been proven; now just practice in a dedicated and unconcerned way, without being obsessed over your results.

The Warrior is quite likely to be accused of selfishness, simply because he no longer gives himself unreservedly to the agendas that others would like to impose on him. They see the Warrior as unresponsive to their needs and will quite literally persecute him in order to coerce him back into the envelope of what they consider acceptable. Authentic traditions are all full of hundreds of stories over millennia to corroborate this fact. Why is this so?

1. People who live by and worship the ego find life in search of the Absolute disturbing and threatening on a very deep, subconscious level.

2. Fallen human beings are easily provoked to a hatred for any way of life they do not understand. No matter how tolerant they may appear, worldly people can very quickly turn into real fascists when it comes to something strange and foreign.

3. This is even more likely if what is "strange and foreign" (note

that in many languages, these two words are identical!) is an authentic way of life and one that implicitly exposes the lie they are living.

When worldly people complain that the Warrior is selfish and unresponsive to the needs of others, what they really mean is that the Warrior is not willing to allow the mistaken priorities of others to dictate how he uses his time and crafts his approach to life. The subtext behind all their bitterness is that the Warrior is not falling in with their common way of life, which they take as a personal condemnation and insult.

The specious "helpfulness" and "responsiveness to others" of many worldly people, their willingness to volunteer their time for various activities, is very often driven by inner neuroses. I confront this all the time in pastoral practice. People assume that "giving of themselves" is a good, loving, and therefore Christian thing to do. Well, yes and no! When the impulse behind the volunteerism is the psychological need to be needed or valued, or to keep busy in order not to deal with uncomfortable inner realities–both very common neuroses in the Western world–the result is always further disintegration rather than healing. One of the basic laws of life is that to benefit others in a meaningful way you must first purify yourself inwardly and become an authentic human being. People today are thirsting for love, compassion, joy, and tenderness, but you cannot help them unless you first acquire these gifts for yourself. St. Isaac the Syrian warns us:

> Many have accomplished mighty acts, raised the dead, toiled for the conversion of the erring, and have wrought great wonders; and by their hands they have led many to the knowledge of God. Yet after these things, these same men... fell into vile and abominable passions and slew themselves, becoming a stumbling block for many... For they were still sickly in soul, but instead of caring for their souls' health, they committed themselves to the sea of this

THE 5 PILLARS OF LIFE

world in order to heal the souls of others, being yet in ill health themselves.[56]

Yet another paradox in the process of inner transformation is this: The transformation we seek depends on a kind of "reverse selfishness." In the words of Fr. Sophrony, "[The Orthodox Christian] in his 'selfish' regard for his own salvation relinquishes everything else as unnecessary."[57] Our society has very curious ideas about what it means to be "good." A good person, so we are taught, is someone who is always at everyone else's disposal.

We're getting into a very subtle area here. All authentic traditions are built on the foundation of obedience, a topic covered in detail in chapter 7. Obedience contains the notion of carrying out the will of the other, particularly of a spiritual guide. But in more general terms it also carries the connotation of being responsive to the demands of everyone around you. There are many misunderstandings of obedience, and one of them is precisely this notion that you should be unreservedly and at all times open to the demands of others and 100 percent available to everyone. The Warrior knows that many of the demands that others make of him are based on their own passions and won't give them any real benefit. To go along with these demands and with the energy behind them will only mire the Warrior more deeply in his own passions and slow down his progress. Real life often comes down to a choice between being obedient to the path you have chosen or to the deluded agendas of other people. You cannot do both.

So obedience to the wrong person at the wrong time is not a virtue. It is an error and a very costly one. When Joseph the Hesychast went to the Holy Mountain in the early twentieth century, he spent over two years traveling around the peninsula to find an experienced guide who would show him how to pursue the particular kind of monastic life he knew he was called to. And this is a man who understood the virtue of obedience in all its unfathomable depths. Yet he himself scrupulously avoided obedience to anyone who would compromise his way of life.

The fine line for everyone who wants self-transformation is this: Am I just seeking my own comfort and disregarding others in order to get it? Or am I really seeking self-transformation? Is my search genuine or am I deluding myself? Am I building up the ego or undermining it? Am I running from worldly responsibilities or am I preserving my inner noetic integrity from the assault of the unnecessary and ludicrous demands of this world? These are the hard questions we have to ask ourselves all the time. The line between delusion and reality can be very, very fine and difficult to pinpoint. And this, by the way, is one of the most important reasons for having a support community of like-minded seekers, as well as someone well trained in an authentic tradition who can help you distinguish between the two.

Changing a toddler's diapers may not be your favorite job, but please don't try to tell me or anyone that it's upsetting your inner peace and noetic concentration! "If you can actually rectify your mind and cultivate your body," writes the Preserver of the Truth, "then if you have… a wife and children, you can enjoy them, and if you have dealings with people, you can use them for refinement. So householders too can become sages, wizards and Buddhas."[58] However, there will be demands that divide up your inner being, rouse your passions, and rob you of energy on every level, pulling you back into a mental world that you had decided to leave. These are the demands that you need to identify and avoid.

The real basis of our progress is love for others, so we have to avoid seeing them as an obstacle. And sometimes we have to work at it, because certain other people may actually be an obstacle in reality. St. Theophan the Recluse wrote about the dangers of seeing worldly life as an obstacle. He noted that if you see it in your mind as an obstacle, it will become insurmountable, whereas if you make an effort to see it as an opportunity, you will much more easily be able to profit from it.

THE 5 PILLARS OF LIFE

The real obstacle is not other people; it is the passions and delusions of others that, paradoxically, also live within us. The problem comes when you realize that others want you, consciously or unconsciously, to share their passions, to "go along" with their way of life.

Warriorship involves, to a certain extent, saying "To hell with the world, I will do what I want." And the result of this apparently insane selfishness will be the purification and refinement of your inner being — which is the only real and imperishable good you can bestow on those you love. You see, this "insane selfishness," as others will call it, is inherently healing, and the negative reactions they have to it are caused by the fact that it provokes violent and hidden passions within them.

Fallen man always wants others to follow his way of life and is deeply offended when this is not the case–hence the stifling social conformity so characteristic of many cultures. And, by the way, some of the bitterest opposition usually comes from those closest to you, especially those who purport to follow the same ideals and tradition you do. It's no accident that many of Orthodoxy's most celebrated figures were viciously persecuted by relatives and friends simply because they chose another way of life. And this was within Orthodox countries! So you see, the merciless mocking that a young child will face from his peers, just because he is different in some unimportant way, has its equivalent in the adult world. As Christ Himself said, "Woe to you when all men speak well of you" (Luke 6:26; RSV) and "If they have persecuted Me, they will also persecute you" (John 15:20; translation mine). If you are really on the path of self-transformation, you are de facto defying the norms of society, even a traditional society, and you will be given a hard time. Every authentic tradition has been persecuted, even on its own turf.

Before ending this chapter and, in fact, this group of chapters dealing with inner refinement, intent, and strategies, I would like to leave you with one thought. And I would like you to come back to this mind-bending thought every day and to use it like Abba Moses' "carpenter's rule" to judge your actions against:

"When there is something to strive for, don't give rise to ideas of gain or loss. Whether there is something to do or nothing to do, let the mind always be at rest."[59] When you have thoroughly integrated this thought into every area of your life, you will enter into a great mystery. An enemy is no longer an enemy, an obstacle is no longer an obstacle. Gain and loss, life and death, it is all the same. And the ego that has so tortured you all your life withers away, and you enter into a place of spaciousness and freedom whose existence you never suspected before...

CONCLUSION

When you have tried to put all these strategies into practice, you will have developed an experiential knowledge of realities you did not suspect before. Old-fashioned ideas, like "virtues" and "vices," long relegated to the dust heap of the Western mind in its rush to divest itself of the oppressive chains of a stifling and gloomy moralism, will have come to your attention with great force. So, to help you understand some of the helps and hindrances you have found so far on your path, the next two chapters deal with the most effective levers in self-transformation and how to defeat the most common obstacles you will encounter.

Key to entering the Warrior's world: Make every single act a pure act, where nothing else exists.

Chapter Seven

VIRTUE: RECLAIMING the POWER of LOVE

S elf-transformation depends on character development and virtue. "The central issue," writes the Preserver of the Truth "is an upright mind and a sincere intention."[1]

Western society currently associates virtue with superficiality and hypocrisy, so inevitably there is a suggestion that being "naughty" or "sinful" is much more fun and exciting. This suggestion is all around us in contemporary culture.

However, nothing could be further from the truth. Based on millennia of experience, authentic traditions contend that real virtue always has a surprising and refreshing quality about it, whereas everything egotistical and evil seems by comparison somewhat flat and boring.

But even the word *virtue* has acquired an amorphous meaning, so that most people, if asked to define it, probably wouldn't quite know what to say. For our purposes we can say this: Virtue consists of exem-

FEIGNING VIRTUE

When I was growing up, my family attended a large liberal Protestant church in downtown Toronto. Even as a child, what always struck me was the artificiality of the whole exercise. It was plainly obvious to me that people were vastly more polite, friendly, and considerate toward each other in the coffee hour after church than they ever were in any other setting. Everything was decorous and pleasant and everyone was the epitome of "nice."

As children in the church, we always had to dress up and put on our Sunday best—the last thing a kid ever wants to do, because you can't play in clothes like that. Even the adults basically spared no effort at looking their best. And to us as children, all this simply added to the artificiality of the whole exercise. We quickly learned that there was one standard of behavior for church and another standard for real life. In other words, we learned that virtue was an external act to be undertaken when it suited us, but that it had nothing to do with real character.

plary character traits and resulting behaviors that, according to authentic ancient traditions, are invariably associated with transformed persons.

Of course, virtue can be feigned externally and become part of a hypocritical and self-serving behavior that does not accurately reflect your internal world.

By reducing virtue to a way of behaving in public that buys you social acceptance, Western religious culture enslaved the concept of virtue to an oppressive moralistic system. And this moralistic oppression inevitably bred rebellion. The ontological approach found in authentic ancient traditions, in contrast, leaves people feeling liberated instead of oppressed, so no civilization has ever rebelled against it.

Moralism only exists where the ontological dimension of virtue has been long forgotten. And without an ontological understanding of how

THE 5 PILLARS OF LIFE

virtues fit into the fabric of the universe, there is no possibility of carrying them out in your inner being. Without the noetic dimension, virtue is nothing more than socially acceptable behavior. It actually then becomes an ego prop, tied to objective recognition, reputation, and social standing. It becomes the basis for moral self-assurance, which ironically makes true virtue and especially humility impossible. This is why St. Maximos the Confessor tells us that virtue and vice must both be transcended.[2] Real virtue opens you up to the Absolute; feigned virtue imprisons you in the narrow cage of the individual ego.

The Western mind automatically associates virtue with the "commandments" of the Judeo-Christian tradition in their later Western interpretation. If you believe that God is an external authority, then "conforming" will be understood as "doing as you're told." This uniquely oppressive scenario has caused thousands of Westerners to flee to the impersonal Absolute of the Far East. However, a personal Absolute is not necessarily interpreted this way. If God is the *Logos* – the source or pattern of creation — then "conforming" is a matter of the ontological transformation of your inner being. You are no longer obeying an external authority; instead you are refining your inner being and optimizing its potential by conforming it to its prototype. So the "commandments" are a reflection on earth of the life of the Absolute.

Commandments are hardly unique to the Judeo-Christian tradition: Buddhism and Taoism are full of them. Here are a very few examples from among hundreds:

- Buddhist[3]

    - Keeping in mind the evils of gluttony, use just enough food to keep yourself fit.
    - Avoid friends and followers who are detrimental to your peace of mind and spiritual growth.
    - Avoid useless conduct and actions.
    - Having made the Great Renunciation, do not permit the

body, speech, or mind to become unruly, but observe the
three vows: poverty, chastity, and obedience.

- Taoist[4]

  - Get rid of anger and hatred.
  - Relinquish attachment to the physical body.
  - Tolerate ignominy and endure dishonor.
  - Forgive people and defer to others.
  - Do not be deluded by alcohol or sex.
  - Do not take a liking to excitement.
  - Do not crave fine food.
  - Sleep less and work more.

Wang Liping's biographers give an ontological interpretation of how
and why Wang Liping "honored his father and his mother" (to use the
biblical formulation so familiar to us): "He looked upon the life of his
parents as part of his own life. The present life is temporal, but primal
life in its most proximate stage depends directly on nurturing by the
parents. Even though people are independent of their parents' bodies
after birth, nevertheless their roots are still there, and their destiny is
still there. *So respecting one's parents is in reality also strengthening the
foundation of one's own life.*"[5] [emphasis mine] In other words, virtue
causes your psycho-physical organism to function properly.

So virtue will connect you with the deepest roots of your own being
and open the door to communion with the Absolute. On a more ordinary level, it eliminates sin committed outwardly, which throws your
inner equilibrium into disarray and cuts you off from the Absolute.
That's a sophisticated way of saying it stops you from hurting yourself.

Of course, you can still harm yourself by using your mind alone.
This is the reason why Christ himself made a point of saying things
like: "You have heard it said to those of old, 'You shall not commit adultery.' But I say to you that whoever looks at a woman to lust for her has
already committed adultery with her in his heart" (Matt.5:27-28; translation mine). This shows two things. It shows first that virtue has deep

ontological roots that must not be ignored if virtue is to become authentic. And it also shows the necessity of beginning from the outside in. In other words, we implement the most external elements of a virtue first; we stop the lustful looks and the angry words before going on to transmute the energies behind lust and anger into the powerful positive forces they may become.

This brings up the whole problem of hypocrisy. "I am polite to person X only because of my practice; otherwise I'd strangle him!" Having thoughts like this does not make you a hypocrite, however. You're a hypocrite only if you identify with the critical thought and especially if you're simply restraining yourself to manipulate the situation in your own favor.

"If one were to distill Lao Tzu's teaching on human conduct," says Fr. Damascene, "it would be simply that one should do what is natural. To be natural, *however, one must first find the original nature of man.*"⁶ [emphasis mine] Only once you have uprooted the historical conditioning that binds you do you have any hope of performing virtue automatically and effortlessly. This is what Lao Tzu called "superior virtue," but to get there you must train yourself in virtue starting today, even though the training will leave you feeling stretched, exhausted, and sometimes "hypocritical." When at last you do find your original nature, then superior virtue will manifest itself automatically, welling up from within you, because this superior virtue is pure art. In the words of Herrigel's archery master, "The right art is purposeless, aimless."⁷

CULTIVATION OF VIRTUE

To arrive at this spontaneous virtue, which is real and not at all feigned, you have to reverse the natural process. And the only way to do this is to deliberately train virtue in your life. You train it in order that it may become internalized and spontaneous. The hypocrite is someone who has never done this and can simply put on an act of virtue for reasons of personal gain.

There are many different lists of virtues and not all of them are in complete agreement. But here's a partial list of the ones that are most important for you at this stage. Please note that these are in no particular order:

- Patience
- Meekness (controlling your temper)
- Kindness (mercy)
- Openness (not judging or prejudging people or situations)
- Gentleness (treating persons, animals, and even "inanimate" creation gently)
- Empathy (readiness to listen to, sympathize, and help others)
- Courage (not absence of fear, but doing the right thing in spite of fear)
- Decisiveness
- Forthrightness (being unafraid to speak the truth — the opposite of political correctness)
- Honor (keeping your word, being trustworthy)
- Faith (trusting in the experience of authentic ancient traditions, the results they have achieved, the methods used; trusting in the inherent goodness of yourself, of others, and of the Absolute; trusting that Truth will prevail in the end, though not necessarily within the confines of this short life)
- Obedience (to the Absolute and to your guide, and also to everyone in general, as far as the latter is possible)
- Humility (attributing all good things to the Absolute, and

none to the individual initiative of your own ego; seeking to remain unnoticed)

- Temperance (moderation in using and consuming whatever is necessary for biological survival)
- Chastity (channeling sexual energy in an appropriate way)
- Hope (keeping focused on the ultimate joy to be acquired through self-transformation, a joy that is "beyond the reach" of corruption and death)
- Purposefulness (working toward appropriate goals in a consistent and disciplined way)

Question: How you can train these qualities in your life so that you assimilate them on a deep level? The following exercises are some proven methods for doing exactly this.

ROCK SOLID LIFE PRACTICE 7.1: TREAT ONE PERSON GENTLY TODAY

Treat one person gently today. This could be a colleague whose work is not up to par or the child that you usually ignore. In any case, the idea is to find someone that you usually treat harshly or have a reason to treat harshly in a particular instance. But today you are going to do the opposite.

ROCK SOLID LIFE PRACTICE 7.2: BECOMING AN EMPATHETIC LISTENER

The key to empathy is to become a listener. So today you will seek out opportunities to listen. Think it through ahead of time and find one or more people to have a chat with, but let them do most of the chatting! And don't just seem to be interested, but force yourself to take an active interest in that person's troubles. Ask interested questions. Prove that you are interested even if in your deep heart of hearts you do not feel interested. The idea that virtue is easy to do is completely mistaken — at the beginning it takes a lot of hard work.

ROCK SOLID LIFE PRACTICE 7.3: PRACTICING FORTHRIGHTNESS

The idea of forthrightness is to bring the light of truth into a situation in which the truth has been compromised. Stating the truth may hurt you, especially in our politically correct world, since lies are a social convention designed to protect the interests of unworthy people. Stating the truth in a matter-of-fact, diplomatic, and a nonconfrontational way is going to be your task.

ROCK SOLID LIFE PRACTICE 7.4: FINDING A CHARITY TO SUPPORT

Find a charity or an individual who is in need of your support in one way or another. They could be in financial need, or they could require your time and effort. In either case, decide to take on this charity or individual as a project and to give to it either financially or in some other way on a regular and sustainable basis. The amount you give has to be sustainable, but it also has to take you beyond your comfort level to a moderate degree.

ROCK SOLID LIFE PRACTICE 7.5: BECOMING OTHER -CENTERED

All of the virtues listed here have one common theme — as spontaneous manifestations in real people they express the

THE 5 PILLARS OF LIFE

fact that the ego is no longer the center the universe, but rather the other person is. In other words, virtue overcomes self-cherishing. For this assignment you have to do the three following steps:

1. Read material that convicts you deeply of the truth that the key to progress is placing the other in the center of your universe.

2. For one whole day you will hold in your heart one person and his or her welfare. This person need not be someone you have face to face contact with, and must not be anyone you have a strong emotional connection with, whether negative or positive. Dedicate all your efforts of the day to that person. Even if you never get the chance to do something good for him or her directly, you can still explicitly dedicate the good you achieve with your daily struggle for self-transformation to the welfare of this person. Next, you will graduate to someone you see often but with the same restrictions regarding emotional content.

3. For this stage, the welfare of everyone is your concern. When talking to others, resolve that no one will leave your presence without feeling consoled, warmed, and cared for. When you are not actively with others, hold various people and situations in your heart.

Now you've reached a crucial stage, since you've done away with much of the disarray of your previous life and embarked on a whole new manner of living that is vastly more interesting and challenging. In essence, you've plugged all the leaks in your life; you have developed solidity, willpower, and focus. Now, if you're not careful, all of this

MIRACULOUS
ANCIENT FORMULA
《《《《《《 8 《《《《《《

Abandoning Yourself to
Heaven

《《《《《《《《《《《《《《

PARADOX
《《《《《《7.2《《《《《《

By applying the ancient
training methods to your
life, you can easily become a
vastly more effective, integrated, and satisfied person.
But, if you do not take the
next step, your very success
may destroy you!

《《《《《《《《《《《《《《

will become trappings of the ego, leaving you in a far worse state than you
were before.

The only way to avoid this trap and
to achieve real victory is to take your
life and offer it freely and without
reservation to the Absolute. This is the
only way that you will be able to overcome self-will, which is the instinctive
drive of the ego for biological and psychological survival in this world.

Your concept of the Absolute Reality
doesn't really matter at this point. What
matters is your willingness to offer your
life in a practical way and to go beyond
any sense of *your* self and *your* virtue
and *your* accomplishments.

As Herrigel learned from his Zen
archery master, "His conquests and
spiritual transformations, so long as they still remain 'his,' must be
conquered and transformed again and again until everything 'his' is
annihilated." Speaking of his own training, Herrigel said,

> If ever the least flicker of satisfaction showed in my face,
> the master turned on me with unwonted fierceness. 'What
> are you thinking of?' He would cry, 'You already know you
> should not grieve over bad shots; learn now not to rejoice
> over good ones. You must free your self from the buffetings
> of pleasure and pain and learn to rise above them in easy
> equanimity, to rejoice as though not you, but another, had
> shot well. This too you must practice unceasingly — you
> cannot conceive how important this is.'[8]

What holds us back from abandoning ourselves to the Absolute? Fear
alone. Fear of losing what we have or what we are. The irony is that

everything we cling to so desperately in an egotistical way — our physical bodies, our relationships, our possessions, our reputations — all these things we lose anyway. Death will have the final word in this world. Naked we came into this world and naked we shall leave it. This is the final and brutal truth of existence in this fallen, tragic, and imperfect world.

> ### PARADOX
> 《《《《《《7.3 《《《《《《《
>
> You can never become a real person as long as you live life according to your individual will and preferences.
>
> 《《《《《《《《《《《《《《《《

Having said that, facing up to this brutal reality can be one of the greatest inspirations on the path to self-transformation. Milarepa's biographer tells us that Milarepa "was one who had been profoundly impressed from his early youth by the transient and impermanent nature of all conditions of worldly existence, and by the sufferings and wretchedness in which he saw all beings immersed."[9] So it's not surprising to find among the precepts of the gurus of Milarepa's lineage the following adage: "Seeing that when we die we must depart empty-handed and on the morrow after our death our corpse is expelled from our own house, it is useless to labor and to suffer privations in order to make for oneself a home in this world."[10]

So, if you have the courage to face up to the brutal truth, and to face up to it not just intellectually but with your whole being, then review the material from chapter 6 on the Warrior's acceptance of death, and come listen to the haunting funeral verses of St. John of Damascus at www.rocksolidlifecom.

The fear that holds us back tries to suggest to us that by taking no thought for ourselves we are leaving ourselves completely unprotected. Really abandoning yourself to the Absolute is torture for the ego; it leaves you with the feeling of being stripped, of having no one to catch you when you fall, that you're exposed to every danger. But the truth is quite the opposite. As Father Joseph the Younger says, the Absolute looks after those who abandon themselves to it with "a system of motherly guardianship."[11] The reality of this divine protection is testified to by every ancient tradition. It is what allowed Christ himself to

Facing up to the truth that we will ultimately lose everything belonging to the world of corruption and death gives us the impetus and energy needed to overcome the bondage of the ego.

say, "Blessed are the merciful, for they shall obtain mercy."(Matt.5:7; RSV) Lao Tzu discovered this principle himself and wrote, "For heaven will come to the rescue of the merciful, and protect him with its mercy."[12]

From all this it should be quite clear to you intellectually that you have nothing to fear by abandoning worldly security. Of course, there is more to it than that: You may be convinced intellectually that you are perfectly safe the first time you go skydiving, but this doesn't mean that you'll be any less scared when the time comes to jump.

> When I met him [Elder Joseph the Hesychast], he was a true God-bearer, a spiritual general par excellence, most experienced in the battle against the passions and the demons. It was impossible for a person to come and stay with him and not be cured of his passions, regardless of how many and how strong they were, *as long as he was obedient to him*".[13][emphasis mine]

> Once, someone from Switzerland who was a monk for many years came to us because he had three terrible, incurable diseases. He had spent a fortune on medicines, for he was a rich man. Someone had recommended that he come to me and tell me his thoughts; I felt very sorry for him. So I told him that he would get well immediately, if he would only believe that God is able to cure him. Anyway, if I were to write the whole story of what I went through to convince him, I would have to write four pages, because neither would he leave, nor did he want to believe, until finally God intervened and he distinctly heard a voice saying, 'Why don't you listen so that you may get well?'

And in this way he was delivered: I demanded that he eat the opposite of what he was told (he was saying that he would die if he did so) and leave everything to God, laying knowledge aside and following faith; that he eat once a day instead of ten times, as he had been doing. Merely three days were enough for God to test him. I was praying ardently for him. Then at night, I saw in my sleep two fearsome vultures which had grabbed him to devour him, and a snake which had wrapped itself tightly around his neck. He was calling to me with wild cries to save him. So then I wrestled with all of them, killed them, and then I woke up.

Then he came to me and said, 'I have become entirely well, as I was when I was born!' Indeed, his flesh was renewed as if he were a small child. He had medicines and two cases of syringes. I told him to throw them all down the cliff onto the rocks, which he did. After that he lived in good health, eating once a day. [14]

We've now arrived at the most neglected aspect of self-transformation. Unfortunately it's also a vital aspect, because if it's not understood correctly and practiced diligently our chances of achieving success are extremely remote. When it comes to the great mystery of obedience, most of us are just like the Swiss monk in the preceding story: We are weak, hesitant, and uncomprehending.

To a Westerner, obedience smacks of a kind of slavery in which you willingly and foolishly allow yourself to be manipulated, used, and abused by a person or institution. Were not all the tragedies of the twentieth century built on blind and foolish obedience? Did not millions of Germans blindly obey Hitler and unleash a war that killed fifty million people? It was with good reason that Winston Churchill referred to the Wehrmacht as "the dulled, drilled, docile brutish masses of Hun soldiery." So by surrendering our own power and ability to make decisions are we not then creating conditions ideal to the resurgence of such great evils?

And besides that, obedience is clearly the opposite of freedom. To be free means to be able to choose, and if you can no longer choose, then it stands to reason that you're not free. And we all know that freedom is the greatest good in human life, the cornerstone of our society and of democracy in general, and that it is the inalienable right of every human being.

Moreover, surrendering our power to think for ourselves and to use our critical faculties to search out the truth, we are denying our own God-given intelligence and, in effect, performing a lobotomy on ourselves. This clearly goes against the very image of God that each of us possesses.

Pretty compelling arguments, are they not? When applied to obedience as commonly understood, all of these arguments make perfect sense. But the obedience that authentic ancient traditions talk about has actually nothing to do with any of this. Practiced properly and with discernment, there is never any danger of being manipulated and abused by the other. Only through obedience can you discover what real freedom is — as opposed to the false and ephemeral freedom championed by our own political propaganda — and only through obedience do you have any possibility of refining your mind and consciousness to the point of discovering your real God-given intelligence.

The criticisms of obedience mentioned previously all assume that obedience is a juridical category. And that is the limit of our experience of obedience in our society. We obey either out of fear for the other party's coercive force (as when we obey schoolteachers or police, or serve in the Armed Forces), or we obey out of self-interest (my boss's decision is crazy, but in the interest of my career it's best that I don't say anything to oppose it).

But now it's time to take a journey into the mysterious land of true obedience, where alone you have the possibility of discovering your true nature and your true face before birth. All followers of authentic ancient traditions discovered and practiced, and continue to practice,

ILLUSIONS OF FREEDOM

We have all been taught since we were children that freedom means freedom of choice — my ability to do whatever I wish to do as long as it doesn't harm someone else. But this logic deserves serious reexamination. After all, if you subscribe to the idea that self-transformation is possible — that weak, foolish, and tormented man can become a fully integrated personality with all of his faculties working in perfect harmony (let alone that he can be filled with perfect love and overcome death itself), then the idea that freedom could depend only on external circumstances seems rather pathetic. If you subscribe to self-transformation, then in effect you're saying that the ultimate good in human life is to be found within, and the corollary is that unless this change takes place in you, your life inevitably remains tormented and unsatisfactory. And if you are tormented, it is because you've allowed yourself to become a prisoner of the ego, operating through its proxies, the passions, which enslave you to the environment of persons, events, and things. How can such a person possibly be "free," since he or she is a slave by definition?

the principles of this true and spiritual obedience, whose characteristics are the following:

- This obedience must be voluntary.
- It must be given in love.
- It must be based on genuine respect for the one you obey.
- It must be given for a transcendent purpose: self-transformation.
- And it is not merely an event or series of events, but a complete approach to life.

The fall of the human being is repeated in the life of each person — what the Taoists would call "going along with the natural process." Rationalism leads to hyperactivity of thought and emotion, which

> **INNER PRINCIPLE**
> ⸢⸢⸢⸢⸢⸢**7.3**⸢⸢⸢⸢⸢⸢
>
> Practiced correctly, obedience restores us to our primordial state and to childlike simplicity of being.
>
> ⸢⸢⸢⸢⸢⸢⸢⸢⸢⸢⸢⸢⸢⸢⸢

gives rise to fear. Fear leads us to seek pleasure and avoid pain. From this our attention becomes completely focused on our apparent self-interest and comfort, so that the ego or false self takes over our very existence. Cut off from the Absolute, we fall into individualism. That is, our awareness of the consubstantiality of the human race fades away and we begin to see others as separate from ourselves and the natural world as a strange and hostile place that must be tamed or exploited. This egocentric obsession is the origin of self-will, which is really nothing more than our old friend "the biological and psychological self-defense of the ego" — in other words, sin.

When voluntarily and out of love we submit our practice of self-transformation to someone more advanced than ourselves, we take the first step toward shedding this terrible burden of individual self-will, toward discovering our own true will. This allows the Absolute to work within us, so that bit by bit we can begin to remove the ego from the center of our universe and replace it with the *other*. Day by day, our awareness of the deep connection we have to other people and to the entire created world returns to normal. "To love is to live for and in the beloved, whose life becomes our life. Love leads to singleness of being," writes Father Sophrony.[15] Even better, all of the actions of our daily lives acquire a different quality and power because they are no longer the fruit of individual initiative but are perfected, filled with and blessed by the transcendent power of the Absolute.

Among "real" people there is no possibility of discord. In the real world of real people — and this world alone is real — there is only one will that reigns, and it does so with the warmth, comfort, and gentleness that convince us that we have found our true home.

Elder Joseph the Hesychast understood the dynamic of obedience in all its depth and majesty. "On a very profound theological and anthropological level," writes his biographer, "the Elder understood submission and obedience in rational beings not as a mere commandment — a mark of those subordinate to the supreme Authority — but as something more essential, that has to do with the depths of being. Obedience is the principle and the means whereby created things are reconnected with their Creator. Created things remain in harmony and in life only insofar as they stay in constant touch with the Creator, and therefore within his influence. Obedience, then, is nothing other than the Law of dependence and the lifeline of rational beings; while disobedience, and therefore the cutting off of this dependence, leads to corruption and death."[16]

"Both Christ and Lao Tzu likened this state of self-abandonment to the mind of a little child who has not yet developed a mature ego, *who has not yet become accustomed to trusting his problem solver* (i.e. the rational mind)," writes Father Damascene.[17] Over the centuries this has been a constant and almost predictable reaction to meeting a holy person — to notice that he or she has become innocent and childlike. Children who met St. Seraphim, the Wonder-worker of Sarov, used to say, "He's one of us." And the affection was mutual! Wang Liping's biographers have noted that, "he'll be somewhat out of sorts if too many days pass without having the chance to play with children."[18] It is as if everything artificial, stuffy, and false, which so often characterizes adult personalities, has been stripped away so that the "real" person, who is purely spontaneous and open to reality without preconceived notions, can emerge.

The stories in the tradition about how obedience protects both physically and spiritually those who practice it are almost infinite. The flip side, of course, is that if you don't put yourself under obedience voluntarily or, even worse, if you ask for advice and then fail to put it into practice just because it's difficult or inconvenient, you forfeit this protection. In either of these two kinds of disobedience, you will never see for yourself how much suffering your self-will is causing you, and

> ## INNER PRINCIPLE
> ### ❮❮❮❮❮❮❮7.5 ❮❮❮❮❮❮❮❮
>
> The more you renounce self-will, the better you will feel, and the more you will realize that this was not your own will at all. You will realize that the will of the Absolute is your true will and that it alone offers true and imperishable bliss.
>
> ❮❮❮❮❮❮❮❮❮❮❮❮❮❮❮❮

you have no chance of making progress beyond the most superficial level.

We've already seen that obedience in this context has nothing to do with a blind adherence to commands dished out from the transcendent external authority, who will punish us if we don't obey. First of all, it's quite clear that the principal victim of our disobedience is ourselves. Second, there is no authentic ancient tradition that has ever interpreted the Absolute as some sort of divine dictator with the bad temper imperiously demanding the allegiance and adoration of his subjects.

Indeed, the picture of the Absolute who rules by fear and metes out vengeance is pretty much unique to Western Christianity, to the god whom the contemporary Greek Orthodox theologian, Christos Yannaras, rightly called "the terrorist God of juridical ethics."[19] The irony is that the original Christian understanding of God is very different: God forgives everyone for everything all the time. Our problem is that we refuse to assimilate this forgiveness and be transformed. It is not God we need to fear, but ourselves — our only real enemy! In the words of Lao Tzu, "The Tao of heaven is to benefit, not to harm."[20]

Granted, not all ancient traditions have identical understandings of the Absolute, but all nevertheless have understood the virtues we require to remake our life as it was meant to be.

As we progress on the path of obedience, our prayers and deepest desires for the true benefit of ourselves and others will come to pass more frequently. Obedience allows us access to the current of the divine energies by expanding our being and integrating us organically into the life of the Absolute in varying degrees. Recall the story from chapter 3 about several people who were obsessed with finding a spouse, but who only found one after they had given up the search and decided to accept whatever the Absolute had in store for them. By surrendering to the will of the Absolute, the Absolute granted their wishes because they could now receive their heart's desire without harm.

So if we fail to practice obedience and to plumb its depths, we risk remaining on the surface of self-transformation and not recouping our investment. The following story told by Father Sophrony relates to just such a case. Sometime before the First World War, a great Russian ascetic from the

PARADOX
⟪⟪⟪⟪⟪⟪**7.4**⟪⟪⟪⟪⟪⟪

When you give up your individual will to do the will of the Absolute, the Absolute will in turn begin to do your will.

⟪⟪⟪⟪⟪⟪⟪⟪⟪⟪⟪⟪⟪⟪⟪

Caucasus named Father Stratonikos came to visit the monks of Mount Athos in hopes of learning something that he himself did not already know about Orthodox life. Father Stratonikos was well known as a spiritual Father and had already made great contributions to the spiritual lives of many monks in Russia. He made the acquaintance of a young monk named Silouan (the future St. Silouan of Athos), and asked to visit him the next day. Silouan had noticed that Stratonikos seemed vague on how the human will and the will of God come together. When Stratonikos arrived, Silouan asked him three questions:

- "How do the perfect speak?"
- "What does surrender to the will of God mean?"
- "What is the essence of obedience?"

Admitting his ignorance, Stratonikos asked for the answers. Silouan replied, "The perfect never say anything of themselves. They say only what the Spirit inspires them to say." Fr. Sophrony notes that, "at this point Father Stratonikos evidently entered into the state of which Father Silouan was speaking. And a new mystery of the spiritual life, unknown to him until then, was disclosed to him. He saw his shortcomings in the past. He realized how far he still was from perfection — that perfection which he had sometimes thought to possess because of his obvious superiority over other monks (and he had been in contact with many remarkable ascetics). He cast Father Silouan a grateful look."[21]

The point here is that Father Silouan understood the one and only cure for the kind of subtle self-absorption Stratonikos was suffering from unknowingly — obedience. He had found that ever-so-subtle current of true obedience and its inseparable partner — humility — and latched onto it with all his strength (paradoxical as it may seem to say so). Whoever finds this subtle current experiences a reality that is extremely difficult to express in words: It is not only a feeling of deep peace, but also an urge to be unknown and obscure, and an attitude of waiting moment by moment with no prospects and no plans, simply open to the Absolute.

Unless you seek this current, you may end up doing nothing more than refining the ego. Lama Trungpa refers to this as "spiritual materialism," a special quality belonging to one of the so-called six realms, the realm of the Gods. Each of the six realms is, on one level, a kind of psychological archetype characterized by a unique obsession that binds those in it to the endless suffering of conditioned existence:

> The realm of the Gods is realized through tremendous struggle, is manufactured of open fear. The fear of failure and the hope of gain build up and up and up to a crescendo. One moment you think you are going to make it and the next moment you think you're going to fail. Alternation between these extremes produces enormous tension. Success and failure mean so much to us: 'this is the end of me,' or 'this is my achievement of ultimate pleasure.' Finally, we become so excited that we begin to lose the reference points of our open fear. We lose track of where we are and what we are doing. And then there is a sudden flash in which pain and pleasure become completely one and the meditative state of dwelling on the ego dawns on us. Such a breakthrough, such tremendous achievement. And then pleasure begins to saturate our system, psychologically and physically. We no longer have to care about hope or fear. And quite possibly we might believe this to be a permanent achievement of enlightenment or union with God.

THE INSIDE OF THE CUP

During the day I often drink herbal tea. Since I use the same teacup, I have to wash it with soap every day. But despite that, the cup develops a kind of film over the inside as a result of the herbal tea, and this film doesn't seem to come off readily with soap and hot water. The film is hardly noticeable and certainly not harmful, but it's very persistent and difficult to remove. In fact, the only way to remove it is to use a scrubbing pad of some kind.

In the New Testament, Christ himself talked about cleansing the inside of the cup. The ordinary practice of self-transformation in all its rich variety is analogous to the soap and water — in other words, it will remove nearly any kind of dirt and stain, and effectively disinfect the cup. And yet for all that, its effectiveness is not perfect because the most difficult stain to remove is the subtle but powerful grip of the ego. And this can only be removed by the scrubbing pad of obedience.

[In fact, this is nothing but] the ego's having lost track of its intelligence. This is the absolute, ultimate achievement of bewilderment, the depths of ignorance — extremely powerful. It is a kind of spiritual atomic bomb, self-destructive in terms of compassion, in terms of communication, in terms of stepping out of the bondage of ego.[22]

One of the other pitfalls of practicing self-transformation without practicing obedience is that we will not learn how to love or be loved.

Elder Joseph the Hesychast explains: "Practical love is impossible without submission. How is it possible to offer love and to serve others if you do not submit to the others' will? ... Those who are obedient offer a double work: practical faith in the person who gives the command, and applied love through the service that they offer."[23]

You can never learn to love anyone else — whether that is a friend, a spouse, or even an enemy — unless you are willing to submit to the will of the other. As a spiritual guide, I often see cases in which a marriage is on the rocks, although the people involved claim to love each other. But when I dig more deeply I realize that despite protestations of love, they are incompetent at *acts* of loving kindness. Because they are not busy fulfilling *each other's* wants and desires, each of them feels unloved and unappreciated. However, if they would simply become "obsessed" with the welfare of the other, all of their problems would take care of themselves. As Joseph the Hesychast puts it: "Every difficulty in the complex spiritual law is smoothed out within the framework of obedience."[24]

OBEDIENCE TO WHOM OR TO WHAT?

The practical question you have to ask yourself, of course, is to whom or to what are you to be obedient?

Some would say your only obedience is to the Absolute. And this is a valid statement of principle. Others would say you are to be obedient to the tradition. This is also valid. But we Westerners can't translate either statement into real life since we've spent years making ourselves oblivious to the subtle presence of the Absolute and since our feel for the tradition (our intellectual knowledge of the tradition, even if excellent, is not enough here) is minimal.

Not surprisingly, every authentic ancient tradition has come to the conclusion that real obedience has to be obedience to a person. And while we need to learn to practice obedience as a general principle to all the people around us, every tradition is adamant that we need one particular person to whom we are obedient and responsible and accountable. That person is our guide.

"If I rely upon a spiritual guide," writes Lama Gyatso, "he or she will lead me along the spiritual path, which is the only way I can solve all my problems and make my life meaningful. I shall gradually draw closer to the attainment of full enlightenment."[25]

In other words, you need to have faith in your guide and this faith is based on three factors.

First, it is based on an exact understanding of the ontological reasons why obedience works: The only way to find our true will — that is, the direction in which our nature inclines on its own when it's in its true state — is to stop listening to the self-will. That is why Abba Dorotheos of Gaza said, "I know of no fault that does not come from trusting one's own judgment."[26] And the only way to do that, so the ancient traditions have told us, is to listen to someone else.

And second, your guide is one link in a long historical chain of teachers and students that may go back decades, centuries or millennia. Authentic ancient traditions must be learned from a person. And although this is a long forgotten principle in the West, the authentic Christian tradition is exactly like this. If we look at the history of Orthodoxy in Russia for example, we see that there were long lines of holy Elders, male and female, and that these lineages gave rise to the majority of known transformed people over the past 1,000 years. Tibetan Buddhist master Tomo Geshe told the future Lama Govinda that the guru "forms a living link in the chain of initiated teachers and pupils who have transmitted the Dharma in an unbroken line from the times of [the] Shakyamuni [Buddha]."[27] All authentic ancient traditions are very similar in this regard and, in fact, this is something of a litmus test of a given tradition's authenticity.

By the way, don't become too obsessed with finding a guide who can trace his or her lineage back a thousand years! There are many patterns of obedience in the traditions. Some people were the disciple of a single master. Others, like St. Silouan, or St. Anthony the Great, learned from a larger number of people. The tradition says that they were like "wise bees," taking nectar from many beautiful flowers. And then of course there's the more radical situation where sincere seekers simply cannot find a guide at the necessary level. These people usually put themselves under obedience to the best person they can find, and so this obedience is rather limited and conditional, as you will see shortly.. But nevertheless, because of their great sincerity and willingness to work, these people master self-transformation and become guides themselves, thus reestablishing the lineage where one had perhaps been lost.

In general there are three types of guides. The terminology used in this list is not completely identical with that of any single tradition, but is a clear way of describing it in English:

1. *Elder:* The Elder is a transformed person, corresponding to a God-Bearing Elder (Greek *gerondas* or Slavic *staretz*) in Orthodoxy, a guru of Mahayana Buddhism or a Taoist immortal.
2. *Teacher:* The Teacher is someone who is more advanced than you are, who has an excellent understanding of the tradition, and has proven to be capable of applying it in his or her own life.
3. *Companion:* The Companion is someone who is more or less at your level and is someone you can share the journey with on a more or less equal basis.

It goes without saying that selecting a guide is a very delicate process and should not be rushed. Some of the recent guides in Orthodoxy, including Father Silouan, have openly stated that they believe that the lack of true Elders has made the model of a life of absolute obedience to such a person impractical for most of us in the modern setting. And this is definitely the case!

CHOOSE WISELY!

In the Orthodox tradition many people are confused by two apparently contradictory lines of thought about selecting a guide. One line of thought, of which St. Silouan is a perfect example, is that it is not terribly important who your guide is, because as long as your obedience is sincere you will be protected. And Silouan himself was given incorrect advice on at least two occasions. However, by sincerely submitting himself to the advice and attempting to put into practice, the Absolute showed him beyond any doubt that it was erroneous and so he abandoned the practice. So here we have the idea that obedience will protect you from bad advice.

The counterpoint to this is expressed by St. Ignaty Brianchaninov:

> The healing of the passions] cannot be accomplished by a guide's fallen will when the guide himself is still enslaved to the passions... 'If you wish to renounce the world and learn the life of the Gospel,' said St. Symeon the New Theologian to the monks of his time, 'do not surrender (entrust) yourself to an inexperienced or passionate master, lest instead of the life of the Gospel you learn a diabolical life.'... Perhaps you retort: the novice's faith can take the place of an incompetent Elder. It is untrue. Faith in the truth saves. Faith in a lie and in diabolical illusion is ruinous...[28]

The solution to this apparent contradiction is the following. St. Silouan was living in a high-level Orthodox monastic milieu, where the vast majority of people he would have considered submitting himself to were extremely reliable. St. Ignaty, on the other hand, was living in a much more problematic environment and had probably seen many people go to their ruin by following false guides. No matter which, if any, tradition we belong to, our situation much more closely resembles the latter, unfortunately, so we need to exercise extreme caution in selecting a guide.

The explicit or implicit denial of the passionate part of the soul leads to a rationalistic approach to life and all the usual consequences that stem from it — the growth of a false personality, slavery to the environment, and a thousand physical and mental ailments.

((((((((((((((((

It is critical to note that the obedience you should practice to each of these three kinds of guides is different!

The Elder

Total and unquestioning obedience is appropriate only to the Elder. Because the Elder has already been transformed, he or she not only teaches about the tradition but has actually become the tradition, so that the Absolute manifests itself through him or her with great clarity. In Orthodoxy it's very clear that such person is to be regarded as Christ himself. And the Mahayana Buddhist regards the genuine guru as a Buddha: "I realized," writes Milarepa's biographer, "that it was irreverent feelings of familiarity with my guru that had caused me to look upon him as merely a human being... what a dull, stupid person I was! Ought I not to have known that Milarepa had obtained perfect enlightenment, in fact was a Buddha?"[29]

A word of caution, though: the modern world has presented the Elders and Teachers of ancient traditions with an unfamiliar patient — the neurotic personality, whose feelings, emotions, and psychosomatic energies (such as the sex drive for example) have been repressed rather than integrated into the personality. And this is a problem of extreme importance in the contemporary Western world, where centuries of moralizing, together with the weapons of shame and guilt, have led to chronic emotional repression. Even the simple fact of not having your emotions validated can lead to this. For example, as a child you express anger or jealousy, but are in effect told that these are feelings you should not have. You react with feelings of inadequacy and by trying to repress these "unacceptable" emotions. Other people have been taught to ignore their own feelings and emotions completely. These unprocessed emotions inevitably explode in some way later in life, either through psychosomatic ailments of various kinds, such as anxiety disorders, depressions or compulsive behaviors, or they take the opposite route — a pathological obsession with emotions.

If parents in particular or society in general are ill at ease with the powerful energies of desire or vehement feeling, they will try to isolate and ignore them in favor of "higher faculties" — which in this case is a euphemism for the rational mind. A lack of emotional support from parents or a situation of parental ineffectiveness that forces the child to take responsibility for him- or herself or for others too soon can also cause this kind of hyper-rationalism.

The inevitable result is "living in the head"- an overly intellectual approach to life which isolates the ability to think and reason from the ability to feel. The lives of such people are often filled with tragic emotional content, but because they themselves are incompetent to understand or process the emotions, the result is a nameless and ill-defined emotional pain. It is not uncommon for such people to turn to substance abuse simply to help them forget their suffering. And indeed, many alcoholics fit this description.

The irony is that suffering people often look to religion for comfort. Unfortunately, though, religion provides the perfect justification for their inability to deal with emotions, because of its frequent hostility to the emotional part of the soul. It legitimizes their inability to express desire and vehemence. Second, it makes them believe that their suffering has some form of redemptive value. It confirms them in their inability to deal with emotional content, as well as in their tendency to intellectualize life and to pretend that the body does not exist.

Father Vasileios Thermos points out, however, that "Despite external similarities, in reality this is not equivalent to the domination of the *nous* over irrational desires as recommended by the ascetic literature."[30] Indeed, it is functionally the opposite: when the *nous* reigns

INNER PRINCIPLE
((((((**7.11** *((((((*

The "religious" idea that bearing this suffering is redemptive is a completely false interpretation of reality. Pathological conditions that obstruct self-transformation only become redemptive if you work to cure them.

((((((((((((((((((((

over the reeducated powers of desire and vehement feeling, there is no repression or imbalance of any kind, but rather perfect harmony. Moreover, the neurotic, puritanical approach confuses the ability to desire or to express vehement feelings (the quantitative element) with sinful desire or sinful expressions of vehemence (the qualitative element). To feel desire or anger is not the same as acting on the feeling, let alone acting inappropriately. The emotions themselves are not evil — they are simply energies that must be acknowledged and processed if great and unnecessary suffering is to be avoided.

Unfortunately, representatives of authentic traditions won't always give a more accurate diagnosis and treatment. I have seen many times with my own eyes (and Father Vasileios presents many analogous cases as well) that both experienced teachers and even Elders have frequently given counterproductive advice based on a wrong diagnosis. The case of George, discussed in chapter 3, is a case in point. As Father Vasileios puts it regarding many contemporary spiritual guides, "...he adjusts his diagnosis and therapy to his own abilities rather than submitting himself to the ascesis inspired by the person before him, or at least asking for the help of a specialist."[31]

Ancient traditions assumed a non-neurotic population and built their therapeutic methods accordingly. I myself noticed in talks with monastic Elders in Greece and on the Holy Mountain a few years ago that many of them are no better acquainted with life in the urban industrialized West than you and I are with life in the Andromeda Galaxy. Many of them are people who, notwithstanding their indisputable achievement of self-transformation, grew up in small villages in the 1930s or 1940s and continue to give advice based on the only experience of life in the world that they have ever known. Of course, to be fair to the Elders, the neurotic person does not walk around wearing a sign that says "I'm neurotic — treat me accordingly!" And because the neurotic doesn't usually understand the sources of his emotional pain, he is often unable to articulate what he is really feeling to his guide.

You might retort with the theory that the Elder doesn't give his or her own opinion but acts as a conduit for the truth from on high. Although this is true in theory and frequently in practice, it is not invariably true, so even holy Elders sometimes give inappropriate advice. And teachers, who are the vast majority of guides, are far more at risk of doing exactly this.

Natural energies that have been repressed because of feelings of inadequacy, anxiety, fear, shame or guilt cannot be transformed by the Absolute until they have been acknowledged and processed correctly. What you do not have you cannot transform. In the words of a Father of long ago:

"The things which are beyond nature do not negate that which is according to nature, but produce them and urge them forth, so that they might be able to gain the power which is beyond their nature. There is no place for that which is beyond nature if one's nature is not according to nature."[32]

So let's go over some inner principles that are absolutely vital to successful self-transformation here and now:

- Feelings, emotions, and psychosomatic energies or drives that have not been accepted, validated, and integrated into the personality will eventually explode as symptoms of mental or physical illness.

- The explicit or implicit denial of the passionate part of the soul leads to a rationalistic approach to life and all the usual consequences that stem from it — the growth of a false personality, slavery to the environment, and a thousand physical and mental ailments.

- Most "religions" inadvertently validate this kind of illness and provide their adherents with a rationale to avoid facing it. This often results in the illness being perpetuated in future generations.

- The "religious" idea that bearing this suffering is redemptive is a completely false interpretation of reality. Pathological conditions that obstruct self-transformation only become redemptive if you work to cure them.

- Guides from authentic ancient traditions are not invariably able to give appropriate advice to people in this condition.

- Authentic ancient traditions require you to face up to, understand, and process the contents of the mind, including the faculties of desire and vehement feeling, and view emotional repression as a sure road to disaster.

- For an energy of the soul to be transformed and reach its full potential through the practices of self-transformation,, it must first exist as an acknowledged and accepted element of the whole person.

The Teacher

The Teacher, in contrast to the Elder, receives a more conditional obedience. This kind of obedience is still very genuine, but in this situation you are more conscious of making sure that the advice you receive accords with the tradition. *Genuine* means that when you approach your guide for advice, you really are utterly committed to receiving the advice you're given and putting it into practice, unless it's blatantly obvious that the advice goes against the tradition in some radical way.

Openness to the advice we receive and this desire not to contradict it in any way is extremely important if we are to receive any help that goes beyond the merely human level. St. Silouan brought up exactly this point with one of his own guides, Father Missail. When he asked Father Missail how someone could learn the will of God, the old man replied: "He must accept my first word as the will of God. Divine grace rests upon him who does so, but if he resists me, then I, as a mere mortal, will back down."[33]

This story is extraordinarily important because it shows us that the level of accomplishment of our guide is not the most important issue. Even an infallible guide becomes fallible when confronted with an insincere disciple. An insincere disciple is one who resists the advice he is given and injects his own will into the discussion. "Man's will is like a wall of brass between him and God," said Abba Poemen in the fourth century.[34]

If we look upon a conversation with our guide as some sort of spiritual equivalent of a secular psychological counseling process, we will be wasting both his or her time and ours. Not that a psychological counseling session is a bad thing, but it is not even on the same plane of existence as a session with your guide. A session with your guide is not an academic discussion or an exchange of views — it's about setting aside your false, individual will in order to enter into a totally different and mysterious reality. Everyone wants a guide these days, but very few are willing to enter the mystery that allows the guide to work effectively!

The Companion

The Companion is a different situation in many ways. Elder Joseph the Hesychast and Father Arsenios were Companions in their ascetic lives.

INNER PRINCIPLE

7.14

For an energy of the soul to be transformed and reach its full potential through the practices of self-transformation, it must first exist as an acknowledged and accepted element of the whole person.

They inspired each other, spurred each other on, and kept each other on the right track. This is the ideal role of the Companion — to function as a reality check. There is much less chance of two people who work together going off the rails than there is of one person alone falling into a sidetrack.

Normally, each Companion would also have a guide — an Elder or Teacher — unless circumstances prevented this.

FINAL THOUGHTS ON OBEDIENCE

You need to be very cautious in searching for the right guide, because deluded people love authority and will masquerade as guides. Part of the danger here is that your own psychological predispositions may be setting you up to fall into a kind of cult-like pseudo-obedience. True obedience to a guide and the pseudo-obedience you find in cults may look superficially very similar, but on the inside they are completely different. Cults are innately oppressive and evil, leading to forms of mind control and manipulation. Real obedience, however, leaves you free and with an inner feeling of peace and refreshment.

Note that your guide does not have to occupy an official institutional position within a given tradition. There is a kind of unresolved tension here. Orthodoxy, for example, has always maintained that the divine energy will work through any priest to cleanse the inner being of anyone who genuinely desires change. On the other hand, we know from great saints like Varsanuphios the Great and Symeon the New Theologian that the cleansing of sins is a high spiritual gift that can come to anyone regardless of position, title, age, or sex. So there is an inherent tension between the institutional and the charismatic. Of course, one person may be both. And this tension is never resolved, precisely because it is inherent to the fallen world.

If you try to resolve it on a rational level, as the Roman Catholic Church has done, you automatically end up with a human institution giving itself the right to define truth, with the demise of the genuine spiritual tradition, and with the rather bizarre theory of institutional infallibility. In this case, whatever the current, duly constituted representatives of the institution say is automatically correct and binding. In Orthodoxy, though, official statements by church hierarchies or councils have frequently been repudiated as misguided and, in fact, nearly every deviation in history was started by an untransformed person in a position of power.

In conclusion, we come back to the necessity of practicing a generalized obedience to everyone around you. If we look at things in this light, then we realize that we are surrounded by an endless number of "teachers":

> They meet us at every step in our daily life, if only we recognize their voices. Your wife wants you to take your raincoat with you: do as she wishes, to practice obedience. Your fellow-worker asks you to walk with her a little way: go with her to practice obedience. Wordlessly the infant asks for care and companionship: do as it wishes as far as you can, and thus practice obedience. A novice in a cloister would not find more opportunity for obedience than you in your own home. And likewise at your job and in your dealings with your neighbor.
>
> Obedience breaks down many barriers. You achieve freedom and peace as your heart practices nonresistance. You show obedience, and thorny hedges give way before you. Then love has open space in which to move about. By obedience you crush your pride, your desire to contradict, your self-wisdom and stubbornness that imprison you

within a hard shell. Inside that shell you cannot meet the
God of love and freedom.[35]

So obedience is closely linked with service to others. And since the
transformed person lives for the good of the other, this sort of generalized obedience is absolutely essential to making progress.

ROCK SOLID LIFE PRACTICE 7.6: ASSIMILIATING OBEDIENCE

For the purposes of this exercise, let's assume that your guide is
a Teacher and not an Elder.

1. Having received instructions from your guide,
    rearrange your Program to accommodate these instruc-
    tions. For example, if I give someone a specific Program
    to follow, then I expect him or her to do it every day
    without fail. Likewise, I myself am equally responsible
    for putting into practice the advice I've received from
    my own guide.

2. During the day, meditate on or keep in mind the guid-
    ance you've received and strive to live by it. To do this
    you will have to have the advice you have been given in
    front of your eyes constantly. Put it on cue cards, post
    it on your fridge, write it on the back of your hand! In
    other words, do whatever you need to do in order to
    remind yourself on a constant basis what you should be
    doing.

3. Find the biography and/or writings of a transformed
    person from the past, someone who resonates with you
    personally. Read it carefully and make a few notes on

what impresses you the most. And for a one-week period, take this person as your "guide" and try to live by the advice that this person would likely give you.

Part 3 is especially suited to people who don't have close contact with a qualified guide. However, it can be used beneficially by nearly everyone. Of course, if you already have a guide you should get his or her blessing to do this. The only trap in this exercise is that it is a relatively inexperienced person trying to interpret the transformed person — and this is something of a hazard because you'll probably still end up doing your own will imperceptibly, and you risk attempting things that are either beyond your level or completely inappropriate to your life situation. So proceed carefully!

As elaborated by St. John Klimakos, in *The Ladder of Divine Ascent,*

> Many of these holy fathers became experts in active life and in spirituality, in discernment and humility. Among them was the awesome and yet angelic sight of men gray-haired, venerable, preeminent in holiness, still going about like obedient children and taking the greatest delight in their lowliness. I have seen men there who lived in total obedience for all of fifty years, and when I begged them to tell me what consolation they had won from so great a labour, some answered that having arrived thereby at the lowest depths of abasement they could repel every onslaught, while others declared that they had attained complete freedom from the senses and had obtained serenity amid every calumny and insult. [36]

Humility is a great mystery. It gives incomparable inner sweetness, but you can only know it by experience. There is no feeling like this — nothing so wonderful or so liberating. And when you find it you will know. Humility flows from obedience and is one of its children.

Humility is the ultimate lever of self-transformation. What? Not love? No. Not faith and hope? No. Not universal compassion? No.

You see, none of the other virtues can exist without humility, and if you acquire humility the rest will land in your lap without effort. Does that sound good? Then let's get started.

FOUNDATIONS FOR PRACTICING HUMILITY

You already began to lay the foundations for practicing humility in chapter 6 when we talked about the Warrior's assuming responsibility not only for his own actions but also for those of others and even for circumstances. You see, humility depends absolutely on the ability and willingness to say (in a non-neurotic way), "I am to blame; others are doing the best they can." As absurd as this may seem to a worldly mentality, it hides a deep ontological truth. By taking responsibility for your brothers and sisters in the human race, you erase the imaginary line dividing yourself from them, the false, individual perspective of life, which is perpetuated by the ego. You then discover the consubstantiality of the human race — your single nature and your deep ontological connection with each other on both the biological and noetic planes of existence. Moreover, and this is a crucial point, you begin to live this truth in a concrete, incarnate fashion. Theory is irrelevant: Principles must be given flesh and blood in your life or they will never help you.

This way, you begin to repair your own inner being, weaken your ego, and stop the cycle of evil in the world around you. And all with such a simple practice!

A great Tibetan Lama said:

> As long as we regard ourselves as superior to others or look
> down upon the world, we cannot make any real progress.

As soon, however, as we understand that we live in exactly the world which we deserve, we shall recognize the faults of others as our own — though they may appear in different form. It is our own karma that we live in this 'imperfect' world, which in the ultimate sense is our own creation. This is the only attitude which can help us overcome our difficulties, because it replaces fruitless negation by an impulse toward self perfection, which not only makes us worthy of a better world, but partners in its creation.[37]

MIRACULOUS
ANCIENT FORMULA
❰❰❰❰❰❰❰ 10 ❰❰❰❰❰❰

Lowliness Is Greatness

❰❰❰❰❰❰❰❰❰❰❰❰❰❰❰

INNER PRINCIPLE
❰❰❰❰❰ 7.16 ❰❰❰❰❰

Humility is the ultimate key to self-transformation and its most powerful lever.

❰❰❰❰❰❰❰❰❰❰❰❰❰❰❰

When I talk about the ontological roots of humility and why it is organically connected to the very fabric of the universe, there is another dimension you must consider: the Absolute itself is humble.

Humility is the raiment of the Godhead. The Word who became man clothed Himself in it, and therewith He spoke to us in our body. Every man who has been clothed with it has truly been made like unto Him who came down from His own exaltedness, and hid the splendor of His Majesty, and concealed His glory with humility, lest creation should be utterly consumed by the contemplation of Him. Creation could not look upon Him unless He took a part of it to Himself, and thus conversed with it, and neither could it hear the words of His mouth face-to-face. Instead of a robe of honor and outward glory, He was arrayed in this. ...When rational (human) and irrational (animal, plant) creation beholds any man clad in this likeness, it worships him as master, for the sake of its own master's honor, whom it beheld clad and walking therein.[38]

INNER PRINCIPLE
((((((7.17 ((((((

The beginning of the path to inner freedom and humility is the frank and non-neurotic practice of assuming responsibility for the evils in yourself, in others, and in the world in general.

((((((((((((((((

As Father Sophrony once said, all of the divine commands given to the human race are actually reflections of the inner life of the Absolute translated onto the plane of earthly existence. In other words, obedience, humility and love are all characteristics of the Absolute. "All things arise from Tao, and they are nourished by Teh (the operative power through which the Tao manifests itself in the world)," wrote Lao-Tzu, "Thus, the ten thousand things all respect the Tao and honor the Teh. Respect of Tao and honor of Teh are not demanded, but they are in the nature of things." He also noted that although the Tao "clothes and feeds all things, it does not claim them as its own."[39]

Many misunderstand humility as a form of weakness and believe that anyone who practices humility is weak and vacillating and will draw abuse like a magnet. They believe that only pride and arrogance make you safe. Self-assertiveness is security and deference is danger. To be humble is to be taken advantage of by the unscrupulous. See "Captain Kirk Gets Humility" to the right.

Humility has to be practiced consciously if it is ever to become an inner state of being. Here, as everywhere else in this book, proper training methods are absolutely essential to your success. So how do we know if we have true humility?

The default setting of the ego is to put others down while you build yourself up. The transformed person, however, has a very different reaction and default setting, which is, in the words of Father Damascene, "the all-consuming urge to get under everything."[41] This is the inner urge to be a nothing and a nobody, to be unnoticed and obscure, and to rejoice in the good fortune of others.

This is the beginning of the ultimate reversal of the fallen world, of turning *Samsara* on its head. People who reach this point, says Father Sophrony, feel revulsion at the mere idea of dominating other

CAPTAIN KIRK GETS HUMILITY

For those of you who are *Star Trek* fans, you may remember that both the original *Star Trek* series and *Star Trek: the Next Generation* featured episodes in which the respective captains' "aggressive" side was removed from their personalities. They then became unfit to command, weak and vacillating.

This shows the currency of this idea in ordinary culture, the idea being that a complete personality somehow integrates negative and positive traits. Nothing could be further from the truth. When we read the biographies of transformed people or if we are fortunate enough to meet one in the flesh, we realize that they are very strong in character. As Joseph the Hesychast said, decisiveness is one of the traits of the true human being. Transformed people sometimes deliberately allow themselves to be mistreated by others in order to overcome the vestiges of their own egos. And this requires vastly more inner strength than the proud have, because the proud are weak. The proud are in the grip of emotional consciousness — their perceptions and judgments are clouded, they are completely yin to external energies, predictable in their reactions and unable to master their basic drives and tempers. This is why St. Paul wrote, "When I am weak, then I am strong."

A Tibetan Lama recently wrote: "In Western societies, the distinction between pride and firmness of mind is often confused. A lack of pride is construed to be weakness. Pride is a built up and concentrated form of ego grasping. So in this respect, it is a weakness. A person can have great strength of character and a strong resolve to achieve a goal, such as enlightenment, for example, without pride ever manifesting."[40]

Do you think Mahatma Gandhi was weak? Or the apostles? To resist the powerful ones of this world without resorting to violence yourself requires tremendous discipline and inner strength. Gandhi knew this very well and constantly emphasized to his followers how difficult it would be to follow the path of nonviolent resistance. By contrast, it is very easy to lash out at those who hurt us because this is our default setting in the fallen world.

people. And those who reach this state know the incredible sweetness of humility and so "automatically" pursue this state tirelessly and with all their strength.

So you can see the degree to which self-forgetfulness is part of humility. In fact, all of the usual secular categories related to self-esteem are no longer operative here because the transformed person has left self-image behind:

"When some accomplishment gives you a sense of superiority," writes the Preserver of the Truth, "then you have a self-image, which creates a massive obstacle. How can you attain the state of emptiness of mind? You have to increase your resolve to break yourself under all things, always taking a backseat to other people, thinking you're not as good as others in any way; then you can get rid of pride and your sense of superiority."[42]

Self-image, whether positive or negative, is really nothing more than a manifestation of the ego. It is self-forgetfulness that is the normal human state; positive self-image may be the best the fallen human person can come up with, but it's a poor substitute. Once the *nous* is refined to a high degree, it communicates its newfound purity to the heart, to the center of your being. "When does a man know that his heart has entered into purity? When he sees all men as good and none appears to him to be unclean and defiled, then in very truth his heart is pure."[43] Then the heart comes quite automatically upon the incredible energy of love:

> When beyond measure it descends upon a man, it throws his soul into ecstasy. Therefore the heart of the man who has felt this love cannot contain it or endure it without an unaccustomed change being seen in him according to the measure of love's quantity. And these are its signs: his face becomes fiery, exceedingly joyous, and his body becomes heated. Fear and shame withdraw from him and he is like

one deranged. The power that gathers the mind flees from him and he is as though out of his wits. From henceforth he deems his life as nothing in comparison with his Beloved. He considers death a joy, though it be a thing most terrible. And further, the gaze of his *nous* is fixed inseparably and deliriously upon Him (the Absolute).[44]

> **INNER PRINCIPLE**
> 〈〈〈〈〈〈 **7.19** 〈〈〈〈〈〈
>
> The authentic or holy person has no self-image in the usual sense, having left this behind in the struggle to love the other.
>
> 〈〈〈〈〈〈〈〈〈〈〈〈〈〈〈〈〈

Whoever reaches even the beginning of this state will have left the false self behind and will have no "self-image" left, good or bad.

One of the greatest side benefits of humility is that it eliminates a great deal of our suffering. A great deal of what people suffer is not objective physical or emotional suffering per se, but is based entirely on their perceptions and reactions to the disagreeable changes they are undergoing. Humility has a way of miraculously smoothing out our perceptions of suffering and insulating us from the ups and downs of physical and emotional existence. So the truly humble person is almost invariably at peace and untroubled no matter what the external conditions of life may be. Now, doesn't that sound like a situation you would like to be in? St. Isaac the Syrian describes it this way:

> As a man who drinks wine and becomes inebriated on the day of mourning forgets all the pangs of his sorrow, so the man who in this world (which is a house of lamentation) is drunk with the love of God, forgets all the sorrows and afflictions and becomes insensible to all sinful passions through his inebriation. His heart is made steadfast by hope in God, his soul is as light as a winged bird, and every moment his mind arises out of the earth and soars far above the heavens through the meditation of his thoughts, and he takes delight in the immortal things of the Most High. His prayer is unceasing, and he is like a man who has the wind

INNER PRINCIPLE
⟨⟨⟨⟨⟨⟨ 7.20 ⟨⟨⟨⟨⟨⟨

Humility eliminates most of the subjective experience of human suffering, even if objectively difficult circumstances remain in place on the physical or emotional levels.

⟨⟨⟨⟨⟨⟨⟨⟨⟨⟨⟨⟨⟨⟨

for his steed, so that his enemy cannot overtake him. Every time he seeks him he flies away from him.[45]

This is why St. Silouan was able to say: "You may say, 'my troubles are manifold.' But I tell you, or better, the Lord himself says, 'Humble yourself, and you will see, even to your own astonishment, that your adversities will be transformed into peace, and you will exclaim, 'Why was I so tormented and fretful?!'

...The soul of a humble person is like the sea — for a moment circumstances may ruffle the surface, and then sink to the bottom. Thus do afflictions disappear down in the heart of a humble person because the strength of the Lord is with him."[46]

The ontological consequences of humbling yourself inevitably have this effect. Think about it: By humbling yourself you progressively undo pride and therefore reestablish your inner organic connection with the Absolute as well as with all creation. So by conforming your life to its intended pattern, you become filled with the energy and power inherent in this pattern. And since this pattern created the universe and upholds its existence, you can imagine how much power that is!

Humility also has the immense benefit of silencing the imagination and the rational mind, so that your incessant internal dialogue, which is one of the ego's main support systems, becomes progressively inoperative. This vastly increases the power and effectiveness of your SSDN and all the rest of your inner work as well.

The real secret of finding humility and undercutting the domination of the imagination is this: "The simple and humble believer frees himself from the domination of the imagination by a wholehearted aspiration to live according to God's will. This is so simple, and at the same time so 'hidden from the wise and prudent' that there are no words to explain it."[47] This is how Father Sophrony puts it, admittedly in Orthodox terms. But the whole-hearted aspiration to live according to the Absolute can be applied to anyone. The driving force of Mahayana Buddhism is the bodhisattva's vow to live henceforth for the benefit of all sentient beings, and no longer merely for the convenience of his or her own psycho-somatic life. Since authentic ancient traditions recognize that in some mysterious way the life of love for the other is inseparable from conforming to the Absolute, these two different concepts of motive force are functionally the same. And so it's no surprise that in Orthodoxy as well you also frequently encounter the notion of living totally for the other.

PARADOX 7.5

The proud person, ironically, acquires a feeling of self-sufficiency despite the fact that his or her inability to cope becomes increasingly obvious to everyone, whereas the humble person is demonstrably a far more capable and "together" person.

ROCK SOLID PRACTICE 7.7: THE LIFETIME CONFESSION

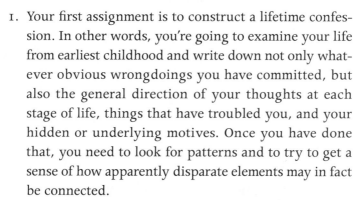

1. Your first assignment is to construct a lifetime confession. In other words, you're going to examine your life from earliest childhood and write down not only whatever obvious wrongdoings you have committed, but also the general direction of your thoughts at each stage of life, things that have troubled you, and your hidden or underlying motives. Once you have done that, you need to look for patterns and to try to get a sense of how apparently disparate elements may in fact be connected.

   Now comes the hard part: you're going to take this confession to your guide and you're going to deliver it to him or her orally and in person. Most people have a very difficult time openly discussing the least pretty trends and episodes from their past with another human being. It's a great act of humility and may leave you feeling broken and crushed, but that's okay.

Many Christians, including not a few Orthodox these days, ask why they should have to do this in front of a person when they can do it "directly to God." The answer is this: Millennia of experience have proven beyond any doubt that only the act of confessing in front of another human being has the therapeutic power to uproot deeply ingrained patterns and habits. You see, people who want to "confess to God alone" are really trying to avoid the painful experience of opening the self and destroying the ego, and so they reap very little benefit.

Nor do you have to be a Christian to carry out this assignment — a qualified guide in any authentic ancient tradition will understand very well what you're trying to achieve.

2. The next step is to analyze your confession again: see how much of what you've suffered during your life was the direct and obvious result of your own doing. Then mentally take responsibility for what you've done and for undoing it if possible. Notice that you've probably not suffered as much as you deserved — rather, you've been somehow mysteriously protected from the full consequences of your actions.

3. Resolve that for one week you will not defend yourself verbally at any time or for any reason. You will offer no self-justification or excuse for things done badly, for things left undone, or for any unintended consequences that your actions may have on others.

The ego lives and maintains itself by self-justification. So by refusing to defend yourself and agreeing to accept the pain that comes from being verbally accused or attacked, you're dealing a devastating blow to your own ego. And whenever someone does reproach you for something, strive mentally to justify his or her reproach and to see how the accusation could be true. This will take more work on your part if the accusation is completely false, but it can still be done. You can use even false accusations against yourself to attack your own ego. But in general, you'll probably find rather quickly that the criticisms of others are pretty much right on target.

4. For one full day hold in the very center of your being and with all your strength the desire to conform to the Absolute in every area of your life — in what you do, think, feel, say, and so on. Of course, there are no limits here. As a Warrior you must assume that there is no limit to what this may cost you.

Now that you have begun to cultivate the fine arts of self-abandonment, obedience, and humility, you are ready to take on some of your main adversaries.

Key to virtue: Retire from the center of your universe — it's a job you've held too long — and place everyone else there for a change.

Chapter Eight

TRIALS and TEMPTATIONS: RECLAIMING a LIFE of VICTORY

If someone were to ask you if you are "passionate about" your hobby or "have a passion" for your favorite food, you would probably answer with a resounding yes. In everyday English, the word *passion* is used as a synonym of zest, enthusiasm, and vibrancy; and these usages are entirely valid, as far as they go. However, the meaning of the word *passion* in the Orthodox tradition is more nuanced. The root is the Latin verb "to suffer," and you will find exactly the same etymology in a great many other languages.

THE PASSIONS: UNDERSTANDING ASSAULT FROM WITHIN

What the various traditions call passions, disturbing emotions, or mental poisons are actually things that we "suffer" — not because all the

> ## INNER PRINCIPLE
> ### ⸨⸨⸨⸨⸨⸨8.1⸨⸨⸨⸨⸨⸨
>
> Passionate thoughts are primarily an ontological phenomenon, not a moral one. You are not responsible that passionate thoughts enter your consciousness, but only for how you react to them.
>
> ⸨⸨⸨⸨⸨⸨⸨⸨⸨⸨⸨⸨⸨⸨⸨⸨

passions are painful at first glance (only some are), but because they're linked ontologically to corruption and death. And so, although a passion like gluttony may appear enticing, indulging in it can result in diabetes, obesity, high blood pressure, digestive problems, and autointoxication — all manifestations of corruption and death. We also "suffer" the passions in another sense: They tend to take over our inner world and coerce us into passively complying with whatever direction they set.

In the Orthodox tradition, even hunger, thirst, and the need for sleep are called "passions." This may seem strange at first glance, but these, too, are things that we "suffer" — they are psycho-physical needs in the fallen world, things that provoke suffering in us until we satisfy them. This proves one very important point: Passion is an ontological and not a moral category, and therefore the fact that passions come upon us is not something for which we are "guilty."

It is difficult to overstate the importance of this principle in the Western context, where so many people have been victimized by false versions of Christianity and perhaps other religions, telling them that they are "guilty" for having "shameful" and "disgusting" thoughts of lust, anger, or other emotions. This inevitably produces the infamous neurotic guilt complex and can lead to severe emotional disturbances in later life. Of course, moralistic approaches like this are designed to maximize social conformity, not collective emotional health. Over against this destructive approach we have Inner Principle 8.1, which imputes no blame and shames no one. It demands of us only that we face up to the realities of our inner landscape and deal with them in a mature, forthright and productive way.

Mahayana Buddhist tradition has a similar concept of passion:

> Soon after we encounter Buddhism, we notice that emotions are described in a different language than that to

THE 5 PILLARS OF LIFE

which we are accustomed. You may think that emotions are an important part of our life, having been taught that life would be boring without attachments, that we would lack self-esteem without pride, and that without jealousy we would not be able to keep our relationships. We may believe that we need anger and that we need to be indifferent to the suffering of the world, otherwise, we would be swept away by the flood of information.

In Buddhism, however, our emotions are called *suffering-causing mind states, disturbing feelings,* or *mind poisons* [emphasis mine]. The only feelings sought are those that arise through direct perception of phenomena and the true nature of the mind. These feelings include fearlessness, which arises when we realize that our mind, the basis for our "ego clinging" and our entire experience, is not a thing and therefore cannot be touched, damaged, or die.[1]

In addition to passions of desire, there is a second type of passion called *vehement feeling,* which gives rise to such strong emotions as anger and fear. Simply put, passions are drives or energies within us that have become disordered and over which we have lost control. The tradition maintains that these drives or energies are not at all evil in themselves, and in fact belong to our nature in its original form. Given this understanding, Orthodox terminology normally calls them "passions" only when they are disordered and drag us down into corruption and death.

From an ontological perspective, if you yield to the disordered passions of desire and vehemence (as opposed to the normal physical passions of hunger, thirst, and fatigue), you surrender your inner integrity to the blind, destructive energies of the fallen world as they express

The various drives within us are not evil in and of themselves, but only because in the fallen world they have become unbalanced and out-of-control.

themselves through the medium of your corrupted psychosomatic being. This obscures the *nous* and grants these energies a certain control over the heart itself — the center of your being. Naturally, this cuts you off from the Absolute and creates a yin state within you, leaving you a slave to the environment. This is why the Preserver of the Truth said, "If you are annoyed or excited on account of things, sickness is already stirring your mind."[2]

Moreover, yielding to passion becomes a vicious circle in which every surrender on our part strengthens the ego, which then provokes further passionate attacks. Father Damascene explains it this way:

> How can the human ego, immersed in its own gratification, hide from the ever present reality of God and the *nous*? How else than by a constant state of distraction into sensual pleasures, thoughts, memories and fantasies? Thus, man's fall into disobedience was at once a fall into distraction, and that was how his consciousness started to become as compounded and fragmented as it is today.
>
> To distract himself from facing his wrongness, man seeks out the very things that made him wrong in the first place: self-love and sensual pleasure. Gratifying himself in this way, he feels "right" again, but only temporarily. Actually, he has only become more wrong, so that now he needs even greater distractions, and even greater shocks, to make him feel that he is right. In this way he progresses further along the path of self-destruction, trying to overcome his predicament by its very cause.[3]

The purpose of our training is to get us off this treadmill so we can make progress. "There can be no progress in prayer while you are energized by the passions," said Joseph the Hesychast.[4] "Once selfish desire arises," says a Taoist source, "the primal spirit is disturbed: the primal energies are blocked, and the training has no effect."[5]

Although many Orthodox sources talk about destroying or uprooting the passions, the real truth is somewhat deeper. What the tradition really says, following on from the idea that the drives behind the passions are themselves neutral and part of our nature, is that the passions need to be reeducated.

> ## PARADOX
> ### 8.1
>
> The war against uncontrolled desire does not lead ultimately to a totally passive or desire-less state, but to a state in which the true, innate desire of our nature manifests itself spontaneously.

And it's very telling that any time in Orthodox history when a kind of hard-core "destroy the passions" idea has been put forward, the tradition as a whole has denounced it in the strongest possible terms.

If you're used to a more or less serious Western Christian milieu, much of what I have said here has probably taken you aback because the Western Christian ideas of sin, passion, and virtue are nearly antithetical to those of the original Christian tradition. To see why this is so, let's take a short historical interlude.

Back in the fourteenth century, a Western monk named Barlaam came from Calabria in Italy to Constantinople. Barlaam was shocked to learn that not only did Orthodox spiritual practices involve the body, but they also leveraged the desiring and vehement powers of the soul. You see, the Orthodox of that time had very little idea of what Christianity in the West was like and were almost completely unfamiliar with the misleading teachings of Augustine of Hippo, on which Barlaam's ideas of Christianity were entirely based.

The great difference was that Barlaam believed that our ability to feel any kind of desire or to express vehemence is evil in itself and that the purpose of spiritual life was to destroy desire and vehemence per se. So for him, the only true spirituality was an escape from the body. And in fact, his idea of prayer was exactly that — the mind had to be raised above the body so that the praying person would essentially pretend to be incorporeal.

The power to pull you forward to total self-transformation lies hidden within you. This hidden wellspring of innate momentum is known in Orthodoxy as the "image of God," in Buddhism as the "Buddha nature," and in Taoism as the "primordial nature."

His opponent, St. Gregory Palamas, defended the true tradition by asking this question: "How is it possible for what God has given us as gifts and has ordained to be part of human nature, to become an obstacle for our salvation?" Knowing that Barlaam's line of thought was a direct attack on the tradition of self-transformation, St. Gregory spared no effort in demonstrating that neither the body nor even our innate emotions and desires are in any way evil. And furthermore, he characterized any practice designed to cut the mind off from these three realities as nothing more than a form of suicide. True self-transformation necessitates the reeducation and realignment of the constituent elements of our nature, and not their destruction. Barlaam's identification of the human person with the rational mind alone is therefore something that Orthodoxy rejects outright.

St. Gregory Palamas was himself a diligent practitioner of the ancient tradition of self-transformation, and based on his profound experience he denounced Barlaam's pseudo-spirituality as "the greatest of Hellenistic delusions [and] an invention of devils."[6]

All this takes on vital importance in the present day and age because of the damage wrought on Western man by this Augustinian line of thought. The alternating extremes of forced repression and unrestrained indulgence so typical of Western history, together with the widespread neuroses of every kind and the pervasive emotional incompetence all have their origin in a false theology sixteen centuries old. The tragedy is that so few people are aware of this. And yet, almost all the counseling I do is related to the historical facts mentioned here.[7]

Let's go back for a moment: Recall that chapter 5 discussed having an innate tendency to move toward the Absolute, which implies that in your natural state you're not completely inert, not noetically stationary. All authentic ancient traditions maintain that human beings are meant to move from A to B, that we are by nature oriented toward a certain goal.

The real teaching of Orthodoxy and other ancient traditions on this particular point is if you remove the factors that obscure your own innate original nature, this nature will manifest itself spontaneously and guide you directly to the goal you were created for: self transformation and union with the Absolute.

INNER PRINCIPLE
8.5

Unless you fight against and ultimately reeducate the passions of attraction offered by such things as food, material wealth, and sexuality, you will not fully realize the suffering they conceal until it is too late.

"Once the human mentality is set-aside, the celestial mind comes back."[8] Or, in the words of Isaac the Syrian:

> When life's concerns do not incur into the soul from without, and she abides in nature, then she does not require prolonged toil to penetrate into and understand the wisdom of God. For her separation from the world and her stillness naturally move her toward the understanding of God's creatures. And by this she is lifted up toward God; being astonished, she is struck with wonder, and she remains with God. When water does not seep into the fountain of the soul from without, the natural water that springs up in her incessantly bubbles forth intuitions of God's wonders. But when the soul is found bereft of these, it is either because she has received a cause for this from some alien recollection, or because the senses have stirred up turmoil against her by means of encounters with objects. When the senses, however, are confined by stillness and not permitted to sally forth, and by its aid the soul's memories grow old, then you will see what the soul's natural thoughts are, what is the nature of the soul, and what treasures she has hidden within herself. … A man, however, does not even know that such thoughts could arise in human nature.[9]

Giving into passion gradually subverts the precedence
of the soul's powers and also
perverts their individual
functions.

According to the Orthodox tradition, your soul has three faculties or powers: the intelligent,[10] the desiring, and the vehement. When these are functioning normally the intelligent power seeks the Absolute and rules over the other two. The desiring power desires self-transformation, whereas the power of vehement feeling arouses us to defend ourselves against the forces dragging us away from our true goal. In short, the intelligent power gives clarity, discernment, and understanding. The desiring power gives warmth, love, and compassion. And the power of vehement feeling gives us courage and decisiveness.

That's the theory, at any rate. In the reality of our present condition, the ego uses the intelligent power to extinguish the *nous* and cloud our perceptions. As for desire, it begins to settle for the deceptive and fleeting satisfaction provided by external objects in an attempt to paper over the feeling of chronic inner emptiness with momentary pleasure, and so the energy of the passions of gluttony, lust, and greed overwhelm the soul from within.

As discussed at some length in chapter 3, neither food nor sexuality are in any way evil or harmful in themselves. As St. Maximos the Confessor rightly says, they become so only when we misuse them, and we misuse them chiefly, if not exclusively, by turning them into pitifully inadequate substitutes for the indescribable bliss of the true life that we've lost.

As for the power of vehement feeling, it begins to produce exactly the opposite of what it provides when it's healthy. Instead of courage we end up with cowardice, and instead of decisiveness we end up with dithering.

It is impossible to judge passions only by their external manifestation. You can be appropriately angry, for the right reasons, with an anger that you control, and even be inspired in so doing. Anger against an obvious injustice is one example. A less obvious example to the Western mind is the use of anger against inappropriate or uncontrolled manifestations of desire or vehemence within you.

"If we want to be angry with something," writes Lama Gyatso, "we should be angry with the 'demon' of our self-cherishing. In reality, anger directed against self-cherishing is not real anger, for it is based on wisdom rather than ignorance and functions to make our mind pure and peaceful."[11] Similarly, Father Sophrony tells us that in spiritual life, anger and hatred must reach their maximum, but that unlike passionate anger and hatred, this kind is directed not against someone else but only against the evil that lives in ourselves.

Using a controlled anger appropriately will not leave any noetic residue in your heart, as you will notice during your SSDN practice. Even if you "hurt" others, it will not become "karma" to you: Those whom you hurt are being hurt only by their own resistance to the truth. A classic example of this kind of anger is Christ's overthrowing the money changers in the temple.

Then there is the uncontrolled anger. When this gets the better of you it makes others around you miserable and will definitely generate consequences that will come back to hit you in the face sooner or later. The Buddhist would call this "karma." Orthodoxy would refer to it as a manifestation of *Pneumatikos Nomos*, the spiritual law: "If you do not want to suffer evil," writes St. Mark the Ascetic, "then do not inflict it, since the suffering of it inevitably follows its infliction. For whatever a man sows he will also reap (Gal.6:7)."[12]

So how many passions exist and what are they called? Well, there is no one answer to this question because several lists of passions exist within the Orthodox tradition, and if you look in other traditions you find a similar state of affairs. But to begin with, let's use the traditional list of the "eight evil thoughts" attributed to Evagrios in the fourth century:

1. Gluttony: attachment to and desire for the pleasures of food and drink.
2. Lust: attachment or desire stemming from an addiction to sexual pleasure.
3. Greed: attachment to wealth or to sensory objects in general.
4. Despair: a feeling of hopelessness, inability to change, inexplicable blackness and depression.
5. Anger: vehement feelings or aversion to persons, events or things.
6. Sloth: laziness or negligence, the feeling of being weighed down or indifferent.
7. Vainglory: the desire to be seen as superior to others.
8. Pride: an inner sense of autonomy, of not needing the Absolute.

The "suffering" involved in these passions is that all of them trap our energy and attention in the world of the senses, of persons, events, and things. Our vision is reduced to the fallen world and, in Buddhist terms, our entire outlook becomes "samsaric." Passions force us into a relation of dependence on sensory objects and material reality. So rather than being above the matrix of persons, events, and things as we are meant to be, we are dragged down into it. From a place of peace and bliss we are dragged into constant storms and dissatisfaction. We lose our sense of internal unity, both physical and mental.

You can see very clearly from this that the problem is not that passions offend God, but that by indulging them we make it impossible for God to help us.

I say "on the physical level" because modern research, particularly in what is called *Psychoneuroimmunology* (a field that studies the relationship between the nervous system and the immune system) has been able to confirm in many cases that indulgence in various passions actually degrades the immune system. One study, for example, found that excessive indulgence in sexual activity — more than twice a week — hindered the production of T-cells.[13]

INNER PRINCIPLE
8.9

"Vices" are not bad because God said so: God said so because they are bad. This is often the case even on the physical level.

There are endless classification schemes for passions or vices. St. Peter of Damascus actually came up with a list of some 298 different ones! At the other extreme, St. Maximos the Confessor once attributed all passions to ignorance, although he typically maintained that the triad of gluttony, avarice, and self-cherishing is at the root of all the others.

The Shakyamuni Buddha listed the six "root delusions" as attachment, hatred, pride, ignorance, deluded doubt, and distorted views. Very similar to this is the traditional list of the "five poisons" commonly used in Tibetan Buddhism: ignorance, hatred, pride, passionate desire, and envy.

Taoist tradition actually mentions joy or happiness as a passion! This may seem shocking at first sight, but there are a couple of reasons for this. First, Chinese medicine has long been known that "extreme joy and laughter slows down and congests heart energy. People with weak hearts can easily die laughing, a phenomenon well-known in Western medicine, and many people have dropped dead from heart attacks upon becoming overjoyed at unexpected good news."[14]

The second reason is that the "happiness" that people experience in the fallen world is not real happiness of all, because that is a result of self-transformation. What most people mistake for happiness is simply the temporary absence of painful occurrences. The irony is that unending "happiness" of this kind would be ruinous for you, because you would fritter away your time in a morass of mindless self-satisfaction that would effectively prevent you from embarking on the path toward self-transformation. This brings to mind an old saying in the tradition, that God allowed physical death to enter the world in order to prevent sin and corruption from becoming immortal.

So, although we always wish for happiness and joy for others, we don't equate this happiness with ordinary worldly contentment, since real happiness can only be found in escape from this world's matrix. And again, escape does not entail going anywhere physically; the path to liberation lies within you.

STRATEGIES FOR REVERSING THE PASSIONS

Many of the most important strategies are discussed in previous chapters. Chapters 2 and 3 show how to get the externals of your life in order, which reduces your vulnerability to the passions. Chapter 4 introduces you to SSDN, which is the most important practice for refining your inner world. Chapter 5 shows how to develop and use Intent, which can enable you to overcome nearly any obstacle at will. Chapter 6 contains a number of "macro strategies" such as meditation on death. This and the Warrior's path in general will steadily undercut the passionate process at its roots.

This childlike state from Inner Principle 8.10 is nothing other than a manifestation of our true nature as it is meant to function. Unfortunately, as we grow up in the fallen world, "discriminating awareness gradually arises, and the encrustation of the senses gradually takes place; the real retreats and the artificial assumes authority. Now even the state of the child is lost."[15]

The key that most people miss in trying to defeat the passions is Inner Principle 8.11.

It is impossible because this conventional or "adult" personality is part of the false self, a creation of the passions themselves. It is about as effective as trying to run while standing in quicksand! Yet this truth can only been known by the practice of inner refinement; otherwise you will never see it for yourself. As one Taoist master said: "The ignorant think the temperament is the real nature, but this is not so. The real nature is the nature as divinely decreed and belongs to the primordial; this is beneficial to people. The temperament is nature created by people and emerges from acquired conditioning; this is harmful to people. How can acquired nature be identified with primal nature?"[16]

We all have our own personal collection of opinions and beliefs that we use to categorize everything — persons, events, and things — saying, "this is good" or "she is bad," fitting everything we encounter into our preconceived notion of reality in order to give ourselves a sense of control, a sense that we have tamed the world and made it safe. We don't realize, though, how much energy we waste in this futile attempt and that all it accomplishes is to solidify the ego's grip on us.

This constant categorization demands an ideology to provide a framework for all of our moralistic judging. Unfortunately, religion provides a perfect alibi for this practice, and fallen man has used it consistently down through the ages for exactly this purpose. He even corrupts authentic traditions and turns them into religions in order to use them in this way. What he doesn't understand is that basic moral evaluations of reality provided by these true traditions were created only to protect him from causing himself harm; they were not intended to be used as bricks and mortar for the foundation of the false self.

The bottom line is that it is only through the consistent practice of SSDN together with the assiduous attempt to suffuse every moment of your life with the stillness you have tasted there that you have any realistic possibility of overcoming your deeply ingrained passions. As discussed in Chapter 4, passionate thoughts develop through a number of stages in our mental continuum. The earlier the stage at which you recognize the development of a particular passion, the easier it is for you to cut it off. This process of takeover by a passionate energy may take several minutes or it may envelope your mental world instantly, depending on the level of your inner attentiveness.

The process of the development of passionate thoughts can be summarized as follows:

1. *Attack:* the passionate energies seek to enter our mental continuum, coming from the environment, hostile noetic entities, or even our own imaginations.
2. *Bare idea:* this energy or "intrusive thought" begins to enter our inner field of vision, though it still has not assumed a definite shape.
3. *Image:* the energy behind the thought produces an image in our inner field of vision as the energy itself slowly gains strength.
4. *Dialogue:* we begin to play with the idea or image. At this point we're putting ourselves in danger, although we have not yet yielded.
5. *Consent:* we surrender our will to the idea.
6. *Action:* we take action on the passionate suggestion concretely.

When we give in to the same passionate energy several times — allowing it to reach stage 4, 5, or 6 — a passionate predisposition develops. Most people these days have several major passionate predispositions which define the kind of traps that they fall into most easily. This is why you know "angry people," "greedy people," "conceited people," and so on. In other words, not everyone is beaten by the same energies. And not everyone notices when they've been beaten: if you simply go along with your passions, you may rest under the illusion that your life is smooth sailing.

Remember that there is no external criterion that can be used to measure someone else's slavery to this or that passion. There are poor people and millionaires alike obsessed with greed, whereas there are other poor people and millionaires who have no passionate attachment to wealth whatsoever!

In general, the way to free yourself from domination by any particular passion involves a twofold strategy: The first is cultivating unceasing inner stillness, which is the principle method of noetic refinement, and the second involves employing specific tactics appropriate to the passion involved.

Furthermore, when you've made progress in integrating stillness into day-to-day life, the solicitations of passionate thoughts that you used to perceive as exciting and enticing come to be felt more as unwelcome disturbances. And this is precisely the measure of victory over any enticing form of passion. According to the exact teaching of the Orthodox tradition, the real meaning of "forgiveness of sins" is Inner Principle 8.14.

Christians in particular should be aware that it is not that you are begging God to forgive you, since in reality God forgives everyone everything all the time without any exception. The central issue is whether you are able to accept this forgiveness and assimilate it on a deep ontological level. It's a question of opening your own being to the Absolute in order to be transformed internally, so that the passionate energies within are reeducated and sublimated. Taoist master Sima Chengzhen likewise affirms that "If we look back at our former cravings after [we have distanced ourselves from them], then we will naturally find them unappealing."[17]

Note: The following exercises require that you keep a journal. As with previous exercises, reflection on your experience is critical to understanding the factors affecting your progress. If a specific passion doesn't have a negative impact on you, then feel free to skip the associated exercise. The following sections are a list of general tactics to use in confronting the eight primary passions.

Gluttony

With gluttony it's important to set up a stable rule for eating and drinking. Most important is not to have on hand anything that would tempt you to abandon this rule. Try not to eat to the point where you are completely full, but instead try to stop eating at a point where you could eat more, where you are still slightly hungry. The basic principle is to give the body what it needs, not what it wants, since, left to its own devices, the body generally craves bad food and lots of it.

ROCK SOLID LIFE PRACTICE 8.1: OVERCOMING GLUTTONY

1. Weeks 1-2: This week you are going to plan your intake of food and drink for next week down to the last detail. First, make sure that you allow your body everything it requires nutritionally–adequate water, protein, fat, carbohydrate, and supplements. Our health Web site at www.rocksolidlife.com/health can help you! Now for the hard part: You will not indulge any of your pet cravings. Give your body what it requires for optimum functioning, not what it wants.

2. Weeks 3-4: For the two following weeks you will maintain your practice of planning your food consumption down to the last detail. However, you'll give

yourself a break! You'll allow yourself to indulge a food craving on two occasions this week, but you'll plan ahead of time exactly when this will happen. Also, the craving must not include anything harmful to your health, such as foods containing refined sugars,

hydrogenated or partially hydrogenated oils ("trans fats"), or other items condemned by our health program (again, see www.rocksolidlife.com/health).

Feel free to enlist the cooperation of those around you; they'll be less likely to sabotage your efforts if they know what you're doing. And if they don't understand inner refinement, just tell them you're doing it to keep in shape, or on doctor's orders.

Lust

The basic strategy against lust, particularly for males, involves avoiding the ever-present seductive sexual images that surround us in contemporary culture. Also important is to cultivate the ability to converse with an attractive person without your will being overcome by the passion. Being overcome means taking delight in the stimulation of the heart caused by the attractive person, and you can easily feel this if you are the least bit attentive to your inner world. The function of this stimulation in the fallen world is to pull us toward biological reproduction for the perpetuation of the species. The aim of self-transformation, though, is to free us from this kind of biological determinism and to place all of our innate drives under conscious control. In the words of an ancient Taoist text:

Practical cultivation is a matter of stabilizing vitality; then the root is strong and living energy flourishes daily. If a lustful attitude is not stopped, the spiritual roots will not be firm; then the accumulation of vitality thins daily, and the production of basic energy lessens daily. Gradually you reach exhaustion and even death. ...So if you want to build up basic energy, first you should stop debauchery and lustfulness; this work must be done with a clean mind free from thoughts.[18]

Again, controlling the passion of lust has nothing to do with sexuality's being somehow innately evil or tainted. Instead, it's a matter of not squandering all the capital of our desiring power on one of the transitory phenomena of this world, and thereby exhausting ourselves physically and sabotaging the noetic integrity on which all further progress toward transformation depends.

ROCK SOLID LIFE PRACTICE 8.2: OVERCOMING LUST

For one week, arrange your life to exclude any and all sexual images coming through the media, however innocuous they may seem. Record the results in your journal. Was it a struggle for you? By the end of it all did you feel better or worse? Was the struggle growing more intense or abating? By the way, whether you felt better or worse, more at peace or more harassed, does not indicate anything in itself; the struggle with this passion can be quite subtle at times. But the ultimate stage is for your heart to be unmoved in the presence of an attractive person of the opposite sex (other than your spouse, of course!).

Greed

The basic antidote to greed is the act of sacrifice. This may sound strange, but the essence of sacrifice in the Old Testament was to take something required for sustaining your biological existence, such as food, and offer it freely to God rather than consuming it. This was a concrete way of saying that life depended on the Absolute and not on biology. In the same way, the greedy person can free him- or herself from the passion by giving away wealth to the point where it becomes painful, because anyone overcome by avarice has the same relationship with money that ordinary people do with food. He or she believes life depends on it. So philanthropy overcomes greed.

ROCK SOLID LIFE PRACTICE 8.3: OVERCOMING GREED

Go over Rock Solid Life Practice 7.4 — have you carried it out to the best of your ability?

Gluttony, lust, and greed are the three main passions of the desiring power. Perhaps the most effective overall strategy for transforming these potent energies is this: "Remain centered, thus bringing about harmony, and desires will not be able to move you. If desires cannot move you, then energy embraces spirit. When spirit and energy follow each other, spirit is clear and energy peaceful and you enter into the vastness."[19] The expression, "when spirit and energy follow each other," signifies the practice of the mind following the breathing, which was outlined in Chapter 4. So by practicing this method assiduously day in and day out, you can gradually learn to control these passionate energies.

Despair

Despair is overcome by the conscious attempt to recall and rehearse all the blessings that you have received and to give thanks for them. Also, turning your anger against yourself when you begin to give in to thoughts of despair is also quite effective. Just a word of caution: These tactics will not necessarily be effective against despair that has evolved into a full-scale clinical depression, or which is caused by biological factors, such as postpartum depression.

For a two-week period, use your journal to keep track of every blessing you receive — this includes every event that brings you joy, any event that, while not "peaches and cream" from your point of view, could have turned out far worse, and even those difficult situations that have taught you something valuable. Force yourself to concentrate on finding these blessings. They really are there, and if you can't find them because you have spent your life seeing the glass half empty instead of half full, then it's time to reeducate your thought processes.

Anger

Anger is overcome by patience, and patience involves not expressing anger that is felt internally. The essential dynamic here is that you no longer accept the angry thought as valid. If you accept it as valid and rehearse it in your mind while merely trying to stifle its external expression, then the anger will eat away at you on the inside, both physically and psychologically. But if you contradict the anger and stifle it, you will find its passionate energy lessens greatly over time.

Use your journal to record every incident that causes you anger over a one-week period. Then, use one or more SSDN sessions to examine your findings and to invalidate your anger: in other words, use your mind to make up reasons why your anger was not necessarily justified. Perhaps you got angry when you found yourself driving behind a slow-moving car, only to realize that the driver was looking for a specific address and had no choice but to drive slowly.

Sloth

Your Program is the main antidote to sloth, coupled with an assiduous program of reading relevant material, guidance from a qualified person, and sharing your experiences with a peer group of people dedicated to the same purpose as you are.

ROCK SOLID PRACTICE 8.6: OVERCOMING SLOTH

Revisit your faithfulness to your Program. Are you entirely free of omitting or postponing parts of it when you just don't "feel like" doing them?

Vainglory

Vainglory is defeated by teaching yourself to accept criticism without reacting, by deliberately rejoicing in the successes of others while trying to stay in the background yourself, and by understanding the vanity of all things. This last element means that you must analyze in the light of your inevitable death your tendency to want to be seen as superior. Only what survives death has any real value; the rest is vanity. The literal translation of the technical term for this passion means "empty glory" – in other words, we impute ultimate value to what is in reality empty or nonexistent.

ROCK SOLID LIFE PRACTICE 8.7: OVERCOMING VAINGLORY

In what areas of your life have you heavily invested in your image? Where does it bother you not to be seen as the expert, the person in authority, the one deserving of special treatment and recognition? Make a list of them.

Pride

Pride is the most subtle and difficult passion to overcome. In general, humility is the only real answer. You have to remember that the hallmark of pride is a feeling of autonomy, and autonomy is overcome by cultivating a relationship of dependence on the Absolute. Authentic traditions tell us this dependence represents our true state; this is how we become yin to the Absolute, reversing our current condition.

ROCK SOLID LIFE PRACTICE 8.8: OVERCOMING PRIDE

Review the results of your work on Rock Solid Life Practice 7.7. Continue to practice parts 3 and 4 of that exercise until they become very familiar.

One of the most effective ways to deal with passion is to analyze a particular passion and deeply ingrain this analysis using your SSDN. If you want to overcome passions based on external objects, the Preserver of the Truth recommends that you dwell on the obvious fact that, "…physical form and things disintegrate before long, ultimately returning to nothing. This is observant insight or understanding; once you can understand, you will naturally be detached from illusions, so delusions and random imaginations spontaneously disappear without having to be eliminated."[20]

To overcome the passion of anger, Lama Gyatso suggests the following:

> When we are harmed by another person we should examine whether it is his or her essential nature to be harmful or whether this is just a temporary fault. If it were true that being harmful was the very nature of this person, there really would be no reason to become angry with him. We do not blame fire when we are burned by it because we know that it is the very nature of fire to burn. On the other hand, if the harmfulness of our aggressor is only a temporary fault, arising in response to changing circumstances, there is also no reason for us to become angry with him. When too much rain falls from the sky we cannot become angry with the sky, because we realize that rain is not part of its essential nature. Rain falls from the sky only as a result of temporary circumstances such as temperature, humidity, and air pressure. Therefore, if the harmfulness of our aggressor is not part of his essential nature, whose fault is it that he harms us? It is the fault of his delusion.[21]

Avoid trying to clash directly with a passionate thought by arguing against it. The usual result of arguing is that the passionate energy becomes even stronger, because whatever the mind dwells on consciously it magnifies. It is far safer to do the following: rebuke the passionate thought powerfully and definitely. This creates internal noetic

> ## INNER PRINCIPLE
> ### ⸨⸨⸨⸨⸨ 8.15 ⸨⸨⸨⸨⸨
>
> One of the most effective ways to defeat passions is to analyze the matter from a traditional point of view and to deeply ingrain this analysis through noetic work.
>
> ⸨⸨⸨⸨⸨⸨⸨⸨⸨⸨⸨⸨⸨⸨

space and loosens whatever grip it may already have on you. Then immediately turn away from the thought and occupy the mind with something else. Many traditions will also tell you that asking immediately for assistance from the Absolute or from transformed people is extremely helpful.

However none of this implies that you will not have to struggle. Overcoming deeply ingrained predispositions can be murderously difficult. Only patience, persistence and the will to fight will get you through this. But what you will quickly discover to your great joy is Paradox 8.3, on page 365.

"Get rid of selfish desire," said Wang Liping's Grandmaster, "entering physically and mentally into quiet stillness, and the primal energy will be buoyant, while the primal spirit will be lively."[22]

In other words, there is something to be said for cutting off a particular passion suddenly and decisively. "Self-government," writes a Taoist master, "is like executing a rebel — you must cut through with one stroke of the sword. Attacking human desires must be like this before it can be successful"[23]

As a spiritual father, I'm constantly amazed by the number of people who continue to be troubled by exactly the same passions over an extended period of time. Yet authentic traditions are therapeutic; they heal our inner sicknesses so that our inner noetic condition continually evolves in a positive direction. When this is not the case — as when same enemy continues to defeat you time after time — the problem clearly lies with your failure to put it into practice correctly.

PEIRASMOI:
UNDERSTANDING ASSAULT FROM WITHOUT

It's often said that the only two sure things in life are death and taxes.

To those we could readily add a third: *peirasmoi*. *Peirasmoi* (pronounced: peer-as-MEE) are life's physically or emotionally painful happenings. The pain itself is not the problem; the problem is whether your response accords with your true nature and carries you forward to self-transformation, or whether it harms your inner being even further.

I use the Greek technical term *peirasmos* from the Orthodox tradition for a couple of reasons. First, because the usual English translation of this word — "temptation" — is quite misleading. "Temptation" in current usage implies a seductive quality, whereas *peirasmoi* may or may not have this. Fear, for example, physical pain and emotional torment are all *peirasmoi*, and yet there is nothing pleasant about them. So it would be much better to translate *peirasmos* as "trial," because they are trying experiences–they put you to the test. The second reason is simply etymology: the root of the word *peirasmos* is *peira*, which means "experience." And this is a profound connection because during the course of your training nothing will be so helpful to you in the end as the trials you have gone through.

Given the constant shifts in our inner and outer circumstances caused by this unstable and corrupt existence we share, it's safe to say that *peirasmoi* — painful and trying experiences — cannot be avoided by any amount of forethought or planning. But we can learn how to reduce their number, lessen their shock and neutralize them, and we can also learn how to use them to our advantage.

Before getting into that, however, you first need a more exact understanding of what *peirasmoi* are and where they come from.

Here are three classic examples of *peirasmoi*:

1. George is sitting at his desk one night paying the bills after a long hard day at the office. Gradually and without noticing he

begins to recall the hurtful comments of a colleague earlier in the day and actually begins to get angry.

2. Jennifer does a breast self-examination one day in the shower and finds what she thinks is a lump that was not there before. Unfortunately, it will be several days before she can have this checked out by a medical professional, and until then she is overcome by feelings of fear bordering on panic.

3. At work, Susan and her fellow employees are called into a meeting by senior management. An overpaid, self-serving, and thoroughly incompetent government bureaucrat subjects them to an hour and a half of lies and deliberate falsifications concerning life in the workplace. Susan leaves the meeting feeling intensely angry and frustrated.

Notice in each case that it was an energy coming from outside the *nous* that provoked passionate response. In the first example, the provoking energy took the form of a thought that slowly insinuated itself into George's mind at a time when he was least able to defend himself. This thought could have come simply from his own memory and inner emotional turmoil or could have been provoked by hostile noetic forces. In the second example, the origin of the *peirasmos* is the physical body itself. And in the third example, the provocation comes from a particular person and circumstance.

Joseph the Hesychast says that *peirasmoi* hit us through three different channels, which he referred to as the inside, the outside, and the surroundings. And these correspond exactly to the scenarios described previously, where the *inside* refers to the inner workings of the mind, the *outside* refers to body, and *surroundings* refers to the external world of persons, events, and things. In each of the three scenarios the external energy gives rise to a passionate response. So passions and *peirasmoi* have a kind of perverse symbiotic relationship. On the more obvious level it is *peirasmoi* that provoke passions and yet, in the mysterious operation of the spiritual law, it is our passionate predispositions that are largely responsible for the *peirasmoi* that hit us.

Here we enter into a very subtle domain. Although our negative thoughts and actions inevitably bring *peirasmoi* down on our own heads, our positive thoughts and actions, while they increase our participation in the Absolute and our invulnerability to *peirasmoi*, do not entirely put an end to *peirasmoi*, since these trials are part and parcel of a world in the grip of death and impermanence.

The idea of karma has become quite well known in the West in recent years, but many people have simplistic ideas about it, thinking that if they follow the Buddha dharma or a similar teaching, then no more bad things will happen to them. The problem is that the fallen world or *Samsara* generates *peirasmoi* as a matter of course — accident, tragedy, illness, old age, the host of other problems, and finally death itself are not going to go away, and there's nothing we can do to become entirely free of them externally.

Fortunately, the *peirasmoi* are not blind — there is an internal logic to the universe and to our lives, so that nothing that happens to us is really "accidental" or "random." The great ascetics of the Orthodox tradition have noted over the centuries that the type and quality of *peirasmoi* vary according to our approach to life. As Joseph the Younger puts it, based on St. Isaac the Syrian and the teaching of his Elder:

> There are the trials of those actively engaged in the struggle, so that they may make additional gains and progress in their struggle. There are the trials of the slothful and the

INNER PRINCIPLE 8.16

If your slavery to anger and desire does not subside over time, if you are continually troubled and overcome by the same passions, this is usually an indication that your practice is not correct. Fix it!

INNER PRINCIPLE 8.17

No amount of forethought and planning can save you from *peirasmoi*, but you can learn how to become more invulnerable to them and to use them to your advantage.

unwilling, to make them beware of things that are harmful and dangerous. There are the trials of those who are drowsy or sleeping, in order to wake them up. Then again there are the trials of those who have distanced themselves and gone astray, to make them draw near to God. Different again are the trials of the righteous and friends of God, so that they may inherit the promise. There are also trials of the perfect, which God permits in order to bring them forward in the Church for the strengthening of the faithful and as an example to be emulated. There is also another kind of trial, again of the perfect, such as those endured by our Lord and the apostles, who fulfilled the law of communion with the world by taking up the trials which are ours."[24].

This shows the educational aspect of *peirasmoi*. It is imperative to understand that the basic difference between a worldly person and a Warrior is not that the former encounters constant evils whereas the latter experiences uninterrupted bliss! The difference is that the Warrior learns how to deal profitably and effectively with *peirasmoi* so as to extract their life-giving nectar, whereas the worldly person reacts incorrectly, wasting the opportunities presented and building up further negative "karma."

Your default setting in the fallen world is to attempt to create life circumstances that are pleasant and to avoid everything painful. So you base your happiness on external factors: romantic relationships, family, children, friendships, career, reputation, official positions and titles, health, financial success, and other such things. But shifting circumstances have a way of dashing your plans. Your relationships fall apart, your children leave home, you get sick, your friends can't be depended upon, your job is downsized, your reputation is attacked, and your financial investments go bad. And no amount of planning can ward off every possible adverse circumstance like this.

The valuable lesson here is that you must begin to base your life on what is eternal instead of what is transitory, because this is the only way to solidify your life and to protect yourself adequately from the constant *peirasmoi* that will inevitably surround you.

The deep meaning of Orthodoxy and other authentic traditions is not about improving our life in the usual sense, because this life is innately unsatisfactory. What these traditions want us to do is to adopt an entirely new existential orientation in the deepest levels of our being. And this is what Orthodoxy refers to as a mode of existence: rather than simply becoming a nicer person — which is all religion will ever do for you (while leaving you fundamentally self-centered) — ancient traditions are about a radical transformation where we replace the idolatry of the fallen self with the "idolatry" of the Other. This is nothing short of a revolution, a 180-degree turn.

Many of the external realities of life may not be any more agreeable than they were before, but our perception of and reaction to these circumstances does change. We become increasingly invulnerable to the constant flux of this world. And it is this that becomes the measure of the effectiveness of our life. In the words of St. Isaac the Syrian:

> If, therefore, the desire of the love of Christ has not become so powerful within you as to render you dispassionate toward every affliction due to your joy in Him, then know that the world is more alive in you than is Christ. When illness, and want, and bodily exhaustion, and fear of bodily harm perturb your mind so as to sway it from the joy of your hope and from your unsullied care to please the Lord, then know that the flesh and not Christ lives within you. *To speak simply, that which you love and which has mastery within you, this it is which lives in you.*[25] [emphasis mine]

Basing our security on the shifting sands of this world not only doesn't

INNER PRINCIPLE
((((((8.18 ((((((

The essence of self-transformation is not about being
nice, kind, and compassionate in the conventional
sense, but rather about
adopting an entirely new
"mode of existence."

(((((((((((((((

work, it enslaves us to an ego game based on fear. There is no way to repair your inner noetic integrity until you've abandoned your senseless search for worldly security, because until then every shift in the sands of the external world will trigger a neurotic, passionate response. But when I say *abandon*, I am speaking of an internal, noetic change and not an external physical one. In other words, two different people could both seek relationships, build careers, take care of their finances, look after their health, and do whatever else life demands of them; one of them could be a slave to fear and the other totally free. The actions are less the issue than is the mentality behind them.

The only way to outflank this fear is to do what it tells you not to do, to go out on a limb, the limb of faith. And this is the constant feature of authentic traditions and explains why so many people in the past did such apparently "crazy" things, such as the Orthodox Christians who went off into the deserts of Egypt or the Buddhists who went to live in caves in the Himalayas.

St. Isaac the Syrian gives us a masterful explanation of the difference between these two modes of existence. For the sake of convenience, he calls the worldly mode of existence "knowledge" and the Warrior's mode of existence "faith":

> Knowledge keeps within the boundaries of nature in all its paths. But faith makes its journey above nature. Knowledge does not allow itself to experience anything that is ruinous to nature and it keeps far away from it. But faith readily submits itself to this and says, "Upon the asp and the basilisk you will tread, and you shall trample upon the lion and the dragon." (Ps.91:13; translation mine). Fear accompanies knowledge, but confidence accompanies faith. The

more a man journeys in the pathways of knowledge, the more he is shackled by fear and he cannot be found worthy of freedom from it. But the man who follows faith straightway becomes a free man and the ruler of himself, and as a son of God with authority he freely wields all things. The man who has found the keys of faith wields all the natures of creation even as God; for by faith comes the authority, after the likeness of God, to create a new creation. And many times faith can bring forth all from nonexistence. But knowledge isn't able to do anything without matter.[26]

It should come as no surprise, then, that the main long-term strategy for dulling the impact of *peirasmoi* is to cut off your bondage to worldly security. And in this endeavor there is no more effective tool than SSDN for recognizing this ego manifestation in all of its numerous disguises.

Once you've made considerable progress in inner noetic work; once you've begun to integrate stillness into your everyday life and can maintain inner vigilance for extended periods, you'll begin to notice that many *peirasmoi* seem almost deliberately fashioned for one purpose: to provoke a passionate response that distracts your noetic concentration. And in fact, the more advanced you become, the more you'll have the feeling that you are being systematically worked against.

Now comes a topic that is very difficult for most contemporary Westerners: Every authentic ancient tradition claims the following, with minor variations:

1.   There are realms of existence other than our own.
2.   Some of these realms are noetic rather than physical, and contain purely noetic beings or powers capable of interacting with us on a noetic or mental level.
3.   Although some of these beings or powers are benevolent, some are, in fact, hostile.

The reason for not having talked about this until this point is the following: Before you have penetrated deeply into the world of self-transformation, the very existence of the noetic world is largely theoretical — you probably have no direct experience of it — so to bring it up would serve no particular purpose.

For reasons peculiar to the West European and North American "religious" experience, secularized Westerners usually do not believe in the existence of "demons" and fall into the temptation to psychologize away the existence of the demonic by confusing it with manifestations of the passions. And in fact, Western converts to Oriental traditions often do the same thing, partly because there are certain elements in some of those traditions which make this rather simple to do at first sight. However, this is a misunderstanding of Oriental traditions.[27]

Orthodoxy's teaching on demonic entities is quite detailed and precise, but most of it is also not relevant to you at this point. What is relevant is that some noetic beings are benevolent (these are conventionally called *angeloi* in Greek, meaning "messengers," although there are actually several different types), whereas others are not. The hostile ones are deeply involved in the process of corruption and death and are quite distressed by your efforts to achieve wholeness and life. You are, so to speak, "ruining their whole day"! So, to paraphrase Joseph the Hesychast, when you fire the artillery shells of your noetic work at them, you cannot expect them to respond by throwing marshmallows at you!

There are several basic strategies that can protect you so well against demonic incursion that you will barely have to think about these wretched creatures ever again. And in fact, that itself is part of the most important strategy:

1. It is extremely important not to become obsessed with the demons, or with the passionate thoughts or *peirasmoi* that they bring. Instead, simply ignore them.

2. In the same vein, you should never debate with intrusive thoughts, because if you do so your *nous* and heart will not

THE 5 PILLARS OF LIFE

emerge "clean," as St. Silouan notes. So when these kinds of thoughts oppress you, your first instinct should be to forcefully rebuke the thought and turn your attention to something entirely different. But the ultimate antidote to the demons, what renders them completely powerless, is item 3.

3. The more you humble yourself and cultivate dependency on the Absolute while sincerely attempting to love even the most difficult people, the more impervious you will become to the demons, to the thoughts they bring, and to the *peirasmoi* that they unleash.

The bottom line is that hostile noetic powers cannot really do you any damage whatsoever without your cooperation. So the most common errors are to disbelieve in their existence and interpret them as impersonal psychological energies — a practice that leaves you ignorant and therefore somewhat defenseless — or on the other hand to become obsessed with them — whereby you end up granting them more power over your life than they are capable of obtaining on their own.

ROCK SOLID LIFE PRACTICE 8.9: DEALING WITH PEIRASMOI

Before *peirasmoi* strike:

1. *Expect them!* To use the colloquial expression, "Shit happens." On a more profound note: "Whenever you wish to make a beginning in some good work: first prepare yourself for the *peirasmoi* that will come upon you, and do not doubt the truth. ... If you have not prepared yourself beforehand to meet *peirasmoi*, then refrain from practicing the virtues."[28]

2. *Anticipate them!* Ask yourself, "What could go wrong

today?" This strategy helps to prepare you mentally to meet whatever obstacles present themselves. Elder Joseph the Hesychast would, "examine with detailed precision the causes and occasions which prompt them [the *peirasmoi*], and teach us how to avoid them as far as possible. His experience centered on this double duty, as he called it: to deal wisely with the causes and occasions of *peirasmoi* so as to forestall them on the one hand, and on the other — whenever they do occur — to confront them bravely with faith and in hope of the ensuing benefit."[29] That said, this procedure is not perfect because there will always be unanticipated problems.

3. *Simplify your life as much as possible!* "Set-aside involvements," writes the Preserver of the Truth, "[self-transformation] cannot have any externals burdening the mind. If you are preoccupied [with numerous] affairs… all of this will inhibit your mind and confuse your essential nature, so you should be very wary of it."[30]

4. *Cultivate the attitudes of the Warrior!* All of the essential aspects of the Warrior's way of life outlined in Chapter 6 will help to keep you safe in the face of *peirasmoi*.

When the *peirasmoi* strike:

5. *Stay mindful of your inner attention!* Fortify your noetic concentration by any means you can, no matter what happens externally. "Even if you are broken and crushed," writes a Taoist master, "just let the mind not move…. if you can keep mindful of the spirit, even if locked in death energy, you can cause the dry bones of seven generations of ancestors to have living energy."[31]

6. *Practice patient endurance!* Condition yourself never to

THE 5 PILLARS OF LIFE

lose your cool no matter what happens, never to give in to anger and frustration, and never to lash out. "Patience is the fortitude of the soul," writes a contemporary Orthodox Abbott, "the support, the deep root that holds the tree when the winds beat against it and the streams strike it."[32]

7. *Run to your guide for direction and protection!* "At the beginning of our stay with the Elder," writes Joseph the Younger, "we usually paid quite frequent visits to him so that he could give us advice and see how we were getting on. Naturally, whether or not we told him what was on our minds, he would explain the meaning of events in detail, beginning from the results and analyzing what had led up to them, right back to the initial provocation. He would explain where these things came from, and why they came and to what extent, with such precision that we were astounded at the place that the 'Law of the spirit of life' (Rom.8:2) held within him."[33]

8. *Remember the sufferings of others!* Whatever you yourself are suffering, it is inevitable that thousands and perhaps millions of your fellow beings are going through a very similar hell at the very same time. Not so many years ago, Father Sophrony wrote:

> For many long years now I have been trying to persuade those who turn to me to apprehend the trials that befall them not only within the bounds of their individual existence but also as a revelation of how mankind lives and has lived in its millennium existence. When in ourselves we live the whole human world, all the history of mankind, we break out of the locked circle of our own "indi-

viduality" and enter into the wide expanses of "hypostatic" [personal] forms of being, conquering death and participating in divine Infinity. …At first, departure from the narrow prison of the individual can seem paradoxical: we ourselves feel crushed by our own sufferings — where shall be find the strength of spirit to embrace in compassion all the millions of people who at any given moment are suffering like us, and surely even more than we are? If we feel joyful, we can manage it better somehow but when we cannot cope with our own pain, sympathy for the multitudes only increases our already unbearable torment. Nevertheless, try this, and you will see how with the profound weeping of prayer for all suffering humanity energy will appear, of another order, not of this world.[34]

9. *Arouse a flaming will to resist!* When you are confronted with an obvious and easily identifiable *peirasmos*, there is nothing as powerful as the determination to win. Joseph the Younger says of his Elder: "The fathers' saying 'give blood and receive the spirit' could be described as the ever memorable Elder's permanent motto. Intrepid and courageous as he was, he left no room for queries or doubts in his life. But his ardent faith also contributed to this excellent combination, and so the results were always positive. Resolve and daring are the chief characteristics of man's freedom which manifests his will…"[35]

Ancient traditions maintain that great and continuous help surrounds everyone who struggles for self-transformation. This help comes from other transformed people who are still living, from transformed people who have departed this life, and from

WORD OF CAUTION

The traditional methods of self-transformation are not meant to be tools that you use to try to peel back the barrier between the worlds. Any deliberate attempt on your part to do so is likely to lead to severe mental instability and delusion. Content yourself with reading about others who have been directly shown the great help that surrounds them, and know that the same kind of help surrounds you too.

St. Ignaty Brianchaninov made note of a particular problem in the mid-19th-century but which also characterizes our own times. The powerful *peirasmoi* of previous eras, involving persecutions, martyrdoms and other open forms attack had given way to an endless number of much less noticeable and less significant *peirasmoi*. But whereas powerful and obvious *peirasmoi* arouse a flaming will to resist, the endless and continuous weaker ones simply drain our energy, distract us and sap our will. We need to pay particular attention to this dynamic because in our chronically busy lives there are millions of distractions and demands constantly sucking us dry.

benevolent noetic beings as well. Unfortunately, you can become easily discouraged because this help is invisible to you in your "normal" state. Orthodoxy explains it this way: There is a barrier between the physical and noetic worlds that remains intact most of our lives, and for your own protection.

When the *peirasmos* has passed:

10. Look for benefit! After a particular *peirasmos* has passed, you need to examine the whole matter and your response to it in order to see what you learned or gained from it. It's true that many *peirasmoi* seem to us unbearable and cruel when we are in the midst of them. But, as Father Damascene notes, "If we are able to look at it

objectively, we will see that, considering the serious-
ness of our condition, the Word [i.e., the Absolute] in
fact acted as gently as possible in effecting the cure."[36]

I promise you that if you implement these strategies in your
own life in a consistent and deliberate way, you will quickly be
able to stabilize your inner state and you will become increasingly yang to the environment, having regained a considerable
amount of your inner noetic integrity.

ALTERNATIONS:
UNDERSTANDING AND COUNTERING INSTABILITY

What Are "Alternations"?
What Orthodoxy refers to as alternations or "changes" are changes in
your noetic integrity. You experience the negative alternations as wan-
ing enthusiasm, flagging concentration, unstoppable waves of
thought, unpleasant mood swings, and in general any change in your
inner disposition that hinders your progress. Positive alternations, on
the other hand, bring peace, calmed nerves, noetic concentration, and
make progress easier.

Where Do Alternations Come From?
St. Makarios the Great outlined the "big four" causes of alternations
seventeen centuries ago: climate, diet, conscience, and hostile noetic
forces. To these I could readily add several others, such as passionate
reactions to events, accepting passionate intrusive thoughts, biological rhythms, hormonal changes, subtle cosmic energies, and illness.
Let's have look at these in more detail:

    I.   *Climatic changes:* These will affect your noetic state first by
        bringing about physical discomfort — you are too hot or cold,

so your attention is distracted. Secondly, cold or wind can overcome the body's protective energy barrier, its *wei qi*, as Chinese medicine calls it, and leave it vulnerable to external pathogens. So you get sick and end up at cause number 10.

2. *Diet:* A diet that's incompatible with your particular physical constitution will cause health challenges that, even if not serious, will be distracting. However, even a diet that your system digests easily may not be compatible with your goals, such as a diet heavy in animal protein and fat, or refined carbohydrates. In both cases the net result is rather similar — the incompatible diet will leave the mind more vulnerable to intrusive thoughts and make it very difficult for the *nous* to sink deeply into a place of rest and stability.

3. *Conscience:* Pangs of conscience over having hurt someone else or having failed to do something you should have done can certainly affect your inner state and distract you for some time.

4. *Hostile noetic powers:* The warfare brought upon you by hostile noetic forces, involving attacks of passionate thoughts and *peirasmoi*, is specifically designed to shatter your willingness to continue on the path — to leave you distracted, drained, and shell-shocked enough that your inner work in particular is ineffective.

5. *External events:* When unpleasant encounters with other people or adverse circumstances happen, they often provoke a passionate response in us, such as anger or fear. For example, if someone insults you, you may feel bitterness or rage and an urge toward self-justification.

6. *Intrusive thoughts:* Accepting an intrusive thought breaks your noetic concentration. Although it's true that not all

intrusive thoughts carry a destructive passionate content, one stage of the attack has already succeeded. Then come the passionate thoughts to seize your distracted *nous* as easily as an eagle seizes a helpless rabbit.

7. *Biological rhythms:* Considerable work has been done in recent years studying this phenomenon, and it is now well established that our energy levels go through cycles based on a number of factors. The female menstrual cycle is an obvious example of a biological rhythm, but everyone also experiences far more subtle biological cycles, and these can easily affect your enthusiasm and willingness to stick to your Program.

8. *Hormonal changes:* The most obvious examples are premenstrual syndrome and the changes associated with pregnancy and childbirth. However, men too are not immune to hormonal changes, and not only during puberty.

9. *Subtle cosmic energies:* Despite the ample evidence that phases of the moon affect mentally unstable people, such phenomena have not yet been adequately investigated scientifically in the West (probably because of the ideological presupposition that astrology is mere superstition). Nevertheless, not only planetary influences but also the influences of sunspot activity and the earth's magnetic field, among other things, deserve more thorough scrutiny.

10. *Illness and injury:* Illnesses and injuries of all kinds can become a noetic distraction, particularly if there is an element of fear, concern, and attachment to the body. Illnesses can also make it difficult to maintain your Program. However, they also grant a great opportunity to go beyond identification with the temporary physical body.

Those are the ten most frequent causes of alternations. Of course, this

THE 5 PILLARS OF LIFE

doesn't explain why it is that we so readily succumb to them. Our vulnerability can be reduced to two main factors: the inherent instability of our personality and hidden causes from the past that result in alternations governed by the spiritual law.

The Inherent Instability of our Personality

Joseph the Younger speaks of "a legacy of parasitic phenomena which came in after the fall: the rupture of our personality, marks of corruption, the constituent elements of death and death itself. Included among these manifestations of corruption and flux are to be found the 'changes and alternations', as the Fathers called them."[37]

When these alternations are caused by factors that we are innately vulnerable to in this life, such as illness or fatigue, the noetic damage is usually minimal and short-term. But when we provoke the alternation by falling into arrogance or negligence, then the harm is greater and the recovery time longer.

Negligence is the failure to stick to your Program, usually out of laziness and love for comfort. When asked to talk about negligence, Elder Joseph the Hesychast once said that negligence is like a drought in which nothing grows, and that it hands us over to self-cherishing, the more general enemy.[38]

As for arrogance, it can arise from a number of situations, the most common of which is probably passing judgment on others or thinking yourself superior to them. This further develops the pride upon which the self-cherishing ego is based. It can give rise to:

> ...trials which are severe and hard to dispel: strange and unusual symptoms of illness and painful wounds, and dereliction that is extraordinary and defies consolation, and all other things that seem impossible and insoluble, giving rise to despair and fear because the heart is devoid of hope. *All these things are consequences mainly of pride*, [emphasis mine] and come upon the person who has been led astray into believing in himself; these are all also the medicines for his healing, to make him sober up

and humble himself and vomit out the bile of this devastating perversion.[39]

Hidden Causes

This second class consists of hidden causes from our past that bring up karma or results based on our past actions and thoughts. These alternations, however painful they may seem, are very carefully orchestrated to cure our inner corruption and return us to our "natural state." What we experience as "the present" is our own creation. "Everything involuntary has its cause in what is voluntary, and man has no greater enemy than himself."[40]

Up to this point the relationship between alternations, *peirasmoi*, and passions may seem a little bit confusing. And in reality it can be somewhat difficult to separate them in a definitive way. That said, it should now be apparent that alternations can provoke *peirasmoi*, and the reverse is also true. Likewise alternations can provoke passions, and passions can provoke alternations. So these three realities have a symbiotic relationship.

Living with and Protecting Yourself from Alternations

What follows are the seven main strategies for dealing with alternations. They will allow you in some cases to avoid alternations or at least their effects, and in other cases will at least show you how to cushion the shock when alternations do hit.

ROCK SOLID LIFE PRACTICE 8.10: WORKING WITH ALTERNATIONS

1. *Stick to your Program ruthlessly:* As the Preserver of the Truth says: "Relinquishing this body without reservation, diligently progressing straight ahead, unafraid of life and death, you are then an individual with determination."[41] Joseph the Younger notes that it is imperative not to pay attention to emotions and to remain

THE 5 PILLARS OF LIFE

indifferent to what happens. So decisiveness is absolutely imperative in dealing with alternations, otherwise we are simply developing our yin qualities, making us increasingly vulnerable to external factors. This brings us to one of the keys to self-transformation that is often ignored:

Ancient training methods of self-transformation are an intriguing combination of two apparently incompatible methods. The first is to come to a detailed recognition of our own flaws and failures and to develop a sense of regret for them so as to humble ourselves. The second is to "act as if" what we want to achieve has already come to pass. So we must both weep as sinners and act like saints, consider ourselves the least worthy of sentient beings but act like bodhisattvas.

> ## INNER PRINCIPLE
> ### ◀◀◀◀◀◀ 8.19 ◀◀◀◀◀◀
>
> You can only become yang to your environment by acting as if you already are.
>
> ## PARADOX
> ### ◀◀◀◀◀◀◀ 8.5 ◀◀◀◀◀◀◀
>
> You must strive to see all the sins and inadequacies of your wretched past and present in order to humble yourself, but at the same time you must act like the person you want to become in your transformed future.

2. *Prepare yourself:* Just as you anticipate *peirasmoi*, anticipate alternations and act accordingly. Think through the events and encounters of the day ahead and how, if at all, each one will affect your inner state.

3. *Have faith and patience:* You don't like the current alternations? Then just wait a few hours! As good weather follows bad, so does your inner disposition change and, in fact, even more frequently than does the weather. Another reason to have faith and patience is that it's possible for you to reach a place where most alternations are

ineffective against you: "When you clear away the defilement of the mind and open up the conscious spirit, this is called cultivating the Way. When you no longer flow in waves, and you merge with the Way and rest in the Way, this is called returning to the root. Keeping to the root is called calm stabilization. After a long time of calm stabilization, illnesses dissolve and life is restored."[42]

4. *Work the dynamics of alternations to your advantage:* "Make hay while the sun shines." If you find yourself in a good state to make progress today, make sure you use it and work hard.
   And when that state alternates to one less conducive to your goal, if not downright difficult, just hunker down, follow your Program and refuse to give in. Constantly push ahead. "You must remain unmoved," says Joseph the Hesychast, "in the midst of the pressures and transformations which the alternations produce in you."[43] Even if SSDN is like pulling teeth and you feel under attack from all sides, just pay no attention and continue. You may well be making considerable progress, even if you think the opposite is really happening. We are not always good judges of our own progress and simply because we assume that unless we feel good and the practice is effortless, nothing good can come of it. This is simply not true.

5. *"Life is but a shadow and a dream":* The more you cultivate awareness of the dreamlike quality of existence as described in Chapter 4, the more you will become detached from external circumstances and even from your own feelings. "Body tranquil, mind free, you can then observe the subtle."[44]

6. *Maintain your inner noetic foothold:* No practice is stronger or more effective than making absolutely sure that your inner attention does not wander. And for this purpose there is no more effective technique

and to pay attention to your breathing, as explained in Chapter 4. "The shortcut to forgetting emotional consciousness is in mind and breathing resting on each other. If the mind and breathing are always resting on each other, then emotional consciousness is naturally forgotten without trying to forget."[45]

7. *Analyze major alternations that have passed:* You may find it useful to consider some of the disagreeable alternations you go through with a view to discovering possible causes so that you can avoid them in the future. "You must discern the causes which have given rise to them," said Elder Joseph to his disciples.[46] Of course, Elder Joseph would do this for his disciples since they themselves were not necessarily capable of arriving at the correct conclusions. Nevertheless it is good for you to try doing this yourself simply so that you can get used to seeing patterns in your own life, because without this kind of self-knowledge you can remain immersed in negative patterns that you're not even aware of. The only caveat is that is: Treat every conclusion you come to as tentative.

Passions, *peirasmoi*, and alternations are the three main obstacles in human life. They are the barriers to self-transformation and at the same time the keys that unlock the gates to it. In this fallen world they are our constant companions, so learning how to deal with them is an essential skill to human life itself, and one among the many useful skills about which our conventional educational system has nothing to say.

One of the more delightful paradoxes of the Warrior's world is that even defeat can be turned into victory. And since we are all so used to defeat, this is a very comforting truth! This approach will turn your struggles into unending triumph. The two-part system is explained in the following sections.

The Infallible Method of Achieving the Impossible:
I call this "the elephant method" because it reminds me of the answer to the question "How do you eat an elephant?" Answer? "One bite at a time!" It allows you to manage your psychological perceptions of the task, keep yourself on track, and give yourself a constant sense of achievement.

Have you ever seen a Chinese martial arts exhibition, where the participants absorb enormous punishment without seeming to even feel it? It looks completely impossible, but I assure you that I know from experience it is for real and in fact not difficult to train. Let me give you an example.

The Qi Gong practice referred to as "Iron Shirt" is a Chinese method for making parts the body impervious to ordinary punches and kicks. In the early stage of training, which lasts for quite a while, your partner hits your body in a prescribed pattern but with very little force. Your body quickly becomes accustomed to this and soon the blows feel like nothing. Then begins second stage in which your partner hits a little bit harder. Then for the third stage he or she will use a bunch of bamboo shoots tied together instead of the hands. For the fourth stage the partner will use a small bag of sand weighing about seven pounds, but again hitting with very little force. Meanwhile, your body has gotten used to steadily increasing force with virtually no effort, and it will do the same with the sandbag. And by the time you can tolerate the sandbag, you will be able to absorb the impact of the average person's punch with no pain or damage.[47]

So how do you apply this method to self-transformation? Well, just as someone training in Iron Shirt knows the general progression of the training ahead of time and all the steps that are to come, so you yourself need to make a map of all the training involved in transforming your life and map it out in a kind of flowchart. Do this on a large Whiteboard or piece of Bristol board and have it on the wall where you can see it. You will find the outline you need in Appendix C.

The second preliminary is to settle in your mind once and for all that you will go through the training step by step, slowly and deliberately, not moving on to the next step until you have genuinely assimilated the previous one. Now you're ready to begin:

1. Set small, manageable goals.
2. Make them incremental.
3. Do one thing at a time, and do it thoroughly.
4. Plan meticulously in advance.

If you follow this method you will soon end up effortlessly achieving ridiculously difficult goals. But what is more important is that you will have a constant sense of enthusiasm because you will be able to see your progress visually. You will have a sense of being an unstoppable force.

Fall and Get Up Again

Despite the universally accepted Warrior paradigm and the frequent military analogies used in many traditions, there are some important differences between the wars of this world and the war of self-transformation. For an army to win a war, it must vanquish its enemies. The Warrior, on the other hand, can lose a great many battles, but as long as he does not quit and leave the battlefield, it is absolutely guaranteed 100 percent that he will win in the end. So surrender is the only form of defeat in the Warrior's world.

There is a famous saying in the Orthodox tradition: "Fall and get up again." This means that no matter how many times you fall, as long as you pick yourself up and continue your training resolutely there is no possible way you can lose in the end.

That is the eleventh miraculous ancient formula. Use it wisely and it is impossible to fail.

Key to overcoming passions, *peirasmoi*, and alternations: The wrestlers of ancient Greece used to slather themselves with olive oil to prevent their opponents from getting a grip on them. The more you abide in stillness and free yourself from temporal conditioning, the less these evil triplets will be able to grab hold of you.

Chapter Nine

The FINAL
CHALLENGE

If you have gotten this far by working your way through the material in this book, and not just by running to the last chapter to see how ends, then congratulations! It has probably taken you the better part of the year to get here — and no doubt it has been a year full of great challenges, great triumphs, and probably a few failures too.

You've done in the space of one year what very few people accomplish in an entire lifetime. And you've done more for yourself and done more good for other people in that short space of time than you possibly could have done by staying on the path of life adopted by the majority of people in our culture.

You probably have a sense of amazement at what you've accomplished, possibly tinged with regret at not having made greater efforts. But what I hope you have is a sense of the boundless possibilities contained within human life and a real feeling of warmth and love toward the people around you.

Now it's time to open that envelope you put away so long ago, that envelope containing the answers to the questions posed in the introduction to this book. Your answers to that questionnaire indicated where you were at in every sphere of your life when you began your journey. Now it's time to take a look at these answers so that you can see objectively how far you've come over these past many months of hard work.

To get the most out of this crucial exercise you should do the following: Go somewhere where you can get away from it all for a day or even half a day so that you can concentrate undisturbed and undistracted on what you originally wrote and can consider everything you've experienced in the interim.

Of course, there is no way to score that original set of questions; it was never intended as a test, but rather as a tool to get you thinking so that you could construct a reference point to return to after having gone through all the material in the book. Once you've gone over your original answers and have a relatively good idea what areas you've made progress in and where you still have some work to do, your next step is as follows:

THE MEASURE OF THE WARRIOR: TAKING THE FINAL TEST

The following questionnaire is a test — have no illusions! Everything in the world of self-transformation as taught by authentic ancient traditions has to do with results. The proof really is in the pudding. You'll notice that there are two different kinds of questions: some deal with your faithfulness to the practices we've taught you, while others deal with the results you've obtained.

Again, you should only do this test if you have worked your way through all the material in the book. And when you decide to take it, you should be in an environment where you're completely undisturbed. So if you're ready to take it, go ahead; the next section explains how to score it.

THE WARRIORSHIP TEST

1. Are you associated with an authentic ancient tradition? (3 points)

2. If yes, are you part of the community of practitioners?

3. Do you have a guide to whom you are responsible in your practice? (3 points)

4. Have you been following your Program since completing Chatper 2?

5. Do you typically follow through with your Program every day without deviating? (5 points)

6. Do you practice no matter how you "feel" at the time? (3 points)

7. Do you feel in control of your time and your life?

8. Have you created a sacred space for your SSDN?

9. Have you managed to spread order and harmony while localizing chaos in your home?

10. Do peace and harmony reign in your heart with respect to your interpersonal relationships?

11. Have you instituted a healthy diet?

12. If you were a smoker, have you quit? (If you were not, give yourself 1 point here).

13.   Are you on an adequate and regular régime of nutritional supplements?

14.   Have you carried out at least one major detoxification? (1 point if you used the supplements and fasting, 2 points if you used colonic irrigation).

15.   Are you on a regular régime of cardiovascular exercise?

16.   Do you stretch in order to maintain your physical flexibility regularly?

17.   Do you maintain your muscle tone with regular exercise?

18.   Have you incorporated "soft" exercise (e.g., Tai chi, Qi Gong, yoga) into your life?

19.   Do you unconsciously move your body in a centered, relaxed, and harmonious way throughout the day?

20.   Have you taken steps to put your financial house in order?

21.   Have you constructed the long-term career/financial plan and taken steps to implement it?

22.   Do you practice in SSDN every day for at least one hour in total?

23.   Do you regularly practice SSDN for longer periods? (two hours or more, give yourself 2 points; four hours or more, give yourself 5 points).

24.   Has inner noetic stillness become your mental default setting? (5 points)

25. Has your inner attentiveness reached the point where random thoughts and emotional waves are unable to disturb you? (3 points)

26. When you decide to do something, do you follow through?

27. Have you proven to yourself by using the Rules of Intent that you can achieve any goal you've set for yourself, so far is it lies within your power? (5 points)

28. When you are with friends or colleagues who are not on a path similar to yours, do you feel an increasing sense of being "different"?

29. Do you attempt to incorporate at least one Warrior attitude or strategy each day? (3 points)

30. Have you eliminated psychological stress from your life?

31. When you are accused of something or attacked verbally, are you able to fight off the urge to defend yourself? (3 points)

32. Have you learned to defend the integrity of your Program against the unreasonable demands of others?

33. Have you made a serious attempt to incorporate the seventeen virtues (described in Chapter 7) into your life? (3 points)

34. Do you always treat people gently?

35. Do you find yourself spontaneously and selflessly concerned with the welfare of others (who are not in your immediate family and whose welfare has no direct impact on your life)? (3 points)

36. Do you find in your heart feelings of warmth, affection, or sympathy for people whom you do not like? (3 points)

37. Do you support a particular charity or charities?

38. Are you sincerely obedient to your guide, following his or her directions as far as you can?

39. Are you spontaneously obedient to those around you (willingly and without internal resistance), as long as their demands do not compromise your pursuit of self-transformation?

40. Do you read something related to self-transformation every day?

41. Have you made a lifetime confession to your guide?

42. When you do succeed at something, do you really believe in your heart that you could not have done so without the help of the Absolute, of your guide, or of your fellow practitioners? (3 points)

43. Is your heart filled with gratitude to others and to the Absolute for everything you have received?

44. Have you eliminated critical and judgmental thoughts and words about other people? (5 points)

45. Is your sexual drive under conscious control?

46. Have you arranged your practice so that you regularly face danger for the sake of your goal?

47. Do you find that your fear of sickness, suffering, and death has abated? (3 points)

48, Do you prepare yourself every day to meet *peirasmoi* and alternations?

49. Do your sufferings automatically lead you to think about and sympathize with the greater sufferings of others?

50. Do you find that *peirasmoi* are largely unable to knock you off track?

51. Do you consciously use the dynamics of alternations to your advantage?

52. Have you ceased to take your own preexisting attitudes, opinions, pet peeves, and emotional states seriously?

53. Does the multitude of changing circumstances throughout the day now seem something like a dream or movie that is unable to disturb you?

54. Are you frequently conscious of the rhythm of your breathing?

55. Do you have an increasing sense of your own noetic impurity (in a non-neurotic way), so that other people all seem to be good in your eyes? (3 points)

Give yourself one point for each affirmative answer unless otherwise indicated. Then add up your points to compute your score out of 100. In general, the score of 80 or more indicates an absolutely superb result! The score between 60 and 80 is still very good. However, unless you are able to answer yes to all of the 5-point questions, you still have some serious weaknesses to deal with and you're probably not ready for the final challenge.

If you have fallen short of the mark of 80 points, don't despair! This simply means that you need to go back and, using the help of the test, work on your weaker areas for a while.

DEEPENING YOUR PRACTICE

Practicing the traditional disciplines outlined in this book may have brought you to a crossroads in your life: You may find that you see everything with very different eyes than you did before. You may be like Herrigel when he had completed his archery training in Japan, and his master said to him:

> I must warn you of one thing. You have become a different person in the course of these years. For this is what the art of archery means: a profound and far-reaching contest of the archer with himself. Perhaps you have hardly noticed it yet, but you will feel it very strongly when you meet your friends and acquaintances again in your own country: things will no longer harmonize as before. You will see with other eyes and measure with other measures.[1]

Training in authentic ancient traditions can make your life in society much more difficult. You may find that you have lost many of the common interests you previously shared with others. It can be really difficult. You may find yourself at times somewhat like Wang Liping after his "resurrection," when he found life in this world banal and was actually quite depressed for a while. As his Grandmaster said: "Who can become a spiritual immortal without going mad?"[2]

The good news is that these feelings are temporary. So, for that matter, is the feeling of being "stuck," of not being able to make further progress. All of these feelings will come and go from time to time and this is perfectly normal.

The real key to deepening your practice lies in three things we have already discussed:

1. Shifting your attention and concern away from your own welfare in this world and onto other realities — onto the Absolute and onto the welfare of other beings: Having spent most of your life obsessed with your own welfare, you must now become obsessed with the welfare of others.

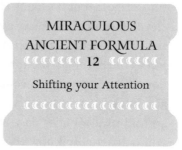

MIRACULOUS
ANCIENT FORMULA
❮❮❮❮❮❮❮ 12 ❮❮❮❮❮
Shifting your Attention

2. Systematically erasing yourself, so that your practice becomes an expression of the Absolute through you:

> If thou could'st empty all thyself of self,
> Like to a shell dishabited,
> Then might He find thee on the ocean shelf,
> And say, "This is not dead,"
> And fill thee with Himself instead.
> But thou art all replete with very thou
> And hast such shrewd activity,
> That when He comes He says, "This is enow
> Unto itself – 'twere better let it be,
> It is so small and full, there is no room for Me."[3]

Only when you are entirely gone will you be entirely there — when you understand what that means by your own experience, you sure won't need this book anymore.

3. Practicing that lever of all levers, which is humility: You must practice seeing the good points in others so assiduously that you begin to see everyone spontaneously as good, worthy and as a reflection of the Absolute, however distant.

All three points are facets of the twelfth Miraculous Ancient Formula. The entire content of authentic ancient traditions is summarized in this formula, but it's much easier said than done! That's why the other eleven formulae are there, along with the detailed explanations. When the Other becomes the center of your universe–not in a neurotic way, but as the natural fruit of noetic realization–then you will understand how the human psychosomatic nature is meant to function. You will also know that we human beings are really all one, and that the world around us is equally part of us. Anyone can say that, of course, but you will actually know this truth by experience or *methexis* (participation), to use the Orthodox technical term.

WHEN YOU HAVE ACCOMPLISHED ALL THIS WITH THE HELP OF HEAVEN...

If this miraculous transformation has begun to take place in you, then you really have done it with the help of the Absolute — with the help of numerous unseen people and forces whose assistance you only half suspect. And I use the word *begun* because this transformation really is without end, and however it may seem to you, you have only just begun.

Now that you've refined your inner being and solidified your life, you are admirable raw material for any authentic ancient tradition, and I for one would give anything to see more of this kind of raw material knocking on my door!

We mentioned earlier that nearly every authentic ancient tradition has been called "the way," and even the Christianity of the first century was sometimes called "the Way" (Greek *odos*). At this point you are slowly beginning to make the transition from simply practicing the Way to becoming the Way, but you still have a very long road ahead of you. And this road is characterized less by doing new and different practices, than by doing the same ones on more subtle levels.

As you continue your training, make it a practice to review the Miraculous Ancient Formulae from time to time, together with the Inner Principles and Paradoxes. These contain much of the distilled wisdom of authentic ancient traditions and can help keep you on

THE 5 PILLARS OF LIFE

track. Also, review the Seven Maxims of Training from the introduction, and make sure your own training accords with these.

And don't forget to visit the Web site www.rocksolidlife.com from time to time. It has a selection of helpful training materials for you, including home-study units that amplify the contents of this book, together with live workshops and retreats. We will also do our best to keep in touch with you and to let you know about any new material that you may find useful.

If you have made a conscientious attempt to work your way through this book, you are indeed a Warrior in the truest sense of the word. Your life is vastly more rewarding and fulfilling than ever before. Your impact on the world is now a positive one, bringing healing to the Cosmos. Now go forward to discover the immeasurable happiness that awaits all those who align their lives with the Absolute.

Once you can achieve a score of 80 points, you're ready for the final challenge, which is found sealed at www.rocksolidlife.com.

Before you open the final challenge, be absolutely sure that you've worked your way through all the material in this book, because the final challenge is no picnic. It really is a kind of initiation or passage into a larger world and is very demanding. But if you really are ready, then I wish you every success and much courage!

Appendix A

CHOOSING
a FOCUS

ach of the following themes is a noetic practice or focus
Edesigned to turn an ordinary, messed-up human being like you
or me into a highly refined, focused and purposeful seeker of self-
transformation.

If you want victory in the battle to change your life, here are the
nuclear weapons — and these noetic nukes have been around for millennia and have proven their effectiveness in many traditions. But be
warned — just as a nuclear weapon has tremendous power, so does
each of these. Each focus is a major revolution in your inner world and
no small struggle is needed to assimilate it.

And assimilate them you must — one at a time until they form a
rock-solid foundation, until each focus seems totally natural to you.
The effort required is considerable, but the payoff in quality of life
and immeasurable happiness far outweighs any possible earthly effort
or sacrifice.

THE METHOD

Use one focus per day. You begin with a short SSDN session in the morning, and you use this session to ingrain the focus into your mental / emotional atmosphere in a very powerful way. As the day unfolds, of course, it will take considerable effort to hang on to the focus, but be patient because the results will come in time.

Remember that the content of each focus can be easily adjusted to match the authentic ancient tradition of your choice. You can customize each focus for yourself or use it as is.

Each focus consists of a list of "focus points." Once your *nous* is stabilized in SSDN, you begin reflecting on these points until they generate the specific feeling associated with this focus. You then try to hold onto and magnify the intensity of this feeling for a short period. Here is the step-by-step method:

1. Begin your SSDN in the usual way. Tune your breathing so that the *nous* becomes clear and calm (5-10 minutes, or more if you wish).

2. If you pray, now is a good time to pray that you will absorb the content of the focus and retain it throughout the day.

3. Read through each of the focus points associated with the focus you have chosen, and allow your mind — which by now should be quite calm and lucid — to reflect on them.

4. Once you begin to sense in your mind and heart the feeling associated with the focus, stop reflecting on the individual focus points and dwell on the feeling instead.

5. Continue dwelling on the feeling for about 2-5 minutes, until it seems like the centre of your mental universe.

6. Get up very slowly and stretch a bit. Then walk around a little while holding onto the feeling you generated using the focus.

When you first start using these reflections, you should go through the list in order. After that, you can choose your focus of the day on a more random basis. At the outset, try changing your focus each day — this works best for most people because their minds easily tire of the same focus. Later on, though, you may prefer to keep the same focus for several days or a whole week. As in all of self-transformation, experience will teach you.

FOCUS 1: STABILIZING THE NOUS

Focus Points

*   I will never achieve anything truly worthwhile unless the *nous* becomes stable.

*   Clearing out random thoughts and returning to the natural state before thoughts arise is the basis and foundation of all practices of self-transformation.

*   Obsessively mulling over endless rational thought will prevent me from seeing the world as it really is, from finding my true self, from sensing the presence of the Absolute and from loving anyone else effectively.

*   Until the *nous* is stabilized, I will remain trapped in an endless world of fantasy and will be the constant victim of whatever stimuli surround me.

*   Once the *nous* is stabilized, every aspect of self-transformation will be within reach — destructive emotions will evaporate, the physical body will regain strength and health and the basis for a whole new life will lie before me.

Continue this reflection until you are deeply convinced that refining the *nous* is the key to transforming your life.

FOCUS 2: BECOMING IMPERVIOUS TO EXTERNAL INFLUENCES

Focus Points

- Material substance does not really and objectively exist; at least not as we perceive it.

- All phenomena are simply energy patterns in endless flux so, in a way, this whole material world is a kind of hologram, an elaborate illusion.

- The people I know do objectively exist, but their appearance too is part of this illusory world.

- Like all other beings, I am trapped in this illusory world, not physically so much as noetically.

- Most people are noetically trapped — their lives revolve endlessly around their relationship with the world of conventional appearances, with the material world, which causes them constant emotional frustration and hardship.

- I will live this day intensely conscious of the dream-like quality of existence, of the unsubstantial quality of the material world.

Continue until you feel strongly the dream-like quality of life in this world.

FOCUS 3: THE BLESSING OF YOUR LIFE

Focus Points

- I am very blessed to have this precious human life.

- I not only have the necessities of life — food, clothing and shelter — but I have known the joy of loving parents and siblings, of spouse and children, of friendships with others.

- I have been blessed with this physical body which, if I would only stop abusing it, should continue to function well for many years or decades to come.

- Most of all, I have the blessing of this tremendous urge to seek the truth of existence, to live my life to its full potential.

- Many of my brothers and sisters in the human race have not enjoyed the great good fortune that I have — many have suffered poverty, illness, lived under tyrannical regimes, lived through wars, famines and natural disasters where they have lost loved ones. Many are held in the grip of false ideologies which plague their minds and cause them inner anguish or to inflict violence on others.

- By whose compassion and by whose prayers was it that I, the least of all, should have received all these good things which I have in no way merited? I know many people more deserving than myself, and yet they have not been so fortunate. Why me?

Continue until you feel deeply thankful for your life — thankful to the Absolute, to all those who have shown you kindness, and even to those whose evil may have moved you to seek self-transformation. Dwell on this feeling of thankfulness until you feel the need to give thanks for whatever will happen to you in the day ahead.

FOCUS 4: THIS TRAGIC AND INSUFFICIENT WORLD

Focus Points

- The end of my life and of the lives of those I love is in a wooden box, six feet underground.

- The years pass away quickly, and soon I shall depart this world.

- People struggle all their lives to achieve a wealth and fame that will be forcefully taken from them in the end. Human achievements are limited to this world, actually quite futile, and a waste of time and energy.

- This world will never satisfy the gnawing hunger we all have to know and live the truth of existence. Our earthly preoccupations are often futile attempts to fill this inner void.

- When I walk through the cemetery, I see that so many people have departed before their time, taken away by accident, illness, war or other evil.

Continue until you feel this world and its conventional existence to be futile and unsatisfying. When this feeling grows strong, you will feel that even food, sex, money, reputation, power, entertainment and the like — things you previous had a strong passionate attraction to — seem quite banal.

FOCUS 5: THE DANGER OF NOT UNDERGOING SELF-TRANSFORMATION

Focus Points

- Unless I use this precious life to refine the inner contents of my mind and heart, I will remain a prisoner to the energies of the world of persons, events and things.

- This noetic slavery will follow me into the grave and into the next life, where it will continue to cause me untold suffering.

- If I gleefully continue in slavery in this world, then it's absurd to hope that I will somehow inherit a blissful existence after death. Only religions promise that kind of nonsense.

- Moreover, if I continue to indulge my passions, my cravings, my temper and self-will, I will probably succeed in giving myself some horrible degenerative disease. And even if my physical health continues, I will still be leading an unsatisfying and stressful existence for no purpose.

- So it is clearly in my own best interest to travel the road of self-transformation with all my strength.

Continue until you feel a real fear of what will happen, both in this life and beyond, if you continue living the same futile and destructive lifestyle as before. Dwell on this fear and keep it with you all day.

FOCUS 6: THE BLESSING OF FOLLOWING YOUR GUIDE

Focus Points
- By following my guide, I will take much time off my journey of self-transformation. By following someone who already knows the way, I won't waste time in the sidetracks of all those who try to reinvent the wheel.

- My guide's knowledge will protect me from the great dangers that lie ahead, making my journey much safer. Refining away the sludge from my mind and heart will be a thousand times easier.

- Moreover, my guide's prayers will protect me even more, so that even if I take a wrong turn, I won't be harmed.

- The simple act of obeying my guide sincerely will cause the Absolute to protect me and array a whole host of beneficial influences on my side. I will always find beneficial circumstances in this life for practicing self-refinement and will be blessed when I depart from this world.

- All this can be mine, but if and only if I actually follow my guide and try to put into practice what he/she teaches me.

Continue until you feel thankfulness and joy at having a guide, and feel a determination to follow his/her instructions with faith and sincerity.

FOCUS 7: SEEKING MERCY FOR ONESELF

Focus Points
- Since my nature on its own tends toward self-transformation, the key to being transformed is to stop blocking this tendency.

- When I "get out of my own way," I will receive mercy from the Absolute and find blessings all around me.

- Lao Tzu discovered that the Tao is innately merciful. So mercy is all around me, and is mine for the asking, so long as I conform to the Absolute as best I can.

- So the shortcut to finding mercy is to ask for it. This alone is a powerful act that will bring many blessings into my life.

Continue until you feel an intense desire to experience the warmth and tenderness of true mercy within yourself, and the mercy of beneficial circumstances for your life. Determine to keep this feeling of seeking mercy all day long.

FOCUS 8: SEEKING MERCY FOR THE OTHER

Focus Points

- Jesus Christ taught that the surest way to find mercy for one-self is to practice it toward others. So if I do everything I can to be a source of mercy to others, I will receive mercy for myself. The law of cause and effect — the "spiritual law," as Orthodoxy calls it — is immutable.

- Others certainly need to experience mercy in their lives much more than I do. So many are in material or emotional distress. Some of them I can bring mercy to by contributing money, time and attention. For the ones I can't easily reach this way, I can still hold them in my heart and seek mercy for them this way.

- It is not only people who need mercy: animals, plants and this whole world are in sore distress. "The whole creation groans and labors in birth pangs..." wrote St. Paul (Rm.8:22). The world, even so-called "inanimate creation," is a living entity whose welfare depends on me.

- By bringing mercy to others I can not only benefit them, but also free myself from my self-obsession, which is the root of all my problems.

Continue until you feel a deep desire to benefit other people, animals and creation in general.

FOCUS 9: WE ARE ALL THE SAME

Focus Points

- Everyone wishes for happiness and strives to attain it, even if few know where it is to be found or how to get it.

- I am no different from anyone else. I too want to be happy. I too want to experience the same joys in life that others do.

- Like others, I have a physical body; I know what it is to suffer hunger and thirst, to need sleep and rest, to suffer distress and illness.

- We all came from our mothers' wombs and we will all die in the end. We are all the same. Whether we are rulers or beggars, famous or unknown, we all suffer the same fate.

- If we are all the same, it means we all have the same innate potential. Everyone can experience self-transformation and know the boundless joy of a life of bliss, beyond the reach of corruption and death.

- If we all have the same origin, the same fate and the same potential, how can I consider myself to be any more important than anyone else? There is no basis for this erroneous view, none whatsoever.

- So it's obvious that from now on I will have to cherish the welfare of others, and not just my own.

Continue until you feel an unstoppable urge to cherish others, to value their welfare and contribute to it.

FOCUS 10: JUSTIFYING THE OTHER

Focus Points

- A great barrier to cultivating a merciful attitude toward others is their own behavior and the anger it causes in me.

- Why should the behavior of anyone else cause me anger? As long as we are caught in the deluded world of the passions, our actions reflect our delusion. Until the *nous* is cleansed and the ego overthrown, we are all our own worst enemies.

- It makes no sense then, that I should be surprised or distressed by the behavior of others. In a very real sense, they are just doing the best they can with what they have got.

- They do not even know about self-transformation. What little they know about authentic ancient traditions they automatically interpret through the lenses of their inherited culture. Surrounded by religion, they are unaware of the very existence of true therapy.

- Many of them have suffered so much from childhood abuses and emotional traumas, poor parenting, difficult life situations and their own poor choices that they cannot realistically be expected to act as transformed people. They are still strongly controlled by the conditioning of the past.

- So naturally, I need to excuse them for whatever they do.

- In any case, they can only be brought to a more authentic existence through kindness. Being angry with them will not bring the results that I desire and that they so desperately need.

Continue until you feel a compassion and indulgence for the faults of those around you. Hold onto this feeling and deliberately make excuses for others during the day.

FOCUS 11: GOING BEYOND DEATH

Focus Points

- Since my life in this world is short and fleeting compared to what lies ahead, it makes no sense to focus exclusive attention on this life.

- It only makes sense to consider my fate beyond the grave; this will spur me on to greater inner accomplishments in this life and put me in a much better position to enter the next.

- If I waste all my attention on the here and now, I'll become obsessed not only with worldly affairs, but with biological survival. Since my instinct for biological self-preservation is the basis of the ego, I will cause myself great harm.

- So from now on I must broaden my horizons to consider life beyond the grave. Only this way can I undermine the ego, the basis of my suffering.

Continue until you feel your horizon expand and begin to think beyond this world of life and death.

FOCUS 12: ACCEPTING THE WARRIOR'S LOT

Focus Points

- When I committed myself to the path of self-transformation, I bound myself to follow the Warrior's path.

- All those who have worked for self-transformation down

through the centuries are my new family. Now that I have joined their ranks, I must expect to face the same difficulties they did.

- I accept the vicious warfare I will face from my own unhealed passions, from hostile noetic forces and from other people who neither understand nor sympathize with my efforts.

- I accept that others may persecute me, even to death, for my convictions.

- I accept that the love that I deliberately cultivate toward others will sometimes meet with rejection and outright hostility.

- I accept that my pursuit of perfection will lead me through hunger, thirst, sleeplessness, and a thousand and one physical discomforts.

- I accept that this war is not about me or about any one person. It is a great conflict of cosmic dimensions and I am merely a humble servant of the Absolute Goodness.

- I accept that there are casualties in war and that this war may cost me my life in this world.

- I accept that the only way to find unchanging peace and happiness is by passing through this conflict with the help of my guide, my fellow-strugglers and the Absolute.

- I accept that this day may be my last and surrender my life without hesitation or regret.

Continue until you feel a zeal, a fighting spirit arise in you.

FOCUS 13: MAINTAINING AWARENESS DURING IMPACT

Focus Points

- Although I can arrive at noetic stillness during SSDN, it is very difficult to maintain my inner noetic foothold, my calm inner awareness, when people or events impact on me.

- Preserving continuous awareness, undisturbed by whatever contacts I may have with other people or with the world in general, is absolutely critical to my further progress.

- So I should spare no effort to practice this so thoroughly that I master it. And I should make this an immediate priority, since so much else depends on it.

- I will use every opportunity this day presents me with to practice this.

Continue until you feel the urgency of the matter. When this feeling is strong and vivid, try to visualize what it would be like to maintain your awareness unabated during an encounter with another person.

FOCUS 14: ACCEPTING RESPONSIBILITY

Focus Points:

- Since the law of cause and effect means that we live in exactly the kind of world we deserve, I have no basis for complaining about my lot.

- Moreover, most of what I would be tempted to complain about is transparently the result of my own choices, so my complaining would be inaccurate and unjustified.

- Since every action or thought I have influences everyone and everything for good or ill, I can hardly complain about adversity that comes my way or about the behavior of others.

- If I had not wasted so many years in an unsatisfying self-centered existence, it is quite possible that many of these evils around me would not exist.

- And if someone mistreats me, it is probably because I have done the same to them or to someone else. So they are, in a way, allowing the Spiritual Law to teach me a much needed lesson.

- So ultimately, the only way out of this predicament is for me to take total responsibility for the world around me and everyone in it.

- If I try to justify myself, I will only strengthen the ego and face more suffering. So my only realistic alternative is to cut off self-justification and assume responsibility.

- As far as I am concerned, from this moment on, I alone am responsible for the world around me. The buck stops here.

Continue until you feel deeply convinced that you and only you are responsible for your life. Now visualize someone blaming you for something, and how you will react!

FOCUS 15: WARMING THE HEARTS OF OTHERS

Focus Points
- Since self-transformation depends on cultivating a disinterested love for others, I must work on this love at all times.

- The more compassion I lavish on others, the more mercy I will receive in turn. More importantly, my ego will be progressively weakened and I will be more at peace.

- So many of my fellow beings are suffering, and yet it often seems I am powerless help more than a few people. Nevertheless, I can help the people with whom I have contact.

- If I could use every personal encounter I have with others to impart mercy, compassion and blessings to them, that could make a tremendous difference in the lives of a large number of people over the years.

- For this whole day, not one person will leave my presence without feeling better about him/herself, so far as it lies in my power.

Continue until you feel a strong urge to behave compassionately toward everyone you meet. Once the feeling is strong and stable, visualize how this would work in reality.

FOCUS 16: NOT JUDGING

Focus Points
- The main barrier to my progress is passing judgment on others. And it's not just on people that I come into contact with: I also constantly pass judgment on situations, politics, the situation at work, and countless other elements in the world of persons, events and things.

- The amount of energy I wastefully invest in this pastime is enough to light up a city for a month. It is a huge burden that I needlessly put on myself.

- Each time I pass judgment, I build up my already huge ego, fall off the path to the bliss of self-transformation, create unpleasant repercussions for myself in the future and cut myself off from the healing energies of the Absolute. And all for what? For a momentary feeling of superiority, when I myself have committed worse offenses? It's just not worth the price.

- By ceasing to judge the whole universe, I will slowly regain my inner peace and allow myself to benefit from practicing self-transformation.

Continue until you are feel revulsion to the whole notion of passing judgment on or condemning others.

FOCUS 17: PLACING THE OTHER AT THE CENTRE OF YOUR UNIVERSE

Focus Points
- As long as I am obsessed with my own welfare, I cannot make any real progress.

- If I continue to think and act as an individual, under the illusion that I am independent of everyone and everything else, I will just increase my own torment.

- On the other hand, if I were to place the welfare of others at the centre of my universe, I would deliver another blow to my ego and create the conditions for future blessings for myself and others. And even now I would begin to feel better.

- The problem is that placing the welfare of others at the centre of my universe seems too abstract. So what I will do is choose one person today whose welfare I will keep in mind at all times. If I can contribute to his or her welfare materially or emotionally, I will. If not, I know that contributing noetically through compassionate attention is extremely powerful.

Continue until you feel it's essential to replace yourself with the other. Once the feeling is powerfully established within you, choose a particular person.

FOCUS 18: THE BLESSING OF OBEDIENCE

Focus Points

- Obedience is the door of the mysteries of existence. I realize that until I undertake true and sincere obedience to my guide, all my other endeavors at self-transformation will meet with only limited success.

- I know that obedience reverses the Fall and returns us to our original, natural state. And I understand that this obedience is a relationship of love and not an authority relationship, as it is in fallen human society.

- I acknowledge that obedience is the only way to overcome self-centeredness and self-will.

- There are so many opportunities for obedience throughout the day, and yet I find excuses to ignore them, stubbornly preferring to do my own thing.

- Today I will make the maximum use possible of every opportunity for obedience. Whenever someone asks me for something, I will do whatever I can to help, so long as the request is not a harmful one. I will stop living for myself and put myself at the disposal of others.

Continue until you feel a deep desire to subdue your will to the will of others, and for their benefit.

FOCUS 19: LOVE OF THE ABSOLUTE

Focus Points

- Since every authentic ancient tradition maintains that love is the defining characteristic of the transformed person, it is obvious that love must also be a defining characteristic of the Absolute.

- If I could focus my desiring power fully on the Absolute, then my lower, passionate cravings would dissolve on their own and my loving desire for the only thing worth desiring would increase dramatically. My *nous* would be clarified, my life would be set firmly in the right direction and I would make great progress.

- This would be one of the fastest ways to cure my noetic illness and to reunite the *nous* with the heart. I would become a fully functioning person for the first time.

- What's more, I would receive loving energy a hundredfold to distribute to others. I would become holy, a real person, and receive blessings beyond imagination in this world and the next. And all this for simply trying love the Absolute.

Continue until you feel a strong desire to love the Absolute.

FOCUS 20: FOLLOWING THE ABSOLUTE PERFECTLY

Focus Points

- It's obvious that all of humanity's problems come from refusing to follow the pattern (the Logos or Tao) of their existence, from ignoring the path of unimaginable happiness the Absolute had laid out for them.

- Instead, people drown out the voice of the Absolute with a thousand distractions.

- Only refining the *nous* will allow me to hear this voice again. But if I refine my being thoroughly, I can learn to follow the Absolute perfectly.

- By doing so, I will be conforming my will to my own nature. This will heal my inner being because I will no longer be acting against myself. All my thoughts and actions will finally become expressions of health instead of illness.

- By sparing no effort to conform to the Absolute in every area of my life, I will reach my goal of self-transformation and receive true and indestructible happiness.

Continue until you feel a strong urge to conform your will to the Absolute.

FOCUS 21: NEUTRALIZING EVIL

Focus Points
- The height of love is to desire to suffer in the other's place in order to free him or her from suffering. This is the exact teaching of Orthodoxy and it also explains why part of the Boddhisattva's way of life is to take on all the evils faced by others so they will attain happiness.

- To do this in reality either means that my self-centered, egotistical mind has already been healed, or else the practice itself will destroy what remains of my egocentrism.

- By alleviating the sufferings of others, I will cause them immediate benefit and perhaps be able to set them on the path of self-transformation. Whatever happens, I will destroy my self-obsession and thereby create favorable circumstances for the future.

- Today I will alleviate the sufferings of others whenever possible. I will help them out of their difficulties in a concrete way whenever the opportunity presents itself, and if it doesn't, I will at least cultivate a willingness to do so. Moreover, I will remember any sufferings I come across or hear about this day and keep those involved in my heart.

- If anyone inflicts evil on me today, I will accept it with patience and not return evil for evil. By returning good for evil, I will put an end to the evil and heal both myself and the other.

Continue until you feel a strong urge to absorb the misfortunes of others so that they can experience joy.

Your PROGRAM PLANNER

Here is your personal Program planner. Please make as many copies as you like from here (and enlarge them with a photocopier, if you wish), or use the downloadable version from the Web site.

The virtue of this chart is its extreme simplicity, which allows you to adapt it to all of your training needs.

TABLE A.1: Personal Program Planner

TIME	MON.	TUE.	WED.	THUR.	FRI.	SAT.	SUN.
Focus of the day							
SSDN times							
Reading & times							
0600							
0700							
0800							
0900							
1000							
1100							
1200							
1300							
1400							
1500							

Continued on page 426...

THE 5 PILLARS OF LIFE

...continued from page 425

1600							
1700							
1800							
1900							
2000							
2100							
2200							
2300							
2400							
0100							
0200							
0300							
0400							
0500							

Appendix C

The TRAINING PROGRAM at a GLANCE

The times given here to complete each step of the training program are quite generous, and provide enough training material for about 21 months. Of course, a diligent person could well finish the program within a year. The important thing to keep in mind, though, is that this is not a race! It's about thoroughness, not speed! A strong foundation is the one essential thing in self-transformation and nothing will ever make up for its absence. It is far better to do a few things well than everything badly. For my part, I'd be ecstatic even if people would master chapter 4 and nothing else!

To return to our truly natural state takes great commitment and persistent training, but nearly anyone can do it. Just remember that everyone has particular strengths and weaknesses that will modify the time needed to obtain results in this or that area. Moreover, you will have to return to some exercises over and over again in order to master them. Another dynamic to consider is that some exercises can be undertaken concurrently with others. Once you get to chapter 4, for instance, you should start practicing SSDN every day without fail, whatever the other assignments happen to be. And some of them have to be done within SSDN sessions.

- Exercise 2.1: Building a Program (4 weeks)
  - Week 1: Logging all your activities
  - Week 2: Enforcing the boundaries
  - Week 3: Cleaning the Green
  - Week 4: Refining the program
  - Taking Stock: Reviewing your experiences

- Exercise 3.1 : Creating external peace and order (6 weeks)
  - Week 1: Building a sacred space
  - Weeks 2-3: Analyzing your household's paper system
  - Weeks 4-5 Analyzing the grocery, garbage and recycling, and laundry systems
  - Week 6: Localizing chaos

- Exercise 3.2 Your primary relationships (1 week)

- Exercise 3.3 Stop judging (1 week)

- Exercise 3.4 Refuse to contradict (1 week)

- Exercise 3.5 Warming the hearts of others (1 week)

- Exercise 3.6 Treating your enemy well (1 week)

- Exercise 3.7 Praising others (1 week)

- Exercise 3.8 Shut up and Listen! (1 week)

- Exercise 3.9 Showing gratitude (1 week)

- Exercise 3.10 Building Health, Immunity and Longevity (ongoing)

- Exercise 3.11 Evaluating your Sexuality (2 hours)

- Exercise 3.12 Your Life's Work and Financial Wellbeing (ongoing)

- Exercise 4.1 Practicing SSDN (4 weeks)

- Exercise 4.2 Practicing perpetual inner stillness (3 weeks)
  - Week 1: Co-opt the thinking process
  - Week 2: Uniting energy and spirit
  - Week 3: Living in a dream

- Exercise 5.1: Maintaining your focus

- Exercise 5.2: Winning with Intent

- Exercise 5.2.1: Transforming the body (4 weeks)

- Exercise 5.2.2: Undoing an addiction (2 weeks)

- Exercise 5.2.3: Mastering a relationship (1 week)

- Exercise 5.2.4: Using intent to enforce your Program (1 week)

- Exercise 6.1: Adopting a focus (4 weeks)

- Exercise 6.2: Determining your belief structure (1 week)

- Exercise 6.3: Tossing out the garbage (2 weeks)

- Exercise 6.4: Replacing the junk (2 weeks)

- Exercise 6.5: Building a noetic diet (2 weeks)

- Exercise 7.6: Assimilating obedience (3 weeks)
  - Week 1: Integrating your guide's instructions into your Program
  - Week 2: Integrating the instructions into daily life
  - Week 3: Patterning your life after a transformed life

- Exercise 7.7: The lifetime confession (4 weeks)
  - Week 1: Preparing and doing your confession
  - Week 2: Analyzing your findings
  - Week 3: Refusing to justify yourself
  - Week 4: Conforming totally to the Absolute

- Exercise 8.1: Overcoming gluttony (4 weeks)

- Exercise 8.2: Overcoming lust (1 week)

- Exercise 8.3: Overcoming greed (1 week)

- Exercise 8.4: Overcoming despair (2 weeks)

- Exercise 8.5: Overcoming anger (2 weeks)

- Exercise 8.6: Overcoming sloth (1 week)

- Exercise 8.7: Overcoming vainglory (1 week)

- Exercise 8.8: Overcoming pride (2 weeks)

- Exercise 8.9: Dealing with *peirasmoi* (3 weeks)
  - Week 1: Preparing for *peirasmoi*
  - Week 2: Confronting *peirasmoi*
  - Week 3: Analyzing *peirasmoi*

- Exercise 8.10: Working with alternations (3 weeks)
  - Week 1: Preparing yourself
  - Week 2: Working with the alternation cycle
  - Week 3: Analyzing the results

- Exercise 8.11: Mapping your training program (1 week)

The FORMULAS, PRINCIPLES, and PARADOXES of TRAINING

- **Miraculous Ancient Formula #1**: Program and Training: A carefully worked out program combined with correct and consistent training cannot fail.

- **Miraculous Ancient Formula #2**: Always Begin from the Outside In

- **Miraculous Ancient Formula #3**: The Power of Inner Stillness

- **Miraculous Ancient Formula #4**: Harnessing the Power of Intent

- **Miraculous Ancient Formula #5**: Eliminate Stress by Embracing Struggle

- **Miraculous Ancient Formula #6:** Beyond Self-Defense

- **Miraculous Ancient Formula #7:** Selfless Selfishness

- **Miraculous Ancient Formula #8:** Abandoning Oneself to Heaven

- **Miraculous Ancient Formula #9:** Obedience

- **Miraculous Ancient Formula #10:** Lowliness is Greatness

- **Miraculous Ancient Formula #11:** Winning All Battles

- **Miraculous Ancient Formula #12:** Shifting your Attention

- **Inner Principle 2.1:** If you seek to learn a new step on the syllabus without having mastered the previous one, especially the foundational practices, you will sabotage any possibility of reaching a high level of accomplishment.

- **Inner Principle 2.2:** Encouraging individual creativity blocks the manifestation of transcendent creativity.

- **Inner Principle 2.3:** Identify those skills that, according to tradition, give the quickest and most comprehensive results and train them, though without neglecting other necessary skills.

- **Inner Principle 2.4:** The training must be carried out during every moment, because training that is limited to certain times of the day or week has insufficient force to effect deep existential change.

- **Inner Principle 2.5:** This is not more stress in your life but less.

- **Inner Principle 3.1:** When you set about transforming your life, you must begin with your external circumstances, partly because these hold clues to your inner state of being.

- **Inner Principle 3.2:** Creating external order in your surroundings is of pivotal importance in gaining inner peace.

- **Inner Principle 3.3:** You can easily create external order in any room of your dwelling by analyzing the systems that intersect it and then modifying these systems.

- **Inner Principle 3.4:** If you seek ego satisfaction in your interpersonal relationships by trying to make yourself the center of someone else's universe, you will inevitably fail miserably. Real people make others the center of their universe because this approach, and only this one, creates happiness and bliss for everyone.

- **Inner Principle 3.5:** You will never arrive at genuine and spontaneous affection for everyone unless you force yourself to act as if you already have it.

- **Inner Principle 3.6:** In the beginning, building bodily health is a prerequisite for inner refinement in self-transformation.

- **Inner Principle 3.7:** The secret lies not in caring for health or neglecting it per se, but in the intentional elevation of your life beyond biology.

- **Inner Principle 3.8:** It is grossly mistaken to conclude that because noetic refinement is the central issue in self-transformation, bodily health is irrelevant.

- **Inner Principle 3.9:** The person is an energetic manifestation that gives rise to a physical body; he or she is not a biological phenomenon that has energy and life because of some internal chemical processes.

- **Inner Principle 3.10:** If you do what everyone else does, you will get the results that everyone else gets.

- **Inner Principle 3.11:** You must adopt a strategy of deliberately creating health. Do not adopt a strategy of fighting disease.

- **Inner Principle 3.12:** The principles of sexual morality outlined by authentic ancient traditions were intended to prevent people from harming themselves. "Religions" have misappropriated them and used them to cause severe emotional harm.

- **Inner Principle 3.13:** Sexual energy is the basic created energy of the human psychosomatic composite.

- **Inner Principle 3.14:** In its crude, unrefined form in the fallen world, sexual energy expresses itself as sexual lust. In its most refined form, it becomes an "erotic" love of the Absolute and universal love and compassion toward all people, creatures and things.

- **Inner Principle 3.15:** In the fallen world, this energy has but one direction and "purpose," which is to ensure the perpetuation of the species, even though it expresses itself as a desire for sexual gratification. It becomes a blind, impersonal urge that attempts to dominate your mind and will.

- **Inner Principle 3.16:** One of the principle tasks of self-transformation is to free you from this kind of biological determinism by "personalizing" your sexual energy, refining it, and bringing it under conscious control.

- **Inner Principle 3.17:** You can personalize, refine, and control sexual energy either by using it within a loving relationship of enduring commitment that is freely entered into, or by sublimating and refining the energy directly in a life of celibacy.

- **Inner Principle 3.18**: Use of the sexual energy for pure self-gratification has destructive side effects on the personality and increases the grip of the false self or "ego," the source of all torment.

- **Inner Principle 3.19**: Millennia of experience have proven that involvement in an appropriate sexual relationship does not constitute a barrier to self-transformation. Therefore, any notion that sexual activity is inherently evil or tainted is completely false.

- **Inner Principle 3.20**: Sexual energy in itself is ontologically good (you would be dead without it!) and morally neutral; only its use or abuse can make it therapeutic and transformative on the one hand, or destructive on the other.

- **Inner Principle 3.21**: Whatever career path you choose in life, your overriding goal is to free yourself from worldly cares and distractions.

- **Inner Principle 3.22**: There is no particular financial approach linked to the process of self-transformation. The Warrior may choose whatever path suits his or her personal uniqueness. Nevertheless, in this area as in all others, the Warrior seeks to understand, process and release inner emotional fetters.

- **Inner Principle 3.23**: To change your financial circumstances, you must not only learn more about financial matters than you do now (i.e., acquire factual information), but you must principally find a way to process the inner, emotional "knots" that would prevent you from using new information constructively.

- **Inner Principle 3.24:** If you make serving others your goal you will never lack for money.

- **Inner Principle 4.1:** Before doing, you must be. To benefit yourself or others you must refine your inner world.

- **Inner Principle 4.2:** A "spirituality" of external good deeds that is not solidly based on inner refinement may benefit others, but only in a limited way, and will harm you in the long run.

- **Inner Principle 4.3:** Reason is not evil in and of itself, but in the fallen world it begins to dominate our inner being and cause inner turmoil, disintegration and death

- **Inner Principle 4.4:** When this inner balance is lost and reason is given free reign, it wreaks mental, emotional, and spiritual havoc.

- **Inner Principle 4.5:** Refining the *nous* refines the human energy system and automatically improves physical and mental health. However, working directly with the energy system alone will not refine the *nous* significantly

- **Inner Principle 4.6:** Unless you push through the barriers of physical discomfort and boredom, you will never succeed at refining the mind and undermining the ego; you will be merely "going along with the natural process" and will never find the "way of return."

- **Inner Principle 4.7:** Just as your state of mind influences your breathing pattern, so modifying your breathing can alter your state of mind.

- **Inner Principle 5.1:** You have within you a natural drive and energy pushing you toward self-transformation.

- **Inner Principle 5.2:** Self-transformation depends on your willpower, and your willpower is derived from the congruence of all the elements in your life

- **Inner Principle 5.3:** Your chances of achieving your goal in nearly any endeavor decline radically if you have no support group

- **Inner Principle 5.4:** Success depends on the guidance and support of others. Your willpower cannot make up for the lack of these critical factors.

- **Inner Principle 5.5:** Because our very being is communal by nature, it is unnatural and counterproductive to travel the path of self-transformation without the guidance and support of others

- **Inner Principle 5.6:** Self-transformational practices only unleash their power in your life if you hold self-transformation to be vastly more important than anything else.

- **Inner Principle 5.7:** The key to victory is to consider every goal a fight to the death.

- **Inner Principle 6.1:** The primary difference between the Warrior and the ordinary person is precisely this: the Warrior chooses his cultural paradigm and chooses his attitudes, all quite deliberately.

- **Inner Principle 6.2 :** Regular contact with a bona fide bearer of your authentic tradition of choice, and/or a peer group immersed in that ethos, is a very powerful lever of self-transformation.

- **Inner Principle 6.3** : Faith grows in direct proportion to knowledge — the more you experience the truths of an authentic tradition in your life, the more your faith increases. Therefore, how much faith you have depends on the depth of your practice.

- **Inner Principle 6.4:** Unless you believe you can succeed, you will certainly fail! But this in no way implies believing that you don't need "outside" help.

- **Inner Principle 6.5:** In every sphere of your life you have a certain amount of prior conditioning that must be acknowledged and uprooted if you are to become inwardly free enough to pursue a productive course of action.

- **Inner Principle 6.6:** If you are responsible for all the events and circumstances in your life, you have the power to transform your life in the present and future.

- **Inner Principle 7.1:** Virtue strengthens all mental, emotional, noetic, and physical functions precisely because it causes all these powers to function properly.

- **Inner Principle 7.2:** Facing up to the truth that you will ultimately lose everything belonging to the world of corruption and death gives you the impetus and energy needed to overcome the bondage of the ego.

- **Inner Principle 7.3:** Practiced correctly, obedience restores us to our primordial state and to childlike simplicity of being.

- **Inner Principle 7.4:** The more you are obedient, the more you are protected; this is not a tit-for-tat arrangement — it happens because obedience opens your being and allows the Absolute to protect you quite naturally.

- **Inner Principle 7.5:** The more you renounce self-will, the better you will feel, and the more you will realize that this was not your own will at all. You will realize that the will of the Absolute is your true will and that it alone offers true and imperishable bliss.

- **Inner Principle 7.6:** Because individualism abhors obedience, the individualist can never experience the deep mysteries of love. Hence, his or her life always remains tormented.

- **Inner Principle 7.7:** On the path of self-transformation it is absolutely imperative to have a guide, irrespective of our current level of achievement.

- **Inner Principle 7.8:** Feelings, emotions, and psychosomatic energies or drives that have not been accepted, validated, and integrated into the personality will eventually explode as symptoms of mental or physical illness.

- **Inner Principle 7.9:** The explicit or implicit denial of the passionate part of the soul leads to a rationalistic approach to life and all the usual consequences that stem from it — the growth of a false personality, slavery to the environment, and a thousand physical and mental ailments.

- **Inner Principle 7.1o:** Most "religions" inadvertently validate this kind of illness and provide their adherents with a rationale to avoid facing it. This often results in the illness' being perpetuated in future generations.

- **Inner Principle 7.11:** The "religious" idea that bearing this suffering is redemptive is a completely false interpretation of reality. Pathological conditions that obstruct self-transformation only become redemptive if you work to cure them.

- **Inner Principle 7.12:** Guides from authentic ancient traditions are not invariably able to give appropriate advice to people in this condition.

- **Inner Principle 7.13:** Authentic ancient traditions require you to face up to, understand, and process the contents of the mind, including the faculties of desire and vehement feeling, and view emotional repression as a sure road to disaster.

- **Inner Principle 7.14:** For an energy of the soul to be transformed and reach its full potential through the practices of self-transformation, it must first exist as an acknowledged and accepted element of the whole person.

- **Inner Principle 7.15:** The Absolute only manifests itself in the degree to which we are open to receiving its manifestation.

- **Inner Principle 7.16:** Humility is the ultimate key to self-transformation and its most powerful lever.

- **Inner Principle 7.17:** The beginning of the path to inner freedom and humility is the frank and non-neurotic practice of assuming responsibility for the evils in yourself, in others and in the world in general.

- **Inner Principle 7.18:** The true test of humility is whether or not the urge to dominate, to be superior, has been reversed.

- **Inner Principle 7.19:** The authentic or holy person has no self-image in the usual sense, having left this behind in the struggle to love the other.

- **Inner Principle 7.2o:** Humility eliminates most of the subjective experience of human suffering, even if objectively difficult circumstances remain in place on the physical or emotional levels.

- **Inner Principle 8.1:** Passionate thoughts are primarily an ontological phenomenon, not a moral one. You are not responsible that passionate thoughts enter your consciousness, but only for how you react to them.

- **Inner Principle 8.2:** Yielding to the passions inevitably involves pain and suffering, even if the first appearance of certain passions appears to offer satisfaction or delight.

- **Inner Principle 8.3:** The various drives within us are not evil in and of themselves, but only because in the fallen world they have become unbalanced and out-of-control.

- **Inner Principle 8.4:** The power to pull you forward to total self-transformation lies hidden within you. This hidden wellspring of innate momentum is known in Orthodoxy as the "image of God," in Buddhism as the "Buddha nature" and in Taoism as the "primordial nature."

- **Inner Principle 8.5:** Unless we fight against and ultimately re-educate the passions of attraction offered by such things as food, material wealth and sexuality, we will not fully realize the suffering they conceal until it is too late.

- **Inner Principle 8.6:** Giving into passion gradually subverts the precedence of the soul's powers and also perverts their individual functions.

- **Inner Principle 8.7:** Anger is a legitimate and necessary weapon against inappropriate and disordered desires and dispositions.

- **Inner Principle 8.8:** Our actions and thoughts on this plane of existence will generate desirable or undesirable consequences for us even within the span of this short life. These consequences have educational value if we examine them closely because they function as correctives, pushing us onto the right path.

- **Inner Principle 8.9:** "Vices" are not bad because God said so: God said so because they are bad. This is often the case even on the physical level.

- **Inner Principle 8.10:** We are seeking state of rest, undisturbed by drives, tendencies, thoughts and willful direction. This state is commonly referred to in all traditions as "childlike."

- **Inner Principle 8.11:** It is impossible to defeat the passions from within the confines of our conventional personality with all its opinions, tendencies, habits and quirks.

- **Inner Principle 8.12:** Inner noetic self-awareness on a continuous basis throughout the day is the key to overcoming passionate energies and to reeducating and redirecting them.

- **Inner Principle 8.13:** Stillness is the greatest weapon against all obstacles. When stillness is integrated into your whole being and every move, passions have no foothold.

- **Inner Principle 8.14:** The sign that we have assimilated God's forgiveness is that we find our former desires and vices repulsive.

- **Inner Principle 8.15:** One of the most effective ways to defeat passions is to analyze the matter from a traditional point of view and to deeply ingrain this analysis through noetic work.

- **Inner Principle 8.16:** If your slavery to anger and desire does not subside over time, if you are continually troubled and overcome by the same passions, this is usually an indication that your practice is not correct. Fix it!

- **Inner Principle 8.17:** No amount of forethought and planning can save us from *peirasmoi*, but we can learn how to become more invulnerable to them, and to use them to our advantage.

- **Inner Principle 8.18:** The essence of self-transformation is not about being nice, kind and compassionate in the conventional sense, but rather about adopting an entirely new "mode of existence."

- **Inner Principle 8.19:** You can only become yang to your environment by acting as if you already are.

- **Inner Principle 8.20:** A Warrior may suffer many setbacks, but the only way that he can suffer irrevocable defeat is by choosing to give up.

- **Paradox 3.1:** People tend to implement changes that leave intact the very inner dynamics that have given rise to the life-situations they do not like. Consequently, they recreate similar life situations over and over.

- **Paradox 3.2:** You do not spread order by trying to create order, but by developing efficient strategies for localizing chaos.

- **Paradox 3.3:** Worldly people are surrounded by others but often they feel lonely, isolated, and depressed, whereas transformed people enjoy a rich, deep, and tremendously fulfilling communion with all humankind, whether or not others are physically present.

- **Paradox 3.4:** You may strive for familiarity in your interpersonal relationships, thinking this will provide intimacy. And yet very often, it actually blocks intimacy instead.

- **Paradox 3.5:** Progress in self-transformation involves the ability to care for the body and to ignore the body — each in precise balance.

- **Paradox 4.1:** The more you rely on your reason, the more easily you are enslaved to the powerful emotional energies and the less "rational" you become.

- **Paradox 4.2:** Obsessive self-protection is the chief cause of all suffering. The more you flee physical and emotional pain, the more you become vulnerable to it.

- **Paradox 4.3:** Self-transformation demands working closely with body and mind in order to integrate the two, while ultimately forgetting them both. This cannot be adequately explained in words.

- **Paradox 4.4:** You are fighting to win and detached from the outcome at the same time. Fighting to win goes this far: Your preparation is flawless and you endure the discomfort. Then you let go. Detachment means that you accept the results with equanimity, whatever they may be.

- **Paradox 5.1:** Human beings are completely helpless and yet wield total control over their own fates.

- **Paradox 5.2:** Success is built on failure, so the willingness to fail is an essential precondition of success.

- **Paradox 5.3:** The true Warrior can never lose, because he or she has learned how to win even in defeat.

- **Paradox 6.1:** The only path to unchanging peace is to work through conflicts and difficulties

- **Paradox 6.2:** Your participation in True Life is directly proportional to your acceptance of death.

- **Paradox 6.3:** Accepting death actually preserves biological life

- **Paradox 6.4:** To build a meaningful future, you must assume you have no future in this world.

- **Paradox 6.5:** You acquire true well-being on every level by forgetting about your own individual biological ease, comfort, and even survival.

- **Paradox 6.6:** The personal mode of existence brings you into a deep, ontological communion of being with others, while maintaining your personal distinctiveness.

- **Paradox 6.7:** The individual pursues pleasure, but ends up with pain. The person accepts pain, but ends up with pleasure.

- **Paradox 6.8:** Unless you sell yourself into voluntary slavery to your Program, you will remain forever an involuntary slave to your own passions and to the influences of the outside world.

- **Paradox 6.9:** Embracing the inner struggle of self-transformation not only does not add to psychological stress and all its physical and mental symptoms, but actually defeats stress by tearing it up by the very roots.

- **Paradox 6.1₀:** The Warrior's task is to learn not to defend himself on every level of his being, in order to collapse the ego.

- **Paradox 6.11:** The Warrior's way of life may seem to violate the natural process, but is actually engaging a far deeper natural process.

- **Paradox 6.12:** Self-transformation demands apparent selfishness, and this "selfishness" is the only way to arrive at true self*less*ness.

- **Paradox 6.13** (The Most Impossible Paradox): Even though the Warrior deliberately uses strategy to move toward certain defined goals and objectives, once he begins to act, he banishes from his mind all thought of gain and loss, victory and defeat. His only focus is the integrity and quality of his own actions, whatever the result may be.

- **Paradox 7.1:** True virtue is a spontaneous manifestation of your being in its natural state; but since you are not yet in your natural state, you must actively and deliberately train yourself in virtue.

- **Paradox 7.2:** By applying the ancient training methods to your life, you can easily become a vastly more effective, integrated, and satisfied person. But, if you do not take the next step, your very success may destroy you!

- **Paradox 7.3:** You can never become a real person as long as you live life according to your individual will and preferences.

- **Paradox 7.4:** When you give up your individual will to do the will of the Absolute, the Absolute will in turn begin to do your will.

- **Paradox 7.5:** The proud person, ironically, acquires a feeling of self-sufficiency despite the fact that his or her inability to cope becomes increasingly obvious to everyone, whereas the humble person is demonstrably a far more capable and "together" person.

- **Paradox 8.1:** The war against uncontrolled desire does not lead ultimately to a totally passive or desire-less state, but to a state in which the true, innate desire of our nature manifests itself spontaneously.

- **Paradox 8.2:** The moral philosophies of authentic traditions protect the humble, but the proud use them to commit onto-logical suicide through terminal self-righteousness.

- **Paradox 8.3:** The more you struggle, the better you will feel. You come to realize that the "feeling better" offered by slack-ing off and negligence is but a pale imitation of true inner health.

- **Paradox 8.4:** Worldly people constantly generate new *peiras-moi* for themselves, but then squander the opportunities they represent; Warriors undo the causes of many future *peirasmoi*, and then gain great profit from those they cannot avoid.

- **Paradox 8.5:** You must strive to see all the sins and inadequa-cies of your wretched past and present in order to humble yourself, but at the same time you must act like the person you want to become in your transformed future.

PRINCIPLE
SOURCES

Colliander, Tito. *Way of the Ascetics*. Trans. Katharine Ferré; San Francisco, CA: Harper and Row, 1982.

Damascene, Hieromonk. *Christ the Eternal Tao*. Platina, CA: Valaam Books, 1999.

Elder Joseph ("the Younger"), *Elder Joseph Hesychast: Struggles, Experiences, Teachings (1898 – 1959)*. Mount Athos: The Great and Holy Monastery of Vatopaidi, 1999.

Ephraim, Archimandrite, ed. *Monastic Wisdom: The Letters of Elder Joseph the Hesychast*. Florence, AZ: St. Anthony's Greek Orthodox Monastery, 1998.

Ephraim, Archimandrite. *Counsels from the Holy Mountain: Selected from the Letters and Homilies of Elder Ephraim.* Florence, AZ: St. Anthony's Greek Orthodox Monastery, 1999.

Evans-Wentz, W.Y., ed. *Tibetan Yoga and Secret Doctrines: Seven Books of Wisdom of the Great Path.* London: Oxford University Press, 1980.

Evans-Wentz, W.Y., ed. *Tibet's Great Yogi, Milarepa.* London: Oxford University Press, 1980.

Govinda, Lama Anagarika. *The Way of the White Clouds: a Buddhist Pilgrim in Tibet.* Boulder, CO: Shambhala, 1970.

Gyatso, Geshe Kelsang. *Meaningful to Behold: View, Meditation and Action in Mahayana Buddhism.* Cumbria, UK: Wisdom Pub. 1980.

Gyatso, Geshe Kelsang. *The Meditation Handbook.* London, UK: Tharpa Publications, 1998.

Gyatso, Geshe Kelsang. *Transform Your Life: A Blissful Journey.* Ulverston, UK: Tharpa Publications, 2001.

Guidance Toward Spiritual Life: Saints Barsanuphius and John. Trans. Fr. Seraphim Rose. Platina, CA: St. Herman of Alaska Brotherhood, 1990.

Herrigel, Eugen, *Zen in the Art of Archery.* Trans. R.F.C. Hull; New York: Random House, 1971.

St. Hesychios of Jerusalem. "On Watchfulness and Holiness," in *The Philokalia,* vol.1. Compiled by St. Nikodimos of the Holy Mountain and St. Makarios of Corinth; trans. G.E.H. Palmer, Philip Sherrard and Kallistos Ware, London: Faber and Faber, 1980-84.

St. Ignaty Brianchaninov, *The Arena: an Offering to Contemporary Monasticism.* Jordanville, NY: Holy Trinity Monastery, 1982.

Ioannidis, Klitos. *Elder Porphyrios: Testimonies and Experiences.* Athens: Convent of the Transfiguration, 1997.

St. Isaac the Syrian. *The Ascetical Homilies* Brookline, MA: Holy Transfiguration Monastery, 1984.

Kaiguo, Chen and Shunchao, Zheng. *Opening the Dragon Gate: The Making of a Modern Taoist Wizard.* Trans. Thomas Cleary; Boston, MA: Charles E. Tuttle Co., 1998.

Mails, Thomas E. *Fools Crow: Wisdom and Power.* Tulsa, OK: Council Oak Books, 1991.

Matthew the Poor (Matta Al-Miskin). *The Communion of Love.* Crestwood, NY: SVS Press, 1984.

The Philokalia, vol.1-3. Compiled by St. Nikodimos of the Holy Mountain and St. Makarios of Corinth; trans. G.E.H. Palmer, Philip Sherrard and Kallistos Ware, London: Faber and Faber, 1980-84.

Po-Tuan, Chang and I-Ming, Liu. *The Inner Teachings of Taoism.* Trans. Thomas Cleary; Boston, MA: Shambhala, 2001.

Practical Taoism. Trans. Thomas Cleary; Boston, MA: Shambhala, 1996.

Reid, Daniel. *The Complete Book of Chinese Health and Healing: Guarding the Three Treasures.* Boston, MA: Shambhala, 1995.

Rinpoche, Tenzin Wangyal. *The Tibetan Yogas of Dream and Sleep.* Ithaca, NY: Snow Lion, 1998.

Romanides, John. *The Cure of the Neurobiological Illness Sickness of Religion.* © 1997 by J.S. Romanides. See www.romanity.org.

The Sayings of the Desert Fathers. trans. Benedicta Ward, New York: MacMillan Publishing Co., 1975. (also found under the title "*The Desert Christian*)

Sherrard, Philip. *Christianity and Eros: Essays on the Theme of Sexual Love.* Limni, Evia, Greece: Denise Harvey, 1995.

Sophrony, Archimandrite (Sakharov). *His Life is Mine.* Trans. Rosemary Edmonds; Crestwood, NY: SVS Press, 1977.

Sophrony, Archimandrite (Sakharov). *Saint Silouan the Athonite.* Trans. Rosemary Edmonds; Essex, UK: Stavropegic Monastery of St. John the Baptist, 1991.

Sopko, Andrew J. *Prophet of Roman Orthodoxy: The Theology of John Romanides.* Dewdney, BC, Canada: Synaxis Press, 1998.

Spencer, Robert L. *The Craft of the Warrior.* Berkeley, CA: North Atlantic Books, 1993.

The Syriac Fathers on Prayer and the Spiritual Life. Trans. Sebastian Brock; Kalamazoo, MI: Cistercian Pub. 1987.

Thermos, Fr. Vasileios. *In Search of the Person.* Montreal: Alexander Press, 2004.

Taoist Meditation: Methods for Cultivating a Healthy Mind and Body. Trans. Thomas Cleary; Boston, MA: Shambhala, 2000.

Trungpa, Chögyam. *The Myth of Freedom and the Way of Meditation.* Boulder, CO: Shambhala, 1976.

Vasileios, Archimandrite (Gondikakis), *Hymn of Entry: Liturgy and Life in the Orthodox Church*. New York: St. Vladimir's Seminary Press, 1984.

Vlachos, Hierotheos. *A Night in the Desert of the Holy Mountain: Discussion with a Hermit on the Jesus Prayer.* Trans. Effie Mavromichali; Dorset, UK: Element Books, 1991.

Vlachos, Bishop Hierotheos of Nafpaktos. *Orthodox Psychotherapy: The Science of the Fathers*. Trans. Esther Williams; Levadia, Greece: Birth of the Theotokos Monastery, 1994.

Yannaras, Christos. *The Freedom of Morality.* Trans. Elizabeth Briere; Crestwood, NY: SVS Press, 1984.

ENDNOTES

CHAPTER ONE

1. Pages 1-3. The order of the elements in this quotation has been slightly rearranged for the sake of clarity. Several Orthodox writers of the twentieth century noted that the word "religion" as commonly used among peoples of European ethnic origin does not correspond to Orthodox Christianity.
2. From www.carm.org. This is a Protestant anti-NAM website.
3. At the present time, Taoism in North America seems to be more susceptible, whereas Buddhism seems to be somewhat better at protecting the integrity of its teachings. This may be due to Buddhism's stronger communal or institutional aspect.

CHAPTER TWO

1. Ephraim 1998, p.55.
2. Kaiguo and Shunchao 1998, p.23.

3. Herrigel 1971, p.69.
4. Ibid., pp. 69-70.
5. Gerontikon, St. Anthony the Great, #13.
6. Elder Joseph of Vatopedi Monastery, disciple and biographer of Joseph the Hesychast, in Elder Joseph, p.174.
7. Practical Taoism 1996, p. 17.
8. More than 1,500 years ago, Abba Isaac the Syrian described exactly how the fallen human mentality and the civilizations it produces are enslaved by egocentric fear. I would encourage anyone who really wants to evaluate our modern western society to read his Homily 52 "On the Three Degrees of Knowledge."

CHAPTER THREE

1. Elder Joseph 1999, p.173
2. Ibid., pp.200-201.
3. Vasileios 1984, p.129.
4. St. Isaac the Syrian 1984, Homily 5, pp.51-2.
6. Monastic Constitutions, #4.
7. Taoist Meditation 2000, p.32.
8. Reid 1995, p.328.
9. Sophrony 1991, p.241.
10. Ephraim 1998, Letter 49. This in no way implies any general prohibition against alcohol within Orthodoxy. Even Orthodox monks are allowed to drink alcohol.
11. Po-Tuan and I-Ming 2001, pp.40-41.
12. See Mails 1991, especially chapters 1&2. Fools Crow is a fascinating example of a recent Native American holy man and healer. His blend of the native shamanism he was trained in and the Western Christianity he was taught is in some ways astonishingly close to Orthodoxy.
13. Reid 1995, pp.68-9.
14. Kaiguo and Shunchao 1998 1998, p.122.
15. Sherrard 1995, p.23.
16. Ibid., pp.76-7.
17. Reid 1995, p.154.
18. Po-Tuan and I-Ming 2001, pp.72 &94. He cites dozens of further examples.
19. Practical Taoism 1996. p.34.
20. A pronouncement by this or that bishop, or by anyone else within the Orthodox Church, does not necessarily carry any weight. The teaching must be supported by the consciousness of the whole Church.

CHAPTER FOUR

1. St. Isaac the Syrian 1984, Homily 4, p.32.
2. Neptic" comes from the Greek "Nepsis" and means inner vigilance or watchfulness of the mind. "Ascetic" comes from the Greek "askesis", meaning practice, and refers to exactly that: practice of the methods that lead to self-transformation.
3. Vlachos 1994, pp. 29-30. Vlachos cites here two different works of Fr. Romanides.
4. Sophrony 1991, p.133.
5. On Watchfulness and Holiness" (hereafter "OWH') #27, in The Philokalia, vol.1
6. St. Makarios the Great of Egypt, Homily XV. St. Makarios the Great, not to be confused with his contemporary and friend, St. Makarios the Egyptian, lived from about AD 300 to 390. He was an ascetic in the Egyptian desert at the time of the great flowering of monasticism there in the fourth century. While the stories about him in the Sayings of the Desert Fathers are unquestionably authentic, some have questioned his authorship of the "homilies" bearing his name. But since the content of the homilies is completely reliable, it doesn't really matter from our perspective who wrote them.
7. Ephraim 1998, Letter 4, p.55.
8. *Practical Taoism*1996, p.20. This is from the "Discourse on the Mind" by the Celestial Teacher of Emptiness and Tranquility.
9. Damascene 1999, p.305.
10. *The Syriac Fathers on Prayer and the Spiritual Life*, Philoxenos #3, p.129.
11. Damascene 1999, p.277.
12. Sophrony 1991, pp.165-166.
13. Po-Tuan and I-Ming 2001, p.36.
14. See Fr. Sophrony's discussion of the imagination in Sophrony 1991, pp. 153-170.
15. Damascene 1999, pp.320ff.
16. Elder Joseph 1999, p.169.
17. St. Isaac the Syrian 1984, Homily 52, p.254.
18. Matthew the Poor 1984, p.140.
19. St. Hesychios of Jerusalem #21 in *The Philokalia* vol.1.
20. If you take the Greek speaking world alone, which is only part of the larger Orthodox world, there were numerous deified human beings there during the twentieth century. Even latterly, Fathers Paissios and Porphyrios, and Mother Gavrila all passed away during the last decade of the century, as did Fr. Sophrony, who was a Russian living in England and well known for his biography of his spiritual father, St. Silouan of Athos. There are many more spiritual giants still in the flesh, but in deference to their wishes I must refrain from naming the ones that I am aware of.
21. Yannaras 1984, p.47.
22. Kaiguo and Shunchao 1998 1998, p.273.
23. *Practical Taoism*1996, p.29.
24. See St. Ignaty Brianchaninov 1982, chapters 9-11.
25. See Sophrony 1991, p.132.

26. *Practical Taoism* 1996, p.23.

27. St. Hesychios of Jerusalem #49 in *The Philokalia* vol.1. Notice the allegorical interpretation of the Old Testament Exodus story. If we read such accounts merely on a historical level, they are just history, but if we look deeper, we find that these biblical records are manuals for inner transformation. "Egyptians" is a standard biblical image for both evil thoughts and hostile noetic entities. The Egyptians preferred to call them "Ethiopians". What the Ethiopians call them, I don't know!

28. St. Theophan the Recluse (Russia, late 19th century) talks a good deal about this. For some examples of structured thematic meditations, see St. Peter Damascene in *The Philokalia*, vol.3.

29. B.K Frantzis describes a Taoist variant of this in his books, *Relaxing into Your Being* and *The Great Stillness*. (Fairfax, CA: Clarity Press, 1998 and 1999).

30. *Practical Taoism* 1996, p.27.

31. See Yannaras 1984. Yannaras demonstrates how the Orthodox understanding of sin has nothing to do with the moralistic and juridical Western concept of sin and why, if you believe in the latter version, your ability to progress will be seriously limited.

32. "Treatise on Sitting Forgetting" in *Taoist Meditation* 2000, pp. 85 & 99.

33. Reid 1995, pp.48-9.

34. Tao Te Ching, p.71.

35. Damascene 1999, p.286.

36. Ephraim 1998, p.194.

37. Kaiguo and Shunchao 1998, p.252.

38. *Practical Taoism* 1996, p.70.

39. For more on this topic, see John Romanides, "Franks, Romans and Feudalism", available at www.romanity.org, part2.

40. The theory of the five aggregates is rather complex and goes beyond our scope here. For an easy to understand explanation, see Mike Butler's article at http://dharma.ncf.ca.

41. Alexander Kalomiros, *The River of Fire*, p.115. This lecture by Dr. Kalomiros is one of the most insightful comparisons of Orthodox and Franco-Latin views on salvation ever written.

42. St. Hesychios of Jerusalem #5 & 6 in *The Philokalia*, vol.1.

43. *Practical Taoism* 1996, p.25

44. Damascene 1999, p. 307.

45. *Taoist Meditation* 2000, p.113.

46. Ephraim 1999, p.342-344.

47. The first popular classics on this topic were Frithjof Capra's *The Tao of Physics* and Gary Zukav's *The Dancing Wu Li Masters*.

48. Ioannidis 1997, p.37.

49. Kaiguo and Shunchao 1998, p.41.

50. See *The Cloud of Unknowing and the Book of Privy Counselling*: New York: Image Books, 1973.

51. Rinpoche 1998, pp.90-91. Note that the author, Tenzin Wangyal Rinpoche, is a representative of the pre-Buddhist Bön faith, though the presuppositions and methods of the two are quite similar.
52. Ibid., p.91.
53. For Fr. Sophrony's superb explanation of stillness in Orthodoxy, see Sophrony 1991, Chapter vi – "Pure Prayer and Mental Stillness."

CHAPTER FIVE

1. Po-Tuan and I-Ming 2001, p.32
2. *Practical Taoism* 1996, p.16
3. St. Isaac the Syrian 1984, Homily 56, pp.278-279
4. Ibid., Homily 3, p.16. The implication here is not that the concerns of life need to cease, although that would be helpful, but that they cease to disturb the *nous* and the heart.
5. Ibid., see Homilies 56 and 62.
6. St. Hesychios of Jerusalem #4, in *The Philokalia*, vol.1, p.63. Note that all authentic traditions agree that unrepented evils in this life lead to even worse sufferings after the death of the body.
7. For a discussion on the *sangha*, see the magazine *Buddhism Today*, vol.7, 2000.
8. Mark Victor Hansen and Robert G. Allen in *The One Minute Millionaire*. New York: Harmony Books, 2002, p.162.
9. *Practical Taoism* 1996, p.45
10. Ephraim 1998, Letter 5, p.57
11. Elder Joseph 1999, p.92
12. St. Isaac the Syrian 1984, Homily 54, pp.271-272
13. This gem has been variously attributed to Vince Lombardi or Napoleon Hill, though some say the source is unknown.
14. St. Isaac the Syrian 1984, Homily 73, p359.
15. Gyatso 1998, p.79
16. *Practical Taoism* 1996, pp.14-15.
17. Elder Joseph 1999, p.196
18. Po-Tuan and I-Ming 2001, p.37
19. *Practical Taoism* 1996, p.46
20. In *Maximum Achievement*, New York: Simon and Schuster, 1995. p.41.
21. Ephraim 1998, Letter 17, p.111
22. See Ibid., Letter 8.
23. Castaneda, Carlos. *The Fire From Within*. New York: Simon and Schuster, 1984, p.176. Although there are compelling reasons for doubting Castaneda's claim that his books are really "non-fiction," none of this invalidates the many excellent points the

author makes. Despite this, however, the system he presents is not entirely compatible with any Authentic Ancient Tradition I know of.

24. *Taoist Meditation* 2000, p.56
25. *Rich Dad's Retire Young, Retire Rich*. New York: Warner Books, 2002, p.51.
26. See www.orthodoxchristianity.net
27. Ephraim 1999, p.204
28. For examples of Buddhist martyrdom, see, Gyatso 1980, pp.239-246.

CHAPTER SIX

1. St. Ignaty Brianchaninov 1982, see chapters 8 and 48.
2. Sophrony 1991, p. 423
3. Ephraim 1998, Letter 16, pp. 107-8.
4. *Shambhala: The Sacred Path of the Warrior*. Boston: Shambhala, 1984, p.28.
5. Po-Tuan and I-Ming 2001, p.27. and *Practical Taoism*, p.5.
6. Kaiguo and Shunchao 1998, p. 72.
7. Robert L. Spencer, *The Craft of the Warrior*, Berkeley, CA: North Atlantic Books, 1993.
8. *Practical Taoism* 1996, p.46
9. Sophrony 1991, p.52
10. *The Sayings of the Desert Fathers*, Amma Sarah #9, p.230: "It is I who am a man; you who are women."
11. For Orthodoxy, refer to the *Sayings of the Desert Fathers* and similar collections, including the newly revised *Synaxarion* (the lives of saints) published by the Holy Monastery of Simonos Petra on Mt. Athos. For Taoism, see Thomas Cleary's translation titled: *Immortal Sisters: Secret Teachings of Taoist Women*, published by Shambhala and Eva Wong's translation of *Seven Taoist Masters: a Folk Novel of China*, also published by Shambhala.
12. *Seven Taoist Masters: a Folk Novel of China*. Trans., Eva Wong. Boston: Shambhala, 1990, pp. 121ff.
13. Barber, p.4.
14. Barber, p.9.
15. St. John Cassian, "On the Holy Fathers of Sketis and on Discrimination", *The Philokalia*, v.1, pp. 95-96.
16. See www.fatheralexander.org for material on St. Seraphim.
17. *Guidance Toward Spiritual Life* 1990, p.32.
18. *Practical Taoism* 1996, p.24.
19. Kaiguo and Shunchao 1998, p. 270.
20. In his letters (Ephraim 1998), Elder Joseph refers to this and many similar experiences.
21. Vasileios 1984, pp.126-130.

22. Gyatso 2001, p.79.

23. *Taoist Meditation* 2000, p.83.

24. Ephraim 1999, p.332.

25. *Practical Taoism* 1996, p.14.

26. Gyatso 1998, p.37.

27. *Practical Taoism* 1996, p.46

28. Ibid., p.30.

29. Ephraim 1998, p. 158.

30. Matthew the Poor 1984, pp. 116-117.

31. An expression coined, I believe, by the late Fr. Alexander Schmemann, former dean of St. Vladimir's Orthodox Theological Seminary in New York, and one of the better known theologians of the twentieth century.

32. Gyatso 2001, p.189.

33. Ibid., p.143.

34. Fr. Sophrony has perhaps become the most influential Orthodox monastic writer of the last hundred years. For a more complete picture of his incredible journey towards inner transformation, see his autobiography, *We Shall See Him as He Is*, and his book *On Prayer*, as well as his earlier work *His Life Is Mine*.

35. Sophrony 1991, pp. 145-6.

36. Damascene 1999, pp.337-338.

37. Sophrony 1991, p.218.

38. Gyatso 2001, p.147.

39. Journey to Ixtlan: the Lessons of Don Juan. New York: Simon and Schuster, 1974, p.120.

40. Elder Joseph 1999, p.174.

41. Ibid., pp.174-175.

42. Second century master Wei Boyang, "Triplex Unity", cited in *Practical Taoism*, 1996 p.72.

43. Prayers after Reception of the Holy Mysteries.

44. Prayers after Reception of the Holy Mysteries.

45. Reid 1995, p.333.

46. It is ironic that some believe Christianity proposes a dualistic body/flesh versus mind/spirit view of the human person. Although, to be honest, any experience with Western Christianity is bound to lead to that conclusion. The deification of reason and the loss of the spiritual tradition of *hesychasm* in the West made this approach inevitable. But, on the other hand, the idea that Oriental or other authentic non-Christian traditions see no conflict between the "flesh and the spirit" is totally fallacious. The truth is that both of these views are gross oversimplifications of real life, which is *never* as cut and dried as we like to think.

47. Vasileios 1984, p.94.

48. "First Century on Love", # 70, in *The Philokalia*, vol.2

49. Lama Anagarika 1970, p.34.

50. *The Sayings of the Desert Fathers*, Abba Anthony, #9.

51. See note 34.
52. St. Isaac the Syrian 1984, Homily 71, pp.344-345.
53. Kaiguo and Shunchao 1998, p.194.
54. From part 2 of his *Franks, Romans and Feudalism*. See www.romanity.org.
55. However, for Christians alone, the Communists in the twentieth century martyred more of the faithful than their nearest rivals, the Iconoclasts of the eighth and ninth centuries, who in turn martyred more than all the pagan Roman emperors combined.
56. Homily 4, p.32.
57. Sophrony 1991, p.233.
58. *Practical Taoism* 1996, p.55.
59. Ibid., p.8

CHAPTER SEVEN

1. *Practical Taoism* 1996, p.36.
2. To understand this critical issue more fully, see Yannaras' masterpiece, *The Freedom of Morality*, especially pp.36ff and 146ff.
3. These examples belong to the Kagyu lineage of Tibetan Buddhism. A complete list can be found in Evans-Wentz 1980a, pp.67-100.
4. Liu I-Ming in Po-Tuan and I-Ming 2001, pp.36-39.
5. Kaiguo and Shunchao 1998 1998, pp.235-236.
6. Damascene 1999, p.235.
7. Herrigel 1971, p.34.
8. Ibid., pages 11 and 69.
9. Evans-Wentz 1980b, p.36.
10. Evans-Wentz 1980a, p.81.
11. Elder Joseph 1999, p. 81.
12. Tao Teh Ching, #67.
13. Ephraim 1998, p.20. (our italics)
14. Letter # 30, in Ephraim 1998, pp.155-56.
15. In Sophrony 1977, p.29.
16. Elder Joseph 1999, pp.216-17.
17. Damascene 1999, p.321.
18. Kaiguo and Shunchao 1998, p.247.
19. Yannaras 1984, p.47.
20. Tao Teh Ching, chapter 81, in Damascene 1999, p.242.
21. Sophrony 1991, pp.56-58.
22. Trungpa 1976, pp.24-25.
23. Elder Joseph 1999, p. 217.
24. Ibid., p.218.

25. Gyatso 1998, p.31.
26. Discourses and Sayings, p.126.
27. Lama Anagarika 1970, p.34.
28. St. Ignaty Brianchaninov 1982, pp.44–45.
29. Evans-Wentz 1980b, p.44.
30. Thermos, p.42.
31. Ibid, p.45.
32. Leontios of Byzantium (6th century), in his *Against the Aphthartodocetists*, cited in Thermos, p.66.
33. Sophrony 1991, p.80.
34. *The Sayings of the Desert Fathers*, Abba Poemen, #54. See also Sophrony 1991, p.333.
35. Colliander 1982, p.44.
36. Step 4, p.96.
37. Tomo Geshe Rinpoche in Lama Anagarika 1970, p.34.
38. St. Isaac the Syrian 1984, Homily 77, pp.381-2.
39. *Tao Teh Ching*, #51, 65 & 34.
40. Kunzig Shamar Rinpoche in *Buddhism Today*, vol.12 Spring/Summer 2003.
41. Damascene 1999, p.381.
42. *Practical Taoism* 1996, p.22.
43. St. Isaac the Syrian 1984, Homily 37, p.177.
44. Ibid, Homily 35, pp.158-9.
45. Ibid, Homily 74, p.363.
46. Sophrony 1991, p.305
47. Ibid., p.158.

CHAPTER EIGHT

1. *Buddhism Today*, volume 12 Spring Summer 2003, p.33.
2. *Practical Taoism* 1996, p.8.
3. Sherrard 1995T, p.282-3.
4. Elder Joseph 1999, p.201.
5. Kaiguo and Shunchao 1998 p.20
6. *Triads in Defense of the Holy Hesychasts*, 1,2,4
7. See, Thermos, chapter 2.
8. *Taoist Meditation* 2000, p.117.
9. St. Isaac the Syrian 1984, Homily 3, p.16.
10. This is not to be confused with the rational mind – the two are different realities.
11. Gyatso 2001, p.58.
12. "On the Spiritual Law," #116, in *The Philokalia* vol.1.

13. The documentary that quoted this study stated this conclusion as a generalization, without reference to age or gender. I would expect that males would be more vulnerable than females, and that the negative results would vary directly with age.

14. Reid 1995, p.79.

15. Po-Tuan and I-Ming 2001, p.65.

16. Ibid., p.66.

17. *Taoist Meditation* 2000, p.94.

18. *Practical Taoism* 1996, pp.33-34.

19. "Secrets of Realization," quoted in *Practical Taoism* 1996, p.60.

20. *Practical Taoism* 1996, p.18.

21. Gyatso 2001, p.338-9.

22. Kaiguo and Shunchao 1998 p.20

23. *Taoist Meditation* 2000, p.64.

24. Elder Joseph 1999, p.183.

25. St. Isaac the Syrian 1984, Homily 56, pp.276-7.

26. Ibid., Homily 52, pp.254-5.

27. Lama Govinda's account of meeting the Oracle Priest of Dungkar (Lama Anagarika 1970, pp.179-191) is a case in point. The Tibetans themselves treated this as the temporary possession of a human being by noetic beings of another realm.

28. St. Isaac the Syrian, St. Isaac the Syrian 1984, Homily 5, p.42.

29. ElderJoseph 1999, p.180.

30. *Practical Taoism* 1996, p.46.

31. Ibid.,, pp. 16 and 24.

32. Ephraim 1999 p.269.

33. Elder Joseph 1999, p.179.

34. On Prayer, pp.115-6.

35. Elder Joseph 1999, p.178.

36. Damascene 1999, p.285.

37. Elder Joseph 1999, p.191.

38. Ibid., pp.196-97.

39. Ibid., pp.184-85.

40. Mark the Ascetic, in "No Righteousness by Works," #104, in *The Philokalia*, vol.1, p.133.

41. *Practical Taoism* 1996, pp.14 & 24.

42. *Taoist Meditation* 2000, p.85.

43. Elder Joseph 1999, p.187.

44. *Practical Taoism* 1996, p.8.

45. Ibid., p.54

46. Elder Joseph 1999, p.187

47. For a description of one Iron Shirt system among many, see *Qigong Empowerment*, pp.239ff.

CHAPTER NINE

1. Herrigel 1971, p.74.
2. 2Kaiguo and Shunchao 1998, p.71.
3. Sir Thomas Browne, quoted in Madeleine L'Engle's *A Ring of Endless Light*. New York: Dell, 1980, p.24.

INDEX

as therapeutic system, 130–131
variations within, 25–29, 27t
Western
historical development of, 26
historical development of "sin" in, 345–346
image of divine dictator in, 312
legalism of, 26
mind-body dualism in, 81–82
neurotic guilt complex in, 342
self-deception in, 151
separation of theory and practice in, 145–146
view of sexuality in, 104–107
virtue as oppressive in, 296
vs Orthodoxy, 25–29, 27t
women under, 221
Churchill, Winston, on blind obedience, 307
Cleansing, in health program, 97
Cloud of Unknowing (text), 169
Cohabitation, 115–116
Cold War, 205
Comfort zone, 23, 177, 186
Commandments
in Buddhism, 297–298
in Taoism, 298
Western conception of, 297
Communists, 39
Community, as lever of self-transformation, 184
Companions, as spiritual guides, 318, 325–326
Compartmentalization, in Religion, 22–23
Complexes, 129. See also Neurosis
Compromise, as form of giving up, 186
Conditioning, cultural, 223, 224
Confession, practice in, 337–339
Consubstantiality
of the human race, 159–160, 257, 281, 310, 330
and man's communal nature, 185, 187
and the power of prayer, 189
Contradiction
practice in avoiding, 76–77
spirit of, 71
Control

in applying intent, 207
as aspect of Religion, 23
of time, 198
Cortisone, 275
Cosmic cemetery, 252–253
Coupling, in process of sin, 143–144
The Craft of the Warrior (Spencer), 217
Creativity, 42
Criticism, 70–71, 279–280
Cults, 326
Cultural values
conditioning in, 223, 224
warrior's examination of, 223–224
of western world, 223

D
Fr. Damascene
on human conduct, 299
on metanoia, 151
on noetic prayer, 133
on obedience, 311
on peirasmoi, 377–378
on the rational mind, 136
on yielding to passions, 344
Death
acceptance of, 210, 245–254
fear of, 12, 129
focus on going beyond, 414
practice in acceptance of, 250–253
as preferable to surrender, 209–210
remembrance of, as lesson, 247
Decisiveness, of warrior, 268–271
Defeat
honorable character of, 208–210
turning into victory, 386–388
Deification
as natural impulse, 177–178
in New Age movement, 31
process of, in biblical text, 161
through noetic prayer, 140–141
Demonic entities, 371–373
Descartes, 139, 273
Desert fathers and mothers
dangers faced by, 248–249
and impact of diet on prayer, 82
Despair, 7, 359–360
Dialoguing, 45

Evangrios, on the "eight evil thoughts," 349–350

Evil
  cycle of, 280
  focus on neutralizing, 422–423

Exercise, internal, 98–99

Existential stance. *See* Worldview

Experience
  as basis for faith, 235–236
  of failure, 208
  interpretation of, 240–241

Extroversion, 127

F

Failure
  in intent, 208–210
  necessity of, 208
  as self-fulfilling prophecy, 238–239

Faith
  and the Absolute, 232, 234
  definition of, 300
  dynamic of, 236–237
  in Far Eastern systems, 236
  introductory, and the transformed person, 235, 238
  as self-fulfilling prophecy, 238–239

Falkland Islands war, 246

"Fall and Get Up Again" method, of self-transformation, 387–388

Fallen state. *See also* Samsara
  Adam and Eve in, 27t
  addiction in, 194
  effect of humility on, 332–333
  external world in, reaction to, 256
  group identification in, 224
  impact of, on nous, 24–25
  "natural" processes in, 118
  reason in, 135
  self-image in, 334
  sexuality in, 109
  social conformity in, 291

Familiarity
  impact of, on interpersonal relationships, 65–67
  vs intimacy, 65–67

Fasting
  as a boulder, 46

  impact of, on immune system, 82–83
  impact of, on prayer, 82

Fate
  control over, 175, 177
  warrior's control over, 255

Fear
  of death, 12, 129, 246
  educational system and, 137–138
  lack of willpower and, 174–175

Fight or flight response, 275

Financial well-being
  practice on, 123–124
  in self-transformation, 121

Five pillars, of transformation, 3–4, 17–18

Focusing
  on accepting responsibility, 416–417
  on accepting the warrior's lot, 414–415
  on the blessing of obedience, 420–421
  on the blessing of your life, 407
  on the blessing of your spiritual guide, 409–410
  on danger of non-transformation, 408–409
  on following the Absolute perfectly, 421–422
  on going beyond death, 414
  on humanity's sameness, 412
  on imperviousness to external influences, 406
  on justifying the other, 413
  on love of the Absolute, 421
  on maintaining awareness during impact, 416
  on neutralizing evil, 422–423
  on not judging, 418–419
  as offensive strategy, 229–230
  on placing the other at the centre of the universe, 419–420
  practice in, 230–231
  on seeking mercy for oneself, 410–411
  on seeking mercy for the other, 411
  on stabilizing the nous, 405–406
  on this tragic and insufficient world, 408
  in transformation, 35
  on warming the hearts of others, 417–418

Fools Crow
  and divine guidance in medical
    treatment, 87
  longevity of, 150
Forgiveness
  continuous, of God, 355
  in disinterested love, 71
Forthrightness, practice in, 302
"Frangopapas," 26
Frankish Empire, 26, 221
Free will, 175, 283
Freedom
  illusions of, 309
  vs obedience, 307–308
Fueling, in health program, 97
Funeral verses, 252, 305

G
Gandhi, Mahatma, 333
Gender differences, in warriorship, 219t,
  220t
Germ theory of disease, 90–91
Germanos, 228
Tomo Geshe Rinpoche
  on responsibility, 280–281
  on spiritual guides, 317
Ghandi, Mahatma, and non-violent
  resistance, 285
Gluttony, 342, 356–357
Gnosticism, 30–31
Goals
  in current life, 12
  as a fight to the death, 209
  focusing in achieving, 229–231
  incremental, 204, 387
  limited, focus on, 197
  measurability of, 201–202, 206
  need for life congruent with, 182–183
God. See also The Absolute
  as Absolute reality, 20–21
  continuous forgiveness by, 355
  Orthodox vs Western notions of, 27t
The Gods Must Be Crazy (film), 137
"Going along." See Natural process
Good and evil, in Religion, 22
Govinda. See Anagarika Govinda

Gratitude
  practice in showing, 79–80
  in relationship building, 73
Greed, practice in overcoming, 359
Group effort
  dream team in, 184
  as lever of self-transformation, 183,
    184–185
  in secular endeavors, 184
  as tool in intent, 200
Group identification
  fallen vs warrior's, 224
  and need to be right, 224
Gyatso. See Kelsang Gyatso

H
Habit, 247–248
Happiness
  five pillars of, 16
  misguided search for, 247
  as passion, 351
Harmartia (sin), 142
Hatha yoga. See Yoga
Healing. See also Medicine
  monasticism as model for, 57–58
  traditional modalities of, 93
Health
  avoidance of extremes in, 85–86
  and benefits of Sitting Still and Doing
    Nothing (SSDN), 149–151
  contradictory statements on, 81
  creating, advantages of, 94
  in current life, 11
  and ending "victim" mentality, 95–96
  four foundations of, Chinese, 150–151
  impact of emotional makeup on, 101
  impact of lifestyle choices on, 93–95
  impact of stillness on, 149–151
  impact of stress on, 7, 275
  in noetic life, 84
  passivity, in attitude toward, 101–102
  as prerequisite for inner refinement, 85
Health program, Rock Solid, 96–101
Health test, online, 103
Heart, 131–132
Heaven, Christian conceptions of, 27t
Hell, Christian conceptions of, 27t

Helpfulness, as neuroses, 288–289
Hermits
    attitude of, towards body, 84
    awareness of needs of others by, 65
Heroism, dynamic of, 260
Herrigel, Eugen
    on art of archery, 398
    on art of superior virtue, 299
    on destruction of egocentric conscious-
        ness, 42
    on overcoming ego, 304
    on patience required in training, 41
Hesychasm. *See also* Stillness
    control of inner world through,
        141–142
    in noetic prayer, 133
    process of, 131
    in reconstitution of true personality, 130
St. Hesychios
    on failure to refine mind, 182
    on hesychasm, 131
    on inner attention, 163–164
    on noetic prayer, 138
    on stillness in meditation, 147
Hinduism, on age of spiritual darkness, 285
History, of humankind, 258
Home, creation of order in, 62–63
Hormonal changes, 380
Human condition, 159–165
Human nature. *See also* Consubstantiality
    potentiality of, 1
    and relation to the Absolute, 161, 258,
        263
Humility
    of The Absolute, 331
    in acceptance of death, 246
    in acceptance of harshness, 74
    as defense against demonic entities, 373
    definition of, 300–301
    foundations for practicing, 330–337
    and freedom from imagination,
        336–337
    inner strength required for, 333
    as product of obedience, 329–330
    as proof of love, 73
    role of confession in, 337–339
    self-forgetfulness in, 334

    of transformed person, 332, 333
Hypochondria, 273
Hypocrisy, 299, 300
Hypostasis (personal identity), 162

I
"I," concept of
    and bondage to the world, 162, 163
    eliminating conditioning of, 163
    social conditioning in, 160–161
    unrealness of, 162
Icon corner, as sacred space, 61
Iconography, 42
Identification, neurosis of, 226
Identity, and the "I" concept, 162, 163
Ideology, 39
    in judging others, 353
    in Western world, 139–140
Illness, self-creation of, 87
Imagination, ending domination of,
    336–337
Immune system
    acceptance of death, impact on, 248
    boosting, through lifestyle changes,
        94–95
    impact of fasting on, 82–83
    impact of passions on, 350–351
    impact of stress on, 101
Incense, use of, in meditation, 154
Individualism
    aversion to obedience by, 316
    as delusion of the rational mind, 24
    impact of, on western culture, 42
    as self-destructive mode, 261, 281
    vs "person" concept, 261
Infallibility Syndrome, 285
Information age, 2
Inner attention
    in confronting alternations, 385
    in confronting peirasmoi, 374
    development of, 163–164
Inner refinement
    centrality of, in integrated life, 229
    daily occupations in process of, 193
    development of, through noetic work,
        46, 85, 133–134
    focusing in, 229–231

energy of, in a pure heart, 334–335
modeling of, in the home, 70
practical, submission in, 315–316
of self, 182
Lust
impact of, on physical health, 110–111
practice in overcoming, 357–358

M
Mail, as source of disorder, 62–63, 64
St. Makarios the Great, on causes of alternations, 378–380
St. Mark the Ascetic, on the spiritual law, 349
Marriage
exception to disinterested love in, 69
and finding a mate, 59
problems within, 114–115
and self-transformation, 113–114, 116
symbolic view of, 107
views of sex in, 104–107
Martial arts
as distraction in self-transformation, 218
"iron shirt" practice in, 386
mastery of steps in, 41
stages of development in, 39–40
Tai Chi as, 98–99
Martyrdom
in authentic traditions, 210
vs self-defense, 281–282
St. Mary of Egypt, 221
Matthew the Poor
on acceptance of death, 249–250
on fear-based educational process, 138
St. Maximos the Confessor
on feigned virtue, 297
on misuse of desire, 348
on passions, 351
on perfect love, 280
McWorld, 226
Mechanistic worldview, 168, 225t
Medicine. See also Healing
authentic traditions in, 86
Chinese
four foundations of, 150–151
human energetic structure in, 99–100

laughter as concern in, 351
traditional
creation of health in, 94
healing modalities in, 93
vs allopathic, 86–92
Western, 88–89
allopathic focus of, 90–91, 223
mechanistic worldview of, 91
pharmaceutical revolution in, 92
vs Chinese, 91–92
Meditation, 41. See also Sitting Still and Doing Nothing (SSDN)
appropriate times for, 154
in current life, 12
dangerous practice in, 145–147
impact of, on physical health, 150–151
posture for, 152–153
sexual energy in, 108
stillness in, 133–134
types of, 147–149
Elder Melchizedek of Yaroslavl Forest, 150
Men, advantages and disadvantages of, 220t
Mental obstacles, 59
Mercy
focus on seeking, for oneself, 410–411
focus on seeking, for other, 411
Metanoia, in inner work, 151
Milarepa, on impermanence of life, 305
Mind-body dualism, 81–82
Modes of existence, 369–371
Momentary disturbance, in process of sin, 143
Monasticism
development of decisiveness in, 271–272
as healing model, 57–58, 140
as setting for achieving stillness, 165
Money
attitudes towards, 122–123
and financial well-being, 123
as source of stress, 120
Money-Mindset test, 124
Mood. See also Attitudes
choice of, 265
choice of, by warrior, 266
definition of, 222
impact of environment on, 265

practice in putting on noetic armor,
267–268
Moralism
concerning passions, 342
concerning sexuality, 105, 117
concerning virtue, 296–297
in social control, 105
trap created by, 196, 197
Mortality, and original sin, 107
Moses the Black, on tactics for achieving
goals, 228–229
Multiplicity, 160
"Musterbation," 52
Mystery, attitude of Religion toward, 23

N
Nationalism, 224
Natural process
compromise as submission to, 186
ego in, 283
in failure of willpower, 174, 175, 179
in fallen state, 118, 309
need for reversal of, 25, 269
reversing, through virtue, 299–300
and sexual drive, 118
violence in, vs warriorship, 218–219
Natural world. *See also* Phenomenal world
western vs traditional perceptions of,
225t
in western worldview, 222–223
Negligence, in following Program,
194–195, 269
Nepsis (watchfulness, in prayer), 133,
163–164
Nervous system
effect of breath control on, 158
effect of light on, 154
effect of meditation on, 150–151
stabilization of, 100
Neurosis, 67, 140
of guilt complex, 256, 258, 342
of "helpfulness," 288
of identification, 226
as issue in spiritual guidance, 320–323
lack of, in traditional culture, 137, 140
need to be right as, 224, 226
origin of, in false theology, 346

and rational thought, 135, 136
self-defense patterns as, 284
New Age movement, 29–31
failure of spiritual warfare in, 216
misrepresentations of sexual yoga,
111–112
and stillness, failure to respect, 147
Newtonian physics, 168
Noetic armor, putting on, 267–268
Noetic diet, 243–245
Noetic energy, 24–25
Noetic integrity, alternations in, 378–380
Noetic prayer. *See also* Prayer
attentiveness and watchfulness in, 133
deification through, 140–141
and martyrdom, 282
in Orthodox context, 103
stillness in, 131, 133–134
thematic meditation as inspiration for,
148
watchfulness during, 163–164
Noetic work. *See also* Focusing
development of refinement through, 46
need for "how to" in, 46–47
practice themes for, 403–405
requirements of, 38–39
transcendence of natural laws in, 84–85
Noetic world, demonic entities in,
371–373, 379
Nonviolent resistance, 285
Nous
in authentic traditions, 134
in body's energy system, 145
and breathing, connection between,
157–158
effect of emotions on, 264
experience of, in western world, 134,
138–142
focus on stabilizing, 405–406
and the human heart, 131–132
impact of Fall on, 24–25, 132
physical senses and, 132
reading for refinement of, 243–245
refinement of, through prayer, 133–134
stabilization of, 99
Nutritional supplements, 97

THE 5 PILLARS OF LIFE

ABOUT
the AUTHOR

Doctor Symeon Rodger is a priest and spiritual father of the Eastern Orthodox Church in Ottawa, Canada. For over thirty years he has immersed himself in the practical "how-to" details of the life-transforming methods of Orthodoxy, Buddhism, Taoism, and other authentic ancient traditions.

He has studied various Oriental martial arts for thirty-five years. Symeon is proficient in the theories of Traditional Chinese Medicine and has led numerous workshops on Qi Gong (Chinese exercise systems) and on various aspects of health and immunity.

Dr. Symeon Rodger also teaches Orthodox theology in English and French at the Université de Sherbrooke in Montreal. He has worked for the Canadian government in eight languages. He is a contributing author to Stephen E. Schmitt's best-selling *Wake Up... Live the Life You Love: Inspirational "How to" Stories.*

ORDERING INFORMATION

Core Systems Press books are available online and at your favorite bookstore.

Quantity discounts are available to qualifying institutions.

All Core Systems Press books are available to the booktrade and educators through all major wholesalers.

For more information, call the publisher at 1-800-648-1546 or visit www.RockSolidLife.com

CORE SYSTEMS PRESS